DATA COLLECTION
AND ANALYSIS

Southampton
SOLENT
University

DATA COLLECTION AND ANALYSIS

Second edition

edited by

Roger Sapsford and Victor Jupp

SAGE Publications
Los Angeles • London • New Delhi • Singapore
www.sagepublications.com

in association with
The Open University

First edition published 1996

Second edition published 2006

Reprinted 2006, 2008

SAGE Publications Ltd
1 Oliver's Yard
55 City Road
London EC1Y 1SP

SAGE Publications Inc
2455 Teller Road
Thousand Oaks
California 91320

SAGE Publications India Pvt. Ltd
B 1/I 1 Mohan Cooperative Industrial Area
Mathura Road, New Delhi 110 044
India

SAGE Publications Asia-Pacific Pte Ltd
33 Pekin Street #02-01
Far East Square
Singapore 048763

British Library Cataloguing in Publication data

A catalogue record for this book is available from the British Library

ISBN-10 0-7619-4362-5   ISBN-13 978-0-7619-4362-4
ISBN-10 0-7619-4363-3 (pbk)   ISBN-13 978-0-7619-4363-1 (pbk)

Library of Congress Control Number: 2005927680

Typeset by C&M Digitals (P) Ltd., Chennai, India
Printed by Cpod, Trowbridge, Wiltshire.
Printed on paper from sustainable resources

Contents

List of Figures

List of Tables

List of Boxes

Preface

This book is about collecting and analyzing research data, but this does not mean that it teaches just the *techniques* of research. Research does indeed involve technical matters, but they are not in fact very difficult to grasp. What is more important to social science research than the technical questions is the frame of mind in which you approach it. Both of us regard empirical research as a part of theory-building, on the one hand, and of good professional practice on the other. Elsewhere (Smith, 1975), the prerequisite for good research has been described as 'the methodological imagination'.

Based originally on material prepared for Open University course DEH3I3 *Principles of Social and Educational Research* in the 1990s, this volume has been re-edited and in some places re-written for a wider market. The original material was targeted at the reader of research rather than the practitioner; its aim was to equip students to understand, evaluate and use evidence in their academic and professional work. The needs of students who have projects to carry out now receive greater emphasis, and each chapter ends with a 'running activity' which will help you to build up a plan or proposal for your own research. We have also suggested further reading in each chapter. The book is designed for students from a wide range of disciplines (including sociology, social psychology, social policy, criminology, health studies, government and politics) and practitioners and readers in a number of applied areas (for example, nurses and other medical practitioners, social workers and others in the caring professions, workers in the criminal justice system, market researchers, teachers and others in the field of education). The second edition has brought some of the examples up to date and added chapters on research issues and methods which have emerged as of importance over the past decade.

The first part of the book covers *design* issues which are closely bound up with how data are collected: the basic logic of different kinds of research studies, and the 'technology' of sampling. Part II deals with the basic research activities of observation and asking questions (using methods exhibiting varying degrees of structure) and the use of documents, published statistics and databases for research purposes. Part III covers (a) statistical analysis of quantitative data, from simple tabular analysis and the graphical presentation of data to complex multivariate techniques using regression or analysis of variance, and including a chapter on the preparation of data, and (b) the qualitative analysis of text and interview transcripts from both an 'ethnographic' and a 'critical' point of view. Two detailed examples of qualitative analysis can also be found on the website www.sagepub.co.uk/sapsford. The 'statistical' chapters do not assume any prior knowledge of statistical techniques. They also do not require more than very simple calculations. Although it is not necessary for the work outlined in this book, we are assuming that those who go on to do research which requires extensive statistical calculation will arrange access to a computer (by far the most sensible way to do statistical analysis). Finally, Part IV looks at the broader ethical, political and conceptual issues that are important at all stages of research.

Acknowledgements

The material on which the first edition of this book was based was originally prepared for an Open University Course Team, and we should like to acknowledge the substantial amount contributed by the Team. Our thanks are due particularly to Martyn Hammersley, Kevin McConway, Keith Stribley and three colleagues who have died since the original course material was written and who are sorely missed – Judith Calder, Betty Swift and Michael Wilson.

Grateful acknowledgement is also made to the following sources for permission to reproduce material in this book:

Figures 1.2 and 1.3: D. Campbell (1969) 'Reforms as experiments', *American Psychologist,* vol. 24; © The American Psychological Association.

Figure 3.1: adapted from B.H. Junker (1960) *Field Work,* University of Chicago Press; © The University of Chicago.

Figures 8.1 and 8.9: P. Abbott (1988) *Material Deprivation and Health Status in the Plymouth Health Authority District*; © Professor Pamela Abbott, Glasgow Caledonian University.

Table 2.3: M.F. Weeks, B.L. Jones, R.E. Folsom Jr and C.H. Benrud C.H. (1984) 'Optimal times to contact sample households', *Public Opinion Quarterly,* vol. 48; © The Trustees of Columbia University.

Tables 8.1, 8.5 and 8.8: P. Abbott (1988) *Material Deprivation and Health Status in the Plymouth Health Authority District*; © Professor Pamela Abbott, Glasgow Caledonian University.

Table 9.2: M. Conway, G. Cohen and N. Stanhope (1991) 'On the very long-term retention of knowledge acquired through formal education: twelve years of cognitive psychology', *Journal of Experimental Psychology,* vol. 120, no. 4, December; © 1991 by the American Psychological Association. Reprinted by permission.

Table 9.7: G. Cohen, N. Stanhope and M. Conway (1992) 'Age differences in the retention of knowledge by young and elderly students', *British Journal of Developmental Psychology,* vol. 10, Part 2; © 1992 by the British Psychological Society.

Box 3.1: N. Flanders (1970) *Analyzing Teaching Behavior,* Addison-Wesley; © Ned A. Flanders.

Box 10.1: M. Hammersley and P. Atkinson (1983) *Ethnography: Principles in Practice,* Tavistock Publications; © Martyn Hammersley and Paul Atkinson.

Box 10.3: A. Strauss and J. Corbin (1990) *Basics of Qualitative Research: Grounded Theory Procedures and Techniques,* Sage Publications Inc.

Box 11.1: J. Scott (1990) *A Matter of Record: Documenting Sources in Social Research,* Polity Press.

List of Contributors

Roger Sapsford is Reader in Social Research Methods at the University of Teesside and before that he taught research methods at the Open University. He is author of *Life Sentence Prisoners: reaction, response and change* and (with Pamela Abbott) of *Community Care for Mentally Handicapped Children* and *Research Methods for Nurses and the Caring Professions*. He was also lead editor of *Theory and Social Psychology* and *Researching Crime and Criminal Justice*.

Victor, Jupp is a principal lecturer at the University of Northumbria at Newcastle on Tyne, with special responsibility for criminology and social research methods. He was previously a lecturer in research methods at the Open University. He is author of *Methods of Criminological Research*, co-author of *Invisible Crime: their victims and their regulation*, and lead editor of *Doing Criminological Research*.

Pamela Abbott is Vice-Rector of the Kigali Institute of Science, Technology and Management in Rwanda and Professor of Social Policy at Glasgow Caledonian University. She has written a large number of books and articles but is best known as the author of *Women and Social Class, The Family and the New Right* and *Introduction to Sociology: feminist perspectives*.

David Boulton was a principal lecturer in the Department of Applied Community Studies at Manchester Metropolitan University at the time when this chapter was written. His teaching was entirely focused on undergraduate and postgraduate research methods, and his research on ways in which the construction of data influences policy outcomes, with special reference to issues surrounding policing.

Judith Calder was a senior lecturer in research methods with the Institute of Educational Technology at the Open University. She contributed to undergraduate and postgraduate courses in research methods and statistics and undertook research consultancies for the British Council, the ODA, the DfE, the Council of Europe and the World Bank. It was with deep regret that we learned of her death a few years before this second edition of the book was published.

Ruth Finnegan was Professor of Comparative Social Institutions at the Open University at the time when her chapter was written. Her publications include *Oral Literature in Africa, Literacy and Oracy: studies in the technology of communication,*

The Hidden Musicians, and a jointly edited CD-ROM entitled *Project Reports in Family and Community History.*

Peter Foster was a senior lecturer in education at Manchester Metropolitan University at the time when this chapter was written. He is author of *Practice in Multiracial and Antiracist Education* and (with Roger Gomm and Martyn Hammersley) *Constructing Educational Inequality.*

Martyn Hammersley is Professor of Education and Social Research at the Open University. His substantive research has mostly been in the sociology of education, but much of his more recent work has been concerned with methodological issues. He is author of *The Dilemma of Qualitative Method, Reading Ethnographic Research, What's Wrong with Ethnography?, The Politics of Social Research* and (with Paul Atkinson) *Ethnography: Principles and Procedures.*

William (Bill) Schofield was a developmental psychologist and statistician at the Cambridge University Department of Experimental Psychology at the time when this chapter was written and now works at the University of Sydney. He is author of a large number of reports on research into physical and mental growth, morbidity and malnutrition, is responsible for the WHO/FAG equations for the prediction of basal metabolic rate and has been consultant to international organisations and major drug companies.

Betty Swift was a lecturer in research methods in the Institute of Educational Technology at the Open University and author of a large number of reports on the University's teaching. She died in 1993, not long after the original unit was written on which this chapter is based, and she is sorely missed.

Michael Wilson was a senior lecturer in research methods in the Faculty of Social Sciences at the Open University, and before that a researcher and lecturer at Imperial College London, the University of Leeds and the University of Cardiff. His death in 1995 is deeply regretted by all his colleagues.

PART I

DESIGN ISSUES

1

Validating Evidence

Roger Sapsford and Victor Jupp

> In this chapter we shall be looking at the issues which logically (and generally in practice) precede data collection itself – what cases to select, and how the study should be designed. The major concern is with *validity*, by which we mean the design of research to provide credible conclusions: whether the evidence which the research offers can bear the weight of the interpretation that is put on it.

Every report of research embodies an argument: 'on the basis of this evidence I argue that these conclusions are true'. Within this, the evidence presented is, again, the product of a series of arguments. The authors collect certain information in certain ways from or about certain people or settings, and the research report argues that this information may be interpreted in certain ways to lead to true conclusions about a certain population. What has to be established in order that the report's conclusions can be believed is that the arguments embodied in the report are *valid* ones: that the data *do* measure or characterize what the authors claim, and that the interpretations *do* follow from them. The structure of a piece of research determines the conclusions that can be drawn from it (and, more importantly, the conclusions that *should not* be drawn from it).

We shall argue, throughout this book, that the same questions have to be answered by research studies in widely different styles and arising from widely differing epistemological bases. Some research takes an essentially *positivistic* approach to the nature of knowledge about the social world: it takes the nature of the world as relatively unproblematic – the main problems being how to measure it adequately – and it emphasizes the neutrality and separateness of the researcher from that which is under investigation. Such work is typically *reductionist*: it seeks to explain the whole by measurement and correlation of the behaviour of parts or aspects of it. Typically, it is *quantitative*: it works by measurement and analysis of relationships between the resulting numbers; and, typically, it aspires to the methods of the natural sciences. Other studies may take a more *interactionist* perspective, looking at the meaning of situations and actions for people, conceived as something not fixed and determinate but negotiated from moment to moment. Studies from this perspective are more likely to be *naturalistic*, trying to eliminate the reactive effect of research procedures on what is studied, and to proceed by observation and participation in the situation as a whole or by relatively 'open' or 'unstructured' interviews with actors in it. Others again will proceed from a more *constructionist* perspective, regarding the space within which meanings are negotiated as a product of history and of social structure, rather than just of immediate negotiation. Work of this kind is likely to proceed by the analysis of interviews or written/printed texts for models of the social world that are implicit in the text and give clues to the framework within which the writer or speaker is working. Other studies again may be more concerned with *reflexive* awareness and deal not with how things are but with how they might be – not with human nature, but with human capability, for example (see Stevens, 1995, for a discussion of this) – and these again are likely to proceed by analysis of what people say, and observation of what they do, in a holistic manner.

Whatever the form of the research and whatever its epistemological grounding, when reading a research report we shall be trying to assess whether the conclusions follow validly from the evidence. We shall therefore be asking who was researched, by what methods, and whether the logic of the comparisons made in the report is sufficient to bear the interpretation placed upon it.

Counting Cases: Measurement and Case Selection

A part of the argument in a research paper entails showing that the subjects or cases investigated can be taken as typical or representative of the population under investigation; the technical term for this question is *population validity*. A second obviously important topic is *validity of measurement*: the question of whether the measures which are used really do deliver what the researcher claims for them, or whether they give vague and error-ridden results, or even a competent measurement of something that turns out to be different from the researcher's claims. (In many ways the second of these is even more important than the first; there is no point in taking great care in selecting the sample if the measurements taken from it are uninterpretable!)

We shall begin our exploration of these two topics, in this section, with a consideration of government administrative statistics and three surveys around the topic area of crime and criminality. (The first also serves to remind us that not all research collects fresh data; valid research can equally be carried out on data already collected by someone else; see also Chapter 5.) At the end of the section, however, we shall look at a study of a rather different kind to show that the same questions may validly be posed.

Examples from UK Government Statistics

Government statistics always look authoritative and are frequently presented as carrying authority; they are, after all, prepared by government statisticians and used by government ministers for planning purposes. In fact, however, they differ very much in their quality as evidence.

At one extreme, we might look at the statistics of births and deaths. Births *have* to be registered, both by the parent(s) and by the hospital or doctor; this includes not only live births but also stillbirths and abortions. Deaths *have* to be registered before a funeral can take place. There are presumably a very few births and deaths which remain concealed – cases of murder or infanticide – but we may reasonably take these statistics as virtually accurate counts of what is occurring, as an accurate representation of the 'population' of births and deaths.

At the other extreme, let us consider *Criminal Statistics*. These are published annually by the Home Office, and they contain (among other things) a supposedly complete count of crimes recorded by the police. We may be tempted to take this as a valid measure of what crimes have been committed during the year, but it would be a mistake to do so without further thought.

Activity 1.1 (allow 5 minutes at most)

Why might it be a mistake to take the count of crimes recorded by the police as a valid measure of crimes committed?

We know that some crimes are uncovered mostly by police action (e.g. road traffic offences), but that others (e.g. burglary, car theft, rape) depend mainly on private individuals reporting them to the police. There is, therefore, an element of personal discretion in what comes to the notice of the police in the first place. (We know from other evidence that most car thefts are reported, for example – for insurance purposes – but only a minority of rapes.) Once the complaint reaches the police, the police officer may decide to record or not to record, depending on his or her assessment of whether a crime has actually been committed, or to initiate further investigation before recording. Thus, at least two levels of individual discretion are involved before an actual occurrence appears as a crime statistic; what appears in *Criminal Statistics* is not an unedited record, but one that has passed through a 'filtering process'. We would therefore handle 'crimes recorded by the police' with some caution as a measure of the 'population of crimes committed'; their validity in this respect is in doubt.

There are very many sets of official statistics that have this discretionary character – more than there are statistics that can safely be taken as neutral records of events. To take one more example, death statistics may be a valid and reliable measure, but the same cannot be said for the 'cause of death' tables. These depend on decisions made by GPs, hospital staff or coroners and are prone to human error and the uneven working of discretion as to what to record in cases of multiple causation.

Three Kinds of Crime Survey

Surveys of the victims of crime have been influential tools of criminological research, particularly in the 1980s and 1990s (for a good review of such surveys, see Walklate, 1989). Their popularity has been given impetus by official policies relating to law enforcement and also to communities taking responsibility for crime prevention. On a methodological front, further impetus was given by the widely held view of social researchers that official statistics on crime, such as those published in *Criminal Statistics*, failed to provide accurate measures of the true level of crime. Victim surveys involve the selection of a representative sample from the population. Questions are asked of sample members: whether they have ever been victims of crime within a specified period of time and whether they reported the event to the police. A major landmark in the development of victim surveys was that these large-scale surveys reported a much higher incidence of victimization than was recorded by the official statistics on crime.

Closer to home, Sparks and his colleagues carried out a much smaller and more localized survey in 1977, involving a representative sample of three areas of Inner London; this found that nearly half the sample claimed to have experienced actual or attempted crime in a 12-month period and reported an 11:1 ratio of victim-perceived to police-recorded crime. Subsequent surveys from Merseyside (Kinsey, 1986) and Islington (Jones et al., 1986; Crawford et al., 1990) have come up with broadly similar figures.

Activity 1.2 (10 minutes)

Two questions about validity of measurement:

1 What do you think are the strengths and weaknesses of victim surveys in measuring the extent of crime, compared with the official statistics?
2 If a victim survey asked whether the respondents had experienced a crime (a) in the last year and (b) in a 12-month period 10 years ago, would the comparison of these two sets of figures provide valid data for examining changes in victimization over time?

The faults of the official statistics are well known; as discussed above, *Criminal Statistics* records not what crimes were *committed* during the year, but what crimes were reported *and determined by a police officer to merit recording*. However, victim surveys are also not without their problems, which need to be taken into account when they are interpreted.

1   They are based on sample surveys, and often on relatively small samples, so there will inevitably be some degree of sampling error (see Chapter 2).
2   They involve asking people whether they have been the victims of crime, and the act of questioning sets up a social situation which may affect the answers: the

form of the question or the politics of the situation could lead respondents to lie (in either direction), or to stretch the truth to provide what they perceive as an answer acceptable to the researcher (see Chapter 4).

3   An element of judgement is involved: the survey has to take as given the respondent's judgement of what constitutes a crime. This may lead to some over-estimation of the 'true' amount of crime. For example, a broken window may be attributed to vandalism, whereas in fact it was caused by adverse weather conditions. In other cases, judgement may lead to an under-estimation. For example, in social situations and settings where violence is the norm, a victim of a beating may not view himself as the victim of a crime, even though a court of law might well judge otherwise if the case ever came to court. (The second is a more complex example than the first because judgement is required on both sides; the courts could as easily be misjudging the situation as the victim in terms of who started the fight and whether the degree of violence used was excessive.)

4   The count depends on the respondent's memory. It is possible that some events will be forgotten. More likely, however, is that the count will be inflated by crimes which occurred outside the period of the question: if you ask for everything that happened during the year from March, it is not always easy for the respondent to remember whether a given incident occurred in April, March or even February of last year.

This problem of memory is obviously even more acute for questions about what happened 10 years ago. Our memories are reconstructed in the light of present concerns, and we tend to be vague about precisely when things happened where a long time period is involved. We would hesitate, therefore, to accept a contemporary 'one-shot' survey of this kind, which asks individuals to reflect on the past, as adequate evidence of changes over time.

Activity 1.3 (5 minutes)

See if you can think of two alternative ways of collecting data about crime victimization over time which would produce more valid data than the retrospective 'one-shot' survey.

One way around the problem of retrospective data collection is to examine findings from a succession of one-shot surveys carried out at different points of time: a *time-series design* or *trend design*. For a sound base of comparison, what we need are successive surveys which sample the same population, are constructed in the same way and are uniform in their definition and operationalization of variables (that is, the translation of the concept into something measurable). For example, the General Household Survey (carried out annually by GSO) has asked questions about burglary victimization in several years of its operation, allowing comparison over time for this limited category of crime. The most notable recent example, however, is provided by the British Crime

Survey (BCS; see Mayhew and Hough, 1982). This was carried out by the Home Office Research and Planning Unit in 1982, 1984 and 1988, and there are plans to continue it every four years. While the individuals questioned are not the same at each period of time, they are sampled in the same manner and asked the same or similar questions about the crimes of which they have been victims. The main analysis provides data on crimes of different kinds, reported and not reported to the police. As with other victim surveys, the BCS uncovers substantial under-reporting of crime; it also testifies to the great fear of crime among the general population, and particularly among women, older people and those living in inner-city areas – fear out of all proportion to the measurable likelihood of becoming a victim of crime. The analysis also provides insights into the respondents' reasons for not reporting crimes. Perceived triviality of the offence is by far the most important reason, but perceived lack of interest and impotence on the part of the police are also important. Given that the same questions are asked at each point of time, there is the facility for making comparisons over time and therefore the basis for making assertions about social changes and social trends.

However, if your interest is in change in *individuals* over time rather than the changes in *populations* over time, it is a bad strategy to take unrelated samples in two time periods; if you find changes, you cannot know whether people have changed or whether the population has recruited a new kind of member. Because different individuals are chosen at each sampling point, time-series designs are not appropriate for examining changes in individuals or for studying individual development. This is the hallmark of the *longitudinal* or *cohort* design. A celebrated British example is the National Child Development Study, which selected a national sample of children born in one week in 1947 and followed them until they were in their late twenties (Douglas, 1964, 1976). Within British criminology, and the study of delinquency and the causes of crime in particular, the longitudinal or cohort study is typified by the Cambridge Study in Delinquent Development, carried out by Donald West and his colleagues.

The aims and broad strategies of the Cambridge Study were very much influenced by the previous work of the Gluecks in the USA (Glueck and Glueck, 1950, 1962), which had indicated the important influence of early family socialization and family circumstances on who did or did not subsequently become delinquent, although, by the admission of its director, it 'began as a basic fact-finding venture without strong theoretical preconceptions and without much clear notion of where it might lead' (West, 1982: 4). However, it departed from its American predecessor by using a prospective (or longitudinal) rather than a retrospective ('one-shot' or cross-sectional) design. In other words, it involved examining which individuals, out of an initial sample, subsequently became convicted of delinquent acts, as opposed to studying retrospectively the backgrounds of those who had already been convicted. The reasons for this were that

> Research with established delinquents can be misleading. Once it is known that one is deal-ing with a delinquent, recollections and interpretations of his upbringing and previous behaviour may be biased towards a preconceived stereotype. Moreover, deviant attitudes may be the result rather than the cause of being convicted of an offence. (West, 1982: 3)

In 1961, a sample of 411 working-class boys aged about 8 was drawn from the registers of six state schools in a London area, reasonably close to the researchers'

London office and with a reasonably high delinquency rate. Girls were not included in the sample, and only 12 boys came from ethnic minority groups.

> In other words, it was an unremarkable and traditional white, British, urban, working-class sample. The findings are likely, therefore, to hold true of many similar places in southern England, but they may tell us nothing about delinquency in the middle classes or about delinquency among girls or among immigrant groups. (West, 1982: 8)

The sample members were contacted at six designated ages between 8 and 21, and sub-sections of the sample were purposively selected and re-interviewed at later ages (persistent recidivists, former recidivists not convicted of an offence for five years, and a random sample of non-delinquents). The main findings (but, for more detail, see West, 1969, 1982; West and Farrington, 1973, 1977) were that five clusters of factors were predictive of delinquency:

- coming from a low-income home
- coming from a large family
- having parents considered by social workers as having performed their child-raising unsatisfactorily
- having below-average intelligence
- having a parent with a criminal record

Activity 1.4 (allow 5 minutes)

What key features of longitudinal studies are exemplified in the Cambridge Study?

The Cambridge Study typifies longitudinal studies in a number of ways. First, it is *prospective* as opposed to retrospective, following 411 8-year-old boys through their teens and twenties. Secondly, in doing so it focuses on *individual development*, especially in relation to the generation of delinquent behaviour and subsequent criminal careers. Thirdly, the study is *descriptive* in that it describes individual development and change, but also *explanatory* in the way the analysis seeks to identify factors which can explain why some sample members became delinquents. Fourthly, the study seeks to be *predictive* by investigating how far delinquent and criminal behaviour can be predicted in advance. Finally, the study illustrates a feature of longitudinal research which has not been emphasized so far in this text: that it is often closely related to policy formation.

> The major policy implications of the Cambridge Study are that potential offenders can be identified at an early age and that offending might be prevented by training parents in effective child-rearing methods, preschool intellectual enrichment programmes, giving more economic resources to poor parents and providing juveniles with socially approved opportunities for excitement and risk-taking. (Farrington, 1989: 32)

During the summer of 1991 the then Home Secretary, Kenneth Baker, held a number of seminars with teachers, clergy, magistrates, social welfare professionals and others to discuss the rising crime rate and especially the problem of youth crime. Subsequently, he outlined, in general terms, policies to identify potential offenders at an early age and to introduce the kind of preventive measures described above. His decision was influenced not only by the seminar discussions but also by the conclusions of the Cambridge Study (see *Guardian*, 19 September 1991, p. 19).

Activity 1.5 (5 minutes)

Now list the strengths and weaknesses of longitudinal cohort studies and time-series designs, as you perceive them in the light of all you have read so far, especially with regard to collecting valid measurements.

Unlike one-shot cross-sectional designs, neither time-series designs nor longitudinal cohort studies are dependent on the collection of retrospective data in seeking to relate past experience to present-day attitudes and actions. Cohort studies go beyond this in being able to collect a wide range of data about a large number of variables at different stages of the same individual's life. As Douglas, a leading exponent of longitudinal surveys, points out:

> A cohort study allows the accumulation of a much larger number of variables, extending over a much wider area of knowledge, than would be possible in a cross-sectional study. This is of course because the collection can spread over many interviews. Moreover, information may be obtained at the most appropriate time: for example, information on job entry may be obtained when it occurs, even if this varies from one member of the sample to another. (Douglas, 1976: 18)

So longitudinal surveys allow the collection of more data, and also its collection at the most *appropriate* time. The enhanced validity of measurement consequent upon sampling through time adds to the *overall* validity – the overall plausibility of the argument. This is further enhanced by the fact that the explanatory value of cohort studies is greater: the longitudinal dimension provides direct evidence of a time-ordering of variables and so gives more credibility to causal inferences which link contemporary attitudes and actions to previous background, experiences and events.

On the negative side, however, longitudinal studies are very costly compared with cross-sectional studies or even time-series designs, and they produce results very slowly. They require key members of the research team to make a long-term commitment to the project, and they also require research funding bodies with patience and foresight as to the long-term benefits of such research. With regard to the sample, there is always a risk that members will change their attitudes or behaviours as a result of being part of the study. What is more, the sample runs the risk of being seriously depleted by drop-out over the years – known as 'sample attrition'. A survey of major North American longitudinal studies (Capaldi and Patterson, 1987) found that the average attrition rate was 17 per cent; one in six of the original respondents was lost to the survey on re-interview for a range of causes, including disinclination to be interviewed, death, emigration or simple failure to notify a new address. What matters here is not just the size of the drop-out but the question of whether the representativeness of the remaining sample is seriously affected. Research on children with severe adjustment problems (Cox et al., 1977) found that they tended to be over-represented among the drop-outs. West and Farrington (1973) found that parents who were uncooperative or reluctant to participate in the study were more likely to have boys who subsequently committed delinquent acts. In attitude studies, those who are most likely to have flexible attitudes are those most likely to be geographically mobile. In workplace studies which use volunteer informants, it is quite clear that those who volunteer readily very often have different things to say about the organization than those who are not much interested in participating in the study.

A further problem shared by all research with a time dimension to data collection is that variables collected at early stages may not anticipate theoretical developments at a later stage, with the result that crucial data may not have been collected. This is sometimes referred to as 'the problem of fading relevancy'.

> Because a long-term longitudinal study takes a long time to carry out, there is a risk that the theoretical framework that served as a basis for the design of the study, for the choice of variables and for the construction of indexes and so forth, has become obsolete by the time the data collection is complete and the results can be published. (Magnusson and Bergman, 1990: 25)

It is, of course, possible to introduce different variables at later stages of either a cohort or a time-series design, but there is no way that analysis of them can benefit from the strength of the designs, which is *the comparison over time*.

A final problem common to all quantitative surveys is precisely that they are quantitative. This sub-section of the chapter has tended to concentrate on sampling and the comparison of samples, but we also need to keep measurement and the validity of measurement in mind. In order to cover large numbers of cases, it is generally necessary to degrade information to numbers – 'readings' on scales – or to collect what data can readily be counted (i.e. *size* of family rather than what it is *like* to live in families of various sizes).

In the next sub-section we shall look at a very different kind of study which provides much richer and more 'naturalistic' data. We shall be suggesting that it has the same concerns as survey research, however, and equal though opposite problems. The focus will be on case selection – what we can say about the population on the basis of cases selected from it – and the extent to which valid conclusions can be drawn from what was said to the interviewers (a question akin to 'validity of measurement').

A Study of Mothers

In the early 1980s, Abbott and Sapsford (1987b) carried out an interview project in a 'new town', interviewing mothers of children with learning difficulties (at that time labelled as 'mentally handicapped'), plus a sample of mothers whose children were *not* identified as 'handicapped'.

> Sixteen families were contacted from a list extracted for us from the school rolls of two Special Schools in the new city (one designated for the mildly handicapped and one for the severely). We carried out two interviews with each mother, separated by about a year, not

using a formal questionnaire but rather trying for the atmosphere of a friendly chat about life and work between neighbours. Although the interviews were tape-recorded, it seemed to us that this atmosphere was readily attained in most cases – the more so because Abbott was very evidently pregnant during the early interviews. ... Although we cannot claim that [this study] had a sample statistically representative of the population of mentally handicapped children, we would claim that [it covers] a good part of the range – from the mildest of borderline handicaps to the very severe. These data are contrasted with a parallel series of interviews with mothers of children who have *not* been labelled as mentally handicapped. (Abbott and Sapsford, 1987b: 46)

The target sample was obtained from two schools for children with learning difficulties, which between them covered the whole range. In one, the researchers picked names at random from the roll and wrote to them, building up a sample from those who replied and were prepared to be interviewed. In the other, the head teacher wrote to families (excluding those she knew to be in substantial distress at that time and one or two who were known to be uncooperative), and those who volunteered to be interviewed contacted the interviewers. The comparison sample was obtained by asking the mothers of children with learning difficulties to name two or three other mothers they knew in their neighbourhood, whose children had not been so labelled, and picking the one whose family composition most nearly resembled that of the mother who nominated them. (As the new city consists of areas which are very different in terms of class and occupational distribution but is reasonably homogeneous *within* areas, asking for local mothers to be nominated yielded a sample matched to a large extent for social class.) The interviews were of a loose 'life-history' variety (see Chapter 4 for a discussion of kinds of interviews), covering the women's lives (including paid employment) up to marriage, from marriage to the birth of their children, what changes the children had brought about in their lives, and the history of themselves and the children from birth.

Looking at the mothers' lives, it was evident that the same kind of physical work was involved in bringing up all young children, but the work of the mothers of children with learning difficulties went on for longer and was consequently more intense; if a child remains incontinent until 6 or 7, or even into his or her teens, the bulk of cleaning and washing tasks is very great. The most severely damaged child in the sample was blind, deaf and had no control of limbs; she needed help to sit up or turn over in bed, and washing her hair required two people (one to hold her over the sink while the other did the washing). Some help was received from family and friends (though *less* by the mothers of children with learning difficulties than the other mothers), but six of the 16 mothers in the sample received no help at all, and in five other cases the help was comparatively trivial.

At a broader level of analysis, the families of children with learning difficulties had 'social tasks' to perform over and above those of other parents. Accepting the child at all can be emotional labour:

> For about a month after I found out I didn't have any feeling for her in any way – she wasn't my baby, she was just a baby that had got to be looked after and fed and kept clean. I couldn't pick her up and cuddle her or nothing ... And I walked past the pram one day and she looked up at me and she smiled ... she just smiled ... after that I was all right.

There are social adjustments to be made, and the decision about how to 'put a public face' on the fact of handicap:

The sooner people knew, I thought, the nicer for them, because there's nothing worse than looking in a pram and it's a friend, and thinking, 'Oh goodness, what can I say?'

Some children fit well into their local communities:

He chucks his wheelchair around the street and everyone knows him, he goes in next door and has an hour in there and a cup of tea and biscuits, and then he goes off down the road, the old people love him.

But there can be problems, even with immediate family:

Let's put it this way, there were relations we have not seen since we found out about Trevor ... [and] we have only been invited to tea with Trevor once to my brother-in-law. He thinks we should put Trevor away.

Most wearing of all is not knowing, but *thinking*, what attitude other people are taking:

When I talk to people and I say, 'Mark is mentally handicapped', and as soon as they know he is coming up to sixteen, you see, you know what I mean? I don't want to put it into words, but you see it even before they say it ... It is an unspoken look. I suppose maybe I would be guilty in the same way, but there is that fear of 'danger to my daughter'.

The authors summarize the overall results of the study thus:

having a mentally handicapped child and caring for him or her at home presents a child's parents with two major tasks which are not faced in the same way by parents of 'normal' children. They have to come to terms with the fact of the child's handicap and its implications for the way in which the family is able to conduct its normal life in interaction with others. At the same time they have to deal with the way our society labels and stigmatises mental handicap – including the way that the historically determined stereotype of mental handicap spills over as a courtesy stigma for the whole family – and this means renegotiating the nature of the family's identity and building a style of life compatible with the renegotiated identity. The task is made none the easier by the fact that the parents are themselves members of the culture which stigmatises them and their children, may project their own feelings of spoilt identity onto the world at large and share to some extent the very attitudes which they are forced to combat. (Abbott and Sapsford, 1987b: 55–6)

It is worth noting that, contrary to expectation, it was not always the child with learning difficulties who was 'the problem' for the family. One mother, for example, was more worried about her eldest child, who had a spell of truanting from school in response to bullying by local children which followed his evident grief at his grandmother's death. Another mother had a child suffering from cystic fibrosis who required daily medical and nursing attention. Another had a child who had been 'teacher's pet' at a small village school and was not adapting to the transfer to a larger secondary school in the new city.

Activity 1.6 (allow 20 minutes)

Look back over the foregoing description in the light of the issues raised so far in this chapter, and make notes on how far it is possible to generalize from the sample and how the nature of the information differs in this study from the ones discussed earlier. Also consider the role of the comparison group in the research.

In terms of representation, this study is clearly inferior to the others already described. The studies we have looked at so far either count all of a class of events or draw a sample which is calculated to be representative in detail of the parent population. In this case we have a sample which cannot be guaranteed to be representative; when the authors say that six of the 16 families did such and such, it would be a mistake to suppose that 37.5 per cent of the parent population would do likewise, and we have no basis for saying how large the error in estimation of percentages actually is. In fact, we know that the sample is biased: it is a volunteer sample – so those who volunteered are likely to have had something they wanted to say – and one of the two schools deliberately excluded certain categories of potential informant (those known to be in distress). The aim was to talk to a typical range of cases, and this may well have been achieved, but we are unable to say the extent to which the sample is unrepresentative of the population.

Beyond this, it is typical of studies of this kind that the data are not precise measurements but rich and complex conversational material. What was picked out of the conversation and included in the analysis was what the authors thought it was important to present to the reader. Even in the full report it would not have been possible to include unedited transcripts (an hour's conversation typically running to 20 pages of transcript). In terms of counts of, for example, amount of help given, the report is undoubtedly factually accurate (within the limitations of decisions about what counts as 'giving help', which is a problem shared by more quantified research). When describing the lives of the mothers, a degree of interpretation necessarily intrudes; although the authors quote a fair amount of what was said to them, this is illustration rather than, strictly, evidence. Where they are framing overall conclusions about the mothers' lives or classifying them into types, what they are doing is to 'give an account' of what they perceive to be true of the data – to 'tell a story' on the basis of the factual evidence.

Furthermore, it is a story based on data which are themselves presented as a story. The informant tells her story, in particular circumstances and to particular interviewers, with a particular perception of what the interviewers are looking to learn and what, therefore, it is relevant to discuss. The interviewers, in their turn, interpret what is said in order to 'tell a story' – or a series of stories of increasing abstraction – based on the material that they have been given. One needs to be well aware of the circumstances of the interview and the predilections of the analysts before what they have to say is acceptable as a plausible account of people's lives.

Against these undoubted weaknesses can be argued the strengths of this kind of approach, all of which revolve around the richness of the data obtained and the comparative lack of structure in the method by which they are collected. One may argue, for example, that even one typical case researched in depth tells us more about a group than superficial information on every member of it: for example, that a thorough exploration of one person's views on religion gives us more insight than figures on church attendance for a whole population. Further, all structured methods involving systematic observation, counting or questionnaires, require decisions *beforehand* as to what is to be relevant, while the relatively unstructured methods used in this study allow surprising information to surface and may question the researchers' preconceptions more readily than more structured approaches.

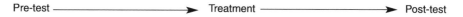

Pre-test ────────────────▶ Treatment ────────────────▶ Post-test

Figure 1.1 *Diagrammatic representation of simple action research*

Comparing Groups: the Logic of Design

In this section we look at a broader aspect of research as evidence: the logic of the arguments that can be based upon it. Whether the research study is structured to make a particular point from the start or the argument is imposed *post hoc* in the process of writing a report, all research reports embody an argument: this or that is the case, on the basis of the evidence presented. The basic point is that most research depends on *comparison* to establish its conclusions.

We have already looked at the importance of comparisons as tools for drawing conclusions, particularly in the study of mothering children with learning difficulties. In this section we look at how comparison is managed, for what purpose and with what success, in those styles of research which are most explicitly based around comparison of groups or 'conditions': quasi-experimental comparisons and true experiments.

Quasi-experimental Analysis: Road Traffic Fatalities

The classic and most often quoted comparison of naturally occurring groups – capitalizing on changes happening 'in the real world' rather than changes introduced by a researcher – concerns the Connecticut 'crackdown' of the 1950s. This was a drastic public programme in one American state re-inforcing police action to curb excessively fast driving, on which a secondary analysis of published figures was carried out by Donald Campbell (Campbell and Ross, 1968; Campbell, 1969). After an unprecedentedly bad year for traffic fatalities, the governor of Connecticut introduced a programme of administrative orders which made it more certain that drivers who exceeded the speed limit would be caught and, if caught, punished. The net result was a decrease in traffic fatalities within the state of roughly 12 per cent. As it stands, this action has many of the qualities of the simplest kind of *action research*, where researchers/practitioners introduce some kind of change and monitor its effects (except that in this case the change was introduced by the authorities, not the researchers). Figure 1.1 illustrates this kind of research diagrammatically.

Activity 1.7 (10 minutes)

What problems do you see with the conclusion that the governor of Connecticut's action caused fatalities to fall by 12 per cent? Stop and make notes on alternative explanations for the results.

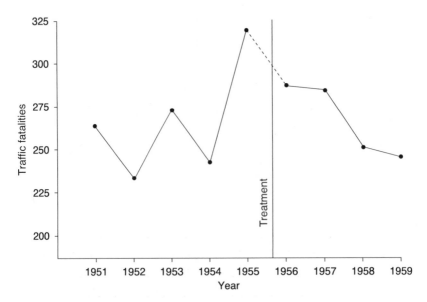

Figure 1.2   *Connecticut traffic fatalities, 1951–1959 (Campbell, 1969: Figure 2)*

Several problems occurred to Campbell, but most of them were answerable by further analysis.

1   There could have been a *trend effect* – the figures could have been going down over the years in any case – coupled with a *regression effect*. (*Regression to the mean* is the technical term for what happens when you look at figures which fluctuate widely around an underlying mean or average trend. Because there is a mean or trend it is very likely, if you have picked an extreme fluctuation, that any other figure will be closer to the mean – and you will remember that the crackdown was initiated because of an *unprecedented* fatality rate.) To explore this we need to compare figures over a longer period than just two years, which is what Campbell did (Figure 1.2). As you can see, there is no obvious trend to explain the decrease in 1956; the figures tend upwards to 1955 and downwards thereafter.

2   There was the possibility that recording practices had changed: for example, by police being less willing to attribute road deaths to speeding. The mere fact of introducing a public programme could have an effect on the record-keeping as well as the driving. Such an effect may well have occurred and the research design is powerless to guard against it.

3   Other equally possible explanations might include: changed weather, changes in petrol prices, changes in drinking behaviour; anything, in fact, that might change driving behaviour. It was possible to guard against most of these, however, by the design of the analysis. What Campbell and his colleagues did was to compare Connecticut with a 'control group' – a set of four comparison states in which the crackdown had *not* taken place. Traffic fatality figures from these four states over

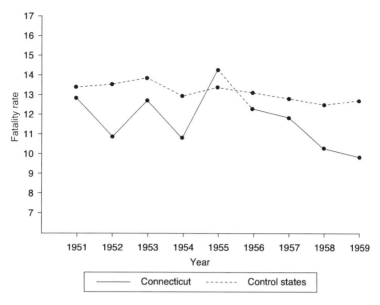

Figure 1.3 *Control series design comparing Connecticut fatalities with those in four comparable states (Campbell, 1969: Figure 11)*

the same period failed to show the downward trend visible in Connecticut (Figure 1.3), and it is therefore likely that none of these factors was responsible for the decrease.

The use of comparison between an 'experimental group' and a 'control group' is a very regular feature of studies which try to show the causal force of treatments, and it is logically very strong. To the extent that the control and experimental groups are alike before treatment, and only the experimental group is treated, if they differ after the treatment the difference must logically be attributable to the treatment. Diagrammatically, this kind of design may be represented by Figure 1.4 (see p. 16). The measurements for the two groups will seldom be identical before the treatment, but the real interest is in the difference between pre-test and post-test measurements. In Figure 1.3, for example, the experimental group shows a marked decline from the point of treatment while the control group does not.

Activity 1.8 (5 minutes)

Pause and think: can this design cope with the problem of changes in recording practice listed in Point 2 above?

The use of a control group does not eliminate factors *confounded* with the treatment – things which vary with or as a result of the treatment and therefore cannot be

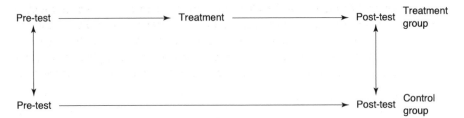

Figure 1.4   *Diagrammatic representation of comparative research using a treatment group and a control group*

distinguished from it. If there were changes in recording practice in Connecticut, for example, these would be specific to the treatment group (they would be part of what happened when the treatment was applied) and could not affect the control group, so the presence of a control group does not eliminate them. What it does make less likely is that a factor *independent of the treatment* was the cause of the decrease in fatalities.

Experiments in HIV Counselling

Consider the following studies:

1   80 pregnant drug users participating in a methadone maintenance programme were assigned at random to a six-session cognitive/behavioural programme or to a 'control group' who received no such intervention (O'Neill et al., 1996).
2   119 drug users were randomly assigned to a 50-minute or a 15-minute counselling session (Gibson et al., 1999).
3   295 drug users participating in a heroin detoxification programme were randomly assigned to a 50-minute individual counselling session (discussing options and trying to increase condom use) or to receive a package of brochures which covered the same ground (Gibson et al., 1999).
4   152 cocaine users were randomly assigned to an experimental programme of three two-hour small-group counselling sessions or to an information programme presenting material on video and in print (Malow et al., 1994).
5   50 people on methadone maintenance were assigned randomly, either to a programme of active presentation of HIV information in small groups, or to receive only brochures (Sorenson et al., 1994).

In all these studies there were pre-intervention measures of AIDS knowledge and self-report measures of condom use.

Activity 1.9 (10 minutes)

Compare these studies with the Connecticut Crackdown and your notes on the Abbott and Sapsford research. What is the function of control/comparison groups in each case, and how effectively does each use this feature? What is distinctively different about the five studies described above?

The five studies all follow the clean lines of the comparative design which we examined above and illustrated in Figure 1.4. One group of subjects received the treatment and the other, picked to be similar to the first, did not, or two treatments are compared; both were tested before and after treatment was applied to one group. The five studies differ from the others described earlier in two important respects:

1   The researchers had control of the treatment. In both the other studies the researchers were looking at 'naturally occurring' variation: in one case, an administrative change to police and court procedure, initiated by a state governor, and, in the other, the natural experience of having and bringing up a child with learning difficulties. In the five studies, on the other hand, it was the researchers who determined what the treatment should be and how it should be run. This clearly gives more opportunity for eliminating possible alternative explanations for the results.
2   The similarity of the groups can to a large extent be guaranteed in the five studies; groups were picked randomly from the same population, which maximizes the chance that anything of importance will be equally distributed between the two groups. In the other studies, the researchers had to 'make do' with naturally occurring dimensions of difference. Campbell and his colleagues had to argue quite carefully and extensively for the validity of the comparison of Connecticut with the four 'comparison states': the extent to which the states used for comparison were really comparable with the state where the 'treatment' occurred. Abbott and Sapsford made some attempt to match the two groups, on social class and family composition, but the success of their efforts is by no means guaranteed.

The difference between the five studies and Campbell's work is that the five studies are *experimental*, while Campbell's is at best a *quasi-experimental* design (to use Campbell's term). An experiment (also called a *controlled trial* in the medical world) is defined as a study in which:

1   The allocation to treatment or control group is under the control of the researcher and can be arranged to maximize the likelihood of having comparable groups.
2   The treatment is under the control of the researcher and can be arranged to minimize the likelihood of other alternative explanatory factors being confounded with its effects.

Activity 1.10 (5 minutes)

What do you see as the advantages of experimental over quasi-experimental designs? Are there corresponding *dis*advantages?

The same logic underlies both kinds of study. The advantage of experimental designs is that the logic is more clearly applied, eliminating a greater number of possible alternative explanations by the design of the study itself. If you measure the state of a group of people at the outset, then administer a treatment, produce measurable changes and *can guarantee that no factor other than the treatment could have produced the effect*, then you are on strong ground in arguing that the treatment produced the effect. Quasi-experimental studies, which capitalize on existing differences between people and/or their circumstances rather than direct manipulation by the experimenter, can never quite offer this guarantee: there are always other potential explanatory factors which might have produced the observed effect. The best you can do is to explore and eliminate those which occurred to you and on which you therefore collected data, by means of statistical control at the analysis stage (see Chapters 9 and 10).

We should note that logical design does not guarantee results which uphold the researcher's prior expectations. In these five studies, for example, the results were:

1   No difference in reported condom use was reported by either group at three months or at 12 months after the study.
2   There was no difference between the groups nine months after the study.
3   Six- and twelve-month follow-up studies indicated no difference between the groups.
4   Both groups showed a significant reduction in sexual risk-taking three months later, but there was no significant difference between them. However, there was a trend for previously high-risk 'players' on the experimental programme to show greater reduction than those on the information programme.
5   Both groups showed enhanced knowledge immediately after the programme, with those who had attended the active small-group programme knowing significantly more than those who had received only brochures. The difference between the groups was not apparent at three-month follow-up, however.

In other words, none of these studies suggests that counselling or the active provision of information has a lasting effect on subsequent behaviour. It is characteristic of good research design that what the researcher wants to support stands a good chance of *failing* to achieve support; unbiased design provides good support for conclusions, when it does so, precisely *because* the result could have gone the other way.

Four major disadvantages or weaknesses of experimental studies occur to us:

1   It is not possible, even in principle, to *guarantee* that no factor other than the treatment could have produced the effect. You can control for what you know to be important, by the design of the study or by statistical control after the event (see Chapter 9), and you can use randomization techniques to try to even out every other difference between groups, but you can never be sure that you have succeeded. It may still be necessary to control for sources of variation.
2   Some factors cannot be manipulated. Studies of gender, class, age and so on will always have to be at most quasi-experimental because we cannot allocate people to different conditions of them. Similarly, the comparison of risk-takers and others in the fourth study is quasi-experimental; it capitalizes on pre-existing difference.
3   Even where the explanatory variable under consideration does lend itself to manipulation and to the allocation of people to one condition or another, ethical considerations may require us to confine ourselves to a fairly small manipulation,

and this may trivialize what we are studying. (The ethics of social research are discussed in more detail in Chapter 13.)

4   An added factor about experiments is that they are often very obviously 'research', and this could provide an alternative explanation of any results obtained. If people know they are in a research situation, this in itself can change their behaviour or attitudes. (This is not a *necessary* characteristic of experimental research, however; for example, some experiments are unobtrusive and not obvious to their subjects, while most surveys are obviously a 'research situation', which may well affect the nature of the response).

Activity 1.11 (allow 20 minutes)

The experiment appears to follow a very clear and indisputable form of logic: if we have two identical groups, intervene to administer a treatment to one and not to the other (or administer two different treatments), control all other possible differences and produce a difference in outcome, then the outcome must have been due to the intervention. There are still problems with it, however; spend some time thinking about such research and see if you can identify them.

The weakness of experimental logic, as outlined here, is that it omits to consider part of the context of the argument.

1   In the perfectly designed and executed experiment it may be possible to show *what* caused the effect, but it will not be possible to show *why*. An experiment does not demonstrate the truth of a theory; a variable may have its effect for the reason the researcher posits or for a wide variety of other reasons.

2   The logic of an experiment argues from cause to effect via control of other variables. In many cases, however, the argument that other variables have been controlled, or are not related and may be ignored, will itself rest on a body of theoretical assumptions, and these are not tested by a given experiment but taken for granted. Thus, when an apparent disproof is produced, we shall not know whether the fault is in the theory being tested or in one of the assumptions being taken for granted.

3   Finally, and perhaps most importantly, what the variables mean is not a thing measured but something interpreted on the basis of a whole body of theory. Again, if a negative finding is produced, we shall not know whether the fault lies in the theory under test or in the wider body of theories which define the situation and the meaning of what is being measured.

In these five studies the interpretation is not helped by the inherent difficulty in precise definition of the independent variable (the intervention). All of the papers cited go to considerable lengths to define what *kind* of counselling or cognitive work or information provision is on offer to the experimental group, under what circumstances, how often and for how long. Nonetheless, if there were positive results and they failed to replicate (to be repeated in another precisely similar experiment) it might be because of subtle but important differences in the different applications of supposedly the same counselling or information provision, by different counsellors or teachers, to subtly different populations.

We might go on to question some experimental programmes from another angle – that is, their ethics. It is a perennial ethical problem of research into medical or psychiatric treatments, for example, or into new and efficient ways of schooling, that the efficacy of the treatment can best be demonstrated by applying it to some but withholding it from others. You will note that most of the five studies above do not withhold treatment or information from the control/comparison group but contrast one form or duration of intervention with another. The ethical problems of research which causes pain or distress to its subjects or informants, or in some way disadvantages them, are not confined to experimental research, though they tend to be most obvious there. One may reasonably ask, for example, whether it is justified to cause distress to people who have suffered in the past by opening up the areas of their suffering and pursuing them in interview, simply 'to pursue the truth'. External examiners of academic courses frequently have to ask whether students who explore areas such as AIDS or sexual abuse for their compulsory research dissertations have legitimate access to the area already – for example, they are already doing counselling in the area – or whether they are just trading on human misery in order to do an exciting third-year project. The whole question of the use of people and their experiences as 'research fodder' – the treatment of people as objects by researchers – has been opened up in recent years by, for example, feminist theorists (see Mies, 1993). It is a question to which we shall return in Chapter 13.

Establishing Boundaries in Qualitative Studies

So far we have looked mostly at 'quantitative' studies: research which yields data in the form of numbers to be analyzed by means of comparisons. The logic of comparison also has a large part to play, however, in 'qualitative' studies – ones where the data are in the form of people's words or the researcher's descriptions of what he or she has observed and experienced. For example, in the Abbott and Sapsford (1987b) study which we considered above, if you describe the lives of *mothers who have children with learning difficulties* you are necessarily at the same time describing *mothers with children*; the two are inevitably confounded. It is only by having a group of mothers whose children do *not* have learning difficulties that you can draw more specific conclusions with any degree of validity. What the two groups have in common will be what is true of 'having children', but the areas in which they differ will be aspects specific to 'having children with learning difficulties'. The presence of a comparison group acts to draw a boundary around the conclusions, enabling the researcher to say what is true of the larger group and what holds only for the target group.

This kind of use of a comparison group is a special case of a more general principle of design, which we can illustrate best by means of a fictional example. Suppose we had an interest in why girls tend not to go into science and mathematics at school, except for biology, and to be over-represented in the arts and humanities. We start by 'exploring the field' in a relatively unfocused way, watching and listening to classes, visiting homes, hanging around places where young people go in the evening, and so on. (Already we have used a form of sampling: sampling of the range of contexts in which young people are active and learn and express their ideas.) Gathering data, we progressively focus our original vague question down into something more concrete and explorable. We find, let us say, that among working-class girls it is difficult to say what puts them off the sciences and mathematics because everything seems to push in the same direction: teachers, parents, friends and boyfriends all seem to express surprise at or distaste for a girl becoming involved in the sciences. Among middle-class girls, however, we might find that parents and teachers are positively supportive of any interests they might have in the sciences. Their friends, however, and particularly their male friends, seem to treat them as something strange if they opt for the sciences. We have a tentative model of what is going on, then: something in the 'boy/girl culture' is having the effect of making some curriculum choices less attractive than others.

A first stage of drawing boundaries would be to sample classes which were very similar to the ones we used initially – possibly other classes in the same school. If the model fits them as well, then at least it has some generality; if it does not, then there was something idiosyncratic about the particular classes with which we started. Let us say that it does turn out to have some generality. We should then want to sample more widely, to see *how much* generality it has. Does it hold for other classes in the same city? Does it hold for other regions? Does it hold for other English-speaking countries? Each of these comparisons is an attempt to see how widely the idea generalizes: to find the boundaries within which an idea is useful, or the conditions under which a theory holds.

Finally, we might want to start testing particular ideas and assumptions by careful sampling of unlikely milieux. Our tentative model is beginning to be cast in terms of a Western English-speaking 'culture of femininity', let us say. Does it hold, therefore, in schools where the predominant 'culture of femininity' has a potentially different origin? We could test this by finding schools where the majority of students are of Asian origin, say, and seeing whether the same model holds. Above all, our model is about the interaction of the genders, so a very interesting 'crucial case' would be to see what goes on at single-sex schools. If the matter is determined simply by school interaction, then the model should not be as useful in single-sex schools. Suppose, however, that the girls who went in for science and mathematics were seen differently even within single-sex schools. It *could* still be gender-related: there could still be 'masculine' and 'feminine' stereotypes, with the cross-gender roles taken by people of inappropriate gender in single-sex schools where those of the appropriate gender are not available. In that case, we might expect wider stereotyping – that these people acquired inappropriate sex-linked stereotypes outside the field of their academic choices as well. It might be that we were quite mistaken, and gender is not the determining variable that we were inclined to think it was. It could be that the influence of parents or boyfriends outside the school was greater than we had supposed. Whatever the case, there would be further research to be done before we came up with a satisfactory model of what was going on.

In other words, without a carefully constructed basis of comparison we are not able to say precisely what it is that has been found out. We cannot say what is specific to girls in schools without contrasting them with boys, nor whether it is specific to the mixing of girls and boys in classes without contrasting mixed schools with single-sex ones.

Conclusion

We can see that the act of comparison is a central logical device for establishing the validity of a line of argument within research. We use comparison to say why a group is interesting, what about it is interesting, and by how much it differs from expectation.

Planned comparisons are a central element of research design: they are what enables us to draw conclusions and to determine the range over which our conclusions hold true.

Unplanned or *ad hoc* comparisons in the course of a research programme may also shape the initial idea into a firm conclusion and allow it to be put forward as a finding, supported by evidence as well as argument. We know very little about anything except in comparison with something else. In experimental and survey research another crucial issue is validity of measurement – the extent to which what is measured and analyzed does actually reflect what the researcher is seeking, and the extent to which the reader can clearly tell that it does so.

In less structured research we do not have 'variables' to 'measure', but it is still important that the circumstances of the data collection assure us that the evidence which is brought forward is plausibly interpreted.

Comparison between groups may be equally as important here as in more 'quantitative' research, in allowing us to establish boundaries for the group about whom our conclusions are true.

Key Terms

Confounded variables/elements   aspects of the data which generally cannot be separated even by statistical means (e.g. age and historical period in which born, in a one-shot survey), or biological gender and experience of having been socialized as a male or a female.

Control   the imposition of structure on data in order to distinguish the effects of different factors or variables.

– *Design control*: designing data-collection to ensure that no variables are *confounded* (see above) – as in the experiment.
– *Statistical control*: distinguishing the effects of variables at the analysis stage, as in most survey analysis.

Constructionism   a view of the social world as a product of history and developing structures, and of human behaviour as societally and historically more than biologically defined.

Experiment   a study in which precisely measured interventions are applied to groups selected by the experimenter (randomly or by matching characteristics) as identical at the start of the research, so that any measured outcomes can unambiguously be attributed to the intervention.

Holism   treating the research situation as a whole – the opposite of *reductionism* (below).

Interactionism a view of the social world as a product of the interacting meaning-systems, and actions of people and groups and of human behaviour as socially more than biologically defined.

Longitudinal (cohort) survey designs ones which take measurements, repeated over time, from the same people or units.

Naturalism trying to disturb the natural situation as little as possible; acknowledging that the research situation modifies the natural situation and therefore trying to minimize the amount of imposed structure.

One-shot surveys surveys which collect data at one point of time only (often involving retrospective measurement of what has occurred in the past).

Positivism the view that social scientific research should follow the principles and methods of the physical and biological sciences, that the major problems are problems of measurement and that the researcher can and should remain external to the research.

Quasi-experimental analysis analysis of survey data which tries to follow the logic of *experimental* research (see above) but were collected from naturally occurring rather than experimenter-selected groups.

Reductionism identifying the logical elements of a situation or process, for separate and uncontaminated study.

Regression to the mean if there is an underlying trend in figures, with data-points varying randomly around it, and if you select a data-point reasonably remote from the mean, then it is highly probable that the next data-point will be closer to it.

Time-series (trend) survey designs studies which take repeated measurements over time but draw a fresh sample each time.

Validity the extent to which the research conclusions can plausibly be taken to represent a state of affairs in the wider world.

– *Population validity*: the extent to which a sample may be taken as representing or typical of the population from which it is drawn.
– *Validity of measurement*: the extent to which we are assured that the measurements in the research do indeed represent what the researcher says they represent and are not produced by the research process itself.

Further Introductory Reading

Jupp, V. (1989) *Methods of Criminological Research*, London, Allen and Unwin (Chapter 2).
Sapsford, R.J. (1999) *Survey Research*, London, Sage (Chapters 1 and 2).
Sapsford, R.J. and Abbott, P.A. (1998) *Research Method for Nurses and the Caring Professions*, 2nd edn, Buckingham, Open University Press (Chapter 1).

Summary Activity: Preparing Your Research Proposal

One of the key aims of this book is to develop the ability to read research reports critically, in a way that facilitates the assessment of validity. A second aim is to develop abilities in the production of research ideas and, more specifically, research proposals and strategies for examining such ideas (for example, proposals for thesis/dissertation research). The aim is to be able to plan research that will produce conclusions that other readers will find valid and credible. For this reason, you will find an activity at the end of each chapter which relates to the production of a research proposal. Each time the activity recurs it will provide a set of questions or prompts relating to material in the chapter. Not all of these questions will be relevant to your own proposed research, but they are all worthy of being addressed – if only to rule them out after assuring yourself that the issues *have* been addressed.

You add to your proposal as you progress through each chapter and as you move from considering design issues through to data collection, data analysis and the drawing of conclusions from such analysis. Cutting across these stages are questions concerning the choice of quantitative as opposed to qualitative data, the choice of primary data collection as opposed to secondary analysis, and questions about the ethics and politics of your research. The first version of the activity draws on material from this chapter and asks you to address questions such as 'Who should I include in my design?' (case selection), 'What data should I collect about them?' (data collection) and 'Over what period of time?' (comparison over time).

1 This chapter has emphasized the importance of validity: that is, designing research such that possible conclusions about the research problem can flow logically from the evidence generated. Valid answers start with clear questions, so what is the research problem or question at the centre of your proposed research?

2 Given the aim of seeking to reach valid conclusions about the research problem, what form of research design (or combination of these) would seem appropriate?

- one based on secondary analysis of data?
- survey-based research?
- naturalistic or qualitative research?
- quasi-experimental analysis?
- an experimental design?

3 With regard to case selection:

- what cases should be selected (individuals, groups of individuals, interactions, social settings, etc.)?
- how should these be selected (at random, using volunteers, taking naturally occurring groups, events or settings, etc.)?
- are the cases to be selected typical or even representative of the population of individuals, groups or contexts about which you wish to draw conclusions?

4 (a) In what ways does your case selection facilitate comparison between individuals, groups or settings (for example, comparison of the answers of different groups of individuals to the same questions, comparison of the behaviour of the same people in different settings, comparison of figures from different years, comparison of present experience and remembered experience in the past, comparison of documents produced by differently 'situated' sources)?

(b)   Are these comparisons appropriate to the research problem you are addressing, and will they be able to yield valid conclusions about the problem?

5   In what ways does your case selection allow comparison over time, and how does this relate to the research problem in terms of, say, examining changes in society (trend studies) or changes in individuals (cohort studies)? Is comparison over time at all relevant to your research question?

6   What measurements, if any, does your research problem require, and how will these be collected (for example, at first hand or by accessing secondary data)? Is it likely that the figures produced will be justifiable as measurements of what we want them to measure (validity of measurement).

2

Survey Sampling

William Schofield

This chapter is about the methods and problems of designing and undertaking sample surveys. The contents are relevant to other quantified
research methods, however, since inferences about population values
from sample measurements will be at the heart of all of them. Even at the
simple level of a survey conducted on one occasion, possibly by questionnaire, or structured interview, or planned selective observation, inference
is involved. What is being inferred is a characteristic, or characteristics, of
the population, and this is inferred from the subset of measurements
obtained from the sample. Behind this process are mathematical models
and theorems which underpin the validity of the inferences so made.

Already in this introduction a number of technical terms have been
used, and you will probably be uncertain of their meaning. This is nothing
to be concerned about. A specialist topic such as sampling methodology
is bound to need a specialized terminology, and the first objective of the
sections that follow is to explain this terminology and to give examples.
The overall aims of the chapter can be summarized in two sentences:

1 It will introduce methods for obtaining representative samples of
appropriate size from a population, and for providing estimates of how
accurate statistics calculated from any such sample are likely to be.
2 It will present and discuss problems in applied survey sampling, for
example non-response, unreliable or invalid measurement, sample
loss, incomplete data, and ways of reducing the effect of these on the
final results.

Sampling

A *sample* is a set of elements selected in some way from a population. The aim of sampling is to save time and effort, but also to obtain consistent and unbiased estimates of
the population status in terms of whatever is being researched. The important point to
note here is the very restricted meaning given to the term *population* in statistics, which

is quite different from everyday usage. Thus, a population could be all the children in some group of interest, perhaps all the children in one school, or all the children in a specified age range in a certain district, or city, or in the UK overall. A population consists of individuals, or *elements*, and these could be persons, or events, or cabbages, nuts or bolts, cities, lakes, patients, hospitals or thunderstorms: anything at all of research interest, including observations, judgements, abstract qualities, etc.

Usually, in survey research, we will be interested not just in the characteristics of a sample, but in those of the population from which the sample has been drawn. Descriptive statistics for a population are called *population parameters* to contrast them with *sample statistics*. Usually, the aim of a research project is not exact measurement of population parameters, such as is undertaken in a general census, but the collection of sample data to be used both to calculate sample statistics and to estimate how close these are to the unknown population parameters, i.e. to estimate the extent of *sampling error*, a concept which will be explained fully in this chapter. Thus, matters of interest in applied sampling include:

1 What methods are available and what are the advantages and disadvantages of each of them, theoretically, in practical terms, and in terms of cost?
2 How close will statistics calculated from samples be to the unknown population parameters?
3 How much will sample size influence this?
4 Which will be the most effective methods of drawing representative samples (that is, minimizing sampling error as much as possible) and in which circumstances?
5 Given that a sample has been appropriately drawn, how can the effects of non-response, or sample loss in any form, be estimated?

Researchers and statisticians have developed techniques for dealing with matters such as these, and they have also developed a specialized terminology so that they can be defined and discussed. The objective of the section is to introduce you to the essential basics of this terminology.

Defining the Population to be Sampled

The first step in sampling is to define the population of interest clearly and accurately. Such definition may seem obvious to a novice, but it is where survey design can all too easily be defective. For example, the intended population might be housebound single parents of young children, but if these were found *via* the records of a social or health service agency then a substantial bias might be introduced by the exclusion of parents not using, or not known to, such agencies. A further obvious example is using the telephone to contact respondents; this limits representativeness to persons meeting selection criteria, but only if they also are available by telephone. Such individuals might differ in very relevant ways from the intended population of interest. Problems such as these can be avoided by defining a population as the total collection of elements actually available for sampling, rather than in some more general way. The words 'group' and 'aggregate' get close to what statisticians mean by a population (Kendall, 1952). A useful discipline for the researcher, therefore, is to bear firmly in mind precisely which elements were available in the intended population

and which were not, and to use this information to limit the extent of the claims he
or she makes about the generalizability of the results.

Sampling Units

For the purposes of sampling, populations can be thought of as consisting of *sampling units*. These are collections of elements which do not overlap and which
exhaust the entire population. For example, if the elements were fingers, and the
population all the fingers in the UK, then the sampling units could be geographical
regions, provided they covered the whole of the UK and did not overlap. Or the sampling units could be families, or individual persons, or hands. If the elements were
persons over 60 who lived alone but who were currently receiving nursing care in
hospital immediately following major surgery, and the population were all such individuals in the UK, then the sampling units could be geographical regions, or hospitals, but not cities, because these might not exhaust the population of interest.
Sampling cities might, for example, exclude individuals living in rural areas.

The Sampling Frame

When a survey is being set up, the sampling units are organized by the researcher
into a *sampling frame*. A sampling frame is whatever is being used to identify the
elements in each sampling unit. Remember that each sampling unit could contain
many elements, in the case of geographical regions, or just one, in the case of simple
random sampling from the voting register. Whatever the circumstances, the sampling
frame provides access to the individual elements of the population under study,
either via sampling units, or directly when these and the population elements are
identical (for example, where we are sampling people from a finite population and
we have a complete list of the names of the population).

The sampling frame could be anything at all provided that it exhausts the total
population. For example, it could be company employment records, or school class
lists, or hospital files, or the voting register. Such lists and records will always contain mistakes, but they may be the only method of finding the sample elements so
that the population can be surveyed. The survey results, when they are available, will
give some information on the extent of inaccuracy of this sort, for example by providing a count of voters no longer resident at the address given in the register. It will
then be possible to see whether or not these inaccuracies are fairly evenly spread
across the sampling frame. It is possible that greater housing mobility will be more
typical of certain sample elements than others, leading to bias in the survey results.
(Incidentally, the term *bias* has a precise meaning in statistics. In this chapter it refers
to an effect on the sample data from anything that moves the value of a statistic calculated from that sample (such as a mean) further from the true population value
than would have been the case if that effect were not present.)

Another and more invidious source of bias in sampling is faulty selection of the
sampling frame itself. In the real world of survey research, a sample is not really a
random set of elements drawn from those which define the population being
researched; researchers can only strive to make it as close to this as possible. In practice, a sample can only be a collection of elements from sampling units drawn from
a sampling frame, and if that *sampling frame* is not fully representative of the

population to be described, then the sample will also be unrepresentative. For this reason, great care should be taken in deciding just what sources will provide the sampling frame for a survey before the frame is set up and the sample drawn.

It is important to understand that if a sampling frame is a biased representation of the population to be studied, increasing sample size will not help – the bias will remain. Even an up-to-date electoral register might not provide an accurate frame for selecting a sample from the population of voters in an approaching election. This is because it will include people who did not, in the event, vote, although they may have intended to do so when surveyed, and these individuals might differ in relevant ways from those who did vote. It will also include those who have moved away, or died, and will not include those who have actively avoided registration for some reason; for example, to avoid jury service or a local tax.

These points have been stressed because, until one is faced with the task of accounting for an unexpected or even improbable result in survey research, locating the elements of a population might seem to involve only the practical issues of gaining access to records or lists. Clearly, there is much more to it than this.

Selecting a Sample

Having identified the population to be researched, and arranged access to it via an accurate sampling frame, the next step will be to decide how the sample itself is to be selected. The objective will be to obtain estimates of population parameters, and some methods will do this more accurately than others. The choice of method will be a question of balancing accuracy against cost and feasibility. The methods available fall into two main categories: probabilistic sampling and non-probabilistic sampling. *Probabilistic sampling* includes simple random sampling, stratified random sampling and, if selection is at least in part random, cluster sampling. The most widely used method of *non-probabilistic sampling* is quota sampling.

Sampling will often be the only feasible method of obtaining data, quite apart from questions of time and cost. But do not assume that extending a sample to include all elements in a population (i.e. conducting a census) would necessarily give better information. In some circumstances, a sample will be more accurate than a census, as well as cheaper, quicker and less invasive of the community. Some sources of discrepancy between the estimated (measured) and true population value, which will hereafter be referred to as *error*, are more likely in a large-scale census than in a small and tightly managed sampling survey.

Activity 2.1 (10 minutes)

Write a brief account (100–120 words) of what you think might be greater problems for a census than for a sampling survey, assuming a fairly large, and dispersed, population (as in the national census).

Answers to activities are given at the end of the chapter.

Error is another word with a specialized meaning in sampling theory. It is not synonymous with 'mistake', and does not mean 'wrong', although a mistake by an interviewer or a wrong answer to a question would each contribute to error in a survey, whether a sample survey or a census. In addition to this, for many things measured there will be variation from many sources, including individual variation, and looking at this from the perspective of a summary statistic such as the mean, this will also be error.

In your answer to Activity 2.1 you probably mentioned some factors such as field-work problems, interviewer-induced bias, the nature or insensitivity of the measuring instrument or clerical problems in managing large amounts of data. Bias from sources such as these will be present irrespective of whether a sample is drawn or a census taken. For that reason it is known as *non-sampling* error. It will be present in sample survey results, but will not be attributable to the sampling method itself. This is an important distinction.

Error which *is* attributable to sampling, and which therefore is not present in census-gathered information, is called *sampling error.* Since a sample has both kinds of error, whereas a census only has the former, you might conclude that the advantage really does rest with the census. The point from Activity 2.1 was, however, that the scale of census-taking makes it difficult to reduce the risk of non-sampling error, and that this can be easier to do in a well-planned sample survey. Also, as you will see later, sampling error can be controlled (or at least the extent of it can be estimated, which amounts to the same thing). Thus there are occasions when a survey could produce less error overall than a full census.

As mentioned above, there are two basic methods of sampling: *probability sampling* and *non-probability sampling.* The former includes simple random sampling, stratified random sampling and some forms of cluster sampling. The latter, sometimes called *purposive,* includes (at its *most* sophisticated) quota sampling and (at its *least* sophisticated) what is sometimes called 'opportunity' sampling: the simple expedient of using as a sample whoever is available and willing (e.g. a 'captive' school class). A practical approach to each of these will be given in the following paragraphs.

Probability samples have considerable advantages over all other forms of sampling. All samples will differ to some extent from the population parameters, i.e. they will be subject to sampling error. Thus, suppose we sampled 100 children, and the average height of the 100 children was 1.2 metres. If the average for all the children in the population from which the sample was drawn was 1.1 metres, then the error attributable to drawing the sample rather than measuring the whole population would be 0.1 metres. For probability samples, very accurate estimates can be given of the likely range of this error, even though the population value will obviously not be known. This involves a fundamental statistical process, the randomization of error variation. Because randomization is missing from non-probabilistic methods, they have no such advantage. Just what this means will be explained in the next section (on simple random sampling).

Simple Random Sampling

The fundamental method of probability sampling is *simple random sampling.* Random sampling means that every element in the population of interest has an *equal and independent* chance of being chosen. Here the word 'independent' means that the selection of any one element in no way influences the selection of any other. 'Simple' does not mean that random sampling is easier to carry out than other methods, but that steps are taken to ensure that nothing influences selection each time a choice is made, other than chance. In theory, this requires selection with replacement – any element sampled should be replaced in the sampling frame so that it has a chance of being chosen again – or else the probability of being selected would change each time an element was removed from the sampling frame and placed in the sample. In practice, however, samples in survey research will generally be comparatively small in contrast with the number of elements potentially available for sampling, and the effect of non-replacement will be trivial and need not concern us further.

Beginner researchers sometimes think that if they do nothing, but simply take what comes along, then this will somehow amount to 'chance' or 'random' selection. However, *setting the probability* of selecting elements from a population cannot be left to chance. 'Random', in sampling, does not mean 'haphazard' or following no thought-out plan in obtaining sampling elements. Possibly even worse than the beginner who does nothing is the experienced scientist who thinks he or she can select randomly, near enough. There is much literature showing that this is not the case. Even for something as simple as selecting wheat plants from a field for the study of growth characteristics, experienced researchers trying to choose randomly have been shown to introduce strong biases. For samples taken when the plants are young there tends to be over-selection of those that are tallest, whereas a month later, when the ears have formed, there is a strong bias towards middle-sized, sturdier plants (Yates, 1935).

Simple random sampling might not be at all simple to achieve, depending on circumstances. For example, it might be very difficult to achieve a random sample of serving seamen in the merchant navy, even if an accurate sampling frame could be compiled. Random sampling does not just mean stopping individuals in the street. Which individuals? Which street? Obviously, there would be a risk of stopping only individuals who looked as if they would be helpful. Or of choosing a well-lit, safe street. The flow of passers-by might be influenced by some biasing event: a store sale, an office or bureau somewhere in the not too immediate vicinity, etc.

Random sampling is similar to tossing a coin, throwing a dice or drawing names from a hat, and in some circumstances procedures such as these might be adequate, but usually random number tables or computerized random number generators will be used. The first step is to number in order the individual elements in the population, as listed in the sampling frame. Sometimes this numbering will already be present, or will be implied. If tables are to be used, the next step is to enter them at some random place; for example, by dropping a small item on to the page and selecting the number nearest to it. This then provides the first random number. From this start the required set of random numbers is achieved by stepping forwards or backwards or sideways through the tables in any systematic way. Until recently, statistical texts usually contained tables of random numbers, but nowadays most researchers use readily available computer programs.

Many surveys will not have used true random sampling, but something called *systematic sampling*. If, for example, you have a list of 100 names from which to sample 10, an easy way to obtain a sample is to start from a randomly chosen point on the list and take every tenth item (treating the list as circular and starting again at the beginning when the end is reached). The great advantage of systematic sampling over simple random sampling is that it is easier to perform and thus provides more information per unit cost than does simple random sampling. Also, because it is simpler, fieldworkers are less likely to make selection errors. For example, constructing a simple random sample of shoppers leaving a certain supermarket might be very difficult to achieve in practice, but selecting one at random, and then subsequently stopping every twentieth shopper, would be less so. A systematic sample is more evenly spread across a population than a simple random sample, and in some circumstances this could be advantageous, for example in monitoring items on a production line, or for choosing a sample of accounts for detailed auditing. Mostly, systematic sampling will be adequate as a form of random sampling, but only to the extent to which there is no 'pattern' in the sampling frame and the placing of any item in it really *is* independent of the placing of other items. This is by no means always the case. If we were using the Electoral Register, for example, we would expect the members of each household to be listed together and, as there are seldom as many as 10 people in a household, the selection of a given household member would guarantee the exclusion of all other household members if we were to take every tenth name. Worse, systematic sampling can occasionally introduce a *systematic bias*: for example, if the names in a school class were listed systematically as 'boy, girl, boy, girl ...' and we sampled every second name, we should obtain a sample made up of a single gender from a class made up of both genders in equal proportions. When such risks are known, they can be avoided by choosing a suitable sampling interval; or, after a set number of elements has been sampled, a fresh random start can be made.

Stratified Random Sampling

One problem with simple random sampling is that sample size may need to be disproportionately large to ensure that all subgroups (or *strata*) in the population are adequately represented. For example, a researcher who intends surveying the attitudes of school leavers to further training might see age at leaving school as important. A simple random sample would need to be large enough to remove the risk of inadequate representation of the ages of leaving with least frequency in the population. This could be avoided by dividing the population into age strata, and randomly sampling from each of these. The objective would be adequate representation at reduced cost.

To draw a *stratified random sample,* the elements of a population are divided into non-overlapping groups – *strata*. Simple random samples are drawn from each of these, and together they form the total sample. If the proportion of the sample taken from each stratum is the same as in the population, then the procedure is called *proportionate* stratified random sampling, and the total sample will match the population. In some cases, however, this might result in small strata of interest not being represented adequately in the final sample. This can be avoided by increasing sample size in all such strata, but not for other strata, and still with random selection. The result would be *disproportionate* stratified random sampling.

Here the sample will not match the population, but it will differ from it in known ways which can be corrected arithmetically. (An unbiased estimator of the population mean will be a weighted average of the sample means for the strata; that is, the contribution of each subset of data to the population estimates will be in proportion to its size. Estimates of variance and of sampling error can also be weighted.)

You may well wonder: why not always stratify, and thus reduce cost? One problem is that stratification is not always a simple matter. In any reasonably sized survey, a number of variables will be possible candidates to govern stratification. Deciding which can be no easy matter. Decisions which seem clear cut when the sample is being selected are sometimes reassessed as unfortunate when the survey results are interpreted.

Further, although the purpose of stratification is to increase precision by reducing sampling error without increasing cost, it can, in some circumstances, lead to less precision than simple random sampling. For example, in a national educational survey, stratification could be made in terms of education authorities, on the grounds that these vary greatly in size and character, and also for administrative convenience, but there could be other units unequally distributed within authorities, such as type of school district or level of institution, with greater variability than between authorities. Unfortunately, this might remain unknown until the survey results are analyzed, when it would become clear that a simple random sample of the same size would have provided better population estimates.

Even so, for many surveys, an advantage is seen for stratification, and it is possibly the most popular procedure in survey research. Money is saved by reduction in sample size for the required degree of statistical precision. Fieldwork costs, such as time, travel, interviewer and administration fees, and the printing and processing of questionnaires, are reduced.

Table 2.1 illustrates proportionate and disproportionate random sampling from a population of 6,000 school leavers in a provincial city. The objective of the survey was to find what proportion of the school leavers were in full-time education or employment 18 months after leaving school. The researchers were asked to provide a breakdown of the findings by sex and any other factor found to be relevant when the sample data were analyzed. For the purpose of the example, it will be assumed that sample size was limited to 400.

Activity 2.2 (allow 30 minutes)

The columns in Table 2.1 for proportionate and disproportionate sample size for the separate strata have been left blank. Calculate and enter on the table the missing figures. Before reading further, make a note of which method of sampling you think ought to have been used on this occasion and, very briefly, why. Check your calculations against the completed table given at the end of this chapter.

Table 2.1   *Proportionate and disproportionate stratified random sampling from 6,000 school leavers*

School leaving age	Population size	% of total in each stratum	Proportionate		Disproportionate	
			Sample size	Sampling fraction	Sample size	Sampling fraction
16	2,730	45.5	182	1/15	134	1/20
17	1,950	32.5	130	1/15	134	1/15
18+	1,320	22.0	88	1/15	134	1/10
Total	6,000	100.0	400	1/15	402	1/15

ᵃThe denominators for the disproportionate sampling fractions have been rounded to give whole numbers.

The decision as to whether proportionate or disproportionate stratified random sampling should be used in this case cannot be made on statistical grounds. If the overall population parameters are the main interest then proportionate sampling will give the best estimates of these. But is this likely to be the case? A breakdown by sex has been requested and, assuming that the school leavers are about half female and half male, the oldest leavers will be represented by about 44 boys and 44 girls. Considering that the researcher will break these down into those who are employed, unemployed, or in further education, then group size will be getting very small. And what about other groups of potential interest, such as race, or new immigrant categories: is it likely that the client will want information on sex differences within these as well?

When making decisions on sampling, the researcher will have to balance these various potential needs, and there will have to be compromise. In general, if there is a risk that subgroups of interest will be insufficiently represented in some strata of the sample, then sample size will need to be increased, and the cost of this will be less if the increase is made only in the strata where it is thought to be needed. This could then compromise some other aspect of the findings, by reducing sample size in other strata if the same total sample size needs to be maintained, and mostly there will be no completely satisfactory answer to problems of this kind in practice.

For the present example the preferred method would be simple random sampling, with a sample size big enough to provide adequate numbers in the smallest groups of interest. As an adequate size for the smallest subgroup could mean 40 or more children, this would be unrealistic. Consequently, disproportionate random sampling would be used. This would cost more per element sampled because of the need to include age strata as a sampling criterion, but overall it would be cheaper because fewer elements would be required. In the full sample, however, there would be over-representation of minority groups and the sample would not accurately reflect population characteristics, although this could be taken into account in calculating and interpreting statistics.

Cluster Sampling

Cluster sampling improves on stratified random sampling by further reducing costs, but with a risk of increasing sampling error. A *cluster sample* is a probability sample in which the elements are all the members of randomly selected sampling units, each of which is a collection or cluster of elements from the population sampled. Cluster sampling is advantageous when a sampling frame listing population elements is not available, or is not easily obtained, or is likely to be very inaccurate, and also when the cost of conducting the survey will be unduly increased by the distance separating the elements. This distance is usually in the geographical sense, but it could also be in time; for example, when supermarket customers, or people brought into a police station or casualty clinic, are sampled at designated time periods during a week. For a genuine probability sample, both the time periods, or any other form of cluster, and the individuals surveyed should be chosen at random. Simply accepting all the individuals who turn up or pass by at some specified time or times until the required number has been obtained would not constitute cluster sampling, which is a probability method. Cluster sampling can be proportionate or disproportionate, as described above for stratified random sampling. Further, in many contexts there will be another level of selection within clusters, either by random selection or by additional clustering.

In a study of teacher/parent relationships within one large local education authority, interest centred on the final two years of infant education and the first two years of junior school. This is an age range when there is an emphasis on learning to read, and on improving reading skill and vocabulary. Some infant and junior classes were within one school, under one headteacher, but in other cases infant and junior schools were separately housed and administered, although intake at the junior school was always from its related infant school. Further, the schools were of different sizes, ranging from one to three parallel classes.

For sampling purposes, children attending school in the authority in the four relevant school years were the population, and clustering was in non-overlapping blocks of all classes within the two infant and two junior years at the same school or schools related by intake. The survey was, in fact, to be conducted four times, at yearly intervals, so that children in the first infant year at the beginning of the study could be followed in subsequent years and compared with parallel previous and future year groups, both within and between schools. The study thus matched a design described in Chapter 1, but it is important to understand that the sampling plan for a repeated (longitudinal) survey, or for an intervention project, could be basically the same as for a once-only survey.

For the purpose of this example, assume that six of these clusters were chosen at random for the survey. This would give clusters containing disproportionate numbers of classes, i.e. ranging from a total of four to 12 depending on school size. A random sample of children could have been chosen from each of these clusters or, if intact classes were required, one class could have been chosen by lottery from each school year within each cluster.

As mentioned above, cluster sampling is cheaper than other methods because the cost of data collection can be greatly reduced. In the example, a sample size of between 600 and 700 children would be expected in the first year. Clearly, interviewing or testing would have been more time-consuming and costly if these had been randomly selected from all the authority's schools, instead of being concentrated in just a few. The task of following and individually testing these children as they progressed across the four school years would also have been considerable.

In this hypothetical research (modified from Tizard et al., 1982), there would be the risk that the clusters had unfortunately fallen by chance on a small group of schools that were unrepresentative, either totally or to some significant extent, of the other schools under the authority's care. There is no way that this risk could be ruled out without taking into account information from outside the survey findings, since these would only include material on the selected schools. Clearly, any such information could be taken into account in the first place and used to formulate selection criteria. These criteria could then be used to select clusters larger than needed and from which random selection could take place. Sometimes cluster samples are non-probability samples at every level, except that if there are treatment and control groups then these are allocated to those conditions randomly. It is essential that this one element of randomization is preserved, and even then the sampling is not strictly cluster sampling but is of the non-probabilistic, opportunity variety.

Sometimes cluster sampling is the only option realistically available – for example, for surveying the unemployed and homeless, when compilation of a sampling frame would in practice be impossible or in cases where lists of the elements in a population may exist, but are unavailable to the survey researcher or are known to be unredeemably defective.

Much policy-related survey research is undertaken in developing countries and can influence the funding policy of aid agencies. Sample findings which did not generalize to the population in need of aid could have disastrous consequences, yet random or stratified sampling from population lists is not likely to be possible. Cluster sampling will usually include at least some element of randomization which, in contrast with a totally haphazard method, will permit qualified estimates of the extent of sampling error. Common sense and professional judgement are likely to be needed even more than usual when evaluating research results in such circumstances.

Quota Sampling

In the most widely used method of non-probability sampling, the population is split up into non-overlapping subgroups, as for stratified sampling. Quotas of the desired number of sample cases are then calculated proportionally to the number of elements in these subgroups. These quotas are then divided up among the interviewers, who simply set out to find individuals who fit the required quota criteria. They continue doing this until they have filled their quota. A given interviewer, for example, might have to find five middle-class and five working-class women over the age of 30, with no other control over who these people are or how they are located, as long as they fill the criteria. This method is called *quota sampling*.

One reason for using quota samples is, again, to reduce costs, but another is that this method seems to have intuitive appeal to some survey practitioners. For example, quota sampling is widely used in market research. Thus, if a population is known to have 60 per cent females and 40 per cent males, it might require a comparatively large sample to reflect this proportion exactly. It might, however, seem important to the researcher that it should be so reflected, whatever the sample size. This can be achieved, for the present example even in a sample of 10, by selecting quotas of six females and four males.

The major problem with quota sampling is that attempts to deal with one known source of bias may well make matters worse for others not known, or at least not

Table 2.2   *Interlocking quota sampling design for a survey project*

Sex	Odd student number		Even student number	
	18–34	35+	18–34	35+
Male	Middle	Working	Working	Middle
Female	Working	Middle	Middle	Working

Social classes ABCI on the Social Grading Schema are shown as 'middle', and social classes C2DE as 'working'.

known until after the data have been collected and it is too late. Further, as there is no element of randomization, the extent of sampling error cannot be estimated. For example, in an Open University research methods course, students undertook a research project on class attitudes in the UK. A questionnaire designed and piloted by the course team was administered by each student to a small group of respondents. The student then collated the data for her or his small sub-sample, and sent them off to the university to be merged with the data from all other students. For 1991, this produced a national sample of well over 900 respondents, as did the preceding year. Questions were included on class consciousness, class awareness, and aspects of class structure. There were questions intended to identify class stereotypes, and questions seeking biographical information on such matters as sex, age, educational attainment, housing and previous voting behaviour. The intended population was all adults in the UK.

Activity 2.3 (5 minutes)

Write a very brief note saying which sampling method would, in an ideal world, have been best for this study, and what the main advantage of this would be.

In fact, the method chosen, for practical reasons, was quota sampling. Each student was asked to collect data from four respondents in an interlocking quota design, which took into account three criteria: social class, sex and age. This design is shown in Table 2.2. Thus, a student with an even OU student number (right-hand side of the table) found one respondent for each of the following categories:

- male/working class/18–34 years
- male/middle class/35+ years
- female/middle class/18–34 years
- female/working class/35+ years

As you can see from Table 2.2, a student with an odd student number also chose four respondents, but with the position of the social class categories reversed.

When the course was being developed, a pilot study was undertaken using this quota design. The results revealed what appeared to be a strong bias in the sample.

For example, there was an unexpectedly high number of respondents in social class A or B who appeared to have 'left-wing' attitudes. Further, the pilot study did not find some of the differences between the social classes expected from other research. The pilot interviewers had correctly followed the quota procedure but had selected middle-class individuals who were not representative of the national population. The same may well have applied to the selection of working-class respondents. It is easy to think of many possible sources of bias when respondents are selected by interviewers solely to fill sampling quotas.

Although the bias in the pilot study was noted when the results were analyzed, it was decided that in a large sample collected by OU students across all parts of the UK there would be no such problem. In the event, as the years went by, successive waves of students collected and analyzed the pooled data, both regionally and nationally. Invariably it was found that, although students had selected individuals to fill their quotas according to the set criteria, the working-class individuals sampled by OU students differed in material ways from what was expected for that social class in the population at large, and the same was true for the middle-class component of the sample. Random sampling, if it had been possible, would have avoided this persistent and pervasive selection bias, whereas increasing sample size did not. In general, selection bias will never be overcome by increasing sample size, which will merely inflate costs to no avail.

Other non-probability methods – such as 'opportunity' sampling, the simple expedient of including as subjects whoever happens to be available from the population of interest – have already been mentioned. These methods, or lack of methods, are sometimes referred to as 'haphazard' sampling, but the term 'opportunity' is preferred because it implies usually what is the case; that is, the necessity of accepting whatever is available, with no realistic alternative. Thus, in a study of new admissions of the elderly to institutional care, the sample might be all admissions until adequate sample size has been achieved at the only institution, or institutions, available to the researcher.

Alternatively, data collection could be continued until certain predetermined quotas were achieved. For example, a quota could be set for the minimum number of persons diagnosed as suffering from senile dementia. Note that this differs from regular quota sampling, where there is an element of choice in that the fieldworker selects individuals to fill the quotas. It also is not *sequential sampling*, which is a method assuming both independence and random selection, but in which sample size is not predetermined. Instead, random sampling continues sequentially until a pre-established criterion has been met; for example, that the sample includes 30 individuals diagnosed as having senile dementia. The purpose of sequential sampling is to find out what sample size will be needed to reach the set criterion.

Estimation of Population Parameters

To follow this section you need to understand in principle the main measure of central tendency – the mean – and measures of dispersion such as the variance and standard deviation. You will also need to understand how probability can be defined as relative frequency of occurrence, and that it can be represented by the area under a curve – by a frequency distribution.

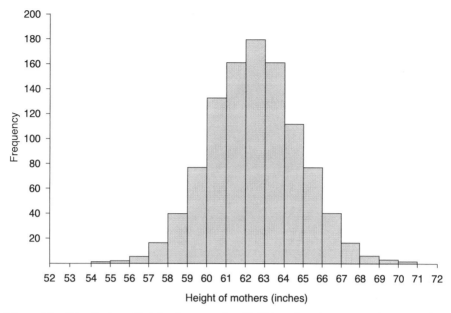

Figure 2.1   *Distribution of heights in a sample of 1,052 mothers (Pearson and Lee, 1902)*

Means, Variance and Standard Deviations

Figure 2.1 is a histogram showing the heights of a sample of 1,052 mothers. The central column of this histogram tells us that about 180 mothers in the sample were between 62 and 63 inches high. From the column furthest to the right we can see that almost none was over 70 inches high. Histograms are simple graphical devices for showing frequency of occurrence.

Figure 2.2 (see p. 40) shows another way of representing this same information – this time by a continuous curve – but the histogram has been left in so that you can see that the curve does fit, and that either method provides a graphical representation of the same information. Mothers' heights are a continuous measure, and in a way the curve seems more appropriate than the histogram. But the histogram makes it clear that what is represented by the area within the figure, or under the curve, is frequency of occurrence. Thus the greatest frequency – the most common height for the mothers – is the 62–63 inch interval. Reading from the curve, we can more accurately place this at 62.5 inches. Check this for yourself.

Now look at Figure 2.3 (see p. 41). Here only the curve is shown, together with the scale on the axis, plus some additional scales and markings. Take your time, and study these carefully. Note first of all that the total area under the curve from its left extreme to its right extreme represents the variation in height of all 1,052 mothers. It is important to understand the idea of the area representing, in the sense of being proportional to, the variation in the mothers' heights. Some other matters need revision before the additional scales shown on Figure 2.3 are explained, and we will also, for the moment, defer explanation of the areas on the figure marked off as 68 per cent and 95 per cent of the total area under the curve.

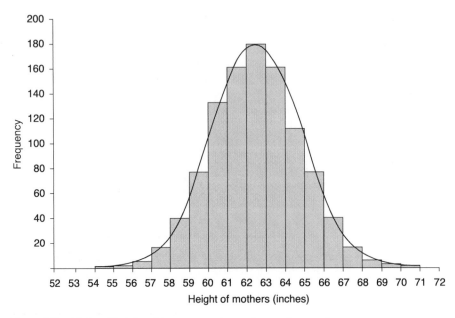

Figure 2.2   *Mothers' heights: histogram and superimposed normal curve*

The *mean* is simply the total height of all mothers, added up and divided by the number of mothers, i.e. the arithmetical average. The mean is at the centre of the distribution
shown in Figure 2.3. Half of the mothers' heights (50 per cent or 0.5 as a proportion) are
above the mean and half are below it. The *standard deviation* is also an average, but not
an average representing where the centre of the distribution is but how it is spread out,
i.e. an average of the dispersion. The standard deviation of a population is found by calculating the mean; finding the difference between each value and the mean; squaring
each of the differences (deviations) so obtained; adding them all up; dividing by the number of values averaged; and finding the square root of the final answer to get back to the
original scale of measurement. If you read through the preceding sentence quickly it
might seem complicated, and standard deviations may remain a mystery. If you are still
unsure on this idea of averaging the dispersion then re-read slowly, and perhaps use a
pencil to re-express the procedures described in your own words.

Activity 2.4 (15 minutes)

Better still, using only the information given in the preceding two paragraphs,
calculate the mean and the standard deviation of the following numbers:

$$(1, 2, 3, 4, 5)$$

and also for

$$(1, 1, 0, 1, 12)$$

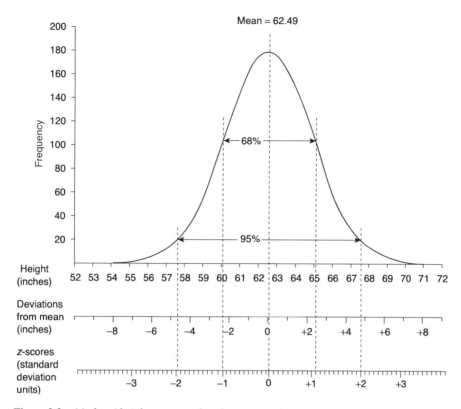

Figure 2.3   *Mothers' heights expressed in deviation and z-score units*

Compare the two means and the two standard deviations, and make a note of any way in which they are similar, or different. Check your results against those given at the end of the chapter.

In the preceding paragraphs, to provide a clear account of what the mean and the standard deviation (s.d.) represent, it has been assumed that the simple set of numbers

$$(1, 2, 3, 4, 5)$$

form a complete population. If, however, they represent a sample from a population, then an adjustment would be needed to allow for the fact that the standard deviation is a biased estimator of the population standard deviation. It does seem intuitively obvious that the dispersion in samples drawn from a population must on average be less than the dispersion in the total population. Also, the smaller a sample is, the greater the comparative effect of this bias will be. For that reason, when the s.d. of a sample is calculated, rather than that of a population, the divisor in forming the average of the squared deviations from the mean is not the sample size n, but $n-1$ (This adjustment will have greater effect on small samples than on large ones).

Now, to return to Figure 2.3: the point about this curve is that it follows a well-known mathematical model, the normal distribution, and is completely described by its mean and standard deviation. Once you know the mean and s.d. of any normally distributed variable, then you can say precisely what shape the distribution will be, and whereabouts within this shape any particular value will fall. This will be a statement about probability of occurrence.

Thus, if you had the height of just one mother there would be a 100 per cent (near enough) probability that it would fall somewhere under the curve shown. There would be a high probability that its actual value would be somewhere between 1 s.d. above and 1 s.d. below the mean, since 68 per cent of the area of the curve in *any* normal distribution is in this range. There would be a low probability of it being greater than 2 s.d. above the mean, because less than 2.5 per cent of the area under the curve is that far above the mean. You can see this in Figure 2.3, where the proportions of area within the ranges of 1 and 2 s.d. above and below the mean are shown.

Before moving on, let us consider one further example. Suppose the mean IQ of a sample is 100 and the s.d. is 15. Then, one individual with an IQ of 145 would be 3 s.d. above the mean. This person's IQ would be located at the extreme right-hand side of the curve. This far out the area under the curve is a very small proportion of the total area. Finding an IQ this high in a sample with mean 100 and s.d. 15 is a rare event. The probability for the occurrence of this event is very low, and can be calculated precisely.

Finally, Figure 2.3 includes two new scales drawn beneath the horizontal axis. The first simply replaces each value by its deviation from the mean. These are *deviation scores*. If you summed them, they would add to zero. They are expressed in inches, as that is the scale of the variable represented, i.e. height. Negative values give inches below the mean; positive values are inches above the mean. Do not read on until you have looked back at Figure 2.3 to check the deviation score scale.

Below the deviation scores is a further scale for the horizontal axis. This is marked out in *z-scores*. These have been obtained by dividing each deviation score on the line above by the standard deviation, i.e. the deviations from the mean are no longer expressed in inches, but in standard deviation units.

The crucial point to grasp is that, whatever units are used on the horizontal axis, the frequency distribution above the axis remains unchanged. All we have is three different ways of representing the same thing. These are mothers' height in inches, mothers' height in deviation scores, and mothers' height in *z*-scores (sometimes called standard scores). You can read from these scales that the average mother is 62.5 inches tall, or that her height as a deviation from the mean is zero, or that her height on a scale of standard deviations from the mean is zero.

These three different scales for reporting mothers' height go beyond just a matter of convenience, such as changing from inches to centimetres. To say that a mother is 62.5 inches high tells us just that. But to say that a mother's height expressed as a *z*-score is 0 tells us that in this sample the mother is precisely of average height. A mother with a height of +2.5 on this scale is a very tall woman, and we could say what the probability would be of finding someone that tall by working out what proportion of the total area under the curve is 2.5 s.d. above the mean. Similarly, a mother with a *z*-score of −2.5 would have a low probability of occurrence. In practice, we will not need to calculate these probabilities because they will be the same for any normal curve and can be found in a table in most statistics textbooks. This is an advantageous characteristic of z-scores, not present when the measurements were expressed in the original scale of inches. Another advantage of z-scores is that they provide a common scale for measurements initially made on different scales.

To conclude, consider that Figure 2.3 represents a random sample drawn from all mothers in the UK early in this century. We have calculated the sample mean, and by using the standard deviation and a mathematical model – the normal distribution – we have found a method of calculating the probability for the occurrence of any individual data item in that sample, which at the same time provides a common scale of measurement for any normally distributed variable, i.e. standard deviation units, or z-scores.

How Sample Means are Distributed

In the previous sub-section a method was developed for calculating the probability for the occurrence of any individual data item in a sample for which the mean and the s.d. were known. This involved the simple expedient of re-expressing the scale of measurement as one of z-scores. We have seen what z-scores are in s.d. units. A z-score of +1.96 is 1.96 standard deviation units above the mean. A z-score of −1.96 is 1.96 standard deviation units below the mean. For *any* normal distribution these values mark off the lower and upper 2.5 per cent of the area under the curve. Thus, a value which is outside the range of ± 1.96 s.d. from the mean has a probability of occurring less than five times in every 100 trials. This is usually written as $P < 0.05$.

The important point to keep in mind for the remainder of this section is that we will no longer be considering individual items of data, from which one mean value is to be calculated, but just *mean values* themselves. We are concerned with mean values because we want to know how confident we can be that they are accurate estimates of population parameters.

Can we use the method of the previous sub-section for finding the probability, not of encountering one individual data element of a particular value – one woman 62.5 inches high – but for finding the probability for the occurrence of a *sample mean* of that, or any other, size? Well, obviously, what would be needed to do this is not a frequency distribution of data values, but a frequency distribution of sample means. Using a statistical package called Minitab, I have generated just such a distribution (Minitab, 1985). I have used a random number generator to draw 100 samples, each with $n = 1,052$, from a population with the same mean and standard deviation as shown in Figure 2.1, i.e. mean = 62.49 and s.d. = 2.435. This is as if I had measured the heights of 105,200 mothers, 1,052 at a time. Just one of these samples is illustrated in Figure 2.4. It has a mean of 62.49 and the s.d. is 2.45. Both are close to the population values. A histogram including this mean and means for the other 99 samples can be seen in Figure 2.5 with the horizontal scale (inches) the same as for Figure 2.4, but with the vertical scale (frequency) reduced so that the columns fit on the page.

The mean of the means given in Figure 2.5 is 62.498, much the same as for the full sample, but the s.d. is dramatically reduced to only 0.074. Clearly, a distribution of sample means is more closely grouped around the central value than is a distribution of data values. So that you can see that within this narrower range the individual means do follow a normal distribution, Figure 2.5 has been redrawn as Figure 2.6, with more bars. Note that the range of mean values in Figure 2.6 is from a minimum

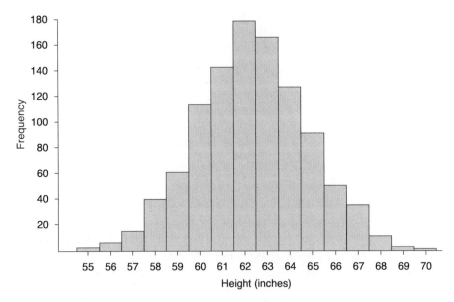

Figure 2.4   *Distribution of mothers' heights in a single simulated random sample,*
mean = 62.49, s.d. = 2.45

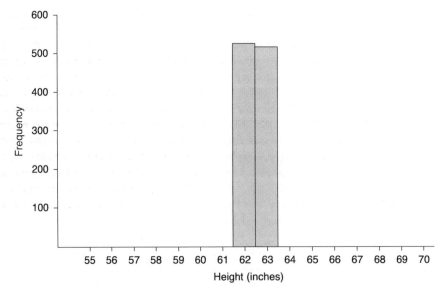

Figure 2.5   *Distribution of mean heights from a hundred simulated random samples,*
mean = 62.498, s.d. = 0.074

of 62.25 to a maximum of 62.75, in contrast to the sample data in Figure 2.4, where
it is from 55 to 70: a range of less than 1 inch, compared to a range of 15 inches.

Armed with the information in Figure 2.6, we can now put a probability on different means, i.e. determine their relative frequency. We can see, for example, that a

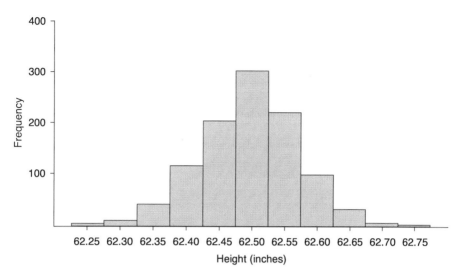

Figure 2.6 *Distribution of mean heights from a hundred simulated random samples, scaled for more detailed display*

mean of 62.75 is in the top extreme of the distribution. This mean would have a z-score of +3.62, and from statistical tables I have found that the probability of obtaining a z-score with this value is only $P < 0.0001$, i.e. only 1 in 10,000. A sample from the present population with this mean would indeed be an exceptionally rare event.

This is all very well, but if a researcher has undertaken a sample survey, and has calculated a mean value for a variable of interest, what would be the good of knowing that if many more samples were randomly selected and a mean calculated for each of them to give a distribution of sample means, then probabilities could be calculated? Fortunately, these are just the kinds of problems where statisticians have come to the aid of researchers and have provided a simple but accurate method of estimating from just one sample of data – provided that it has been randomly sampled – what the standard deviation (which we will refer to as *standard error*, s.e., which is represented here by a capital S) would be for a distribution of sample means from the same population. The formula for doing this, together with an example of the calculations, is:

$$s.e. = s.d./\sqrt{n}$$

i.e.

$$S_{mean} = s/\sqrt{n}$$

where s is standard deviation and n is sample size. We can make these calculations for the data given in Figure 2.4 where the mean is 62.49 and the s.d. is 2.45:

$$S_{mean} = 2.45/\sqrt{(1,052)}$$
$$= 2.45/32.4346$$
$$= 0.076$$

I hope you will be amazed at just how simple this procedure is. The standard deviation which we have just calculated is given the special name of standard error because it is used to estimate the sampling error associated with one specific sample mean. The standard error of a mean is an estimate of the standard deviation of the distribution of sample means.

Now, since the standard error is the standard deviation of a distribution of sample means and these are normally distributed, then 95 per cent of the values in that distribution are within the range of ± 1.96 standard deviations from the mean, i.e. approximately ± 2 s.d. from the mean. In the present example that gives a range from approximately 0.15 below to 0.15 above the mean (2 × 0.076), i.e. from 62.34 to 62.64, from our one sample. We can be 95 per cent confident that the true population mean will be somewhere within this range. Notice how close the value we have just calculated by weighting the s.d. of one sample by the square root of the sample size, i.e. 0.076, is to the true s.d. of the distribution of sample means, which we do have in this case, i.e. 0.074.

Often, survey findings are expressed not as mean values, but as proportions or percentages. For example, a finding might be that 36 per cent of all households use Brand X to wash the dishes. Assuming that this assertion is based on a sample survey for which 1,000 households were sampled, what would the likely margin of error be? Provided sampling was by a probability method – for example, simple random sampling – then an unbiased standard error of a proportion can be calculated. It will not, however, be pursued here. The theory behind calculating descriptive statistics and standard errors for proportions is harder to follow than is the case for means. This is because it involves using what is known as the *binomial distribution.* Every sample statistic – the mean, median, mode, the standard deviation itself, a total or a proportion – has a standard error which can be estimated from just one random sample when it is needed. As we have seen, knowledge of standard error enables statements about probabilities. For example, comparing how far apart two means are in terms of standard errors provides a test of whether the two means differ by more than chance.

Formerly a lot of time could be spent learning formulae and calculating confidence limits and significance levels using standard errors. However, in research, calculations are now done by computer. Thus the details of statistical formulae are not important to survey researchers. What is important is that the method being used and its assumptions are fully understood. In this case you need to understand thoroughly what is meant by a *distribution of sample means,* and how the standard deviation of this distribution can be estimated from one sample. Further, you need to understand the use to which this s.d. is put in its role as standard error of just one sample mean.

A final important point should be mentioned, although space does not permit it to be developed in any way. Very often in social and behavioural science, data distributions do not look at all normal, and it might seem that procedures which assume a normal distribution cannot be used. However, first, various things can be done about this, including transformation of the scale to one which is normal for the measure concerned. Secondly, the relevant mathematical models require that the *underlying* variable which is being measured is normally distributed, and it is to be expected that individual samples (especially small samples) will look rather different. Thirdly, and this is the most fortunate point of all, even if the population distribution is far from normal, as sample size increases the distribution of sample means from that population will move closer and closer to the desired normal form, thus permitting valid statistical inferences to be made about those means. This statement rests on a fundamental theorem in statistics (the central limits theorem). This theorem justifies much of the data analysis undertaken when quantifying and estimating the reliability of survey research findings (Stuart and Ord, 1987).

Error, Sample Size and Non-response

As was mentioned in the discussion of Activity 2.1, there are two categories of error in survey research: sampling error and non-sampling error. Conceptually, the terms sampling error and non-sampling error refer to different entities, and it is theoretically important to consider them as such, but in practice we can never have a true measure of sampling error, but only an estimate of it, and the influence of non-sampling error is hopelessly confounded within that estimate. Both researcher and research evaluator have to ensure that non-sampling error is avoided as far as possible, or is evenly balanced (non-systematic) and thus cancels out in the calculation of population estimates, or else is brought under statistical control. As has been shown, the difference between sampling error and non-sampling error is that the extent of the former can be estimated from the sample variation, whereas the latter cannot. Further, we have seen that sampling error can only be reliably estimated if the selection of respondents has been random. At best, random sampling will allow unbiased estimates of sampling error; at worst, quota and opportunity sampling will provide little or none.

In practice, researchers often overlook or are unaware of these difficulties and quote standard errors, i.e. estimates of sampling error, even for samples where their use is not justified in theory. But at least sampling error *can* be calculated, whether appropriately or not, and if sufficient information is provided then judgements can be made about just how much reliance can be placed on it. The various sources of error grouped together as non-sampling errors are another matter – not because they will be necessarily greater in extent, although this could well be the case, but because they are difficult to control, or even detect. The great virtue of randomization is that it takes care of potential sources of bias, both known and unknown. If it can be assumed that error, whatever its source, will be randomly spread across a sample, and will cancel when statistics are computed, then one does not even need to know what it is that is cancelled. The problem is systematic, non-random error, which will not cancel.

Non-sampling error is often overlooked when survey findings are evaluated, and if an estimate of sampling error is given, then it is often wrongly assumed that this shows the likelihood of total error. For example, in the 1992 General Election in the UK, one survey predicted a Labour Party vote of 42 per cent ± 3 per cent. Presumably the figure of 3 per cent represents approximately twice the standard error, and thus the 95 per cent confidence range for this result would be from 39 per cent to 45 per cent. This says that, if the same pollsters drew sample elements in exactly the same way, and questioned and recorded in exactly the same way, from the same population, with a sample of the same size, then they could expect to obtain a value in that range 95 times for every 100 samples so drawn and tested.

However, this statement tells us nothing whatsoever about whether the sampling frame truly represented the voters of the UK overall, let alone the more restricted set of those who actually did vote. It tells us nothing about interviewer bias, or procedural reactivity, or untruthfulness on the part of respondents. If one took a guess and allowed another 3 per cent for all of these, then the predicted range would increase to 36–48 per cent, which would greatly decrease the usefulness of the survey finding, since in a moderately close election it would be very unlikely to predict successfully which way the outcome would go, because the estimates for the two major parties would always overlap. An advantage the pollsters do have, however, is replication. Many polls are taken, and by different organizations. Taking all into account might give some possibility of balancing some sources of non-sampling error – but not all. It could, of course, be the case that all the polls suffered from similar defects, in which case pooling would not cancel the bias and prediction would be highly unreliable.

Major sources of non-sampling error related to the sampling process itself include sampling-frame defects, non-response, inaccurate or incomplete response, defective measuring instruments (e.g. questionnaires or interview schedules), and defective data collection or management. Some of these are the subject of other chapters in this book, but their relevance here should also be kept in mind. Many of these effects are, or can be, controlled by proper randomization in sampling. For example, in a large survey the error related to small differences in technique on the part of interviewers (perhaps consequent upon personality differences) will be randomly spread across the data, and will cancel out. Any residual effect should be small and would be lost in the estimates of standard errors, possibly here balancing with other small residual effects.

Sample Size

Often, selecting an appropriate sample size has been a hit and miss business of choosing a size which can be managed within the resources available, or a size similar to that used in earlier published work. There is a misconception that sample size should be related to the size of the population under study. As has been shown above, the precision of sample estimates depends very much on sample size (the sample s.d. is divided by the square root of the sample n) and no reference is made to the size of the population sampled.

Assuming that for a sample survey the 95 per cent level of confidence is required ($P < 0.05$), and the maximum error is set to 5 units on the scale of measurement, then the following formula will provide the estimated sample size:

$$\text{Sample size} = 2 \times 1.96(\text{s.d.})^2/5^2$$

If the estimated s.d. is 10, then the required sample size would be approximately 16. If the limit for the difference of interest was reduced from 5 to 2 points, then esti-mated sample size would increase to close to 100, assuming that the s.d. remains unchanged. Note that the researcher had to provide an estimate of the s.d., although the actual value will not be known until the research is concluded.

This is a very simple account of what might appear to be a simple subject, but which in fact is a complex one. Just how big a sample should be is a matter of balancing cost against the level of precision required. True, as sample size increases, the size of the standard error of any estimate of a statistic does decrease. But this needs to be qualified by knowledge that large samples may introduce more non-sampling error (as mentioned in the answer to Activity 2.3) than smaller ones, where measurements and management problems may be smaller. Also, the power of the statistical test to be used must be taken into account and tables have been published for doing this (Cohen, 1969; Lipsey, 1990). Many computer packages now also include routines for dealing with this.

Non-response

Estimating the required sample size needed for a stated level of precision has been discussed. There is, however, little point in reporting that sample size was formally determined to achieve maximum precision, if a sizeable proportion of the sample was subsequently lost through non-response, or because items of data were missing. This is a major source of error in many surveys.

Procedures for dealing with non-response and missing data have to be established when the research is being planned, and not left to desperate *post hoc* remedy. In establishing such procedures, total non-response should be distinguished from failure to respond to individual items in a questionnaire, and both should be distinguished from data which are simply missing (i.e. lost or inadequately recorded). Preliminary data analysis will also lead to further data loss, usually due to the dropping of elements (individuals or cases) found to have been included in the sampling frame by mistake, but which do not belong to the population studied, or because inconsistent or highly improbable values have been found on crucial variables.

Final reports should contain information on the extent of sample loss and missing data, which amounts, at least in part, and sometimes completely, to the same thing. Non-response rates as high as 50 per cent or more have frequently been reported. Some elements of the sample simply will not be found, others will refuse to participate, either completely or in part. In addition, data, and sometimes whole subjects, will be lost due to clerical inaccuracy. The extent of data lost for this reason alone is seldom reported, but is usually surprisingly high, perhaps as much as 8 per cent (Schofield et al., 1992). Response rate is influenced by such design matters as the appearance of a questionnaire, its layout, length and readability. These topics are dealt with in more detail elsewhere in this book. Information on such matters will be sought in pilot studies, in which different versions of a survey instrument can be tested. Sample loss for these reasons is likely to introduce bias because it might increase the proportion of more persistent or better educated respondents.

If the survey involves home interviews, non-response might be related to time of day at which the interview was sought. From Table 2.3 it can be seen that a higher proportion of persons over 14 years of age are at home in the early hours of the evening on Sunday, Monday and Tuesday than at any other time. This, however, is also evening meal time, and a busy time for families with young children. Again, sample loss could be systematic, and it could introduce bias.

If, when a survey is being planned, it seems likely that response rate will be low due to the nature of the information sought, or the accuracy of the sampling frame,

Table 2.3   *Proportion of households with at least one person over 14 years of age at home, by day and time of day*

Time of day	Proportion by day of week						
	Sun.	Mon.	Tue.	Wed.	Thur.	Fri.	Sat.
8.00–8.59 am	(B)	(B)	(B)	(B)	(B)	(B)	(B)
9.00–9.59 am	(B)	(B)	(B)	0.55	0.28	0.45	(B)
10.00–10.59 am	(B)	0.47	0.42	0.38	0.45	0.40	0.55
11.00–11.59 am	0.35	0.41	0.49	0.46	0.43	0.50	0.62
12.00–12.59 pm	0.42	0.53	0.49	0.56	0.45	0.55	0.60
1.00–1.59 pm	0.49	0.44	0.50	0.48	0.43	0.51	0.63
2.00–2.59 pm	0.49	0.50	0.52	0.47	0.45	0.45	0.59
3.00–3.59 pm	0.54	0.47	0.49	0.54	0.50	0.50	0.65
4.00–4.59 pm	0.52	0.58	0.55	0.57	0.57	0.56	0.53
5.00–5.59 pm	0.61	0.67	0.65	0.67	0.59	0.57	0.56
6.00–6.59 pm	0.75	0.73	0.72	0.68	0.65	0.64	0.59
7.00–7.59 pm	0.73	0.74	0.75	0.64	0.61	0.57	0.66
8.00–8.59 pm	(B)	0.51	0.51	0.59	0.74	0.52	(B)
9.00–9.59 pm	(B)	(B)	(B)	0.64	(B)	(B)	(B)

(B) = base less than 20.

Source: Weeks et al. (1980).

or the method used to contact respondents, then sample size could be increased. This might seem to be an obvious and easy solution, but it will be costly in terms of management and material and, in any case, will be unlikely to solve the problem.

Activity 2.5 (10 minutes)

In the planning of a sample survey by questionnaire sent by post it has been calculated that a sample of $n = 200$ will give the required level of precision for estimating population means at the 95 per cent confidence level or better for most items of interest. But only about 40–50 per cent of those sent questionnaires are expected to return them. The researchers propose simple random sampling with sample size increased to $n = 400$. Comment briefly on this proposal. If you were an adviser, what advice would you give?

Increasing sample size to cover expected non-response would, in fact, be more likely to increase than to decrease bias. More money would be spent to no avail. Studies have shown that non-responders tend to be: the elderly; those who are withdrawn; urban rather than suburban, or rural, dwellers; individuals who fear that they will not give the information adequately in comparison to others, or who fear that they might expose themselves, and be judged in some way by the responses they make. To lose such individuals selectively would very likely reduce the representativeness of a survey sample. To increase sample size while continuing to lose such individuals would in no way help, and could lead to comparatively stronger influence from, perhaps, initially small biasing groups.

Whether information is collected by questionnaire or by interview, positive effort should be made to follow up non-responders. Even when second copies of a questionnaire are sent out, or repeat interviews arranged, response rates above about 80 per cent are seldom achieved. The task for the researcher, who wants sample results which truly represent the population studied, plus information which will help evaluate how far this objective has been achieved, is to get as much information as possible on those individuals who are still missing when all possible action has been taken to maximize response rate.

For this reason, the records of individuals who have made only partial, or even nil, response should never be dropped from a data set. Usually, information will be available on some variables; for example, geographical region, home address, perhaps age or sex. Analyses can be made to see if the missing individuals are at least randomly distributed throughout the sample in terms of these measures, or grouped in some way which might help identify the possible direction and extent of bias on other measures for which there are no data.

Even better would be a small follow-up survey of a random sample of non-responders, possibly involving home visits and/or the offer of incentives, so that reliable predictions can be made about the likely characteristics of all non-responders. In some circumstances this could be counter-productive, in that interviewer/respondent reactivity might be increased. One way or another, however, the problem of non-response has to be tackled. Vagueness or, worse, total lack of information on this topic, is no longer permissible.

Conclusion

This chapter has dealt with methods and problems of designing sample surveys, and has related these to the wider research context, where ultimately the validity of findings will rest on how well the sample represents the population being researched. We have seen that the quality of the inferences being made from a sample will be related to both sample size and sampling method. We have seen that, provided a probabilistic method has been used, then a reliable estimate can be made of the extent to which the sample results will differ from the true population values, and that error of this type is known as sampling error. The methods discussed included both simple and stratified random sampling, systematic sampling, and cluster sampling, and also non-probabilistic methods such as quota sampling. Selecting the best method for any particular research will usually involve compromise, and will be a matter of balancing the level of precision required, in terms of the width of the error estimates, against feasibility and cost.

We have also seen that error from many other sources – non-sampling error – will have to be taken into account when planning survey research and

(Continued)

(Conclusion continued)

when evaluating results. Major sources of non-sampling error which have been discussed in this chapter include faulty selection of the sampling frame and non-response. There are many others, including the instruments used for collecting information: schedules, questionnaires and observation techniques. The problem for researchers is that, however well they plan the technical side of sampling and calculate estimates of sampling error of known precision, non-sampling error will always be present, inflating overall error, and reducing representativeness. Estimating the extent of this is a matter not of mathematical calculation, although statistical procedures can help, but of scientific judgement, based on an awareness of what problems are likely, as well as common sense.

Key Terms

Bias   aspects of measurement or sample selection which tend to increase the difference between sample statistics and the population parameters.

Census   a study including (or intending to include) all elements of a population, not just a sample.

Cluster sampling   sampling which selects groups of elements based on geographical proximity.

Element   a single case (item) in a population or a sample.

Error   *see* Sampling error.

Mean   the average of a distribution – calculated by adding all the values together and dividing by the number of cases.

Non-probabilistic   *see* Probabilistic sampling.

Non-sampling error   *see* Sampling error.

Population   the total set of elements (cases) available for study. Your population might be people – all the people in the UK, or all the children in one school, or all the children in a specified age range in a certain district – but it could be incidents, or cars, or businesses, or whatever is being studied.

Probabilistic sampling   sampling in which elements have known probability of being chosen. Samples where this is not the case are known as 'non-probabilistic'.

Quota sample   one collected by interviewers who have been instructed to ensure that the cases they collect match a predetermined distribution on certain key variables (often the known population parameters).

Random sample   one for which every element of the population is guaranteed an equal, non-zero chance of being selected.

Sample   elements selected from a population, by studying which we hope to understand the nature of the population as a whole.

> **Sampling error**   the calculable probability of drawing a sample whose statistics differ from the population parameters. This is contrasted with 'non-sampling error', which is bias built into the design, the sampling frame or the measurement.
> **Sampling frame**   a complete list of the elements in a population.
> **Standard deviation**   a measure of spread or dispersion from the mean, based on the normal distribution.
> **Stratified random sample**   one made up of separate random samples, drawn from sets which together make up the entire population.
> **Systematic sampling**   a sample that consists of every *n*th member of a sampling frame, perhaps from a random starting point.
> **z-score**   the distance of an element from the mean, measured in standard deviation units.

Further Reading

Lipsey, M.W. (1990) *Design Sensitivity,* Newbury Park, CA, Sage.
A short and fairly readable text on statistical power in social science research. It includes charts for determining sample size.

Moser, C.A. and Kalton, G. (1971) *Survey Methods in Social Investigation,* London, Heinemann.
Although somewhat dated, this remains a standard text for material covered in this chapter.

Schaeffer, R.L., Mendenhall, W. and Ott, L. (1990) *Elementary Survey Sampling,* Boston, PWS-Kent.
A further elementary text, recently revised, which includes some of the mathematical derivations of sampling methods, but with many practical examples of surveys and methods. Useful later if you have the task of designing a survey.

Answers to Activities

Activity 2.1

The main advantages of a sample survey over a full census is that it will be easier and cheaper to set up, manage and analyze than a full census. Although the results based on a sample will, in theory, be less accurate than if the whole population had been included (assuming this to be possible), this might not be the case in practice. Many sources of bias – for example, management problems, faulty measurement, lost or corrupted data – will potentially be present whichever method is used, and will be easier to control in a tightly constructed and managed survey than in a full census.

Activity 2.2

Table 2.1, with the missing entries added, is shown on p. 54. The first of these, in the fourth column, is the sample size *(n)* for proportionate sampling. This was found by calculating 45.5 per cent of the total sample of 400. This gave a sample proportion of *n* = 182 for the representation of 16-year-old school leavers. Similar calculations were made to find the other sample proportions. For the disproportionate method, the total sample was divided into three equal groups, one for each school-leaving age, without taking into account the differing incidence in the population of each of these groups.

Compare your note on the sampling method you would choose with the explanation given in the three paragraphs following the activity in the text, where several non-statistical reasons are given for balancing the various alternatives.

Table 2.1   (*completed*)

School leaving age	Population size	% of total in each stratum	Proportionate		Disproportionate	
			Sample size	Sampling fraction	Sample size	Sampling fraction
16	2,730	45.5	182	1/15	134	1/20
17	1,950	32.5	130	1/15	134	1/15
18+	1,320	22.0	88	1/15	134	1/10
Total	6,000	100.0	400	1/15	402	1/15

ªThe denominators for the disproportionate sampling fractions have been rounded to give whole numbers.

Activity 2.3

Clearly, a probabilistic method would be preferable, since this would permit a valid estimate of the extent of sampling error. As the population of interest is all the adults in the UK, a simple random sample would be costly and difficult. Precision relative to sample size could be increased by appropriate stratification, and thus you would recommend a stratified random sample.

Activity 2.4

The mean of the first set of figures is 3, and the mean of the second is also 3. The two standard deviations are, respectively, 1.414 and 4.517. In other words, the two sets have the same mean but very different standard deviations because they differ greatly in the way the individual values are distributed about the mean. The average of this dispersion (the standard deviation, s.d.) is much greater for the second set than for the first.

Activity 2.5

You will probably want to accept the decision to use random sampling, provided that an appropriate sample frame is available, and also that there is sufficient finance to cover the cost of obtaining a sample of the size needed for the required precision. You will then point out that, with an expected response rate of 40–50 per cent, the sample is not likely to be representative of the population of interest, as the non-responders are likely to differ in important ways from those who do respond. Merely increasing sample size will be costly, and will not help. You would suggest that the additional money should be spent instead on making a second, and even a third, approach to non-responders; doing analyses on whatever limited data are available for non-responders to see how they differ from those who do respond; or setting up a small random study of the characteristics of non-responders, perhaps by visiting their homes, or offering an incentive for participation.

Research Proposal Activity 2

This chapter has introduced methods for obtaining representative samples from a population and for providing estimates of the accuracy of statistics derived from a sample. It has also examined issues and problems relating to survey sampling, sample loss and non-response. In outlining a research proposal, you should consider whether the following questions are relevant:

1 What is the population to which you want your results to apply? What are the sampling units in that population?
2 Is a sampling frame available? Is it complete, accurate and fully representative of the population you wish to describe?
3 What methods of sampling will be used (random or non-random) and why?
4 If random sampling is to be used, should stratifying factors be introduced? If so, will the sampling be proportionate or disproportionate to population frequencies?
5 Is there value in adopting a cluster-sampling approach?
6 If random sampling is not feasible, or too costly and time-consuming, is some form of non-random sampling more appropriate?
7 What sources of non-sampling error can be anticipated and how can they be counteracted at the planning stage?
8 What should the size of the sample be? What balance should be sought between cost and level of precision?
9 What steps will be taken to deal with the bias introduced by non-response or missing data?

PART II

DATA COLLECTION

3

Observational Research

Peter Foster

This chapter considers data collection by means of observation – as a main research tool, or as a preliminary or supplement to other methods. It distinguishes between

- 'structured' or 'systematic' observation, where reductionist measurements are collected by observational means to test hypotheses or explore correlations between variables, and
- 'less-structured' or 'qualitative' observation to explore the framework of meaning in as holistic and naturalistic a manner as possible.

A main concern is with ways in which the validity of data collected by these means is assured.

Using Observation

Within everyday life we are all observers. We constantly observe the physical organization of the environment around us, and we observe the behaviour of the human beings who inhabit that environment. Observation involves watching, of course, but information from sight is supported by that received through our other senses: hearing, smelling, touching and tasting (these are even more important for blind or partially sighted people). The information from these various senses is usually combined, processed and interpreted in complex ways to form our observations – our mental images of the world and what is going on in it.

In everyday life we use observation to gain information or knowledge so that we can act in the world. Without observation, participation in the world would be impossible – and when our senses are impaired, that participation becomes more difficult. Observation also informs, and enables us to test our common-sense theories about the social world. We all interact with others on the basis of, often taken-for-granted, ideas about how particular types of people are likely to behave in particular circum-stances. These theories are built up, and continually refined, by observation of the behaviour of others and of ourselves.

Observation fulfils similar purposes in research, but there is an important differ-ence. Again, the aim is the collection of information about the world with the inten-tion of guiding behaviour. However, observation is not usually done simply to enable the researcher to decide how to act in the world or to inform his or her common-sense theories. Its aim is the production of public knowledge (empirical and theo-retical) about specific issues, which can be used by others in a variety of ways. This knowledge may influence the behaviour of those who access it, but its influence will be less direct than is the case with everyday observation.

Activity 3.1 (5 minutes)

Do you think there are any other differences between observation in everyday life and observation in research? Make a note of them before reading on.

I think there are two further distinctive features of observation in research: first, the way it is organized and, secondly, the way observations are recorded, interpreted and used. In research, observation is planned and conducted in a systematic way, rather than happening spontaneously and haphazardly, as it usually does in everyday life. Appropriate techniques are carefully selected for the purposes at hand. Observations are systematically recorded rather than stored only in personal memory, and are carefully interpreted and analyzed, again employing systematic and planned proce-dures. Moreover, the data produced by observational research are subjected to checks on validity so that we can be more confident about their accuracy than is usually the case with observational data produced routinely in everyday life.

As part of research, observation can be used for a variety of purposes. It may be employed in the preliminary stages of a research project to explore an area which can then be studied more fully utilizing other methods, or it can be used towards the end of a project to supplement or provide a check on data collected in interviews or surveys (see, for example, Stacey, 1960; Bennett, 1976; Rex and Tomlinson, 1979). Where observation is the main research method employed, it may be used to obtain descrip-tive quantitative data on the incidence of particular sorts of behaviour or events (see, for example, Galton et al., 1980; Sissons, 1981), or to enable qualitative description of the behaviour or culture of a particular group, institution or community (see, for example, Malinowski, 1922; Whyte, 1981). In the latter case, observation is used as part of a broad approach to research, usually referred to as ethnography, which uses a combination of data-gathering techniques (I discuss this further below). Observation may also be used to develop and test particular theories, and situations or cases may be deliberately selected for observation in order to facilitate this (see, for example, Glaser and Strauss, 1967, 1968; Brophy and Good, 1974).

Advantages and Limitations

Observation as a research method has a number of clear adv
and questionnaires. First, information about the physical
human behaviour can be recorded directly by the researc'
on the retrospective or anticipatory accounts of others. For a ..
accounts may be inaccurate. For example, they may be shaped by the
the person plays in ways that make the account misleading, the information .
have been systematically recorded and may therefore contain errors, or the accou..
may be distorted by the person's concern to present a desirable image of him- or herself. Since observation enables the researcher to note down what he or she sees as it
occurs, observational data are often more accurate.

Secondly, the observer may be able to 'see' what participants cannot. Many
important features of the environment and behaviour are taken for granted by participants and may therefore be difficult for them to describe. It may require the trained
eye of the observer to 'see the familiar as strange' and provide the detailed description required. Moreover, important patterns and regularities in the environment and
behaviour may only be revealed by careful, planned observation by a researcher over
a period of time.

Thirdly, observation can provide information on the environment and behaviour
of those who cannot speak for themselves and therefore cannot take part in interviews or complete questionnaires: babies, very young children and animals are obvious
examples. It can also give data on the environment and behaviour of those who will
not take part in interviews or complete questionnaires because they have not the
time, or because they object, or because they fear the consequences. In fact, some
form of observation (perhaps covert) may be the only way of collecting information
on the behaviour of people who are extremely busy, are deviant, or are hostile to the
research process for some reason (see Taylor, 1984, for example).

A final advantage, which I mentioned earlier, is that data from observation can be
a useful check on, and supplement to, information obtained from other sources. So,
for example, the information given by people about their own behaviour in interviews can be compared with observation of samples of their actual behaviour.

However, there are also limitations to observation as a research method. The environment, event or behaviour of interest may be inaccessible and observation may
simply be impossible (or at least very difficult). This may be because the social
norms surrounding the event or behaviour do not usually permit observation (as with
human sexual behaviour, for example), because the behaviour deliberately avoids
observation (as with many forms of deviance), because the event or behaviour occurs
rarely or irregularly (as with disasters), because the observer is barred from access
to the event or behaviour (as is frequently the case in studying powerful élite
groups), or because the event or behaviour happened in the past. Sometimes events
and behaviour are just not open to observation.

A second limitation is that people may, consciously or unconsciously, change the
way they behave because they are being observed, and therefore observational
accounts of their behaviour may be inaccurate representations of how they behave
'naturally'. This is the problem of reactivity.

A third limitation is that observations are inevitably filtered through the interpre-
tive lens of the observer. It must therefore be emphasized that observations can never

de us with a direct representation of reality. Whatever observational method is
d, what the observer obtains from observational research are constructed repre-
entations of the world. Moreover, observers inevitably have to select what they
observe and what observations they record. Sometimes the basis of these selections
is made explicit, but at other times it is not, and clearly there is a danger that the
researcher's preconceptions and existing knowledge will bias his or her observation.

Finally, it is worth emphasizing that observational research is very time-consuming,
and therefore costly, when compared with other methods of data collection. This
means that the researcher may only be able to observe a restricted range of subjects
or a small sample of the behaviour that is of interest. As a result, the representativeness of observations may often be in doubt. In some cases, interviews or questionnaires may be a more economical way of collecting detailed data which are more
broadly representative.

Structure in Observation

There are a number of different approaches to observational research. One important
distinction is between *more-structured* (sometimes referred to as 'systematic')
observation and *less-structured* (sometimes referred to as 'ethnographic' or 'unstructured') observation. These two approaches originate in different academic traditions,
and have different aims, purposes and procedures.

More-structured Observation   The roots of more-structured observation are in the
positivist tradition in social science, where the aim has been to emulate, to one degree
or another, the approaches and procedures of the natural sciences. The emphasis in
this tradition has been on the accurate and objective measurement of observable
human behaviour, on the precise definition and operationalization of concepts, on the
production of quantitative data, on the examination of relationships between variables
using experimental and statistical techniques, and on the systematic testing of theories using what has been termed the 'hypothetico-deductive' method.

The aim of more-structured observation, then, is to produce accurate quantitative
data on particular pre-specified observable behaviours or patterns of interaction.
These data concern the frequency, duration or, in some cases, quality of particular
behaviours, and may also record the types of people involved, or the physical, social
or temporal context in which the behaviour occurs. It may be used to describe patterns
of behaviour among a particular population or in a particular setting, or, especially
where the data are produced in controlled experiments, to test pre-existing theories
and hypotheses concerning the nature and causes of behaviour.

The essential characteristic of more-structured observation is that the purposes of
the observation, the categories of behaviour to be observed and the methods by
which instances of behaviour are to be allocated to categories, are worked out, and
clearly defined, before the data collection begins. So, in this sense, there is maximum prestructuring. A variety of different techniques is used to record behaviour,
but all involve some sort of pre-set, standardized observation schedule, on which a
record (often ticks or numbers) of the type of behaviour of interest can be made. The
role of the observer is to follow carefully the instructions laid down in the observation schedule, thereby minimizing observer subjectivity.

An example of a structured observation system used to record aspects of teacher–pupil interaction in classrooms can be found in Flanders' interaction analysis categories, as given in Box 3.1. The behaviour, observed at 3-second intervals, is coded into one of 10 categories. The schedule can give useful data on the proportion of class time taken up by different types of activity.

Box 3.1   *Flanders' interaction analysis categories (FIAC)*

Teacher Talk

Response
1   *Accepts feeling.* Accepts and clarifies an attitude or the feeling tone of a pupil in a non-threatening manner. Feelings may be positive or negative. Predicting and recalling feelings are included.
2   *Praises* or *encourages.* Praises or encourages pupil action or behaviour. Jokes that release tension, but not at the expense of another individual; nodding head, or saying 'Um hm?' or 'go on' are included.
3   *Accepts* or *uses ideas* of *pupils.* Clarifying, building or developing ideas suggested by a pupil. Teacher extensions of pupil ideas are included but as the teacher brings more of his/her own ideas into play, shift to category 5.

Initiation
4   *Asks questions.* Asking a question about content or procedure, based on teacher ideas, with the intent that a pupil will answer.
5   *Lecturing.* Giving facts or opinions about content or procedures; expressing *his/her own* ideas, giving *his/her own* explanation or citing an authority other than a pupil.
6   *Giving directions.* Directions, commands or orders to which a pupil is expected to comply.
7   *Criticizing or justifying authority.* Statements intended to change pupil behaviour from non-acceptable to acceptable pattern; bawling someone out; stating why the teacher is doing what he/she is doing; extreme self-reference.

Pupil Talk

Response
8   *Talk by pupils in response to teacher.* Teacher initiates the contact or solicits pupil statement or structures the situation. Freedom to express own ideas is limited.

Initiation
9   *Talk by pupils which they initiate.* Expressing own ideas; initiating a new topic; freedom to develop opinions and a line of thought, like asking thoughtful questions; going beyond the existing structure.
10   *Silence or confusion.* Pauses, short periods of silence and periods of confusion in which communication cannot be understood by the observer.

(Continued)

Box 3.1   *(Continued)*

There is no *scale* implied by the use of these numbers. Each number is classificatory; it designates a particular kind of communication event. To write these numbers down during observation is to enumerate, not to judge a position on a scale.

Source: Flanders, 1970, p. 34

It is possible to use more-structured observation to collect data on a large scale by employing a team of observers, all using the same observation schedule in the same way. As observational procedures are standardized, the data collected by each observer can be collated, and quantitative comparisons can be made on a number of dimensions – for example, different situations, times and subject types. Using the Flanders schedule, for example, we could compare the proportion of school class time taken up by different activities between teachers, schools, curriculum areas, time periods and so on. The results of such research are cumulative, which means we can build up our knowledge of the particular behaviour in question over a period of time. It is also possible to establish the reliability of more-structured techniques by, for example, comparing the data from two researchers observing the same behaviour and using the same schedule.

Less-structured Observation   The origins of less-structured observation lie in anthropology and in the application of its ethnographic approach to the study of communities and groups in industrialized societies, pioneered, for example, by the Chicago School of Sociology (a brief history of this can be found in Burgess, 1982). Research in this tradition has generally rejected the positivist approach to social science and has stressed that, to understand human behaviour, we need to explore the social meanings that underpin it. It has emphasized studying the perspectives of social actors – their ideas, attitudes, motives and intentions, and the way they interpret the social world – as well as observation of behaviour in natural situations and in its cultural context.

Less-structured observation therefore aims to produce detailed, qualitative descriptions of human behaviour that illuminate social meanings and shared culture. These data are combined with information from conversations, interviews and, where appropriate, documentary sources to produce an in-depth and rounded picture of the culture of the group, which places the perspectives of group members at its heart and reflects the richness and complexity of their social world. Less-structured observation is characterized by flexibility and a minimum of prestructuring. This does not mean that the observer begins data collection with no aims and no idea of what to observe, but there is a commitment to approach observation with a relatively open mind, to minimize the influence of the observer's preconceptions and to avoid imposing existing preconceived categories. It is not unusual, therefore, for the focus of the research to change quite dramatically during the course of data collection as ideas develop and particular issues become important. The aim of less-structured observation is also often to develop theory, but here theory tends to emerge from, or be grounded in, the data (Glaser and Strauss, 1967). Rather than developing a theory and then collecting data specifically to test that theory, data collection, theory construction and testing are interwoven. So theoretical ideas develop from initial data collection and then influence future data collection; there is a cumulative spiral of theory development and data collection.

As one of the key aims of this type of observation is to see the social world as far as possible from the actor's point of view, the main technique used is *participant observation*. Here the observer participates in some way with the group under study and learns its culture, while at the same time observing the behaviour of group members. Observations are combined with interviews, conversations and so on, and are generally recorded using field notes and, where possible, audio or video recordings.

Obviously, less-structured observation cannot provide the large-scale comparative data on particular behaviours that is possible with more-structured methods, but it can produce far more detailed data on the behaviour of particular individuals or groups in particular settings. It gives qualitative data which, in combination with data of other kinds, can explicate the social and cultural basis of human interaction. Less-structured observation frequently involves the researcher spending long periods of time in the field, building relationships and participating in social interaction with subjects. The aim is that subjects come to trust the researcher and become accustomed to his or her presence. Consequently, the data produced may be less influenced by reactivity – by the researcher and the research process. Less-structured observation provides data which enable us, as outsiders, to see the social world more from the point of view of those we are studying – it gives us some sense of an insider's perspective. Because we are more able to appreciate the cultural context of behaviour and examine the motives and meanings given to behaviour by subjects, we may be better able to understand their social action. Less-structured observation also gives us the opportunity to examine the way interactions and social meanings change and develop over time, and the way in which social order is actively constructed by social actors through interaction. Finally, the method is particularly suited to the development, rather than the rigorous testing, of theory.

Which observational approach is adopted in a particular research project depends on the nature of the problem or the issue being investigated, the theoretical and methodological sympathies of the researcher, various practical considerations, and sometimes the stage that the research has reached.

To some extent, my division of the two approaches is rather artificial. In practice, researchers often use a combination of approaches. Sometimes research which adopts more-structured observation as its main method may begin with a period of less-structured observation. This may form part of the pilot work, and can help the researchers identify the type of behaviour on which they wish to focus and enable them to become accustomed to the research setting. It is also quite common for research which employs an ethnographic approach to utilize more-structured observational methods at some stage. This may happen when the researcher requires quantitative data on particular forms of behaviour. In my own research (Foster, 1990), for example, I was interested, among other things, in teacher-pupil interaction in multi-ethnic classes. I was concerned with whether teachers gave more of their time and attention to children from certain ethnic groups. My overall approach to the research was ethnographic and my observations were generally less-structured, but in this case I felt the need for more quantitative data on specific aspects of teacher behaviour and so I used a structured observation system developed by Brophy and Good (1970). This enabled me to count the number of different types of interaction that teachers had with students of different ethnic groups (the details of this part of my research are contained in Foster, 1989).

Relationships and Roles

Negotiating Access

Gaining access to settings in order to conduct observational research is a problem for both more-structured and less-structured observation. Whichever observational technique is used, the researcher has to get to a physical position from which he or she can observe the behaviour of subjects, and this usually involves negotiating entry to a group, institution, community or social setting of some sort. However, there are some differences between the two observational approaches. More-structured observation is more likely to involve access, sometimes by multiple and paid observers, for short periods to a relatively large number of settings. For example, in the ORACLE research (Galton et al., 1980) there were nine researchers who observed 58 classes in 19 different schools for three days each term. In contrast, in ethnographic studies, where less-structured observation is the main method, often a lone researcher is concerned to gain access to a single or a small number of settings for a relatively long period of fieldwork. Lacey (1970), for example, conducted fieldwork in one school, to which he gave the pseudonym 'Hightown Grammar', over a three-year period. These differences mean that sometimes different strategies for gaining access need to be adopted.

The problem of access is of greatest significance early in research when the researcher is negotiating entry to the overall setting under consideration – a particular school, factory, village, community and so on – in order to begin observation. But, for ethnographic research in particular, it remains an issue throughout data collection as entry to sub-settings within the overall setting has to be continually negotiated, and sometimes renegotiated, as the research progresses.

A number of different strategies are used to gain access. Which one is adopted depends, in the main, on the nature of the setting (or sub-setting) and what behaviour is to be observed. Settings (and sub-settings) vary in their openness to observation. Public places and events, such as streets, shopping centres, parks, football matches, some religious services or public meetings, are relatively open and may pose few problems of access. Here, usually, no one's permission is required to observe; an observer role can be taken relatively easily since it is common for people in such situations to watch the behaviour of others, and the researcher can remain relatively unobtrusive. The research of Marsh et al. (1978), for example, on the behaviour of football crowds, was conducted in part by standing on the terraces of Oxford United and observing crowd behaviour (while also watching the match!); and research by Lofland (1973), on 'waiting styles' in public places, was conducted by observing in bus depots and airports.

However, this does not mean that observation in public settings is always unproblematic. Sometimes observation, or at least very close or obvious observation, can be inappropriate. This may be particularly the case in public settings, where evasion of social interaction is the norm or where a person's presence in the setting is normally brief or transient. Here the observer may have to adopt techniques to conceal his or her observation or justify 'hanging around', such as observing from behind a newspaper or pretending to be legitimately waiting. It may also be difficult to observe behaviour of a private nature even though it takes place in a public setting. Humphreys (1970), for example, observed male homosexual activity in public lavatories. He had to justify his observation by adopting the role of 'watch queen', which meant he posed as a voyeur and acted as a look-out for the men.

Access to what are considered more private settings will generally prove more difficult than access to public ones. One strategy here is to observe covertly. Access to the setting is obtained by the researcher secretly taking on an established role in the group under study or using his or her existing role to conduct research secretly. No formal permission to do the research is requested. The researcher simply becomes, or already is, a participant member of the group, and he or she uses this position to observe the behaviour of other participants. One example of this type of research is a famous study by Festinger et al. (1956) of an apocalyptic religious sect, in which observers secretly joined the sect as new members. Another is a study by Holdaway (1983), who took advantage of his position as a serving police sergeant to observe the occupational culture of fellow officers.

Covert research is most likely to be used when there is a strong possibility that access is unlikely to be gained using open methods. This may be because groups fear the consequences of research, perhaps because they are involved in behaviour which could be considered deviant, or because they are hostile towards the idea of research itself (see, for example, Homan, 1980). In such cases it may be the only option if the research is to go ahead. Sometimes, as Chambliss (1975) discovered in his study of organized crime in an American city, covert study may be necessary only for the initial period of the research. Once relationships have been established it may be possible for the researcher to become more open and honest about him or herself and his or her purposes.

Covert observation is also used when reactivity is likely to be a problem if research is conducted openly. For example, the Glasgow gang observed by Patrick (1973) would almost certainly have behaved very differently if they had known they were being researched. However, covert research in certain circumstances is potentially dangerous. When researching criminal groups, for example, if the researcher's 'cover is blown', there could be violent consequences. If the researcher's real identity and purposes are discovered, at the very least it is likely that the research will be forced to end. Doubts have also been widely expressed about the ethics of covert research.

Access in covert research is dependent on the researcher's ability to play an established role convincingly, or at least to convince existing members that he or she is a genuine new entrant to the group. This obviously depends in part on the researcher's physical characteristics, but also on his or her ability to use a variety of impression management techniques and to display cultural competence in the setting. For example, in his study of Pentecostal church groups, Homan took an active part in worship and

Bible study and used Pentecostal language and forms of greeting in order to present himself as a new member (Homan, 1980; see also Homan and Bulmer, 1982). However, he did not undergo baptism, as Pryce (1979) did as part of his research on Pentecostal groups in the Afro-Caribbean community of Bristol.

Where observational research is conducted openly, the researcher generally has to seek formal permission from subjects and/or those responsible for them in order to observe in the setting. In the case of laboratory experiments, which generally involve more-structured observation, the researcher deliberately creates the setting; subjects, in agreeing to take part in the study, give their consent to observation of their behaviour in that setting. Subjects are recruited by a variety of methods – by advertising, word of mouth, offering inducements – and researchers will usually explain the purposes of the research and the possible consequences of taking part. Having said this, however, subjects have sometimes been deceived about the true nature of experiments and their potential effect. For example, in experiments on obedience to authority conducted by Milgram (1974), subjects were told that they were taking part in a scientific study of memory and learning. During the study they were duped into thinking that they were administering increasingly severe electric shocks to learners. What was in fact being studied was the extent to which they would obey authority figures instructing them to administer the shocks.

In the case of research in more natural settings – groups, institutions, organizations and so on – the researcher has to negotiate access with a number of 'gatekeepers', perhaps at different levels of an institutional hierarchy (although it is not always clear who the key gatekeepers are). Gatekeepers usually have positions of authority within the group or institution and can grant or withhold permission to conduct research in their particular sphere of authority. They may also be the subjects of the research. For example, if I wanted to gain access to a school in order to study teaching methods, I would probably first have to seek the permission of local education authority (LEA) officers (if the school was LEA maintained), school governors and the head teacher, and then, in order to gain access to sub-settings within the school, I would have to approach heads of department, teachers and perhaps students as well. This would probably involve lengthy discussion and negotiation, a process which can be a useful source of data on the political structure of the group and on the perspectives of key group members.

Gatekeepers will be concerned to protect their own interests and the interests of group members from any threat posed by the research. Consequently, they may refuse access altogether, place limitations on the type of research which can be done, or try to manage the impression of individuals and the group that the researcher receives and documents (for discussion of this in the context of studying military élites, see Spencer, 1973). The last of these strategies may involve presenting individuals, or the group, to the researcher in a particular way, restricting or influencing access to particular areas, times or events, and/or placing constraints on what the researcher can publish. Gatekeepers may also try to use the research for their own purposes. They may, for example, try to use research data to monitor the behaviour of particular individuals or subgroups, or use published accounts to enhance the interests of the group. Interestingly, the Royal Ulster Constabulary (RUC) police officers studied by Brewer (1991) used the research as an opportunity to air their grievances to senior staff.

Activity 3.2 (allow 15 minutes)

Imagine that you are a gatekeeper in a group or institution with which you are familiar. You are approached by a researcher wishing to spend a number of weeks observing in your group or institution:

- What sort of questions would you ask the researcher?
- How would you respond to his or her request and why would you respond in this way?

Make a note of your answers before you continue.

One factor that influences the response of gatekeepers to access requests is their preconceptions of research and researchers. This derives from any previous experience of research they have had, or from the way research is presented to them by others or by the media. Sometimes conceptions of research and researchers are negative and access may be denied. This was Homan's (1980) perception of the Pentecostal church members he studied and was a key influence in his decision to conduct covert research. On other occasions, conceptions may be more positive and the researcher may be welcomed and given considerable assistance. More commonly, the gatekeepers' conceptions consist of a mixture of positive attitudes and scepticism, trust and suspicion.

In negotiating access, researchers try to influence the conceptions gatekeepers have of the research. They adopt a number of techniques. Sometimes they simply explain fully the purposes and nature of the research and the methods to be employed, in the hope that the gatekeepers will be sufficiently interested and willing to allow the research to go ahead. This was the approach adopted by Stenhouse and his team who conducted research on library use in school sixth forms (Stenhouse, 1984). They wrote to head teachers explaining the aims of the project and the research methods to be adopted, and offered to visit the school to discuss the research at greater length. Most of the schools approached agreed to take part in the research.

On occasions, however, the account of the research given may be selective or involve an element of deception. As explained earlier, part of my own research was concerned with whether teachers gave more attention in the classroom to students from certain ethnic groups (Foster, 1990). When negotiating access to classrooms for this part of the research, I did not tell the teachers that this was specifically what I was interested in because I thought that, if I did, they would make a conscious effort to distribute their attention equally. I kept my explanation deliberately vague and said that I wanted to observe teaching methods and student behaviour.

Researchers are also concerned to influence how gatekeepers see them as people. As a result, they use, consciously or unconsciously, many self-presentational techniques to convey an impression of themselves that will maximize their chances of gaining access. They dress and conduct themselves in ways that give the impression that they will 'fit in' and that their presence is unlikely to cause offence, disruption or harm to subjects and that they can be trusted. Delamont, for example, reflecting on her research in a Scottish girls' public school in the 1960s, describes how she 'always wore a conservative outfit and real leather gloves' when meeting head teachers. On the other hand, she wished to give a slightly different impression to the pupils and so wore a dress of 'mini-length to show the pupils I knew what the fashion was' (Delamont, 1984: 25).

Another technique used when negotiating access is to offer inducements to gate-keepers. Researchers may, for example, emphasize the potential knowledge gains to the community as a whole or to the subjects themselves in comparison with the small amount of time or disruption that the research will require. They may offer services in return for access and enter into bargains with gatekeepers. For example, a number of researchers who have conducted ethnographic case studies in schools have taken on a part-time teaching load, in part to facilitate access (see, for example, Burgess, 1983); and, in my research (Foster, 1990), I offered to act as a 'consultant' to the school, which involved encouraging teachers to reflect on and improve aspects of their practice.

Researchers may also offer to protect the interests of subjects by guaranteeing the confidentiality of data, using pseudonyms and/or stressing their commitment to established ethical principles (see, for example, British Sociological Association, 1992). Sometimes gatekeepers are offered some control over the research: perhaps the opportunity to scrutinize, and maybe veto, plans and research techniques, or to control the use of data or the publication of a final report. Walford and Miller (1991), who studied Kinghurst, a new City Technology College, offered the head teacher the opportunity to write an unedited 15,000-word section of the planned book to encourage her to give them access (see Walford, 1991, for a discussion of this). Collaboration with subjects is seen as highly desirable by some researchers (see, for example, Day, 1981). It is suggested that this not only facilitates access, but also respects more fully the rights of subjects to be consulted and involved and means that the research is more likely to address their concerns and produce knowledge which they will find useful.

Another common strategy used in gaining access, especially in ethnographic research, is to use the assistance of a sponsor. This is generally an established and trusted figure within the group or institution who can vouch for the researcher and reassure subjects about the purposes of the research and intentions of the researcher. Sponsors can be very helpful in gaining access to groups or settings which might otherwise remain closed. Taylor (1984), for example, used the assistance of John McVicar (an ex-professional criminal), whom he got to know while conducting research in Durham prison, to gain access to the world of professional criminals. Sponsors can also be useful guides to the structure, organization and norms of the group and can provide invaluable advice on the most appropriate ways of collecting data. They can usefully act as informants, too, providing another valuable source of observational data. Indeed, they may have access to areas which are closed to the researcher, and they may have useful background knowledge which can enable a better understanding of behaviour. The best researcher's sponsor, Doc in Whyte's study of Cornerville, performed all these roles (Whyte, 1981). Without Doc to show him around, introduce him, vouch for him, supply him with information and answer his questions, Whyte's research would probably have been impossible.

On the other hand, there are disadvantages in relying too heavily on a sponsor. Access to certain individuals, subgroups or sub-settings can be restricted by too close a relationship with a sponsor who is perceived by other subjects to be hostile to their interests. Also, the research may be channelled in particular directions by the sponsor's contacts.

Researchers frequently rely upon personal contacts to find sponsors. Indeed, research settings are often selected, and access facilitated, because researchers have some prior experience of, or contact with, the group or institution. In such cases, the researcher has already established some form of identity in the eyes of subjects and can capitalize on this when negotiating access. Gillborn (1990), for example, researched the school he had attended as a pupil, and Cohen and Taylor's (1972) research in Durham prison came about because they were already involved in adult education work with long-term prisoners.

Activity 3.3 (allow 10 minutes)

Suppose you were interested in conducting research in the group or institution for which in Activity 3.2 you were a gatekeeper:

- What methods would you use to gain access?
- What problems would you anticipate in gaining access and how would you overcome them?

Briefly note down your answers before you continue.

Developing Relationships

Researchers are not only interested in gaining physical access to particular settings, they are also concerned with observing behaviour which naturally occurs in those settings. In other words, they desire access to behaviour which has been influenced as little as possible by the researcher's presence or the research process. The latter form of reactivity is, of course, eliminated in covert research because subjects are not aware that they are being studied. The former is not eliminated, however, because the researcher, in his or her participant role, may have an influence on behaviour. For example, Festinger et al. (1956), in joining the apocalyptic religious sect, telling the members fictitious stories about their 'psychic experiences' and joining in group activities, inevitably reinforced the beliefs of the group they were studying.

Researchers who are conducting their work openly adopt a number of techniques to become unobtrusive in the setting and minimize reactivity. They often pay attention to their own physical position in the setting and to the positioning of any recording equipment they are using. They also take care to dress and behave in ways that will allow them to blend into the setting, the aim being to reduce the extent to which subjects are conscious of their presence and of their observation. King (1984), for example, during his research in infant school classrooms, tried to avoid eye contact with the children and at one stage used the Wendy House as a 'convenient "hide"'.

Ethnographers often spend considerable periods of time in the field so that subjects become accustomed to their presence. They also make great efforts to build relationships of trust with subjects in order to facilitate access and reduce reactivity. As with negotiation with gatekeepers, what is involved here is the negotiation of the researcher's identity with subjects. The researcher wishes to be seen as a certain type of person and will try to influence (sometimes consciously, but often unconsciously) the way he or she is perceived by controlling or manipulating the information that the subject receives. Subjects (like gatekeepers) will have certain preconceptions and developing perceptions of the researcher, both as a person and as a researcher.

Activity 3.4 (5 minutes)

Consider a group or institution of which you are a member. A stranger – a smartly dressed, middle-aged woman, carrying a brief case – enters the setting:

- What identity(ies) would you attribute to her?
- If the stranger declares herself to be doing research, what other interpretations of her identity spring to mind?

Make a note of your responses.

Obviously, how you answer this will depend on your conceptions of the possible roles such a person could have in this particular setting and of the characteristics you attribute to a middle-aged woman (smartly dressed and carrying a briefcase) in such roles. It will also depend on your conceptions of researchers generally. This, in a sense, is the researcher's starting point. She (or he) tries to build on, adjust or change these initial conceptions using impression management techniques similar to those discussed earlier in connection with gatekeepers.

What impression the researcher tries to give depends, of course, on the role he or she takes in the group. If the research is covert, then the researcher seeks to give subjects the impression that he or she is indeed a real participant (perhaps initially a novice one) with the characteristics of such a person. If the research is conducted more openly, then the researcher may wish to give the impression that he or she is what Hammersley and Atkinson (1983) term an 'acceptable marginal member'. This may involve dressing in acceptable ways, though not necessarily in clothes identical to those worn by subjects. Parker (1974), for example, in his research with 'down town' adolescent boys in Liverpool, adopted a style of dress – 'black shirt, black jeans, burgundy leather (jacket)' – which enabled him to blend in, but which did not copy exactly the boys' style.

It may also require behaving in ways which enable the researcher to fit into the group. In *Street Corner Society,* for example, Whyte (1981) describes how he 'learned to take part in the street corner discussions on baseball and sex'. He also recounts a mistake he made when, after listening to a man's account of his illegal gambling activities, he suggested in discussion that the police had been 'paid off'. The reaction of his subjects suggested that such a statement was unacceptable in public talk and Whyte felt 'very uncomfortable' for the rest of the evening.

The researcher may trade on existing experience, skills and knowledge in developing subjects' conceptions of his or her identity. Pryce (1979), for example, utilized his identity as a Jamaican and his knowledge of Jamaican religious affairs to establish a rapport with his subjects. And in my own research (Foster, 1990), I frequently made use of my experience of teaching in a nearby school to convey the impression that I was knowledgeable about, and sympathetic to, the teachers' concerns – in a sense that I was one of them, rather than some sort of expert or critic.

On reflection I also, generally unconsciously, presented myself as (for want of a better phrase) an ordinary, decent type of person – someone who was honest, approachable, friendly, sensitive and understanding. I did this by engaging in everyday, sociable conversations, openly discussing aspects of my past and present life and exchanging day-to-day information. This type of self-presentation is crucial in gaining acceptance. Also important is how the researcher actually behaves. One has to demonstrate one's trustworthiness, openness, reliability and so on, since behaviour provides subjects with direct evidence of one's attributes. Indeed, subjects may sometimes actually test the researcher out in these respects.

On occasions, the researcher may be more consciously selective in the self presented to subjects. For example, he or she may play down or conceal certain aspects by disguising or failing to reveal personal views or political commitments. This was the case in Fielding's (1982) research on the National Front. He suppressed his disagreement with the ideology of the organization and presented himself as an 'unconverted sympathizer'. The researcher may also deliberately emphasize other aspects of self. Hobbs (1988), for example, in his study of deviant entrepreneurship and police detective work in East London, cultivated a view of himself as 'entrepreneurial and sharp' and 'sexist and chauvinistic' in order to blend in and become an insider (although, interestingly, he drew the line at racism). What aspect of self the researcher chooses to reveal or emphasize may change during the course of the research, as his or her role changes and as relationships with subjects develop.

Offering services is another means by which researchers negotiate their identity. Anthropologists have often provided simple medical and technical advice in the pre-industrial communities they have studied. In this way they have been able to demonstrate their commitment to the group and avoid being seen as exploitative outsiders. Similarly, ethnographers of institutions and groups in modern, industrial societies have given a whole range of services, such as assisting with teaching and extra-curricular activities in schools, giving legal advice to subjects in trouble with the law, serving as secretaries on committees, or merely lending a sympathetic ear. In fact, the participant role taken by many ethnographers involves working with and therefore helping subjects in the course of their everyday activities. This help is often crucial in building up relationships of trust and openness.

There are, of course, limits to the identities the researcher can negotiate with subjects. Ascribed characteristics such as age, gender, 'race' and ethnicity limit the sort of person the researcher can become and also the sort of relationship that can be developed with subjects. They may therefore restrict access to settings and to data.

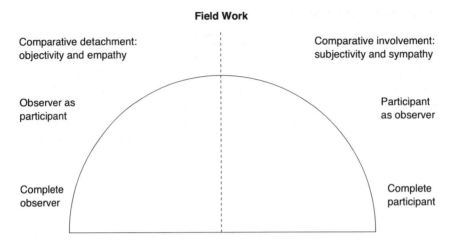

Figure 3.1   *Theoretical social roles for fieldwork (Junker, 1960: 36)*

But ascribed characteristics can also facilitate identities, relationships and access. As a 40-year-old white male, I would find it difficult to present myself as a young 'rap' music enthusiast, or develop close peer-type relationships with school pupils, or directly access the world of radical feminists. On the other hand, I might find it easier to present myself as a mature, professional person, to develop relationships with school teachers, or to access the world of white, male-dominated clubs. In saying this, I do not mean to imply that the researcher must be of the same age, gender or 'race' as his or her subjects. It is simply that sometimes age, gender or 'racial' characteristics can aid in the construction of certain types of identity and relationship. And, as Hunt (1984) pointed out in her research on the police, it is possible to renegotiate identities attributed on the basis of ascribed characteristics. In her research, she was initially perceived by male officers as an 'untrustworthy feminine spy', but, by utilizing a variety of impression management strategies, such as spending time on the pistol range, displaying a skill in judo and 'acting crazy' (in other words, taking unusual risks), she was able to negotiate a more acceptable and productive identity as 'street-woman-researcher'. (See Warren, 1988, for a more general discussion of the influence of gender on relationships in the field.)

Activity 3.5 (5 minutes)

Think about your own ascribed characteristics. In what ways would they limit and facilitate the identities, relationships and access you could negotiate in particular research settings? Note down your response before you continue.

The Researcher's Role

The role taken by the researcher in the group or setting under study varies according to the purposes of the research, the nature of the setting, the means of gaining access and the observational method employed. His or her role is more likely to be that of detached, non-participant observer when the purpose of the research is to collect data on specific observable behaviours using more-structured techniques, and it is more likely to be that of an involved participant when the purpose is the collection of ethnographic data using less-structured techniques. This highlights one key dimension of the researcher's role: the extent of participation in the group or setting. Gold (1958) and Junker (1960) suggest four types of role along this dimension (see Figure 3.1).

The complete observer   The researcher has no interaction with the subjects during data collection. In some psychological research, for example, subjects are observed through a one-way mirror and so do not come into direct contact with the observer. The benefit of the complete observer role is that it should eliminate the reactivity which stems from the immediate physical presence of the observer.

Activity 3.6 (a moment's reflection)

But do you think it eliminates reactivity altogether?

It only eliminates reactivity completely if the subjects are unaware that they are being observed, as is the case with covert research. But sometimes subjects are aware, or at least suspect, that they are being observed. This is often the case in laboratory experiments. Even though subjects cannot see the observer, they know that they are being observed. As a result, they may behave differently from how they would have behaved if unobserved.

Another advantage of this role is that the observer can remain detached from the subjects and therefore uninfluenced by their views and ideas. He or she is also free to concentrate on data recording, and possibly even to discuss data with another observer during data collection.

However, the role of complete observer places limitations on the behaviour and settings that can be observed, especially in natural situations. Also, the researcher may not be able to collect supporting data by asking the subjects questions. As a result, he or she may fail to appreciate the perspectives of the subjects and to understand the social meanings which underpin their interaction. This is one reason why this role is most often used in more-structured observation, where the researcher is interested only in categorizing instances of observable behaviour.

The observer as participant   Here the observer interacts with subjects, but does not take on an established role in the group. His or her role is that of researcher conducting research. He or she may develop more participant roles with some subjects, but the key role is that of researcher. Typically, the researcher is 'the person writing a book about ...' or 'the person investigating ...'. This type of role is often used in more-structured observation in natural situations where the researcher spends short periods of time observing behaviour in a relatively large number of settings. For example, the team of researchers led by Rutter, who investigated the relative effectiveness of 12 comprehensive schools in London, conducted observations of all the lessons taken by one class in each school for one week (Rutter et al., 1979). The researchers made it clear that their role was to observe and tried to keep their interaction with pupils and teachers to a minimum.

This role is also sometimes used in ethnographic work. In such cases the nature of the researcher's identity may be more fully developed and negotiated, and the researcher may be more likely to construct roles which involve greater participation, but the essential role is that of researcher. Woods (1979), for example, in his study of a secondary school, thought of himself as an 'involved' rather than a participant observer. He deliberately did not take an existing role in the school, although he did occasionally help out with lesson supervision and extra-curricular activities.

As with the complete observer role, one advantage of this strategy is that the researcher is more able to maintain his or her detachment from the subjects and take an outsider's view. Participation in a researcher role also enables him or her to move about within the group to observe behaviour in different sub-settings. Consequently, the researcher is able to get a fuller, more rounded picture of the group or institution. It is also much easier to sample sub-settings, events, times, subjects and so on systematically and to develop and test theoretical propositions.

The danger is that the researcher is viewed with suspicion by subjects. He or she may be viewed as an inspector or critic, an intruder or snoop. As a result, subjects may change their behaviour in order to present themselves in a particular way to the researcher, and even react to him or her with hostility. This is particularly likely if the researcher remains with the group for a period of time and fails to negotiate an acceptable identity, or if he or she does not conform to subjects' expectations.

Activity 3.7 (10 minutes)

Think again about a group or institution of which you are a member. How would people respond to the presence of an observer? Briefly note down your answer.

The participant as observer   This involves the researcher taking an established, or certainly a more participant, role in the group for the bulk of the research. In a number of school case studies, for example, researchers have worked as part-time teachers. As mentioned earlier, this was the case in Lacey's (1970) research in a grammar school. He taught alongside the teachers in the school while also acting as a researcher.

Often, taking a participant role facilitates access to the group or institution and to sub-settings within it. Offering to assist subjects with their work in return for access may be part of the bargain that the researcher negotiates with them. And working or living alongside people may help in building rapport and relationships of trust and openness which will help to reduce reactivity. Indeed, it may be that, because the researcher is a participant, subjects forget that he or she is doing research and behave more 'naturally' as a result. At times like this it might be said that the research becomes covert, although it is difficult to tell when this happens.

Activity 3.8 (5 minutes)

Following on from Activity 3.7, do you think your response to an observer would be any different if the researcher was a participant observer? Note down what this response might be before you continue.

The other main advantage of this role is that the researcher is better able to see the social world from the point of view of his or her subjects. He or she has to learn the culture in order to operate as far as possible as an insider, and gain access to information not available to outsiders. In this way, the researcher is more likely to appreciate and understand the subjects' perspectives and the meanings that underpin their interaction. In short, the researcher can put him or herself in their shoes. For this reason, this type of role is usually taken by researchers conducting ethnographic or less-structured observation.

However, a major problem with taking a participant role is that it places restrictions on the data that the researcher can collect. Access to sub-settings within the group or institution may be prevented by rules and norms which apply to the participant role. As a participant, the researcher may be expected to behave in certain ways and may be seen by subjects as having particular loyalties. Pryce (1979), for example, found it difficult to move between different Afro-Caribbean religious congregations in Bristol once he had established ties with one of them.

Developing and playing a significant role may also be very time-consuming and means that little time is available for recording and processing data. It can sometimes be stressful, too, when the expectations of the participant role are in conflict with those of the research role. Lacey (1970), for example, describes the tension he felt between the role of teacher and that of researcher. There is also the possibility that the more the researcher participates, the greater is his or her influence on the group.

An associated problem is what is sometimes termed 'going native'. In its extreme forms the researcher actually gives up the research and becomes a real member of the group. This is rare. A greater danger is of over-rapport with subjects or identifying too closely with them. The researcher loses his or her sense of detachment and adopts an over-sympathetic view of subjects. This may lead researchers to be selective in their observations and interpretations of behaviour so that they present a one-sided, and therefore inaccurate, account. This problem is not confined to the participant observer role – Hammersley and Atkinson (1983: 98–9) argue that Willis (1977), who adopted more of an observer-as-participant role, erred in this way – but it becomes more likely the more involved the researcher is with subjects.

The complete participant   Here the researcher plays an established role in the group and is fully immersed in that participant role, but uses his or her position to conduct research. Sometimes the research may be covert. There are two possibilities here. The researcher may secretly join the group or institution as a new member; for example, the observers in the study by Festinger et al. (1956) secretly joined a religious sect, and those in Rosenhan's (1982) study posed as psychiatric hospital patients. Alternatively, the researcher may already be a member, and thus uses his or her established position to conduct covert research; Holdaway (1983), for example, used his position as a serving police officer to research the occupational culture of fellow officers, and Davis (1959) took advantage of his job as a Chicago taxi driver to study the interaction between drivers and their customers.

The complete participant may also conduct research openly, however. This is the case in much practitioner research in education, where teachers research aspects of their own practice or institution. They work primarily as teachers, but engage in research with the aim of improving professional practice (see, for example, the case studies contained in Hopkins, 1985; Hustler et al., 1986; for a more theoretical discussion, see Elliott, 1991).

Again, the advantage of the complete participant role is that it facilitates access. As I have already pointed out, covert research in a participant role may be the only way of gaining access to certain groups. And where research is conducted openly, the researcher's established role and identity may ease access to sub-settings and individuals. The approach also has the advantages of the insider role explained above, and, in the case of covert research, the particular advantage of reducing that reactivity which occurs as a result of the subjects knowing that they are being observed.

There are, however, limitations similar to those with the participant-as-observer role. The restrictions on data collection are, if anything, more severe as the researcher has to maintain his or her participant role. Sometimes the attention that has to be paid to playing the participant role means that the time and opportunities for data collection are limited. The danger of 'going native' may also be more serious, as will the potential for role conflict and strain on the researcher's sense of identity. There is also a greater possibility that the researcher, as a full participant, will influence the people he or she is studying, or find that his or her research is controlled by a superior.

Changing research roles   It should be emphasized that, in ethnographic work in particular, research roles usually change during the course of the research. For example, the researcher may take on a participant role at some stage during the research. He or she may move from a rather naive, detached observer role in the early stages of the research to a fuller, more participant role in the later stages (see the example of Punch, 1979a, mentioned earlier); or, as in Corsaro's (1981) research in a nursery school, from a complete observer behind a one-way screen to a participant observer; or, as in Lacey's (1970) research, from a participant role in the early stages to a research role later.

It is also the case that researchers take on multiple sub-roles which differ according to the sub-setting and the particular individuals with whom they interact. Woods, for example, in his secondary school study, claims that he played at least five different roles. He was a 'relief agency or counsellor' to pupils and sometimes staff, a 'secret agent' to the head teacher (a role he avoided playing), a person to be 'appealed to' or 'consulted' during 'power struggles', a 'substitute member of staff' and 'fellow-human' (Woods, 1979: 261–2).

Managing Marginality

A major problem faced by researchers adopting a more ethnographic approach is that of balancing the insider and outsider aspects of their role: what has been termed 'managing marginality'. There are clear dangers in the researcher identifying too closely with subjects, allowing this to bias observations and interpretations, and thereby presenting a distorted picture. Over-rapport may also lead the researcher to concentrate on one particular subgroup or setting, which may influence his or her relationship with, and access to, other subgroups or settings. There are also advantages in adopting an outsider position. It enables the researcher to see subjects' behaviour in a relatively detached way with the freshness of a stranger. He or she may be able to see things which participants take for granted and will also be able to take a broader, more rounded view of the group, which includes its various subgroups or settings.

At the same time there are, of course, dangers in remaining too detached, too much an outsider. If relationships of trust do not develop, subjects will remain hostile or suspicious and are therefore likely to behave differently. It is unlikely that they will talk openly about their experiences and views, or that the researcher will develop a knowledge and understanding of the social meanings that underpin group interaction and the perspectives of subjects. As a result, the picture of the group they present may be based in large part on their own preconceptions.

The researcher's aim must be to balance the insider and outsider roles and combine the advantages of both; in other words, to manage a marginal position *vis-à-vis* subjects. Being at one with the group and yet remaining apart, being a 'friend' yet remaining a 'stranger', can be a difficult and sometimes stressful experience. But, as Hammersley and Atkinson (1983) emphasize, it is essential for good ethnographic work.

What to Observe

Focusing Research

The behaviour the researcher chooses to observe and record will depend on the overall topic and research questions being investigated. These will be determined by the researcher's theoretical and substantive interests. In more-structured observation, these ideas will produce categories of behaviour that will be specified in advance of fieldwork in the observation schedule, although sometimes more-structured observation is preceded by a period of less-structured exploratory observation. These prespecified behavioural categories become the primary focus of observations.

In less-structured ethnographic observation, the initial focus of the research is often less clear. Researchers will probably begin fieldwork with certain theoretical and substantive questions in mind – what are sometimes termed 'foreshadowed problems'. They will also bring with them certain sensitizing concepts drawn from previous research. Beynon (1985), for example, was interested in initial encounters between teachers and pupils in secondary schools and so his observations concentrated on the beginning of the school year for a newly arrived pupil intake. He also brought to the research certain concepts, such as teacher and pupil coping strategies, which had emerged from earlier work on teacher–pupil interactions. But, in less-structured observation, ideas are frequently undeveloped and general, and researchers usually try to avoid a commitment to pre-existing theoretical categories. The focus of initial observations is therefore wide, and the researcher is concerned, like any new member, to obtain a broad overview of, and basic information about, the group or institution under study. In addition, he or she will probably record, in a relatively unselective way, any data that appear to be relevant or interesting. As research progresses, theoretical ideas develop in conjunction with data collection. More specific research questions, propositions and hypotheses emerge from an examination and analysis of initial data. These, then, form the basis of, and provide the focus for, future data collection. This gradual refinement of research questions – the concentration of observations on specific issues and areas – is often referred to as 'progressive focusing'.

Research may focus on particular subjects or sub-settings within the overall setting, or it may focus on particular times, events, behaviours or social processes. One strategy sometimes used in this process is theoretical sampling, which you met in Chapter 1. Here different cases – or subjects, sub-settings, times or events within a case – are selected for observation specifically to test and develop hypotheses. Observational instances are often chosen in such a way as to minimize or maximize differences which are thought to be theoretically important. By minimizing the differences, it is possible to clarify the detailed characteristics of a theoretical category. And, by maximizing the differences, the researcher will be able to establish the range of a particular set of categories. So, for example, if I were interested in how teaching style was affected by the number of pupils with behavioural problems in a class, I could look at teaching in classes with a large and small number of such pupils and at teaching in classes with similar numbers of such pupils. In this way I could attempt to identify the differences in teaching style which seemed to be the result of differences in the numbers of behavioural problems.

Theoretical sampling also influences how many observations the researcher should make. Glaser and Strauss (1967) suggest that data are collected on a particular theoretical category until it is 'saturated': that is, until nothing new is being learned about that category.

Representative Sampling

Observational research also often involves representative sampling of different types within the case that is being studied. It is rarely possible for the researcher to observe every subject, sub-setting, event or instance of behaviour in which he or she is interested, and even if it were possible it would not be necessary or desirable to do so. What observational researchers generally do (like researchers using survey/interview methods) is to select samples and base their analysis and conclusions on data from these samples. Observing a sample is obviously much less time-consuming and, as a result, it is possible to collect more detailed and accurate data. But, as with surveys, there is a danger of error arising from unrepresentative sampling. If the subjects, settings, events or behaviour sampled and observed are unrepresentative of the general population of subjects, settings, events or behaviour with which the researcher is concerned, then it will not be legitimate to generalize from the sample.

In more-structured observation, and sometimes in the early stages of an ethnographic study, researchers are concerned to select representative samples of people, places, times, behaviours or events within a case, so that they can make generalizations to the relevant population or establish general patterns in the setting they are studying. Some form of random or systematic sampling is often used. This may involve selecting a random or systematic sample of subjects to observe. So, if I were interested in studying middle managers in an industrial organization, I might select a random sample from this population to observe. It may also involve observing behaviour at a random or systematic sample of times. For example, if I were studying a hospital or hospital ward, I might select a random sample of days or times of the day (including the night shift) to observe. I would at least ensure that I did not conduct all my observations on the same days and at the same times. Where an institution is organized around a periodic cycle of time – as are schools and colleges with their academic years – it would also be important to spread my observations across the organizational cycle. There are obvious dangers of unrepresentativeness if observations are concentrated at particular times of the cycle, unless, of course, it is these particular times that the researcher is most interested in, as in Beynon's (1985) research focusing on initial encounters between teachers and pupils. In such cases, these events or times become the population from which samples are selected.

Time (or point) sampling is frequently used in more-structured observation. Here the researcher records and categorizes the behaviour which is observed at regular timed intervals. In the ORACLE project (Galton et al., 1980), for example, teacher and pupil behaviour were each observed and coded at 25-second intervals. The behaviour occurring at such times was then held to be representative of behaviour in general in the classrooms studied.

Where the researcher has pre-existing knowledge about the heterogeneity of an organization, he or she may also select random or systematic samples of places or sub-settings within the overall setting. In a study of a school, for instance, a researcher might select a sample of departments or corridors to observe. He or she might also select samples of particular events or behaviours. In a school, the researcher might try to observe, say, a random sample of assemblies, department meetings, lesson openings or demonstrations in science lessons. However, it may be difficult to specify and identify events or behaviours in advance so that they can be sampled. In this case, ethnographic researchers sometimes sample from the descriptions of behaviour contained in their field notes. There are, of course, dangers with such a strategy because the behaviours recorded in field notes may be an unrepresentative sample of all such behaviours.

Having said all this, in ethnographic research in particular the selection of what to observe is often not done on a random or systematic basis. Accurate sampling frames may not be available in advance and access to particular subjects, sub-settings, times and events may be difficult or impossible to obtain. Pragmatic considerations in the selection of observations often loom large. What the researcher actually selects to observe may very much depend on the opportunities that arise, the role he or she takes within the group and the relationships that have been developed with subjects. Often observation depends on the cooperation of subjects or gatekeepers, and the researcher has to concentrate on those who are willing to cooperate. One strategy that is sometimes used is *snowball sampling*. Here, one observed subject passes the researcher on to another, vouching for him or her and acting as a sponsor. The advantage of this strategy is that sponsorship encourages cooperation and therefore facilitates access, but, of course, the limitation is that the snowball sample may be unrepresentative.

Recording Observations

One of the greatest differences between more-structured and less-structured observation is the way observations are recorded.

More-structured Observation

As the aim of more-structured observation is to produce quantitative data on specific categories of observable behaviour, the nature of the categories and the procedures for allocating instances of behaviour to them, must be clearly specified before data collection. These form the basis of an observation schedule in terms of which the researcher can code his or her observations.

The nature of categories and procedures obviously varies according to the aims of the research and the particular behaviour to be observed. At a very simple level, a researcher may be interested in a dichotomous variable, such as whether a person is or is not talking. However, it is more usual for researchers to be concerned with several, more complex, multiple-category variables; for example, types of question asked by a teacher during classroom observation.

The researcher may also be interested in distinguishing between the frequency and the duration of observed behaviours. How often a person does something may clearly be a different matter from how much time they spend doing it. *When* a behaviour occurs in time and *where* it occurs in a particular sequence of behaviours may also be important. Thus, some means of recording the temporal location of behaviour is sometimes needed. As Croll (1986) points out, there are three main possibilities.

The first possibility is some sort of continuous recording. In this, a time chart is used and the type of behaviour which occurs is coded continuously on the chart. When the behaviour changes, a new code is used from the time of the change. This type of recording allows the observer to locate the behaviours in time and to record their frequency and duration, and also where they occur in a particular sequence of behaviours. A simple example of continuous recording has been used in research on eye contact in interpersonal interaction. Here researchers have been interested in the frequency and duration of eye contact between two interacting individuals. Often using video recordings, observers note on a time sheet the period over which one, both or neither subject is engaging in eye contact. Other, more complex, variables may also be recorded (see Scherer and Ekman, 1982, for a discussion).

A more complex example was used in research by Vietze et al. (1978), which looked at the interaction between mothers and their developmentally delayed infants.

Observations of the behaviour of both mother and infant were recorded continuously by two observers – one focusing on the mother, the other on the young child. The infant's behaviour was coded into five categories: visual attention to the mother, non-distress vocalization, smile, distress vocalization, and no signalling behaviour. Likewise, the mother's behaviour was coded into five categories: visual attention to the infant, vocalization directed to the infant, smile, tactile play stimulation, and no behaviour directed to the infant. From their observations, the researchers could discover the frequency and duration of particular mother and child behaviours, and also of the combinations of different types in interaction. They also had information about the sequences of behaviour.

However, continuous recording may be difficult where behaviour changes frequently and rapidly, as, for example, with question and answer sequences in a school classroom. It is also difficult to record more than one variable or category of a variable at a time unless more than one observer is used, as in the case above. Moreover, if the nature of behaviour is ambiguous and the coding decision cannot be made until some time after the behaviour has begun, continuous recording will not be possible.

A second possibility is time (or point) sampling. As noted above, this often involves the coding of behaviour which is occurring at regular times – for example, every 25 seconds in the ORACLE research (Galton et al., 1980). The observer can record the behaviour occurring at what is hoped is a representative sample of times, and can therefore estimate the proportion of time taken up by particular behaviours. Time sampling can also involve coding the behaviour which occurred in regular timed periods. At a time signal, the observer notes down whether particular behaviours occurred during the preceding period. A study of science teaching by Eggleston et al. (1975) used such a system. Observers noted whether any of 23 different types of behaviour occurred (categories included types of teacher–pupil interaction and pupil use of resources) during each 3-minute period. The advantages of this method are that a large number of behaviours or events can be recorded and some indication is gained of their minimum frequency. The problem is that the method will underestimate the frequency of behaviours which are clustered in time, and will tell us little about the duration of behaviours.

A third method of recording involves focusing on events. Here, whenever the behaviour of interest occurs, its nature, and sometimes the time at which it occurs (and less commonly its duration), is recorded. A good example of such a system is the Brophy and Good Dyadic Interaction System used for studying teacher–pupil interaction (Brophy and Good, 1970). In this complex system, the observer records the nature of the teacher's communications to pupils, students' responses to these communications, and teacher's responses to students' responses, every time such events happen. So, for example, the observer would record the type of question asked of a pupil, then the nature of the student's response to the question, followed by the teacher's response to the student's answer.

The advantage of event recording such as this is that it gives data on the frequency of events or behaviours, and possibly where they occur in time and in a sequence of behaviours. However, the method does not usually give information on the duration of behaviours and may prove difficult to operate when events of interest occur frequently in rapid succession.

**Activity 3.9 (allow 30 minutes, plus time to try out the
schedule, plus a further 15 minutes)**

Think of an example of behaviour which is fairly easy for you to observe and on
which it might be interesting to collect quantitative data. When I thought about
this I came up with the following ideas:

- Children's play: what types of activity do my young children engage in and
  how long do these last? Are boys' play activities different from girls'? Do
  boys dominate collective play space?
- Family roles: who does what in the home? How often? How much time is
  spent on different activities?
- Shopping: do shop assistants give more time and help to customers of their
  own ethnic group or gender?
- My work: how do I break up my time? What sorts of things do I do? How long
  do I spend on different activities?
- Meetings at work: who contributes and what is the nature of their contributions? Do some contribute more than others?

Devise a simple observation schedule that you can try out during a brief period
of observation. You will need to think about the sorts of categories into which
the behaviour could be divided, and rules for allocating observed instances of
behaviour to them. Think too about how you will select behaviours to observe
and how you will record your observations. When you have devised your
schedule and tried it out, make a note of the difficulties you encountered.

Less-structured Observation

In contrast, the aim of less-structured observation is to produce detailed qualitative
data on behaviour as part of a rounded description of the culture of a particular group
of people. The emphasis is on flexibility and on recording behaviour and events in
their wholeness; that is, taking full account of the social and cultural context in
which they occur, and examining the perspectives and interpretations of participants.
As such, fieldwork data will include records of conversations, discussions and interviews, as well as the observed behaviour of subjects. The usual method of recording
data is in the form of field notes. These are notes taken either during the observation
itself, when this is possible, or shortly afterwards, and they form a running record of
the researcher's observations.

It is obviously impossible to record everything that happens in a particular situation. Selection is inevitable and necessary. What is written down depends on the
initial research questions and the stage the research has reached. During the early
stages, an initial relatively wide focus is adopted and the researcher generally tries
to note down a broad, general outline of what is happening, perhaps making a more
detailed record of incidents that seem particularly interesting or revealing. At this
stage, the researcher may find some behaviour difficult to understand, but will often
keep a record of it, as the data may be understandable and useful at a later stage. As
the research progresses, and theoretical ideas begin to develop, the researcher

focuses more carefully and makes more detailed records of particular aspects of behaviour or situations.

At such times, it is very important to record as much detail as possible about what was said, both verbally and non-verbally. The actual language used may provide key information about subjects' perspectives which can be followed up in interviews and conversations. It is also important to record as much as possible about the physical, social and temporal context in which the behaviour occurred. Detail of such contexts may be essential for later analysis, and also for an assessment of any reactivity. But, of course, the more detail collected on particular behaviours, the narrower the range of events which can be recorded. As Hammersley and Atkinson (1983) note, there is an inevitable trade-off here between detail and scope.

Generally, the more detailed the description, the more likely it is to be accurate, and the less likely to be subject to distortion. But we should always remember that even detailed accounts are the product of selection and interpretation. It is important, therefore, that the researcher reflects carefully on the degree to which his or her own ideas and perspectives, and, of course, behaviour, have influenced the account produced. Indeed, it is useful if what is often referred to as a reflexive account, which discusses these influences, runs alongside the researcher's field notes.

A major influence on the accuracy of field notes is *when* they are made. Notes should preferably be made as soon as possible after the observation. The longer this is left the more is forgotten and the greater the chance of inaccuracies and biases creeping in. Sometimes it is possible to make notes during the observation. I did this, for example, when I was observing lessons in the classroom (Foster, 1990). The teachers, on the whole, if they were prepared to allow me to observe their lessons, did not seem to mind me taking notes. Sometimes, particularly in the early stages of the research, they were curious about what I was writing and what I would do with the data, and I had to reassure them about confidentiality. On occasions, I gave them my notes to read, partly to reassure them, and partly to provide a check on the validity of my accounts (I discuss the assessment of validity later in the chapter). Taking notes in the classroom seemed to be a legitimate activity, perhaps because the teachers felt that in this context they were more publicly accountable or because others engage in the same activity, most notably inspectors and tutors of trainee teachers. But the act of note-taking inevitably affected the teachers' perceptions of me. My conversations with them revealed that they saw me as more threatening, and as more of an evaluator and less of a colleague, because of this.

However, often social norms in the setting do not permit note-taking. For example, I thought it was inappropriate to take notes in the social area of the school staff room. In this case, I had to write up my observations in the evening, or move into the work area adjoining the main staff room and 'make out' that I was working! When the research is covert, note-taking during observation is usually impossible. In most situations note-taking is not a usual or acceptable activity. The exception is when writing is an integral part of the participant role, as it might be if one were observing student behaviour in lectures, for example. Here covert note-taking is feasible. Interestingly, the researchers in Rosenhan's (1982) study of psychiatric hospitals, who posed as patients, found that they could make notes fairly openly on the wards. Their 'continual writing' was interpreted by staff as further evidence of their insanity!

On occasions, it may be possible for the researcher to play a role in which note-taking is expected. Whyte (1981), for example, during his fieldwork, acted for some time as secretary to the Italian Community Club and therefore kept records of meetings. Sometimes researchers can take notes covertly, without the cover of a 'writing role'. Hammersley (1980), for example, jotted brief notes down on his newspaper when observing in the staff room of the school he studied.

Where note-taking during observation is not possible, the researcher will have to retreat to some private area of the field – an office, a tent, even the lavatory – or leave the field altogether for a period to write up his or her notes. Where the field is officially constituted for only part of a day, as with schools and many other contemporary institutions, it may be possible to do this when the field has 'closed down' – the evenings or weekends, for example. At these times, memories and hurried jottings taken in the field can be elaborated, written down, recorded and filed. But it will also probably be necessary to have more substantial breaks from the field, not only to catch up on note-taking, but to organize, examine and analyze data and to reflect on the research itself. These breaks from data collection are essential to plan future data collection effectively and also to recuperate from the stresses and strains of fieldwork.

It is perhaps impossible to over-stress the dangers of spending too much time in the field and too little time recording and analyzing data. As Lacey (1976) pointed out, there is a tendency to fall into the 'it's happening elsewhere' or 'it's happening when I'm not there' syndrome. Researchers often feel that they have to be in the field all the time and preferably in several places in the field at once. If they succumb to this temptation, the result is often forgotten, and therefore wasted, observations and/or an overwhelming mass of unanalyzed data.

Field notes vary in form, and individual researchers usually develop their own particular style and organization. Some use notebooks and divide pages into sections for descriptive accounts and analytical or methodological reflection. My own preference is for files from which I can take out pages easily for copying or reorganization. Some researchers type out their notes in full, others write notes in their own idiosyncratic shorthand. Some make extensive use of diagrams, especially to record the organization of physical space in the field, others prefer the narrative form.

Whatever the style or format, it is essential that notes contain basic information – date, time, place and so on – and any other information about the context of an event or behaviour that may be relevant. It is also important to distinguish clearly between verbatim records of speech, summaries of events, and interpretations, and to note any uncertainties in one's account. Some space should also be given in field notes to an assessment of reactivity and to methodological reflection in general.

Once notes have been made, they must be organized in such a way that information can be located and retrieved fairly easily. This will require some sort of cataloguing and indexing system, perhaps using a computer system. In fact, the organization of data into sections, categories and themes for this purpose forms part of the analysis of the data which proceeds alongside data collection.

Activity 3.10 (allow about 40 minutes in total)

In this activity I would like you to try a short piece of less-structured observation. Again, choose a setting in which it would be relatively easy to observe.

Think briefly beforehand about the sort of things you want to focus on, and then spend a short period (say, about 10 minutes) observing. Try to make notes during the observation. If you are unable to do this, then write down your observations as soon as possible afterwards.

When you have completed your account, go over it carefully:

- Do any fruitful lines of enquiry or analysis suggest themselves?
- What do the data tell you about the perspectives or culture of your subjects?
- Finally, what difficulties did you encounter in collecting observational data in this way?

Using Technology

Paper and pencil are the basic tools of the trade, but in our increasingly 'high tech' world electronic recording devices are frequently used. Whether to use such devices – the most common being audio or video recording – as aids to observation is a question common to both main approaches to observational research. Their advantage is that they provide a more complete and accurate record of behaviour and can be used to supplement or check data records produced by the researcher, such as field notes or tallies produced by systematic observation. They may therefore be useful in assessing the validity of data recorded live. Using audio or video recordings, it is also possible to conduct a more careful and sometimes more complex analysis of data, since we can stop and replay the recording in order to consider the coding or categorization of the data. Audio or video recording may actually be essential in some studies where information is needed on the details of interaction and/or on the specific language that is used, as in conversation analysis. This was the case, for example, in a study by Tizard and Hughes, which compared young children's language development in the home and in nursery schools (Tizard and Hughes, 1984; see also 1991 for a discussion of methodology). The researchers designed tunics for the girls to wear (the study observed girls only) which contained small, unobtrusive microphones. These microphones recorded the actual conversations between parent and child, and teacher and child. These data were supplemented by direct observation to record the context of the conversations.

On the other hand, electronic recording is not cheap and permission to record may not always be easy to obtain. Observation may therefore be limited to certain settings or sub-settings. Where permission is obtained, it is likely, particularly with video recording, that reactivity will increase. This problem may reduce as subjects become accustomed to the presence of recording equipment, and it may be less significant than in the past as modern equipment is more compact and unobtrusive. Nevertheless, reactivity is a serious drawback.

There is also the danger that the researcher may be swamped by a large amount of data far beyond what is necessary or possible to analyze. When electronic recording is possible, there is a great temptation to avoid selection decisions and to try to record almost everything. For the purposes of data analysis, it is usually necessary to have a written record of verbal interaction. Audio and video tapes therefore have to be transcribed, a process which is extremely time-consuming and sometimes difficult if the recording quality is poor.

This last point draws attention to the technical problems that can occur. Recording devices can fail and important data can be lost. Furthermore, it is important to realize that recording equipment cannot provide a complete record of behaviour. Audio recording obviously misses non-verbal communication and video has a restricted visual range. Neither method can adequately record complex verbal interaction between a large number of subjects, such as that which occurs in a school classroom where pupils are working on a variety of assignments simultaneously. Nor can they provide an adequate record of the wider social context in which behaviour occurs.

Audio and video recordings are by no means the only example of technological aids used in observational research. Stopwatches are often used to time the duration of behaviour precisely. Sometimes, still photography has been used to provide a record of behaviour at particular instants or, where repeated photographs are taken, of changing spatial patterns (see, for example, Bell, 1990). Electronic devices are sometimes used to record observations directly into computer data bases. For example, in the study I mentioned earlier on mother–infant interaction by Vietze et al. (1978), observers used a 12-button keyboard connected to a cassette recorder to record their observations. The data were then transferred automatically to computer disc. More sophisticated equipment is becoming increasingly available.

Another interesting example of a technological aid to observation was used by Bechtel (1970) to study standing and movement patterns among museum visitors. He called the device a 'Lodemeter'. It consisted of many pressure-sensitive pads covering the floor of a large room, and every time a person walked on a pad a counter increased by one. In this way, Bechtel was able to build up an accurate picture of which areas of the room were most used.

Of course, technology is not only used as an aid to recording. Sometimes devices are used to ensure that observation is unobtrusive. Serbin (reported in Pellegrini, 1991), for example, used binoculars to observe children's play from a distance. Another, rather amusing, example was the use of a periscope by Middlemist et al. (1976) to help study the effects of the invasion of personal space on stress levels. The setting was a three-urinal men's toilet and the subjects were toilet users whose personal space was 'invaded' by a confederate to the study. Subjects' stress levels were measured by delays in the onset of urination and a shortening of its duration. Urination was observed by a researcher in a nearby toilet stall with the assistance of the periscope! One wonders whether anything is considered private by some researchers!

Assessing the Validity of Observations

As with other research data, we must always be concerned about the validity and reliability of observations. Validity refers to the extent to which observations accurately record the behaviour in which the researcher is interested. One aspect of validity is reliability. This refers to the consistency of observations, usually whether two (or more) observers, or the same observer on separate occasions, studying the same behaviour come(s) away with the same data. Of course, if observational techniques are unreliable they are highly likely to produce invalid data.

Threats to Validity

The validity of observational data can be threatened in a number of ways. First, there is the possibility of reactivity – both personal and procedural. In this case, actual observations of behaviour may be accurate, but subjects do not behave in the way they normally behave. Personal reactivity occurs when subjects behave differently because of the personal characteristics or behaviour of the observer. They may behave in particular ways because the observer is male or female or belongs to a certain 'racial' or ethnic group, or because he or she dresses or conducts him or herself in a particular way. What is important here is how the subjects perceive the observer, how they interpret his or her behaviour, and how they behave as a result. Where two or more observers are involved, as in many more-structured observations, and subjects react differently with different observers, then problems of reliability emerge too.

Procedural reactivity occurs when subjects behave differently because they know they are being studied or observed. They change their behaviour in response to the procedures involved in the process of observation itself. This form of reactivity is most marked in experiments where subjects are often placed in 'artificial' situations and what goes on is deliberately manipulated. However, it is eliminated altogether in covert research where the subjects are unaware that they are being observed. Where procedural reactivity is high, the ecological validity of the observations – the extent to which they can be generalized to other settings – will be in doubt.

A second possible threat to validity comes from the inadequacies of the measuring instruments used in the observation. The preconceived categories of an observation schedule may be unsuitable or inadequate for describing the actual nature of the behaviour that occurs. They may ignore aspects of behaviour which are important given the aims of the research, or may force the observer to code behaviours which are significantly different under the same category. As a result, the descriptions produced by the observation system may be invalid. Techniques used in ethnographic research may also be inadequate. Selectivity in note-taking, and the distortion that can occur when the researcher relies upon memory to write field notes, can be significant sources of error.

A third potential threat to validity comes from observer bias. All observers have particular cultural knowledge and approach observation from particular theoretical and sometimes political standpoints. These subjectivities can affect what behaviour is selected for observation and how this behaviour is interpreted and recorded. They may therefore result in invalid data.

In more-structured observation, precisely what is to be observed is set out in advance and is clearly a product of the researcher's theoretical ideas. But in this type of observation the aim is to minimize the effects of observer subjectivity by ensuring that all observers observe behaviour in the same way and follow the same coding rules. Unfortunately, there is sometimes inconsistency in the way rules are applied by different observers (and sometimes by the same observer on different occasions). This happens particularly when there are ambiguities in the coding system or where coding requires inferences about observed behaviour.

Ethnographers have more often been accused of allowing their theoretical and political preconceptions to bias their observations. Perhaps the potential for this type of bias is greater with ethnography because what is to be observed, and how, is not systematically set out before the observation begins. The work of the anthropologist Margaret Mead (1943), on the island of Samoa, has been criticized on these grounds. Freeman (1984) has suggested that the conclusions she came to about the stress-free nature of adolescence there were to a considerable extent the product of her own pre-conceptions. His observations revealed rather different experiences and behaviour among young people. One of the weaknesses of ethnographic research is that it is largely the product of the ideas, choices and negotiation strategies of an individual researcher. As a result, the picture produced by one researcher of a group or institution may be very different from that produced by another.

A related threat to validity arises from misperception or misinterpretation of behaviour. The observer may simply misunderstand the 'real' nature of the behaviour he or she observes. This is more likely when behaviour is complex or when the observer is unfamiliar with the social situation and the meanings which are in play. For example, in my own research in a multi-ethnic school, I observed a situation in which a white adolescent boy called an Afro-Caribbean boy a 'nigger'. I initially interpreted this as a clear instance of racial abuse. However, I discovered later that the two boys were the best of friends and regularly swapped racial insults as a way of reinforcing a sense of camaraderie. My initial observation was clearly invalid (if we define 'racial abuse' as implying negative evaluation of the person to whom it is directed).

Ways of Assessing Validity

How, then, do observational researchers assess the validity of their observations? One method is to check the reliability of research techniques. The main way of doing this is replication. Sometimes whole studies are repeated using the same procedures, with different observers. At other times, parts of a study may be repeated. Replication is more feasible in experiments and studies involving more-structured observation, where procedures are clearly specified and therefore can be fairly easily repeated.

One form of replication involves examining the extent of agreement between two observers of the same behaviour. This technique is more often used in more-structured observation. Here it usually involves comparing the individual coding decisions of two observers to see to what extent they agree. This is termed *absolute agreement*. Alternatively, it may involve comparing their overall coding results to see whether the total number of behaviours allocated to the categories of the schedule tally. This is called *marginal agreement*. Obviously, absolute agreement is a much stronger test of the reliability of observations, but it is not always possible to conduct such a test with all observation systems. Inter-observer agreement is usually worked out for each variable in the observation system and can be expressed as the proportion of instances when the two observers agree on appropriate coding.

Replication is not usually feasible in ethnographic research. Procedures are not prestructured, and the course of the research is very much a product of the ideas and personal idiosyncrasies of the researcher and the way he or she interacts with subjects. Moreover, procedures are not usually recorded in sufficient detail to allow another researcher to reproduce them in the same way. The nearest ethnographers come to replication is the re-study. The same group or institution is studied again some time after the original study (see, for example, Burgess, 1987). Re-studies provide limited information on reliability because, although the research setting may be the same, the research questions and procedures, the sub-settings, subgroups and individuals studied are often very different. Moreover, in the period of time since the original study, the group or institution will probably have changed considerably and differences in data and conclusions may be the product of these changes.

Techniques such as reflexivity, triangulation and respondent validation are more often used in ethnographic research to assess validity. *Reflexivity* involves the continual monitoring of, and reflection on, the research process. During and after the fieldwork, the researcher tries to assess the extent of his or her own role in the process of data production and how the data were affected by the social context in which they were collected. Reflection during data collection may influence the process of future data collection because it may throw up methodological hypotheses and suggest alternative ways of collecting data. When the fieldwork is complete it forms the basis of the researcher's own methodological assessment of the data.

Sometimes researchers provide readers with a reflexive account of their work in the form of a natural history. These are sometimes contained in methodological appendices to the main work (see, for example, Whyte, 1981) or published separately (see, for example, Burgess, 1984b). These accounts can be useful to the reader in assessing the researcher's role in the production of data and the conclusions of the study.

Triangulation is more a direct check on the validity of observations by cross-checking them with other sources of data. If a researcher's conclusion is supported by data from other sources, then we can be more confident of its validity. Triangulation can involve comparing data on the same behaviour from different researchers (as in reliability checks in more-structured observation) who possibly adopt different roles in the field. Alternatively, it can involve comparing data produced by different methods – for example, observational data can be compared with interview data – or it can involve comparing data from different times, sub-settings or subjects.

Comparing data from the researcher's observations of behaviour with data from the various subjects involved is one form of *respondent validation*. Here the aim is to check the validity of the researcher's observations by reference to the subjects' perceptions. This may take a number of forms. The researcher may discuss his or her observations with subjects, asking them whether they feel the observations are accurate and what their perceptions of a particular incident were. Alternatively, the researcher may ask participants to supply written accounts of a particular instance or period of behaviour. These can then be compared with the researcher's own observations. Ball (1981), for example, in his study of mixed-ability teaching in a comprehensive school, sometimes compared his account of lessons with those provided by teachers. And, finally, the researcher may feed back his or her observations to subjects and ask for their comments (see Ball, 1984).

The advantage of such techniques is that the researcher may be able to access important additional knowledge about the behaviour under consideration – for example, about the thoughts and motives of subjects, their perceptions of the behaviour of others, and about the social context in which the behaviour occurred – which is not available from observation. They may also provide a valuable alternative perspective on the behaviour that occurred, as well as useful information on subjects' perspectives. As Fielding (1982) found in his study of the National Front, they may also be a useful way of encouraging the involvement of subjects in the research.

However, respondent validation does not automatically ensure the accuracy of data. Subjects may be more concerned to manipulate the impression of behaviour which is contained in the data as a way of enhancing or protecting their own interests. Their accounts may therefore present behaviour in certain ways or may give particular interpretations of that behaviour. These accounts will, of course, be influenced by the social context in which they are delivered, and by their perception of the researcher and of the use to which the data will be put. Moreover, it is important to recognize that subjects' accounts of their actions and perceptions are reconstructions from memory, which may not necessarily correspond to their thoughts or perceptions at the time the behaviour occurred. We must recognize and try to assess, too, the potential threats to validity in respondent accounts.

Conclusion

In this chapter I have introduced you to the different styles and techniques used in observational research. I identified two basic styles: more-structured observation, and less-structured or ethnographic observation. Although there are clear differences between the two styles, I do not want to leave you with the impression that they are opposed and mutually exclusive. I must emphasize that observational research often involves both styles and that, at times, both raise similar issues and problems.

All observers have to gain access to subjects. In a narrow sense this means getting to a physical position from which subjects can be observed. But it also often means developing relationships with subjects so that, as far as possible, the way they behave 'naturally' can be observed. Similar ethical problems – concerning deception, invasion of privacy and harm to subjects, for example – are involved in both styles; and in both styles decisions have to be made about what to observe. In more-structured observation, those decisions are more likely to be made before the actual fieldwork; whereas, in less-structured observation, decisions are made during the course of fieldwork itself. Nevertheless, researchers must choose what to focus on and select appropriate samples. The major difference between the two styles is that more-structured observation requires observers to allocate behaviours to preconceived categories of an observation schedule, whereas less-structured observation involves written accounts in field notes describing the nature of behaviour in more detail.

The final section of the chapter considered various threats to the validity of observational data, and the main ways in which researchers check validity. Producers of observational research should always be concerned with the validity of their data. Observational research will only make a useful contribution to the bank of public knowledge if we can be reasonably confident of its validity. Readers of observational research should also keep matters of validity in the forefront of their minds. A consideration of such matters is essential to any assessment of research. As producers and consumers of observational research, we can never, of course, be absolutely sure of the validity of observations, but we must decide and make clear to what extent confidence in that validity is justified.

Key Terms

Ascribed characteristics characteristics which (e.g.) the researcher is presumed by others to have because of some aspect of his or her appearance or behaviour.

Covert research projects where those who are the 'subjects' of the research are not aware of the fact.

Field notes records kept by the researcher (particular participant observers) which record what they have observed, but also detail events, problems, feelings, things said to them, foreshadowed ideas, links to previous knowledge or belief, etc. Field notes may be a valuable source of data in all research and are often the only source for participant observation research.

Gatekeepers people 'through' whom it is necessary to pass in order to gain access to the research situation. These will often be formally constituted as gatekeepers – access to school classes, for example, requires the permission of the Head Teacher, and access to National Health Service premises for research requires the permission of the Local Research Ethics Committee. Others may also be 'unofficial' gatekeepers, however – the experienced 'old hand', or the union representative, without whose approval and cooperation you are unlikely to get the cooperation of anyone else in the setting.

Holism considering a situation or context or person as a whole.

Hypothetico-deductive method the development of theory by deducing hypotheses which have to be true if the theory is true, or which distinguish between theories, and subjecting them to empirical test.

Naturalism trying to disturb the natural situation as little as possible in the course of research

Operationalisation turning concepts into measurable variables. For example, 'intelligence' is measured by the ability to answer conceptual questions or the speed with which problems can be resolved; 'trust' is measured by the number of circumstances in which one person says he or she would feel able to rely on another.

Overt research research where the 'subjects' of it are aware of its existence.

Participant observation conducting research by joining a setting and playing some role within it.

Reactivity the production of difference by the research itself. We distinguish between 'personal reactivity', where the character, appearance, speech or behaviour of the researcher produces effects which might not otherwise have occurred and 'procedural reactivity', where the way in which the research is conducted (or even the fact that the situation is a research one) produces effects different from what might have occurred in the undisturbed natural situation.

Reflexivity awareness of the impact of the procedures and the characteristics of the researcher, and the particular events which happened to occur during the study, on the nature of the data collected. Awareness that the researcher's preconceptions and latent interests may shape the conclusions drawn from the data.

(Continued)

(Key Terms continued)

Replication   running the study again on fresh participants, using precisely the same methods.

Respondent validation   obtaining the view of the respondents on whether the research data and/or conclusions are valid.

Re-study   undertaking a study which attempts to repeat work already carried out with the same or comparable participants.

Triangulation   bringing more than one method or researcher or source of information to bear on the same area of investigation.

Further Reading

More-structured observation

Smith, H.W. (1975) *Strategies of Social Research,* ch. 9, Englewood Cliffs, NJ, Prentice-Hall.
Webb, E., Campbell, D.T., Schwartz, R.D. and Sechrest, L. (1966) *Unobtrusive Measures: Non reactive Research in the Social Sciences,* Chicago, Rand McNally.

Less-structured research

Burgess, R.G. (1984) *In the Field: an Introduction to Field Research,* London, Unwin Hyman.
Hammersley, M.I. and Atkinson, P. (1983) *Ethnography: Principles in Practice,* London, Tavistock.

Research Proposal Activity 3

This chapter has examined ways of carrying out observational research. In outlining your research proposal you should consider the following questions:

1   Is observation likely to be the main research method employed in your study?
2   *If not:* could observation be used with profit in the preliminary stages of the project, to explore an area which can then be studied more fully using other methods, or towards the end of the project to supplement or provide a check on data collected by other methods?
3   What degree of structure should be used in the observation? (In addressing this question, pay attention to the nature of the problem being investigated, your theoretical and methodological approach and the constraints imposed by the social context and by what is practicable.)
4   Will there be problems in negotiating access, and how might these be overcome?
5   What kind of observational role should be adopted? (In considering this question, take account of the research problem, the nature of the setting, the means of gaining access and the degree of structure to be achieved.)
6   What should be observed? Should some form of sampling be involved?
7   How should data be recorded? (In addressing this question, pay particular attention to the type of observational method and observational role to be adopted.)
8   What are the potential threats to validity, and how can they be overcome?

4

Asking Questions

Michael Wilson and Roger Sapsford

Social scientists use a wide range of techniques to collect their data. Structured observational methods, for example, require the systematic observation of behaviour, but without direct questioning of the people observed. Participant observation may involve asking questions, but the questions arise naturally in the course of observation rather than as part of a more explicit researcher's role (though participant observers often do employ more formal interview methods as well). This chapter is concerned with methods of data collection that explicitly involve interviewing or questioning individuals.

Comparison of Methods

Interview and Questionnaire Methods

This chapter covers the following techniques of data collection:

1   *Face-to-face interviews employing an interview schedule*: a standard schedule is used for each respondent, in which the questions have the same wording and are asked in the same order. The ability of the interviewer to vary the wording of questions or the order in which they are asked is strictly limited.
2   *The telephone interview*: a variant on the face-to-face interview using a schedule but conducted on the telephone. This is an increasingly common choice of data collection method because of its speed and comparative cheapness. It is much favoured by market researchers. Telephone interviews are, of course, not 'face to face' and some of the non-verbal cues which affect the interaction between interviewer and respondent are missing – body language, for example – but, in terms of a personal and social interaction between respondent and interviewer, they have much in common with true 'face-to-face' interviews.
3   *Postal questionnaires*: most people are familiar with these because of their widespread commercial use to collect market information. Here, respondents are asked to read the questions and to answer either by ringing or ticking one of the

'answer boxes' provided; or, less likely, to write in their own 'free response' to a
question.

4 *Face-to-face interviews in a free format*: these are conducted, approximately, like
   natural conversations between two people. They are often tape-recorded in full
   for later analysis; although the interviewer may take continuous and contemporaneous notes, this is difficult to do while concentrating on the management of
   the interview. Note-taking can also be more obtrusive than tape-recording.
   Although 'naturalistic', interviews such as these are managed to a large extent by
   the interviewer, who sets the agenda of questions, probes more deeply into issues
   of interest with supplementary questions and records the answers and the discussion. They do not use standardized schedules (like methods 1, 2 and 3) but the
   interviewer will use a list of topics even if the wording of specific questions is
   not standardized.

Three dimensions will be used here to compare methods of asking questions: *procedure, structure* and *context*. Two of these dimensions are closely linked, the procedural and the structural; although they may be distinguished conceptually, it is
useful to deal with them together. The reason for this close linkage will become clear
as you read through the next section.

Procedural/Structural Factors

The first dimension on which methods of data collection may be compared is that of
the *procedures* that are employed. At one extreme of the dimension or continuum of
procedures lie social science methods, such as the laboratory-based psychology experiment, which try to imitate those of the natural sciences: the positivistic methods of
investigation which seek to reproduce the *controls* over variables that the exact or natural sciences hold to be their particular strength. An important set of issues, from the
social scientist's point of view, is concerned with the reaction of human subjects to the
knowledge that they are being investigated – and in this respect human subjects differ
most markedly from the inanimate objects of natural science investigations. Simply to
know that one is a research subject can change the subject's expressions of beliefs and
attitudes, not to mention behaviour, in a way that can produce results that are artificial
and of only poor application to the natural world of human interaction.

At the other extreme of the procedural dimension lies the *naturalistic* interview
between researcher and respondent. This takes the form of a conversational type of
interaction between investigator and respondent. Obviously, the respondent usually
knows that the interview is a research one, but the form of the questions follows a
natural line through the respondent's replies, which are recorded in full for later
analysis rather than being summarily reduced to a 'measurement' or series of measurements. The ideal in the naturalistic or unstructured interview is to approximate
the 'feeling' of the unforced conversations of everyday life. The naturalism of this
sort of interview means that many extraneous variables, which might well change the
information being collected, are uncontrolled. Other people, such as partners, friends
or children, may be present and may well join in the interview and have an effect on
what the respondent says, although the interviewer will try to avoid this if at all possible. The settings of the interviews are everyday ones, such as the respondent's

home or workplace, not the laboratory. Above all, the questions asked and the wording used are not closely prescribed but are 'situational' in order to maintain naturalism. In terms of procedures, then, the naturalistic interview is at the opposite end of the spectrum from the experiment.

As all methods of data collection entail *some* degree of structure, the comparison is between highly structured and less-structured methods. A *highly structured method* of asking questions is one in which the procedures of data collection are carefully laid down so that individual interviewers are required not to depart from them in any way. Questions, for example, are worded in the same way and should be asked as written (in interview schedules and questionnaires), in the same order, and the responses should be categorized according to the *response categories* which the research designer has provided. Often the respondent does not follow the procedures of the interviewer and will ask for clarification of a question's meaning or will give a response which is not easily categorized. In these cases, the interviewer is provided with *prompts*, which allow subsidiary information to be given but which, again, follow a set routine; that is, even the prompts are highly structured and minimize the opportunities for the interview to move towards an agenda of interest which is determined by the respondent rather than the researcher, whether wholly or partly. Highly structured methods also discourage the interviewer or data collector from departing from the design for data collection that the researcher has laid down. Certain types of laboratory experiment (in which the interaction between subject and researcher is prescribed in detail) represent a highly structured method of data collection. So do postal questionnaires, in which each respondent receives a copy of the same questionnaire and is expected to complete it in the same order, following the same questions. As we shall see in the next section, there is little control over the way in which a respondent completes a postal questionnaire, but the principle remains the same: an invariant structure for eliciting information, preferably information given by the respondent and not by someone else!

Less-structured methods of data collection include the naturalistic or unstructured interview. Here, the questions are not asked in an invariant order (although *some* agenda of questions or topics is determined by the interviewer) and the phrasing of each question can be varied according to what has gone before, what the interviewer has already found out, and according to the respondent's understanding. The interview appears less artificial, more natural, than a structured interview and more resembles a conversation between equal participants. The idea of prompts in the structured sense is unnecessary because supplementary questions can be put according to the replies received, in a way that does not interfere with the natural flow of conversation.

There are advantages and disadvantages to both highly structured and less-structured methods; in no sense is it true to say that one is to be preferred to the other or that one is more objective than the other. The examples given in this chapter show the range of ways of asking questions and allow a detailed comparison to be made between methods of differing degrees of structure.

Contextual Factors

The contextual dimension of data collection includes a number of issues and is, perhaps, less of a single dimension of comparison than the procedural and structural ones, but the effect of *context* on responses is sometimes a critical one.

First, the terms on which the interview has been agreed to is important. What status does the interviewer claim (often implicitly rather than explicitly) as giving him or her a right to ask questions about the respondent's personal beliefs, opinions or status? What, in other words, is the legitimacy of the interviewer? At one extreme of this comparison lies the market research interview, conducted in the street or (more commonly nowadays) over the telephone. Although small rewards for cooperation are frequently offered (small sums of money, free samples or gift vouchers), there is little in it for the respondent. At the other end of the spectrum lies a request to take part in 'scholarly' research, which may be of little direct use to the respondent but which enlists a sense of altruism as a motivation.

The context of interviewing affects *response rates* greatly. Market research interviews often achieve a response rate of less than 50 per cent, mainly through refusals rather than failure to contact selected respondents. But 'scholarly' research also often fails to achieve good response rates. Morton Williams (1990) argues that good response rates are most difficult to obtain in surveys of the general public on topics not directly relevant to their lives. For example, Van Dijk et al. (1990), in a large-scale study of the experience of crime in 17 countries, conducted over the telephone, achieved response rates of only 45–60 per cent. At the other extreme, surveys of patient satisfaction in hospitals, where patients perceive that the results might be of direct use to them, often lead to response rates of nearly 100 per cent.

Another important aspect of context is the perception of the interviewer's characteristics by the respondent; that is, the way in which the respondent will *ascribe* beliefs and opinions to the interviewer on the basis of visible characteristics such as accent and dress (perceived social class), ethnic origin, or gender. Ascribed characteristics (or the perception of them) can affect replies received, so that interviewers with different ascribed characteristics will receive different replies to the same questions. This is known as *inter-interviewer variability* and its source lies in the respondents' 'reading' of the characteristics of the interviewer. An experiment (a British one) in which an actor, alternately using a middle-class and a working-class persona (using changes of accent and of dress), approached subjects at a railway station asking for directions, showed how the subjects' perceptions of the 'interviewer' changed their responses (Sissons, 1970). Subjects were chosen randomly so that selection biases were controlled. The different ratings of 'helpfulness' which were received, depending on whether the working-class or the middle-class persona was presented, varied significantly in favour of the middle-class persona.

In general, any ascribed characteristic of the interviewer (that is, one which is relatively unalterable, such as skin colour or accent) can bias the responses obtained in any sort of interview. The best practice to minimize this sort of interviewer bias is to match the ascribed characteristics of interviewers with respondents (so that blacks interview blacks, women interview women, and middle- or working-class people interview their class equals).

Finally, under 'context', the power relations between interviewer and respondent are important. Perceptions that the interviewer is in a position to influence (for bad or for good) the respondent's life chances in a direct way (rather than as a member of a group) can alter the nature of the responses or even the willingness to take part. Simkin's study of the psychological well-being of the long-term unemployed recruited a suitable sample through the local Job Centre (Simkin, 1992). She acknowledged the problems that this caused and the likelihood that she, as researcher, would be associated with the Job Centre regime and particularly with the government's 'availability for work' tests, which seek to disqualify people from unemployment benefit (which is not means-tested and is paid at a higher rate than Income Support) if for any reason they are not immediately available to work – through mental ill health, for example.

Choosing Between Methods

It is probably clear to you that the three dimensions of comparison of data-collection methods are therefore not entirely clear-cut or exclusive. In particular, methods which embody a high degree of structure are also ones in which the procedures for data collection are closely specified. Nevertheless, structure and procedure can be distinguished, and will be in the remainder of this chapter.

The term 'unstructured interview' is also a misnomer because a completely unstructured interview is impossible. Natural conversations have a structure; unstructured interviews also have a structure – often not quite the same structure as that of natural conversations. An interview conducted in an unstructured style still contains a degree of control of the interview process by the interviewer. The fact that the interview is more naturalistic (i.e. it reflects better the normal rules of conversations such as 'turn-taking') should not disguise the issue that the interviewer has a focus (or series of foci) for what is being asked and may introduce topics as she or he sees fit. Thus the term 'less structured' is preferable to 'unstructured' and one should think of the dimension of structure as a *variable,* ranging from highly to less structured methods.

There is no single best way of collecting data; the method chosen depends on the nature of the research questions posed and the specific questions you want to ask respondents. The aim of all methods is to obtain valid and reliable data – true answers to questions, not distorted by the methods of collection or prone to chance fluctuation – which can be used as the basis for credible conclusions. The methods differ, however, in how they guard against threats to validity and what price the researchers are prepared to pay, in terms of potential invalidity in one area, to strengthen their claim to validity in another.

Highly Structured Methods

There are two main structured forms of asking questions: the *interview schedule* and the *self-administered questionnaire.* They share the need for questions to be unambiguous and easy to read, so that what he or she is supposed to do is entirely clear to the interviewer and/or respondent.

Activity 4.1 (10 minutes)

What, if anything, is wrong with the following questions?

1. Gender   Male   Female

2. Age _____

3. Are you married? Yes   No

4. Age of spouse _____

5. Ethnic group: White
             Black Caribbean
             Black African
             Indian
             Chinese/Japanese

6. Monthly take-home pay: Nothing
              Up to £100
              £100–£200
              £200–£400
              More than £400

7. Do you agree with the following?

Family is more important than work	Yes	No
Children's interests come before everything	Yes	No
Children should not be allowed to come to harm	Yes	No

Answers:

- The 'questions' are too abrupt. It would be better to spell them out – 'Which sex are you?', 'What age are you?' – as this will read as more polite on a self-administered questionnaire and will give the interviewer something standardized to read out if the schedule is interviewer-administered.
- Even if an interviewer is being used, the questions need to include instructions on what is to be done – e.g. 'ring one of the answers'.
- Some degree of 'routing' is required after Q3 – a large arrow from 'No' to Q5, or an instruction not to answer Question 4 if the answer to Question 3 was 'No' – to save asking the respondent for the age of a spouse which he or she doesn't have.
- The concept 'married' is thoroughly ambiguous. By 'yes' do we mean

  - legally married and residing with spouse
  - legally married but currently separated
  - ever legally married, even though spouse may now be dead or divorced.

  And what about people who are living together 'as husband and wife' but are not legally married?

- In Q5 the categories do not cover the field: where do people of Pakistani origin or Koreans describe themselves. (At the very least, an 'Other' category is needed.) It is also not clear where someone with a brown skin and Indian parents who regards himself as British would put himself – the question conflates skin-colour and original family nationality very crudely.

- In Q6 the categories overlap – someone taking home £200 per month has two places in which to inscribe him/herself.
- The third item under Q7 is a bad one – what does it mean to say that you *don't* agree with a proposition that children should *not* ... In general, double negatives should be avoided.

Thus a certain amount of work can be done to ensure the success of a structured survey before it ever leaves the office.

Interview Schedules

Although interviewer-administered schedules and self-administered questionnaires have many points in common, the interviewer-administered schedule allows for more control over the interview than does the self-administered questionnaire, which is either sent by post or administered to a group such as a class in a school. The interview schedule should be used by a trained interviewer in order to ensure that it is applied in a standardized way, as we shall see. The self-administered questionnaire is, by definition, controlled by the respondent who is untrained, and it therefore calls for a more sophisticated layout and preparation than one which can be 'corrected' by a trained interviewer in the course of the interview. This is particularly true if the schedule/questionnaire is at all complicated by *routing* instructions, such as 'If you answered "yes" to question 14 go to question 16', or what American social scientists call 'skip questions'. A trained and experienced interviewer will be less confused by such skip questions than a once-only recipient of a questionnaire.

Typically, an interviewer will have been trained to be non-directive and non-judgemental in administering an interview schedule, especially in dealing with queries raised by the respondent. This can make replies sound rather 'wooden' and artificial. If a respondent is nervous about the interview, cold or stilted replies may well intensify his or her reluctance to continue. Interviewers, after training and experience, are encouraged to adopt a positive tone of voice and to smile or nod, whatever the reply, as a way of encouraging the respondent. Such non-verbal behaviour is just as much a prompt as a spoken follow-up question. Both sorts of prompting – verbal and non-verbal – introduce a variation in the social interaction between interviewer and respondent which is far from fully controlled and may introduce an unknown source of *bias* into the recorded responses. But prompting of different sorts is essential to any well-conducted interview, and the effects which it, and certain characteristics of the interviewer, may have on the respondent's replies has to be regarded as a source of *response error.*

Response error covers systematic biases which may affect the responses collected by an interviewer. Systematic bias, as opposed to random bias, is when distortions of the respondent's opinions or beliefs tend to occur in one direction only. For example, *social desirability* responding occurs when answers are altered to show the respondent in a desirable light with respect to the interviewer, including the views that the respondent ascribes to the interviewer on the basis of external characteristics such as social class or gender. It also describes our preference for socially approved responses over those which may not be generally approved. This can be discounted or controlled for by a careful matching of interviewers to respondents so that discrepancies of social class, ethnicity and gender are minimized and/or by careful control of the 'emotional tone' of questions. *Acquiescence* responding is where the respondent is tempted to answer favourably no matter what the question. It should be obvious that social desirability and acquiescence overlap and reinforce each other as sources of response bias. The former can be controlled by careful matching of the characteristics of interviewers to their sample of respondents and the latter by careful phrasing of questions so that they do not seem to invite one sort of response rather than another, but this is not always easy and needs careful *piloting* (see section below).

All this leaves the interviewer using a *standardized* schedule (and the researcher who designed it) in something of a dilemma. On the one hand, he or she wishes to make the interview appear as natural as possible by encouraging the respondent to take part in a 'conversation', although a highly controlled and directed one (which is what is partly meant by a *standardized* method of data collection). On the other hand, the interviewer must be sensitive to the respondent's understanding of the questions asked and be willing to elaborate or prompt in order to ensure that this understanding is genuine. To ensure the latter, it is essential that prompts are used, both verbal and non-verbal.

This leads to a paradox. Interviewers *must* probe or prompt to ensure a full understanding of a question, but even if they follow the 'best practice' in non-directive prompts and non-directive body language, prompts of any sort mean that a different question has been asked of respondents because they answer to different depths of understanding. But the essential feature of standardized methods of data collection is that each respondent is asked the same question, carrying the same meaning, so that responses are comparable across the sample. In an ideal sense, these are difficult principles to reconcile. In practice, given the variability and idiosyncrasies of a team of interviewers, reconciliation of these principles is impossible.

It may be thought that the paradox may be overcome by using one interviewer for all respondents. But no one individual interviewer can hope to present him or herself in exactly the same way to each respondent. Interviewers will change with each different encounter, and so will the necessary prompts, if they are to avoid the 'wooden' artificiality which I noted above as a defect of the standardized method of interviewing. If the interviewer is inflexible, then she or he will either prejudice the continuation of the interview or bias the responses which are obtained.

In summary, the ideal standardized interview schedule consists of the following:

1 The same questions should be asked of every respondent, using the same wording. This is standardization of the questions. The context and procedures of the method of asking questions should also be standardized, by the interviewer introducing the research purposes in the same way and by using the same format for approaching the respondents.

2 There is an assumption that all respondents will understand the question in the same way. If they do not appear to understand the question as asked and want clarification, then the prompts or subsidiary information which the interviewer gives should be non-directive.

3 The respondent should feel motivated to continue to answer further questions; this is partly a matter of context, partly a matter of the length of the interview schedule (measured by the average time to complete the interview), and partly

a question of how well the interviewer maintains a motivation to continue the interview.

4   The interviewer (or a coder[1] working after the event) should be able to categorize the responses to any question into a set of mutually exclusive and exhaustive categories. A simple categorization, for example, is 'yes', 'no' or 'don't know'.

5   A less simple categorization of responses (and one more commonly used) is a Likert scale – named after its inventor, R. Likert. Here the responses are coded by the interviewer, in the field, to one of five or seven mutually exclusive and exhaustive categories. Typical Likert categories are:

- strongly agree (with a particular statement)
- agree
- neither agree nor disagree
- disagree
- strongly disagree

This is a five-fold Likert categorization. Seven-fold categorizations use three categories on either side of the 'neutral' category of 'Neither agree nor disagree'. The language used for the categories will fit the sense of the question and may invite agreement with a given statement or ask for responses to a question which the interviewer has to code into a specific category.

Open-ended Questions in Standardized Interview Schedules

Some schedules use open-ended (uncoded) questions, in which the respondent's reply is written down by the interviewer to be classified later into one of a set of codes. There are rarely more than a few of these in any particular schedule because of the extra work involved in the data-collection process, but they do have an important advantage.

Activity 4.2 (10 minutes)

List the advantages and disadvantages of this kind of question.

Uncoded questions allow the researcher to search the full range of responses obtained before reducing replies to a set of categories, and the 'translation' of replies

---

1 A *coder* is one of the research team who classifies verbatim responses, which have been recorded by the interviewer, into one of a set of codes. The questions which need this sort of *post hoc* coding are known as open-ended or uncoded questions. They are 'coded' but not by the interviewer in the field (see section on 'Open-ended Questions'). Coding is discussed further in Chapter 7.

to coded categories can be done by the researcher in the office rather than by the interviewer in the field. This means that open-ended questions do not constrain the respondent's beliefs or opinions to categories predetermined by the researcher, as fully standardized methods of data collection must do. Although it is not so apparent with interview schedules as it is in self-administered questionnaires, the respondent can also see that his or her reply is being taken down fully rather than summarily reduced to a tick in a box, and the sense that their responses are not constrained can help to improve the naturalism of this method. However, the interviewer has to be relied upon to extract the relevant material from what may be a long response and to discard the irrelevant, and replies to open-ended questions can rarely be taken down truly verbatim; the potential for bias introduced by the interviewer is considerable. Another disadvantage to *post hoc* coding (sometimes called office coding as opposed to field coding) is that it increases the time and cost of the questionnaire survey. Many investigators prefer to avoid using open-ended questions; they are liable to introduce an unknown degree of interviewer bias and to vitiate the advantage of highly structured methods of data collection: standardization, and speed and ease of numerical analysis of the results. Chapter 7 discusses how open-ended responses are coded 'in the office'.

Self-administered Questionnaires

Questionnaires are just as much highly structured methods of data collection as are interview schedules. Their chief advantage over interviewer-led methods is that they are cheap, particularly if they can be group-administered. Even postal questionnaires are much cheaper than the use of interview schedules, and it is far quicker to conduct an investigation by questionnaire than by any other highly structured data-collection method.

However, their response rates are usually low, unless they engage the respondents' interests or the investigation is perceived as being of direct value to the respondent. The critical reader should always look to see what the response rate was for an investigation and also whether any information is given on the characteristics of those who did *not* respond, so that some assessment can be made of the representativeness of the sample. This is desirable, of course, whatever the method of data collection, but it is particularly important in questionnaire investigations because of low response rates.

Both closed and open-ended questions may be used in questionnaires, but where interview schedules may introduce some degree of interviewer bias in the recording of responses, or the use of prompts or the interaction between the interviewer and the respondent, different sorts of bias may arise in the use of self-completed questionnaires. Fundamentally, the investigator has no control over the conditions in which the data are elicited. It may not be the required respondent who actually completes the questionnaire, it may be a group or family effort, and the questionnaire may be completed in any order that the respondent likes, despite the careful ordering of the questions which the researcher may have imposed. The degree of literacy of the respondents must also be carefully considered when evaluating the use of questionnaires. For example, and it is an extreme one, I once received a research proposal which wanted to survey a sample of functional illiterates by means of a postal questionnaire! Completing a questionnaire in a manner satisfactory to the researcher is a lot to ask of many respondents, and *piloting* of drafts of questionnaires on samples which are representative of the target population is essential (see below) both to gauge the length of time which it takes and to investigate whether the questions are properly understood by the respondent.

Piloting

A pilot investigation is a small-scale trial before the main investigation, intended to assess the adequacy of the research design and of the instruments to be used for data collection; piloting the data-collection instruments is essential, whether interview schedules or questionnaires are used.

An important purpose of a pilot is to devise a set of codes or response categories for each question which will cover, as comprehensively as possible, the full range of responses which may be given in reply to the question in the main investigation. For this to work effectively, the pilot sample must be representative of the variety of individuals which the main study is intended to cover. Representativeness is difficult to guarantee with the small samples that pilot studies necessarily use. It is better to construct a purposive sample for a pilot study so that the full range of individuals and their possible responses is covered, as far as the range can be known in advance of the study. Purposive or theoretical samples such as these can be contrasted with probability samples (see Chapter 2), in which the random selection of individuals in large numbers gives a reasonable assurance that the sample represents the population accurately. Pilot investigations do not attempt to represent, in the statistical sense, the correct proportions of different types of individuals in the population because the purpose is not to estimate the true proportions of such types, but to cover the entire range of replies which might be given to any of the possible questions in the first draft of a questionnaire or schedule, By covering the full range of replies, the researcher is then in a position to work out a set of codes or response categories which embraces the entire range of responses which might be given. This is a counsel of perfection and, no matter how good the pilot, responses may turn up in the main study which have not been anticipated in the pilot results.

The response category of 'Other (specify) …' is often included in the codes for closed questions as a way of avoiding a complete foreclosure of the researcher's or the interviewer's options when unexpected and difficult-to-code responses are obtained, even after the pilot results seem to show that the set of response categories is adequate and the main investigation has gone ahead. If the interviewer has (correctly) dealt with a difficult response, it can be treated like a response to an open-ended question; it can be dealt with in the office rather than coded crudely in the field.

There are other aims, besides the devising of comprehensive coding frames for specific questions, when piloting questionnaires and interview schedules. These other aims have to do with the overall design of the instrument rather than with specific questions, except for points 2 and 5 in the list below. These other aims represent criteria for an instrument which works effectively as a highly structured method of data collection. The areas to be explored include:

1   Do the respondents understand the question as initially phrased? This is a matter of using appropriate language according to the sort of research population one is

dealing with. Interviewing a sample from a population of young working-class people will require rather different language from that required when interviewing a sample from a population of young graduates.

2 Are the potential respondents able to think of the whole range of possible responses to any particular question or do they need a particular type of prompting?

3 Does the interview schedule or questionnaire take too long to complete so that pilot respondents are showing signs of impatience?

4 What is the best order for the questions? If questions which are sensitive appear too early this might jeopardize gaining the information required or even the completion of the interview itself.

5 Do the questions *discriminate* effectively between different respondents? Investigations which simply seek to *describe* the frequency of occurrence of particular characteristics in a sample of a population do not need to discriminate in their questions. Investigations which are *explanatory* in purpose, however, do need to discriminate; that is, questions should 'spread' the respondents across the response categories.

Each of these aims or purposes of the pilot will be discussed further.

Activity 4.3 (5 minutes)

How, at the piloting stage, would you go about ensuring that the language of a questionnaire was comprehensible and natural for the respondents?

Appropriate Language   On the phrasing and language to be used in formulating questions the pilot is particularly useful. It is common, in well-designed research, to have a two-phase pilot study. In the first phase, using the sort of theoretical sample I specified above – one covering the whole range of individual types which the main investigation is intended to sample – less structured methods are used; that is, more naturalistic interview methods, in which the interviewer has an agenda of general topics, phrased as broad questions, but not the invariant and specific questions of a finalized questionnaire. The replies can be tape-recorded for later analysis and from them questions in the appropriate language can be drawn up and an initial set of response categories or codes devised. In the second phase, using another sample drawn or constructed in the same way as the first phase, a more-structured technique is used. This is where a draft of a questionnaire or schedule appears and is administered (by interviewer or self-completion by the respondent) in a similar way to the final instrument. How well the specific, rather than broad, questions are understood can be assessed, as can the length of the questionnaire or schedule, measured by how long it typically takes to complete (point 3 above).

Prompting   Point 2 in the criteria for an effective instrument of data collection raises something more subtle about responses to individual questions. Can the respondent be expected to articulate (or even to think of) the full range of possible responses to a particular question? For example, if the research investigation was concerned with the effect of certain stressful life-events on personal health, the investigator might ask the question (among others) 'Have you experienced any stressful problems in the past year?' with a view to relating 'stress' to health status.

Activity 4.4 (5 minutes)

What are the problems of this kind of question, and how would you go about overcoming them?

The problems are that respondents may not realize that their experiences have been stressful, nor remember those that they prefer to forget. In this sort of case, a special type of prompt is often used, called a *showcard*. This lists the full range of possibilities of responses for the respondent, who is asked to indicate which one or ones apply to him or her. An example is Slack's (1992) study of mental health and the unemployed. As part of the study, Slack wanted to know what 'life stressors' people had experienced during the course of the past year, in order to control for the effect of life stressors on any possible relationship between unemployment and mental health. It is unlikely that members of her sample would have systematically reviewed all the unpleasant possibilities which might have happened to them, so a showcard was used which listed a number of stressful events or experiences and the respondent was asked to say which ones had occurred to them. The list of life stressors could have been derived from a pilot investigation (and originally was) but Slack, legitimately, borrowed it from already published work.

Ordering of Questions   This is a complex matter and one that is frequently badly handled. It is generally better to put demographic questions – those relating to age, marital status, family relationships, occupation, etc. – towards the end, if possible. This is partly because they are uninteresting questions to the respondent and one wishes to engage his or her interest in the interview as soon as possible, and partly because, being sensitive, they may be resented. Other topics/questions which should be regarded as sensitive include sexual orientation, health status (particularly mental health status), income, and professional and educational qualifications; such questions should not come near the beginning of an interview or a questionnaire. It is instructive, when reading published research reports, to relate response rates and refusals to the design of the questionnaire or schedule and particularly to the ordering of the questions (if the researcher gives enough information to allow a judgement to be made). Other factors affecting response rates must, of course, be taken into account.

A good questionnaire designer will also think carefully about what is essential to ask as well as the order in which to ask questions. Does one need to know exact income, for example, or will an income bracket do just as well? If it will, then a show card containing income brackets can be given to respondents and their responses need only be A, B, C, etc. This is perceived as less intrusive than insisting on precise figures. However, it may be important in some circumstances to be exact about 'factual' questions, such as income or age, and a show card with income brackets would be insufficient. For a further discussion of the difficulties, see the section on 'Factual Questions' below.

Discrimination   The piloting of individual questions needs to take account of the ability of a question to discriminate between respondents, but only for certain types of investigation.

Activity 4.5 (5 minutes)

For what kinds of research is it important that questions discriminate between respondents, and when might this not matter?

Descriptive investigations are aimed at the accurate estimation of the frequency in the population of certain responses and are unconcerned with spreading the responses across the response categories. If, for example, 90 per cent of responses in a sample of the general British population classify themselves as white/European in response to a question about ethnic origin (as in the 1991 Census), this is not a problem; all the researcher and the critical reader are concerned with is whether the estimation is reasonably accurate. Explanatory investigations, on the other hand, are trying to relate differences on one variable (constructed from responses to specific questions) to differences on another variable. Here, the discriminatory power of a question does matter and the pilot should be testing it. A question which discriminates effectively will show a spread of responses across the answer categories. This is not necessarily an even spread, but one which shows a significant frequency of response in each category.

We can illustrate this latter point. In the United States, McIver et al. (in Zeller and Carmines, 1980) investigated the links between being a victim of crime, the type of neighbourhood the respondent lived in, and the respondent's perception of the quality of the police service which he or she received. This represents three important variables whose intercorrelations were vital to the investigation and to *explaining* the connection between experiencing crime personally and perceiving the quality of the local police service on a scale ranging from poor to good.

One of the questions which they asked, measuring perception of the quality of police service, was the following: 'How would you rate the overall quality of police services in your neighborhood? Remember, we mean the two or three blocks around your home. Are they outstanding, good, adequate, inadequate, or very poor?' (Zeller and Carmines, 1980: 163–4). Another question which they asked, again to do with the perceived quality of the police service, was 'When the police are called to your neighborhood, in your opinion do they arrive very rapidly, quickly enough, slowly, or very slowly, not at all?' If responses across their sample had accumulated heavily on, say, 'adequate' in the first question or 'not at all' in the second question, then both questions would have failed to discriminate between respondents. Too many of the responses would have been alike and would have made it impossible to calculate useful correlations between 'perceived quality of police services' – the underlying variable which these two questions would help to measure – and other variables of importance such as 'criminal victimization'.

In general, when responses to a question are to form a variable for an explanatory analysis, the pilot must show that responses across the sample to a question are divided among the response categories – not necessarily evenly, but 'spread' to a sufficient extent to allow a useful analysis of the correlations between variables to occur. Questions which do not discriminate in this way should be eliminated from an instrument after the pilot stage has explored the adequacy of the interview schedule or the questionnaire.

When reading research based on highly structured data-collection methods, look critically for an account of how the data-collection instruments were piloted. Whether interview schedules or questionnaires were used, piloting should have been carried out and the process by which the questions in their final form were arrived at should be documented. Ideally, some account should also be given of how the respondents' cooperation was obtained (the 'research bargain') and how they reacted to the time which the interview took. Unfortunately, this is likely to prove impossible to find in journal articles because pressure of space (and convention, as well) means that questionnaires are rarely printed with the substantive findings and analyses. Even books, where space is less of a problem, often omit an account of the methods employed in empirical work.

Asking More Complex Questions

Certain topics in data collection prove to be more difficult to gain valid and reliable information about than may first appear. These include: retrospective questions where the respondent is asked to remember past behaviours and opinions; 'factual' information about such things as income and occupational career; and, most difficult of all, the scoring or measurement of 'attitudes', where a number of questions are used to place a respondent on a scale which represents a single continuum of an attitude, or test of attainment for which any respondent has a score derived from a number of separate questions. The latter is a *composite measurement* which is composed of responses or scores from a number of discrete questions. A continuum or a unidimensional scale assumes that there is a single property which is being measured. For example, the property of height is unidimensional; it is assumed that every member of a population may be placed on a particular point of the scale, ranging from low to high. However, social science concepts which denote 'properties' are more complex than physical properties such as height, weight or temperature, and each social science concept may represent a number of different dimensions. The main problem in composite measurement is to disentangle these different dimensions. For example, social class probably consists in most people's perceptions of two dimensions: occupational or status prestige, on the one hand, and income level, on the other. These two dimensions do not overlap perfectly (in fact, far from it) and this is reflected in the popular ideas of 'genteel poverty' and the *nouveaux riches*. With composite measurement, the responses to a set of related questions may be analyzed to show two or more dimensions of an underlying attitude. The aim in analysis is to distinguish the different dimensions so that each can be seen as a single dimension.

Factual Questions

Apparently simple, factual questions can be more difficult than they seem. Oppenheim (1979) gives a good example of the difficulties that even the simplest question might hold, particularly if the researcher is vague as to why the question is being asked. Oppenheim's question was: 'Do you have a TV set?'

Activity 4.6 (a moment's reflection)

Think about this question. What potential ambiguities do you identify?

Who, asks Oppenheim, is the 'you' in the question? Is it the respondent (does the respondent own a set personally), the family, the parent(s) if a child is being asked, the landlord if it is a lodger who is the respondent? Are we interested in whether the TV set is owned or rented? Ambiguity is implicit in the word 'have'. In this simple example, most of the problems can be solved by being clear about the purpose of asking the question and what details it is necessary to know. Some factual questions are more difficult but can be tackled by knowing clearly what is essential and what is not.

Occupational status appears to be straightforward, but it is far from that because the purpose in asking for a respondent's job is often to classify him or her by social class. Occupational labels such as teacher, engineer or manager cover a wide status range, and it is impossible to locate an individual in a social class without knowing more about, for example, whether the job is one which requires the holder to supervise others (and, if so, how many?) and what qualifications are needed to enter the occupation. The need for further details means that prompts will have to be used. This is easier with schedules administered by an interviewer than with questionnaires (self-completion schedules) because the interviewer will immediately know which is a prompt and when it is needed. With questionnaires, great care is needed to keep the question clear and, at the same time, to get sufficient detail for the investigator's purposes. A cluttered and badly laid out questionnaire will risk confusing the respondent.

Retrospective Questions

Van Dijk et al.'s (1990) research, which asked respondents to think back over the past five years and remember if they suffered the theft of a motor vehicle, is typical of the problems that can arise with retrospective questions. Is the respondent's memory accurate enough, leaving aside ambiguities in the question itself? With an interviewer, the situation can be better controlled and, if the answer is clearly outside the time period asked for, a prompt can be used such as 'Has there been anything more recent?' This is much more difficult with self-completion questionnaires, and questions which ask for retrospection should be regarded with suspicion if they are used in self-administered questionnaires.

Accurate answers to questions which ask for periodical behaviour are equally difficult to ensure: not because the respondent is consciously trying to impress the interviewer (though that might be a problem with certain types of deviant behaviour) but because memory is very fallible. Even innocuous questions such as 'How often do you visit your dentist?', besides being vague as to the period under review (i.e. recently, over the past five years), will also suffer from memory lapses. Questions about how much people usually drink per day are also notoriously badly answered. Relatively light drinkers usually overstate the amount of their drinking: if when they drink at all they typically have two drinks, then they will tend to say they drink two drinks a day on average, even though they have these two drinks on only five of the seven days. Heavy drinkers tend to underestimate their drinking; if they typically have four drinks in a night but tend to 'binge' from time to time and have many more, they will typically put their average down as four drinks.

If an accurate estimation of the frequency of a particular behaviour is an important objective of the investigation, a preferred method of data collection is the use of diaries. Another, used by at least one market research firm for measuring consumption of 'consumer non-durables' (supermarket food etc.), is to rely on physical evidence kept by the informant – to 'count the empties', in other words.

Composite Measurement

At its simplest, the idea of 'measurement' in the social sciences is that a response to a question can be used as a means of classifying an individual. Where the question is a simple, factual one, this is relatively straightforward. For example, gender is measured in only two categories; occupational status can be measured more elaborately but, typically, six categories are used (from higher professional/managerial to unskilled manual). These classifications are derived from answers to single questions, although care has to be taken to make the question (and the response) precise enough (as we have already noted).

When we wish to measure more complex and more abstract characteristics such as opinions, personality traits or attitudes, relying on a single response will be problematic. It is possible to measure individual attitudes towards divorce, for example, by asking the single question 'Do you think that divorce should be made more difficult?' and classifying the responses into 'Yes' and 'No', but this seems crude. Even if the question (and the measurement) were made more sophisticated by putting the question in the form of a statement 'Divorce is too easy today', and providing five Likert categories for the respondent to indicate the extent of his/her agreement or disagreement with it, we are still relying on a single response, albeit one which allows five categories of measurement rather than two.

Very abstract entities such as attitudes are *constructs* which are created by the process of investigation; they are not directly observable responses. What we can observe are the responses we obtain when we present the individual with statements or ask questions which will *indicate* whether or not the construct is present. With attitudes, we conceive of the construct as being a continuum, so that authoritarianism, for example, is measured on a scale running from very authoritarian at one extreme to not authoritarian at the other. The probability of accurately locating an individual on such a scale by means of a single question or statement is very low. Partly, this is due to inevitable problems of measurement error, which is a general issue in all investigations, and partly it is because any single question will be a mixture of a 'true' indicator of the construct and error. Respondents may make idiosyncratic responses, particularly to opinion questions. The question above on divorce may be interpreted by some respondents, for example, as a question about the need for tougher laws generally, not just ones on divorce. Such responses, then, would be compounded of general attitudes towards the criminal justice system *and* specific attitudes towards divorce laws as such. In other words, the indicator (the response to the question) may be drawing on two different constructs, the first of which in this example would be 'error'.

Composite measures use batteries of indicators in order to achieve a single measurement of an underlying construct. By using multiple measurements, it is possible to disentangle the specific 'errors' in individual questions from what they indicate about the underlying construct. With a carefully chosen set of questions (often called items in composite measurement) more accurate measurements may be made.

The process of composite measurement usually begins with the assembly of a large pool of items or individual questions which seem, on the face of it, to measure the same theoretical construct. Considerable work is necessary to refine the initial item pool into a form which is short enough to be tolerated by respondents and which satisfies a number of statistical tests. The main requirement of such measures is that they should be single dimensions, and items are selected for final inclusion partly on the basis of how strongly they contribute to a common factor underlying the pool of items. Given the resources needed to create a new composite measure, those that become established in the theoretical literature are widely used by other researchers. Examples of theoretical constructs for which standard composite measures are available include: authoritarianism, Machiavellianism, and Eysenck's (1970) extroversion–introversion. These examples are all personality traits but composite measurement is also used for tests of attainment and for intelligence tests.

To see how the responses to an initial pool of items or questions are used to test whether or not a single underlying attitude is being measured, let us look in more detail at McIver et al.'s study (in Zeller and Carmines, 1980) of the public's evaluation of the US police. Five questions were designed to elicit evaluation of the quality of police services:

How would you rate the overall quality of police services in your neighborhood? Remember, we mean the two or three blocks around your home. Are they outstanding, good, adequate, inadequate, or very poor?

Do you think that your police department tries to provide the kind of services that people in your neighborhood want? [Responses: 'Yes'/'No'.]

When the police are called to your neighborhood, in your opinion do they arrive very rapidly, quickly enough, slowly, or very slowly? [Also coded: 'Not at all'.]

Policemen in your neighborhood are generally courteous. Do you agree or disagree? Do you feel strongly about this?

The police in your neighborhood treat all citizens equally according to the law. Do you agree or disagree? Do you feel strongly about this?

(Zeller and Carmines, 1980: 163–4)

Responses to these five questions were strongly intercorrelated, as they must be if they are designed to measure the same underlying attitudes: attitudes towards the police service (ranging from positive to negative evaluations). However, this is not enough to demonstrate that a single attitude construct is being measured. Using the statistical technique of factor analysis, the researchers showed that two dimensions underlie the patterns of responses: the ability of the police to fight crime, and policing style. This analysis allowed the researchers to develop two distinct scales, one for each of the dimensions.

In general, constructing an attitude or opinion scale, or a complex (indirect) measure of personality or intelligence, involves following most or all of the following steps:

1   Selecting items to form an 'item bank' – probably items which have *face validity* (which look, on the face of it, as though they ought to measure what is desired), but this is not absolutely necessary (see *criterion validity*, below).
2   Applying these to a sample of respondents – preferably representative of the population with whom they will eventually be used – to obtain scores on each, and discarding items where discrimination is low – where there is not a reasonable spread of scores.
3   Checking *internal* or *construct* validity by exploring the dimensionality of the data. Factor analysis may indicate how many distinct dimensions are to be found within the data and, to the extent that these are interpretable, it may be desirable to conceive not of an overall scale but of several subscales measuring rather different things. Calculation of a statistic known as *Cronbach's alpha*, which is based on the intercorrelation between every pair of items in a scale, will assess the extent to which all the items in a subscale are indeed measuring the same thing (by the extent that they correlate with each other) and may allow you to discard one or two items to produce a more unidimensional subscale with less internal error variance.
4   At this stage it may be possible to check *criterion-related validity* or *predictive validity*. If the test is to measure depression, for example, and you have groups of people reliably diagnosed as depressive or not, then the high-scorers on the test should lie solely or predominantly among the diagnosed depressives. (This stage is essential if the items used were not picked for their face validity, being the only way of demonstrating what the test actually measures.) If the test is to measure achievement at mathematics, it should correlate highly with the end-of-year maths examination. Sometimes the test can be correlated with observed behaviour; a test of Conservative sympathy, for example, should identify future Conservative voters and current Conservative party helpers.
5   The reliability of the test should be established – preferably by test–retest methods (readministering it a few weeks later and seeing the extent to which it yields

the same results for each respondent or at least puts them in the same order). Split-half reliability (comparing two halves of the test on a single administration) or Cronbach's alpha give an indication of reliability, but they are not as strong as test–retest methods because they do not give an assurance that the trait or belief or attitude is stable over time.

6 If what is being measured is a trait or ability, or if the test is to be used for diagnostic purposes, the final stage would be to collect results from a very large representative sample, to obtain *population norms* – reliable estimates of how the scores may be expected to be distributed in the population, which in turn will indicate whether the subsequent research sample is in any way extreme or untypical.

The 'police' example above shows the strengths of highly structured methods, provided that they are carefully piloted. A large sample can be used (admittedly, the use of a telephone survey in the McIver study helped here but the point is generally true for structured questionnaires) and sophisticated forms of analysis can be brought to bear on the problem, revealing an interesting duality in the public's perceptions of the police. The way in which structured methods lend themselves to a wide range of numerical and statistical analysis has proved an enduring attraction to investigators. Only structured methods, such as the standardized questionnaire, allow a reasonably large number of respondents to be interviewed within a practicable time span and within feasible limits of cost. It is also the case, of course, that standardized questionnaire surveys (and experiments even more so) seem to be more 'scientific', more like the proven methods of the natural sciences (with all the prestige that science has), and capable of impressing consumers of social research – particularly those who influence or determine political and social policy. In other words, by placing methods in the positivistic traditions of enquiry, this style of social research makes implicit claims to be regarded as a legitimate branch of the exact sciences.

Less Structured Methods

Many social scientists have long held doubts about the validity of highly structured methods of social investigation and data collection. The attempt to study the attitudes, beliefs and perceptions of respondents, using artificial, highly structured procedures, is held to entail an unacceptably high degree of reactivity, no matter how well it is done. And to reduce what the respondent says in reply to a question to one of a set of predetermined answer categories is unnecessarily constraining of the respondent, who may well feel that his or her 'real' opinions have not been correctly represented. Clearly, office coding of responses to open-ended questions goes some way to meeting these criticisms, but there still remains the artificiality of structured methods of data collection and the *procedural reactivity* that such methods entail. Procedural reactivity means that the very artificiality of highly structured methods leads to the respondents withdrawing from the situations in which they normally act. As Hammersley (1979: 94) puts it: 'This [highly structured method] results in the suspension of the relevances and constraints embedded in those situations, which may be important in structuring people's everyday activities, and in their replacement by rather unusual relevances and constraints'. And he goes on to say, 'We must ask, therefore, what the relationship is between what people do and say in these "artificial" situations and what they do and say in everyday life ...' That is, the procedures used to question respondents – to elicit data – may distort or bias what the respondent believes, or how he or she might act in a natural situation. This is procedural reactivity.

Responses in highly structured methods are elicited in social interactions which are very artificial; this is obviously so in the case of questionnaire investigations, but it is none the less true in interviewer methods of data collection. A conversation, as Garfinkel (1967) points out, has a highly normative structure in which there are expectations of 'turn-taking' and of 'equality' between conversationalists. That is, topics are expected to be initiated by both parties rather than just by one, dominant, interviewer. Thus, in naturalistic methods of data collection, social scientists seek as far as possible to conduct their research in natural settings, in places where social activities are already in progress or where 'interviewers' fit into the 'scenery' and where social science investigators play a role in which they disturb the processes of social interaction as little as possible. This is *naturalism,* which seeks to minimize the procedural reactivity of more highly structured methods of asking questions.

> In order to minimize procedural reactivity, ethnographers [i.e. non-positivistic social scientists using unstructured methods of investigation] seek as far as possible to conduct their research in natural settings, in places where social activities are already in progress. Only in this way, they argue, can we hope to avoid unwittingly studying artificial responses, or at least behaviour which is not representative of people's everyday lives. In doing research on such settings, the ethnographer tries to play a marginal role, so as to disturb the processes of social interaction occurring there as little as possible. (Hammersley, 1979: 94)

Observing and Interviewing

There are a number of ways in which the ethnographer plays a role in which he or she disturbs the processes of social interaction as little as possible. Perhaps the most distinctive of these roles is that of *participant observer,* considered in Chapter 3, and the research role in which 'marginality' is most vital. The participant observer may ask no questions in any formal sense; he or she participates in a social group, and questions that are asked are often incidental and arise from the normal social interaction of the group in which the participant observer finds a role. More artificial, because it is more contrived, is the *unstructured interview,* in which a naturalistic conversation is recorded in full (or nearly so) for later analysis. The interviewer cannot hope, in this method of asking questions, to merge with the scenery and to be as unobtrusive as the naturalistic form of asking questions demands. Some explanation of the interviewer's purposes and needs is required and a degree of procedural reactivity is necessarily introduced because people, in everyday life, do not submit to an interview at length, except on well-defined occasions such as job interviews.

However, the unstructured interview typically involves far less procedural reactivity than the standardized format of the interview schedule or the questionnaire; it appears to be more naturalistic, and it is so because the questions asked and the order in which they are asked flow from the respondent's replies rather than being entirely imposed by the interviewer's predetermined list of questions. It must be said, however, that interviews in the ethnographic style are diverse and a single prescription for the ideal unstructured interview would give the false impression of a single interviewing method in ethnographic research; however, very directive forms of interviewing, in which the interviewer openly controls the interview and uses standardized questions, are rarely used and then only to probe the 'fronts' which members of the group may have put up.

An Example of Less Structured Interviewing

An example can be taken from some research which one of us (Wilson) undertook in the 1990s – a study of a sample of 40 people who were in long-term residential care in the 1940s and 1950s. Wilson was particularly concerned to understand the informants' own interpretations of their experience, including the transition which they made from the Home to the world of work and of independent living.

Three waves of interviews were used for each informant: first, one which presented the researcher and his research aims and sought to gain their cooperation in a data-collection process which demanded a considerable period of their time. Because the topics to be covered were sensitive and likely to touch on difficult periods in their lives, it was important to establish a climate of trust, particularly concerning whether their current partner was to know of their background. This preliminary interview was not tape-recorded, but brief contemporaneous notes were taken and more detailed notes written up immediately after each interview had finished. These notes were used in conjunction with my theoretical objectives for the research to prepare a list of relevant topics (or interview guide) which could be tailored to the specific experiences of each informant. This formed the structure for the second interview (which was tape-recorded) and which the informant believed to be the actual beginning of the research. The third interview was, again, unstructured but designed to elaborate topics and interpretations which were gained in the second interview. All interviews took place in the respondent's home and were naturalistic in style.

Some of the topics listed for Interview 2 (before tailoring to each individual in the light of Interview 1) were as follows, in the order of preference, although the order had to be modified according to the respondent.

What are you doing for a living now? (Subsidiary topics/questions to trace work and post-compulsory school histories.)

How many children do you have, their ages/genders? (Subsidiary topics/questions to explore aspirations for their own children *and* begin to probe indirectly into marital histories and stability of family relationships.)

Do you still keep in touch with Sister L. or Sister F. – the staff who had been responsible for the group, both still alive? (Subsidiary topics/questions, exploring the nature of their relationship with the mother-substitutes and inviting comparison with their natural parents.)

Where did you go when you first left the Home? Were you apprenticed? Where were you living? (Subsidiary topics/questions to explore the transition from institution to independence *and* begin to probe early coping strategies and continuing dependence on the Home.)

Very sensitive topics were left towards the end of the interview, if possible – particularly questions on the circumstances in which the informant came to be taken into residential care, including child abuse (sexual or violent or both), illegitimacy, family breakdown, and so on.

Note that we have listed topics rather than actual questions. Specific questions to each informant were phrased naturally, taking into account what they had already said in Interview 1 and the flow of information during Interview 2. Nothing sounds more stilted or artificial than asking a set question regardless of what has gone before. The naturalism of unstructured interviewing requires the illusion that the interview is a 'conversation' rather than a formal interview between researcher and subject – one in which the informant can initiate questions and elaborate answers (without prompting) just as much as the interviewer.

Note also that the structure was a list of *topics* to be covered, not a list of *questions* in a set order. During the interviews, the informant, who is encouraged to speak as freely as possible, is never obviously redirected if she or he veers off on to another topic than the one which the interviewer has succeeded in introducing. The connections between events which the informant makes have to be *understood* by the researcher in their natural context. Apparently disconnected recollections in interviews can be especially revealing of what the informant holds to be significant to him or her.

Let us illustrate most of these general points with an extract from one of the Interview 2 transcripts.

Some background information is necessary to understand the exchanges between the informant, P., and the researcher (M.W.). This is a study of children (now adults) who experienced a long period of residential care in the 1940s and 1950s. They were a group in the care of a large voluntary children's home, founded in the 1860s, which, in the 1940s and 1950s, believed in long-stay residential care (the situation has now changed). The group studied were members of two 'family groups' each in the care of a Sister (Sister L. and Sister F.), both of whom are still alive, but retired. All of the group left the Home between 1954 and 1959. Wilson was one of them.

Follow-up studies of children who have been in care suffer from an extremely poor response rate. Social workers who select a random sample from Local Authority lists typically get a response rate of 5 per cent, with all the unrepresentativeness that such a low figure implies. In addition, the fact that former inmates of residential homes are approached by a social worker risks a personal reactivity which this study avoids. The informants trusted Wilson as one of them; even so there was personal reactivity, but of a different kind.

The following extract is from an interview (second wave) with P., now aged 54. He works as an engineer in the computer industry, has two grown-up children, and has been married for 25 years to a former Sister (an ex-staff member) of the Home. This is an extract from a sensitive part of the interview:

M.W.: What happened to D. [his brother, two years younger]?
P.: He's a bloody alcoholic, hides a bottle of rum under a bush whenever we go and see him. Christ, he's been in and out of work for ages and lives in a ... room in London which is a complete tip and his woman left him I'm not ... surprised how did she put up with him for so long? My Dad's to blame.
drank like a ... fish, never saw anybody in the Navy do it like that and they could ... drink all that ... free rum, and all that.
M.W.: Yeah, never knew anything about your Father tell me about him and your Mum.
P.: Yeah, didn't know anything about yours either we never talked about it did we? (*M.W.:* Right.) Mine split up when I was seven, that's when we were at Doddington remember that you was a right little ...? You were great mates with D. though, you

two were always together until we smashed the place up. Christ you couldn't half throw a brick (*M.W.:* an old saucepan and so could you, and eggs as well! – [*laughter*]) and when they sent us to [another branch of the Home] you two got split up didn't you? After ... [the Governor] caned us in front of everyone else, when we got there, bastard! Remember the baths we had to take afterwards, bloody glass in them too?

M.W.: Yeah never forgot it, but [Governor] is dead now did you know? (*P.:* Yeah, good job.) They put us in [different houses] but we still saw a lot of each other. He didn't like [an area of north London] where they put him in digs did he?

P.: He ... hated it! The job [in a bakery] and the ... landlady who was a right cow and wouldn't let him have any visitors we had to meet in the caff. My Dad went to see him once only time he did and she turned him away wouldn't even tell D. he'd been there.

M.W.: Did your Mum keep in touch?

P.: No never saw her after we went to Doddington, she took up with another man but I never saw him didn't want to know about us I suppose, starting again with another man – had more kids too but I've never seen them.

M.W.: Where is she now, do you know?

P.: Don't know and I don't want to know after all this time.

M.W.: Why do you think D. turned into an alkie, you didn't?

P.: Family I think what with my Dad I don't know about my Mother and D. had a bad time when he first left [the Home] and never got sorted out ... different women and he spent a lot of time then with H. [later convicted of murder and sentenced to life imprisonment] you remember him you three were always together he drank a lot and D. caught it from him I think but I don't really know. He's weak he always was you led him around by the nose and H. too so I suppose he got into the wrong lot and drank too much.

The shared references to mutual experiences between P. and the researcher need to be taken into account when assessing the impact the researcher had on the information collected. There are frequent references to people and events which they had both known, and this gave the interview a more natural feel. It is similar in some ways to the sorts of interview which might arise in a study using overt participant observation following a period in the field studying the group – that is, where there is a sense of the observer belonging to the group and being accepted as a member. In this case the researcher's role is perhaps less marginal than it is for most participant observers. On the other hand, there is reaction by P. to Wilson as an individual, with his memories of me as a boy, what he had been like and his part in his brother's alcoholism. This is personal reactivity, which is an issue in any method of interviewing. One must ask how such reactivity may have biased the responses obtained.

Interviewer Control in Less Structured Interviews

Activity 4.7 (15 minutes)

Look back over the last section. What elements of structure – of control by the interviewer of the flow and direction of the conversation – do you detect?

Notice how, in the extract above, Wilson replied (naturally) to the specific yet partly rhetorical questions which P. asked (e.g. 'Remember the baths ...?') but turned the interview back to the issues which he wanted to explore. Thus he remained in control of the interview, though he appeared to be non-directive and preserved the naturalism of this method of interviewing. A full transcript would show that I had not fully followed the rules of 'turn-taking' and of conversation between equals that real conversations have (see, for example, Garfinkel, 1967). Although Wilson spoke less than P., he nearly always moved the interview on towards topics and issues which were on the research agenda rather than P.'s agenda. In other words, he took control and imposed my structure or agenda on to P. and still maintained an essential rapport with him.

This research example is, perhaps, unusual in that, even though a research interviewer, Wilson had a natural role in the conversation as one of the original group. If the aim of finding an acceptable role without a background of shared participation is to succeed, some role for the interviewer must be found which is accepted by the informant. At the same time the interviewer must remain detached in order to structure the interview according to his or her research interests.

The need to engage with the informant, yet remain detached, is a difficulty of naturalistic methods of investigation. It is most obvious in participant observation studies, where finding a role to play is the first concern of researchers. Lacey (1976) was a teacher at a northern grammar school when he undertook his study of the under-achievement of working-class boys in grammar schools; and, although his role seemed natural and blended into the scenery of the school, he reports the strains between being perceived as a teacher, who was interested in matters not normally discussed by either teachers or pupils, and the need to remain detached, even though the headmaster knew he was a researcher. So it is with one-to-one interviews where the interviewer always has a role in the eyes of the informant, yet it must be a role that allows the informant to think that he or she has been listened to carefully and understood. Nevertheless, it is the interviewer who structures the interview even though he or she may do less talking than the informant. It is the interviewer who changes the subject, asks clarifying questions, refers back to something said earlier, and finally ends the interview. Thus, although the unstructured interview may appear just that, it still contains a structure largely dictated by the researcher rather than by the informant. A common structure, for example, is to apply some element of the 'life-history interview': to take the informant through the chronology of his or her life or job or stay in prison, or whatever, as a good way of letting them tell a story with which they are familiar and so fluent and imposing as little research-determined preconception as possible on the conversation. The opposition between structured and unstructured methods of data collection is in many ways a false one; all are structured, but in different ways. The best one can say is that there are degrees of structure in all methods of asking questions.

One place where a degree of thought and prestructuring will often be applied is at the beginning of interviews. Introductions are crucial: your role and that of the informant are established by the first few things to be said, and these are very difficult to break once established. There is also the 'prescripted' relationship between informant and researcher, a part of procedural reactivity, which determines that informants will want to be helpful and so will try to make sense of the situation in order to find out what you want to know. To avoid telling informants what kind of information you want – and so increasing your chances of getting what is salient to *them* rather than what is salient to *you* – we often prepare bland and open-ended questions to ask at the start, ones which do not 'give the game away'. Interviewing life-sentence prisoners, for example, one of us started the interviews not with 'What do you do to survive this sentence?' but 'What's it like in this prison?' and 'How does it compare with the prison you were in when you were first sentenced?' (Sapsford, 1983). Talking to mothers of children with learning disabilities the question was not 'Tell me about the problems you have with your disabled child?', but 'What's Milton Keynes like as a place to live in?' and 'What's it like as a town for bringing up children?' (Abbott and Sapsford, 1987b). In the latter case this allowed the researchers to discover families where the child with the learning disabilities was *not* the main family problem, something which would probably not have emerged if they had focused in on the disabled child from the start.

Reactivity and Validity in Research Asking Questions

The central problem in data collection in the human sciences is that it usually involves personal, social interaction between the observer and the observed or between the interviewer and the respondent. Even when postal questionnaires are used, there is still social interaction. The respondent is asked to give time and application, usually for little reward except, perhaps, a feeling of satisfaction. Willingness to assist the investigator depends on the *context* in which the respondent is asked to take part. A request to complete a four-page questionnaire which comes from the respondent's family doctor and which is concerned with patients' experiences at local hospitals when referred as outpatients is likely to get a better response rate than a market research questionnaire posted to a sample of new car buyers. There is great satisfaction in being asked for your opinion in a matter which is of great personal concern. The market research questionnaire carries little or no sense of reward; it is simply a chore for most respondents, and response rates in this sort of research are notoriously low.

The context in which respondents are asked to answer questions does not just affect their willingness to respond; it also can alter the responses, and so it is an aspect of the *validity* of the data-collection method. This is so not just in naturalistic face-to-face interviews, in which the way the interview is set up (what is said about the nature of the research, the characteristics of the interviewer, etc.) matters greatly, because the respondent will *react* to his or her perceptions of the nature of the questions and to the characteristics of the interviewer. It applies equally to standardized questionnaires. These are conducted in a context too, and, although they appear to be more 'objective', there is still social interaction between the researcher and the respondent. This applies whether the questionnaire is self-administered or conducted by an interviewer.

Context in data collection is one of the dimensions on which we compared methods in the Introduction to the chapter. Another analytical dimension, by which I distinguished different methods of data collection, was that of the procedures used. At one end of a dimension of differences in procedures of collecting data lies the standardized, apparently impersonal methods of the laboratory experiment. The experimenter uses a fixed set of instructions for each subject and is rarely allowed to vary the wording or to give further information even when subjects ask for it. Frequently, the experimenter will not know the hypothesis which is under investigation. All this is to prevent the experimenter unwittingly biasing the results by indicating, however subtly, what is the preferred response or behaviour (the one which will confirm the investigator's hypothesis). On the face of it, this sort of procedure appears objective and scientific; it is clearly derived from the experimental procedures of the natural sciences, and belongs to the *positivistic* school of the philosophy of science and is open to the same objections. There is known to be less objectivity in experimentation on human subjects than some of the proponents of 'the scientific method' have thought (see Crowle, 1976). In particular, the subjects may lie to the experimenter. The problem is, as Crowle puts it, that 'the human subjects are of the same order of complexity as the experimenters', and may detect what the experiment is really about and alter their behaviour accordingly or give false responses. Subjects may react in undesired ways to the rigid procedures of the experiment, and the data gathered may be biased in unknown ways, thus making interpretation of the results ambiguous. And, by needing to work out in advance the entire procedures of the experiment and not being able to change them, this method of data collection is inflexible and forecloses the possibility of exploring connections and potential analyses that may emerge in the course of the investigation.

It was in reaction to positivistic methods of conducting social research that some researchers long ago adopted methods of data collection that are naturalistic in their procedures, such as the unstructured interview. This chapter has shown that such methods are not unstructured, despite superficial appearances to the contrary. This means that we cannot say that research based on ways of asking questions which are relatively unstructured is necessarily more valid than research using highly structured methods. Less-structured methods minimize procedural reactivity and allow the freer exploration of respondents' meanings and beliefs. They do this at the possible expense of reliability: the ability of another researcher to obtain the same results using the same methods, something which is stronger in highly structured methods. However, less-structured methods do sometimes have a reflexive account of the research in which the investigator *reflects* on the context and on the procedures adopted and tries to assess the impact that these might have had on the responses obtained and on the interpretations placed upon them.

However, procedural reactivity is only one source of bias; there remains *personal reactivity*; that is, the effect that a particular researcher's interactions with respondents might have had on the research. Personal reactivity is maximal in less-structured methods and minimal in highly structured ones. In the experiment, the behaviour of the experimenter is closely controlled, with a view to minimizing the impact of her or his persona on the experimental result; the same is attempted in highly structured interview studies, through standardization of questions and procedures and the standardized training of interviewers.

Validity, then, is a matter of trade-offs: between procedural and personal reactivity, and between reliable and less reliable methods. Whichever method of data collection is chosen, attention must be paid to the objectives of the research, and the methods adopted must be evaluated in this light. I had, for example, considered using highly structured methods of research for my study of the 40 respondents who had been in residential care, but I rejected this because it would have been impossible to have avoided the personal reactivity that would have followed from my knowing them since childhood. More importantly, I wanted *their* understanding of what it was like to be in care, and this would have been impossible without employing a method which allowed me to explore their memories using *their* meanings, rather than to impose mine from the outset.

Conclusion

In this chapter we have looked at different data-collection methods used to ask people questions. These range from the precoded and highly structured interviewer schedule or self-completion questionnaire, through schedules and questionnaires which make use of 'open' questions to which informants can make a free-form response, to the relatively unstructured and naturalistic one-to-one conversational interview or focused group interview.

What these all share is a degree of *structure* – even those methods described above as 'less-structured'.

- The interviewer exerts control over what is covered, even where he or she tries to appear not to do so, and even the postal questionnaire has a clear structure which respondents are expected to follow.
- Beyond this, the research situation is a *socially* structured one, with its own implicit rules about obeying the interviewer and helping him or her and about the degree of personal disclosure which is appropriate. Less-structured interviews may resemble conversations, but conversations also have a social structure and a set of implicit rules for conducting them.
- These two kinds of structural effect are referred to as 'procedural reactivity' and constitute ways in which the data may be a product of how the research is structured rather than a fair reflection of everyday life and understanding.

Whatever the degree of structure, interviews and questionnaires also share the fact that the replies are given to a *person*; even with postal questionnaires the informant will have an idea of the kind of person who is asking the question – a generalized middle-class, socially acceptable other. Personal reactivity is another way in which data may be due to the circumstances of the research rather than to the circumstances under investigation.

Key Terms

Acquiescence set   the tendency of respondents to agree consistently with what is said.

Agenda   the list of topics (and perhaps prepared 'starter' questions) used in place of a fully structured questionnaire by someone carrying out less-structured interviewing.

(Key Terms continued)

Ascribed characteristics characteristics which the informant sees in the interviewer – e.g. gender, ethnicity, class – which may lead to stereotyping.

Correlation the association between two variables, the extent to which values on one can be predicted from values on the other. Variables are said to be *positively* correlated when high values on one predict high values on the other – e.g. physical fitness and running speed. They are said to be *negatively* correlated when high values on one predict low values on another – e.g. height and distance of hair from ceiling.

Cronbach's alpha a statistic calculated to assess the extent to which items in a scale are correlated with each other; they should be highly correlated if they all measure the same thing.

Factor analysis a technique, based on assessing correlation between variables, for simplifying data by looking for groups of variables which are highly correlated and so may be regarded as aspects of a single factor.

Intercorrelation *see* Correlation above.

Interview schedule a set of highly structured questions asked by an interviewer in a face-to-face or telephone interview. See also *questionnaire* below.

Life history interviewing a full *life* history interview would involve many hours of interview to explore someone's entire life in depth. Here it is used to mean a more limited use of the technique, using the person's life as a structuring principle for the interview in order to get them talking in general about what they feel and believe and have experienced, rather than focusing on particular questions of interest to the researcher.

Likert scale an item in an attitude or personality scale where respondents are invited to express their degree of agreement or disagreement with a proposition. Alternatives are *Thurston Scales*, where people answer yes or no to a question, or *bipolar scaling* (also called *semantic differential scaling*) where informants locate their response as being nearer to one of two opposed propositions or characteristics.

Questionnaire as used here, a structured set of questions, containing all necessary instructions, for respondents to fill in by themselves. In many books you will find the work used to encompass interview schedules as well.

Reactivity the extent to which results are due not to the nature of what is being investigated but to the nature of the research.

– *personal reactivity*: reaction to the person of the interviewer (or an imagined, generalized person in the case of self-administered questionnaires) or to his or her behaviour or questions.
– *procedural reactivity*: reaction to the nature of the research situation or to the fact that it *is* a research situation.

Reliability the stability of a measure; the extent to which scores do not change over a relatively short time.

Response categories the categories which appear as possible answers to a question on a highly structured questionnaire or schedule. Also called *codes*.

(Continued)

(Key Terms continued)

Response rate the proportion of the intended sample who actually yield usable interviews.

Routing instructions to the interviewer or respondent to skip certain questions, depending on the answer to previous ones.

Unidimensional measuring a single dimension.

Validity the extent to which the research conclusions can plausibly be taken to represent a state of affairs in the wider world. In this chapter we have talked mostly about aspects of *validity of measurement*:

- *Face validity*: the appearance of measuring what is wanted.
- *Criterion/predictive validity*: assuring validity of measurement against a trusted criterion or by predicting the outcome of a future event or test.
- *Concurrent validity*: assuring validity by comparing scores with those of a test or instrument whose validity is assured is an aspect of this.
- *Construct validity*: here, exploring the structure of a scale to see if the items all measure the same thing. More generally, validating the measure by showing that properties it needs to have to be a valid measure in this circumstance (e.g. reliability) are present.

Further Reading

Burgess, R.G. (1984) *In the Field: an introduction to field research,* London, Allen and Unwin. [A sound basic introduction to less-structured research]

Hammersley, M. and Atkinson, P. (1995) *Ethnography: principles in practice,* London, Routledge. [Another sound basic introduction to less-structured research]

McCracken, G. (1988) *The Long Interview,* Beverly Hills, CA, Sage. [A short but detailed and prescriptive discussion of technique in less-structured interviews]

McQuarrie, E.G. (1996) *The Market Research Toolbox: a concise guide for beginners,* London, Sage. [Lives up to its title. Covers all degrees of structure and is better on group interviews than any of the others listed here]

Oppenheim, A.N. (1992) *Questionnaire Design, Interviewing and Attitude Measurement,* London, Pinter. [The survey researcher's bible – detailed and definitive]

Sapsford, R.J. (1999) *Survey Research,* London, Sage. [A readable and wide-ranging introduction to survey research]

Research Proposal Activity 4

This chapter has been concerned with 'asking questions' of respondents or informants as a form of data collection. In constructing a research proposal, especially one which includes some form of interviewing as a means of data collection, you should address the following questions:

I   What degree of structure should be built into data collection? How much control should the interviewer take over the interview process?

2   What sources of invalidity are likely to be the outcome of the context of data collection and how can you guard against them?
3   Should data collection be based on highly structured or less structured methods, and why?
4   If highly structured methods of asking questions are to be used, should they be interviewer-administered or self-administered? Should questions involving composite measurement be included? Should open-ended questions be included?
5   What piloting procedures need to be put in place?

5

Research and Information on the Net

Roger Sapsford

This chapter looks at available data that can be accessed and analyzed on computer or from the library without undertaking new empirical research, and at the possibilities of the World-Wide Web as a medium for primary data collection from and about its users.

So far in this book we have treated 'research' as if all the relevant data were collected/constructed 'from scratch' by the researcher, asking people questions, or observing behaviour, or counting incidents, or participating in social situations. In fact, as you will have realised, a lot of what upholds the argument of a research paper is not new information, gathered by the researcher, but existing results, interpretations and theorizations which the researcher has distilled from the work of others; the 'literature review' is an integral part of the research plan and the research report. In this chapter we go beyond this obvious statement, however, to look at numerical and other types of information which are already available, having been collected by other researchers and/or as a by-product of an administrative process. Such statistics may be found in published volumes, but a major current source is the Net, or World-Wide Web, where a remarkable range of sources of information is to be found. The Web may also be used as a communication medium or an observable locus of social interaction, to conduct primary research on informants or settings which would not otherwise be accessible. Interpreting web data poses it own special problems, however, which this chapter considers.

Searching the Literature

A problem with being an academic, a researcher or an information officer nowadays is that there is just too much information to handle. Once, the PhD student did a 'literature review' by searching within libraries and bookshops and borrowing from other libraries. Subject indices and annual Abstracts (reporting the title and authorship of articles in a range of journals or other sources and giving a brief abstract of their contents), classified publishers' catalogues and purpose-written Bibliographies were the available means for locating work. A range of strategies were used for tracking down publications – using the reference lists of papers already read (following up references there which looked useful and looking to see if useful authors had published anything since), using general textbooks as a guide to more specialist literature, looking for relevant specialist journals, writing to academics and research units to seek out useful sources and the sheer serendipity of looking along the library shelves at the point where a useful source has been found, or going through back and subsequent issues of journals, to see what came to hand. The aim was to cover everything written on a topic, in order to make sense of what is already known and place the new research question in the context of the existing body of knowledge.

Even in the 1930s or 1940s the task of covering everything was an impossible one. (There are several instances of research issues and scholarly debates emerging in different countries at different times – sometimes, but not always, in different languages – and running surprisingly parallel courses, without any evidence whatsoever that the later set of participants had read the work of the earlier ones.) Now so much is being published that covering everything is out of the question. The advent of the World-Wide Web – the loose network of interconnected servers that links computers across the world – makes so much material available that a lifetime would not be sufficient to cover a small fraction of it. At the same time, the Web puts sources within the reach of people and organisations that would not have been able to afford the time, or the money, to seek them out for themselves. Laborious hand-written notes are more and more being replaced with downloadable text, and photocopying gives way to downloading of text, pictures and even video and audio records.

All the old strategies for seeking out information are still in use, and they may indeed be the best way to start in an academic research area, where what is important in the first instance may be the development of ideas rather than the proliferation of data. The new media, however, have brought new search engines to bear on the researcher's problems. Some time ago the classified 'manual' library catalogue – cards arranged in author or title order, or sometimes classified by subjects determined by the insight of librarians or the demands of cataloguing systems such as the Dewey Decimal System – gave way to computerized catalogues which have the property of being *searchable*. What this means is that you can insert a word or phrase as a keyword and call up everything within the library which has been classified under it – all uses of the phrase or its component words in the title or in an auxiliary keyword cataloguing field, according to the sophistication of the system. A combination of keywords will pick out the broad set which contains any of the components or the narrow subset which contains them all. This gives much more flexibility to searching catalogues, and works from unlikely sources or little-known authors are less often missed; as Ó Dochartaigh (2002) points out, the Web is the answer to marginalization by place or resource or freedom of access.

The strength of the Web as a whole is that, while there is no catalogue of it as there would be in a library, the Web is searchable in just the same way. Every item accessible on the Web has a unique address or page-name, and the text of the items is itself open to searching. The amount of material available is almost incalculably large, but computers work very fast indeed, so that a search that would take a person a year will be a matter of moments on the computer. Search Engines will permit you to enter keywords, as in a catalogue search, and identify sites whose names or contents include those words.

Searching is admittedly something of an art; it is very easy to miss references, or to summon up too many or too few. Selecting keywords involves a great deal of imagination, and searches will generally require several different combinations of keywords to cover the range and then narrow down the selection to an inspectable number. 'Urban regeneration' would yield thousands of entries, for example, and it would be necessary to limit the search to a subfield – by place or period or type of publication or by discipline (psychology, sociology, economics, politics, built environment) or area of intervention (housing, health, schooling, crime, local economy, employment...). It is necessary sometimes to allow for geographical or cultural differences between how things are labelled. It will always be good practice, for example, to explore both English and American spellings of terms, and the same may be true for French and Canadian French. We need also to remember that the clichés of one country are not necessarily shared by another. Two apocryphal stories often told to illustrate this point concern (a) the psychologist interested in applying psychometric tests of pain and control over pain to the experience of going to the dentist who entered 'scaling' and 'pain' into a set of dental abstracts – with predictable results, in hindsight – and the British sociologist interested in unreported work and benefits fraud who entered 'black economy' into a US database. In the latter case the phrase means 'covert or illegitimate work for money' in Britain, but in the US it summoned up thousands of references to the legitimate economic endeavours of African Americans.

Sources found on the Web are particularly useful to the researcher and writer because they are already in electronic textual form. They are themselves searchable – keywords will bring the reader to relevant passages without having to plough through the whole document (though at the risk of the reader misunderstanding the context of the passages so identified). More, they are copyable – you do not have to write down quotable passages to use in your writing but can copy them from the source document and paste them in place. (The corresponding problem here is a very substantial growth in plagiarism which we can only hope is largely confined to the student population.)

Box 5.1 *Useful abstracting services (valid at the time of writing) (Note: many of these are accessible only through libraries that subscribe to them, or offer only limited services to non-subscribers)*

edina.ac.uk/econlit: abstracts from international economics journals.
www.bib.umi.com/dissertations: access to Dissertation Abstracts.
www.bids.ac.uk: social science and humanities abstracts and access to the PsycInfo database of psychology abstracts.
www.dialog.com: This site gives access to several hundred databases covering a range of disciplines – e.g. business studies, medicine, psychology, sociology.

Box 5.1 *(Continued)*

www.isinet.com: The ISI Web of Science site is the leading British source of world-wide social science references. This may also be accessed through wos.mimas.ac.uk.

www.jhuccp.ord/popline: the Popline database of abstracts on population, family planning and related issues.

www.northernlight.com: this is a very flexible means of accessing articles in the site's own database or across the web and paying for full-text versions by credit card. (There is no charge for looking just at Abstracts.)

www.oclc.org: The *Firstsearch Electronic Collections Online* database from OCLC includes a wide range of publications of relevance to the social sciences, including sociology, women's studies, economics and psychology and incorporating access to Dissertation Abstracts.

www.omni.ac.uk/medline: abstracts on medicine, nursing and professions allied to medicine.

www.promo.net/pg/: Project Gutenberg is a full-text database of public-access books (mostly those on which copyright has run out).

Journal articles (abstracts and sometimes full text) can also be accessed via publisher or 'aggregator' sites – e.g. www.blackwells.com, www.ingenta.com, www.sciencedirect.com (Elsevier Publishing), www.swetsnet.nl.

Information on the Net

Beyond books and articles, the Web opens up access to a wide range of other 'publications' which would not have been available in the past except at a local level.

- Government and local government sites include information and articles on a wide range of topic areas, including policy documents, legislation and official documents, local and national government research reports and (often interrogatable) published administrative statistics (crime figures, economic data, statistics of health, housing, education, leisure…). The US output is particularly voluminous (at least in part because of their Freedom of Information Act), but most other countries also make quite a lot available.
- Full-text newspaper reports, with searchable indices, give access to published works across the world.
- University sites generally contain information about research and sometimes access to reports and summaries online.
- Individual research projects sometimes have their own sites, as do voluntary organizations, groups of activists and many other kinds of group. A general search for the name of the group (perhaps limited in terms of country) will generally turn these up.
- Some academics and many others have their own web sites, which may include publications, polemic, reviews, statistics or other potentially useful information.

Box 5.2   *Further useful web sites (valid at the time of writing)*

Government and other 'public' sites
neighburhood.statistics.gov.uk: local and regional statistical information on the UK.
www.access.gpo.gov: access to a wide range of US Government publications.
www.amnesty.org: Amnesty International.
www.census.gov: the United States Census.
www.data-archive.ac.uk: the Data Archive held at the University of Essex, UK, which gives access to a wide range of large-scale social, educational and psychological surveys.
www.hmprisonservice.gov.uk: information on prisons in England and Wales.
www.ifrc.org: the website of the Red Cross/Red Crescent.
www.fedworld.gov: access to a wide range of US government statistics and databases.
www.official-documents.co.uk: full-text versions of UK Command and Parliamentary papers, including the annual reports and statistical returns from government agencies (e.g. police, prisons, health, education).
www.opengov.uk: access to most British governmental information – a 'portal' for identifying other websites.
www.regard.ac.uk: results of research sponsored by the UK Economic and Social Research Council.
www.socialexclusionunit.gov.uk: the UK Social Exclusion Unit – document and research reports on deprivation and urban regeneration.
www.statistics.gov.uk: summaries of UK governmental statistics.
www.ukonline.gov.uk: a second portal to UK government websites.
www.upmystreet.co.uk: a non-governmental source of UK local statistics, including statistics on material deprivation.

News and media
www.ipl.prg/reading/news: access to a wide range of newspapers.
www.ipl.prg/reading/serials/: access to a wide range of online magazines and serials.
www.lexis-nexis.com: the largest full-text collection of newspaper articles world-wide.
www.newslibrary.com: an archive of US newspaper articles.
www.newsline.org: the site of the American Journalism Review – newspapers, magazines and broadcast media.
www.yahoo.com/r/nm: covers a variety of media.

Wire services
www.afp.com: Agence France Press.
www.itar-tass.com: TASS.
www.pa.press.net: Press Association, UK.
www.reuters.com: Reuters.
www.upi.com: United Press International, USA.
www.wire.ap.org: Associated Press, USA.

The problem with using any of this information is the question of how to evaluate its worth. As we saw in Chapter 1, when looking at the statistics of crime and mortality, you need to know quite a lot about other people's statistics before you can be reasonably sure they are valid for your purposes. The same is true of all other kinds of information. Press reports may be 'news', but they cannot be taken straightforwardly as 'fact'; even where there is no governmental or business censorship, two generations of the sociology of the media have demonstrated that many issues other than 'truth' are involved in what gets reported and how it is presented. Journal articles and, to a lesser extent, books, are safer, in that reputable academic journals follow a peer-review process by which submitted material considered by other academics, anonymously on both sides in the case of journals, before they are selected for publication. (You still have to evaluate the arguments and methods for yourself, of course!) Government material will be taken as more or less reliable and valid, depending on one's attitude to Government. Other material is to be treated with caution. As Ó Dochartaigh (2002, p. 18) points out,

> The lonely, the deluded, the obsessive. Individuals who fall into these categories seem to be heavily overrepresented on the Net.

Deliberate fraud is also not to be ruled out: nothing stops me from opening up a website in someone else's name, or the name of a University or other public organization, except subsequent legal action on the part of that person or organization. Case law has demonstrated that even where the name or apparent source of a site is grossly and probably deliberately misleading, it may still be legal if it registered the name first.

Sampling on the Net

Not everyone uses the Net, clearly, and so any conclusions based on Internet samples are likely to be in some ways biased.

Activity 5.1 (a few minutes' thought)

In what ways would you expect Net users to be untypical of the population, and in what ways are samples of them likely to be unrepresentative (a) of Net users and (b) of the general population?

This is not a particular problem of the Net. As we have seen in earlier chapters, even randomly selected target samples finish up to some extent as volunteer achieved samples and not perfectly typical of their population, because of differential non-response/refusal/failure to contact. What we need to know, about a Net sample as about any other, is *in what ways* it is likely to be unrepresentative/untypical of the population. Clearly it is restricted to those who own or have access to computers, which is a substantial limitation. It seems plausible *a priori* that older people, particularly working-class older people, may be less likely to use the web, so that web users are a select and different subset of them, but this seems less plausible when we consider people under the age of thirty, many of whom grew up with it and used it at school or at home to gather material for their homework. The view has been widely expressed that the internet-user population is a dramatically skewed sample of the population at large (Bordia, 1996; Coomber, 1997; Stanton, 1998). Szabo and Frenkl (1996) present concrete evidence that the Net-user population is skewed in just the ways that might be expected – mostly middle-class and well educated and predominantly North American. These views have been challenged, however. Smith and Leigh (1997) compared Internet and non-Internet samples and found that they differed in mean age and gender, but not in terms of ethnicity, education, sexual preference/orientation, marital status or religious affiliation. A study drawing samples *via* the American Psychological Association web page (Krantz et al., 1997) and a student sample found a wider age-range in the former but no difference in gender proportions. Clearly it is not safe to talk about 'the Internet user population'; we need to consider the nature of the sites and their probable readership. We will also want to consider the extent to which it would *matter* if the sample were unrepresentative, particularly in qualitative research, and balance this against the possibility of reaching otherwise untraceable scattered marginal or deviant groups – Coomber (1997), cited above, was a survey of drug-dealers – or drawing samples world-wide.

Most sampling/case selection on the Net entails volunteer sampling: a research instrument or invitation to participate is published on suitable sites or circulated through email mailing lists. This kind of approach allows some degree of targeting but makes it more difficult to demonstrate population validity. Ways of warranting this that have been suggested, include taking very large samples in order to minimize sampling bias (Strauss, 1996), comparing sample size to number of 'hits' on the site over the period of the survey (Hewson et al., 2003), or comparison with non-Internet samples to establish which population is appropriate for comparison (Buchanan and Smith, 1999; Smith and Leigh, 1997; Hewson et al., 2003), sampling randomly from lists of user groups as a form of cluster sampling (Swoboda et al., 1997), or sampling randomly from visitors to a given site (Dahlen, 1998, cited in Hewson et al., 2003).

Questionnaires on the Net

Survey research using the Net is becoming increasingly more common. Many companies or organizations that provide services on the Net are taking the opportunity to present satisfaction surveys or market research surveys to all or some of their users. Questionnaires to all users would be useful on a site visited relatively rarely, but on a frequently used site this kind of presentation would either generate unmanageably large numbers or risk a biased sample by sampling only a short and potentially unrepresentative time period. For frequently visited sites, with the help of a technician/ programmer, it is possible (see above) to organize presentation so that a randomly chosen sample can be generated, and indeed to sample time periods systematically.

For the casual or amateur user – the typical researcher – email presentation is probably the simplest means of delivery. An email is sent to appropriate lists of users asking them to fill in an attached questionnaire and return it as an attachment to the reply. This has the problem that it is difficult for the user to remain anonymous – more so, at any rate, than with unsigned and unnumbered questionnaires returned in envelopes, because email arrives with the address of the sender as part of the message. It has the enormous advantage of cheapness; from the researcher's point of view there is no more expense in sending thousands of copies than hundreds or tens – mailing to each list takes one single operation. There is also anecdotal evidence that those who use computers frequently may be more sympathetic to email than to material received through the post and more likely to reply to it.

Many researchers set up a special email account for the research project and close it at the end of the project, to avoid clogging up their 'working' email account with either responses to the questionnaire or the junk mailings that are often attracted when you post out to unknown recipients. Doing so can also conceal identity, where the topic area is sensitive and the researcher does not wish his or her association with it to become public knowledge, along with his or her address.

With more knowledge or technical help, or the use of one of several software packages now available on the market, the questionnaire can be presented in HTML and made very attractive and interactive. Interaction and differential routing can also be managed by connecting to the 'quiz' routines of a web-based teaching package such as Blackboard. With a bit more knowledge still, or technical help again, the questionnaire can be accessed through a link to a web site, and it is possible to control access to the site (to quota for demographic characteristics, for example) by adding preliminary 'routing' questions. Anonymity of respondents is easier to assure and to demonstrate with Net presentation than when using email.

Activity 5.2 (a few minutes)

What are the advantages, and the drawbacks, of using the Net to deliver questionnaires? List as many as you can think of.

- As was said above, a major advantage is cheapness.
- A second is that the Net and email make some 'difficult to access' populations more accessible.
- A third is that questionnaires filled in on computer are not subject to the same constraints of space as physical questionnaires; while you would want to limit the time the task takes, you do not need to limit the number of pages in order to make it *look like* a quick task.
- It is also possible to route respondents through the questionnaire more clearly than on paper-based instruments if an interactive form is used; this gives some of the advantages of interviewer-administered questionnaires without the element of personal reactivity which these inevitably entail.
- It is possible to obtain very large samples at no extra effort, or to obtain an adequately large sample in a relatively short space of time and little expense; as

Hewson et al. (2003) point out, this makes the Net survey a viable instrument for pilot studies and unfounded projects.

- There is some evidence that response rates are better and answers to open-ended questions longer on email surveys than on postal ones (Schaerfer and Dillman, 1998), though not all studies report good response rates (see, e.g. Couper et al., 1999).

- Finally, with proper design and/or by use of an appropriate software package it is possible to design questionnaires which are machine-readable, where the answers are automatically transferred to an analysis package (e.g. SPSS) or a spreadsheet compatible with one (e.g. Excel). This saves a lot of time and can save a lot of money.

The problems are mostly problems of sampling (see above). Validity is probably not an issue: there is no reason to suppose people are any more likely to lie or misrepresent themselves on email or Internet questionnaires than on postal ones. Possibly there may be problems of procedural reactivity – some people may find computer presentation more remote and impersonal than the paper or interviewer-administered questionnaire – but there is as yet no empirical evidence available to permit us to explore this concern. Given proper design it seems likely that younger respondents will find computer-mediated presentation *less* impersonal if they associate the computer with email and chat-room conversations with friends.

Qualitative Interviewing on the Net

Email is an obvious medium, in some ways, for initiating a conversation and interviewing in a relatively unstructured way. However, the conversation will be asynchronous – replies will not necessarily be posted immediately after the question is asked – and there is a remoteness about written correspondence which is felt to a lesser extent in telephone interviews but not in face-to-face interviewing. It is probably better to think of email data-collection as a different medium from interviews, though sharing many features – something more like an exchange of letters, but far faster and producing less 'mannered' and deeply considered responses. 'Chat rooms' and 'bulletin boards' allow more of the features of spoken, face-to-face conversation to be preserved. Both may seem remote to older informants and so invoke a degree of procedural reactivity, but this is less likely to be the case with younger informants (many of whom use such methods routinely as a means of communication, often with strangers or people known only 'through the computer'). There is little or no opportunity in either means of presentation for drawing on non-verbal cues, as in a face-to-face interview, but the development of video conferencing may overcome this problem.

Good results have been reported by researchers using the computer for immediate communication (e.g. O'Connor and Madge, 2000; Bennet, cited in Mann and Stewart, 2000), reporting that informants were more able than in previously conducted face-to-face research to develop their own themes and elaborations. Reports on asynchronous interviewing are more mixed. Hodkinson (2000) reports that the questions had an undue effect on the communication, which became formal and constricted, while Mann (in Mann and Stewart, 2000, p. 77) experienced no such problems.

The successful use of email to circulate anonymized contributions by other informants as a stimulus for discussion has also been reported (Ferri, 2000).

The Net may also be used to conduct group interviews/focus groups or to set up discussion panels which 'meet' more than once. There has not been a great deal of group research online so far, but the possibilities are immense (Gaiser, 1997; Mann and Stewart, 2000). Groups can be run 'in real time' or asynchronously in the form of chat rooms or bulletin boards, or with purpose-built conferencing software (or, presumably, by serial emails where the content of each message is preserved as it is forwarded to the next participant). Group research online has been used successfully in areas which might be thought too sensitive for group discussion – discussing adolescent sexuality with adolescents, for example (Schnarch, 1997).

The disadvantage, obviously, is that there is no non-verbal interaction between participants, and it is also sometimes found that turn-taking breaks down in real-time computer-mediated interaction between more than two people. However, the advantages are equally obvious. It is much easier to bring a group together on the machine than in the flesh, and differences of power or status make less impact on computer-mediated conversations than in real-time ones. Asynchronous groups are less immediate than real-time ones, but they are useful in overcoming problems of time coordination and also help to iron out differences in typing and writing speed between participants. There are suggestions that asynchronous groups allow more consideration to be given to questions, and to answers, than the immediacy of the real-time group (see Horn, 1998 on the nature of chat as opposed to conversation online).

Participating and Observing

Finally, there are clearly opportunities for observation and participation on the web. Passive observation – looking at pages and sites, including interactive sites such as chat rooms – is a self-evident possibility for research, sharing much with content analysis or critical analysis of printed text. Comparison of sites would permit comparison of imagery or ideology or discourse between different kinds of company or institution, or between the sites of individuals (classified into genders by name, perhaps, or into countries by the suffix of the email/web address). Observation and comparison of interactive sites allows study of the Net itself as an interactive virtual environment – who enters what kind of site (with personal characteristics deduced from details revealed in the interaction – or as stated by the respondent, if you control the site and can ask entrants about demographics), how they behave while on it, what actions they take and what choices they make, what rules of conduct and implicit expectations can be inferred from what people say and do.

Active participation is also a possibility. A researcher could join a chat room or work group with the intention of taking part but also exploring the nature of the group. This would be classic participant observation – taking a (minor) role in a group or context, experiencing the context as a participant, interacting with and talking to other participants, noting their explanations and justifications and exploring the rules and conventions that help to define the nature of the context. (Like 'real-life' participant observation, the entrant to virtual communities may have to become quite deeply immersed before finding or being allowed access to 'rooms' other than the most public and easily accessed – see Kendall, 1999.)

A problem, however, is that it is never quite clear *what* is being explored and *who* the participants are. This is true in all situations, on or off the Net, but it is particularly true of computer-mediated interaction which is not concerned with work issues – chat rooms and the like. It is not just that people *can* lie about who they are or falsify their personal details; it is that they *do*, in large numbers, as far as one can judge anecdotally. A culture has grown up of presenting oneself differently on the Net from in real life, to the extent that the notion of apparently 20-year-old men or women turning out to be in their fifties or pre-teens when computer correspondence leads to face-to-face meetings has become a cliché of fiction-writing. There are even sites where the adoption of a false identity is mandatory – role-play sites where a story is invented and played out in a chat-room according to pre-declared rules (e.g. that participants are vampires or thieves or super-heroes, with declared powers and histories); role-play groups also meet 'in real life', but they are less common than computer-mediated groups. The adoption of false or modified or partial identities is of research interest in its own right – though following up on it would entail researching the 'real' person as well as the fictional image, which is more difficult – and people's behaviour in these identities is also a valid research area (perhaps contrasted with typical behaviour in groups or written text). It has been argued (by, e.g. Mann and Stewart, 2000) that we can only ever observe *virtual* environments on the web, not 'real life'. This is perhaps to overstate the problem; male behaviour on the web, for example, is a case of male behaviour in general and could validly contribute insights to research on gender. The problem of identity on the web does, however, raise interesting reflexive questions about the status and generalizability of evidence, which also have implications for the other forms of Net research described above.

Current ethical wisdom is that research should be overt for the most part, in computer-mediated research as much as in research face to face with participants and for the same reasons. Passive analysis of existing sites will normally not require consent, in the same way that research on published reports and novels does not require consent; websites are in the public domain. Where information is actively collected about participants or where researchers enter an interactive relationship for the purposes of research, it is normally thought that they should make their research identity clear to participants (and probably ask the permission of the person controlling or co-ordinating the site before entering it for research purposes). Permission is also usually asked, even to post advertisements on sites asking for volunteer informants.

Conclusion

Research does not *have to* involve first-hand data collection; it can also be based on material made available by other people. Government departments and other organizations publish statistics covering their area of operation, and these can be very useful, provided due allowance is made for their provenance and some imagination used about allowing, in drawing conclusions, for the way in which they are collected.

(Conclusion continued)

Many of these statistics are available on the Internet, as answers to queries or pre-set tables or even sometimes as data sets that can be re-analyzed. The Internet is an invaluable tool for the researcher. It can be used to locate books, articles and reports in locations which might not otherwise have been accessible. It provides abstracts and often full-text copies of a wide range of sources. Much material is 'posted' on the Net that might not be accessible in printed form or which is never printed. It can be used as a medium for contacting research informants, using survey questionnaires or less structured forms of interrogation and conversation. The content of what is posted on the Net and the interaction between people which occurs naturally in computer-mediated form can also be topics of research in their own right and yield valuable clues to what is thought, said and done in 'real life' contexts.

More even than any other source of information, however, we need to think reflexively about the validity of Net-derived information. *Anything* can be posted on the Net, by anybody. You need no authority to put something there, where it can be accessed by other people, and there are few checks on authenticity. You can pretend to be whom you like or alter your ascribed characteristics; you can lie, or mislead, or simply be mistaken, out of ignorance or as part of wider mental malfunction. Falsehood, bias, bigotry and zealotry are present alongside truth, science and thoughtful analysis. All Net material, including 'first-hand' data, is therefore to be treated with some caution.

Key Terms

Asynchronous presentation   interaction in which the replies may not be immediate but be made at any time. (Email is the most obvious example of this.) The opposite is synchronous/real-time interaction.

Bulletin Board   an asynchronous chat room – a site where different people can leave messages (on an agreed topic) which can be read by all subscribers to the Board.

Chat room   a synchronous Bulletin Board – a site where subscribers to the room can talk to each other in real time and all can read everyone's contributions.

Editable text   text which can be inserted into and worked on within a word-processing program.

Email   one-to-one (or one-to-many) private correspondence using computer links.

Excel   Microsoft's spreadsheet, which allows data storage and simple calculation.

(Continued)

(Key Terms continued)

Hit   a visit to a site. (Most hit-counters cannot say whether a number of hits represents x different people or one person visiting x times.)

HTML   a form of presentation which produces good-looking web pages and can readily be made interactive with the user but which is less suitable for copying into text/word-processed documents.

Internet   (also called Net or Web or World-Wide Web): A collective name for all the sites available by telephone connection.

Keyword   a word or phrase used for searching for references to a given topic. Keywords can often be linked by 'and', 'or' and perhaps 'not' to form flexible and sophisticated search expressions.

Page   an Internet location. *See* Site. (However, some sites may have multiple pages, separately accessible or hierarchically organized.)

Real time   *See* Asynchronous Presentation.

Search engine   a program or routine which will look at a wide range of Internet sites and search for a word, phrase or keyword in their titles or their full text.

Searchable text   text which will allow internal electronic searching for characters or keywords.

Site   a location within the Web which is the 'property' of one person or organization, who post (makes available) on it material which is to be accessible to all comers. (Some sites have passwords for all or part of their contents, so that it is necessary to subscribe and be admitted.)

Synchronous   *See* Asynchronous presentation.

Web   *See* Internet.

Further Reading

Hewson, C., Yule, P., Laurent, D. and Vogel, C. (2003) *Internet Research Methods: a practical guide for the social and behavioural sciences*, London, Sage.

Mann, C. and Stewart, F. (2000) *Internet Communication and Qualitative Research*, London, Sage.

Research Proposal Activity 5

Will you be using the Web at all as part of your research?

1   *For searching the literature, etc.*: what databases will you search for abstracts of journals, books, etc? What other sites might be useful?
2   *For secondary source of statistics – as the main data, or as context for your own empirical work*: what sources are available? Do they have the kind of detail you need? Are there agencies or academics you might contact to get more detail or different figures?
3   *For secondary qualitative sources – as the main data, or as context for your own empirical work*: are there books, brochures, handbooks, governmental

reports, newspaper articles, personal or institutional web pages, that would be useful? Do you have a strategy for locating such material?

4 *Quantitative data collection*: are there pages which might act as your 'texts' for content analysis (see also previous question)? Do you intend to use the email or the web in general to distribute questionnaires? Have you considered questions of access and permission? What kind of a sample are you likely to get, and is this adequate for your purposes?

5 *Qualitative data collection*: are you proposing passive observation of activity or content on the net? Do you propose overt interaction – conversations or interviews on the net? Do you propose covert or overt participation – taking part in, for example, chat-room sessions? In all these cases have you considered the ethics of doing so and the representativeness of the material you would find?

6

Using Documents

Ruth Finnegan

Interviews, questionnaires, observation and experiments – the forms discussed so far – are all important sources of data in social and educational research, and widely drawn on by researchers. But they do *not* comprise all the forms of information gathering, despite what is sometimes implied in 'methods' textbooks. Existing sources, whether in writing, figures or electronic form, are also important bases for research. They can function both as the main source for the researcher's conclusions and to supplement information from other sources.

Some understanding of the use of documentary and related sources is highly relevant in three main ways. First, they form a major source of data in social research. This type of source is often played down, perhaps because, since it is shared with a number of other disciplines, it may not seem quite so distinctive of the social sciences as data generated through questionnaires, surveys or experiments. However, social researchers have, in fact, built extensively on the existence of such sources as government reports, official and unofficial records, private papers, and statistical collections. As with the other forms of information gathering discussed in this book, these sources have both advantages and limitations, and they can be used well or badly.

Secondly, the use of existing sources comes in at various stages of the research process (in so far, that is, as these stages are separable). One phase is that of the preliminary 'literature search'. This usually comes near the start of any research endeavour and so is not highlighted in this chapter, which is concerned primarily with the phase of 'data collection and construction'. However, there is frequently some overlap between these phases, if only because existing sources are not only a source of data for producing research findings in the first place, but are also commonly used for their criticism, or for further development later. Thus, they are doubly important in assessing research.

The third point is that these sources are not neutral asocial data whose import is necessarily self-evident. Their selection and interpretation are affected, not only by practical constraints like access or timing, but also by the researcher's aims and viewpoint. As you will see, this theme needs to be further extended into the question of how the sources themselves come into being. Since there can be selection and interpretation here too, a piece of research building on documentary sources needs to be judged (among other things) by how carefully the researcher considers and explains these aspects of the sources.

It is worth noting at the outset that, although the phrase 'documentary sources' was obviously first used to refer to sources in the form of written documents (still one prime meaning of the term and a leading form of source material), it is nowadays sometimes widened to include other sources, such as radio or film material which are neither primarily in writing nor in 'documents' in the traditional sense. Both in this chapter and elsewhere you will encounter both senses. Indeed, the ambiguity is not without its uses in reminding us that existing sources comprise materials of many different kinds. Most consist of words or numbers, but there are also such forms as maps, charts and photographs; and audio or video sources are also increasingly exploited. The medium for their storage, transmission and consultation also varies. Some are in manuscript, others published in print. Some are on paper, others on microfilm or microfiche, in audio-visual media or (increasingly important and also discussed in Chapter 5) in electronic form.

Documentary Sources

This chapter gives further consideration to principles for evaluating existing sources as data, with the main focus on documentary sources in the traditional sense of textual documents which are written (or otherwise reproduced typographically) largely in the form of *words*. (As you will see, this needs some qualification as we go along, but for the moment we will let it stand.)

There is a reason for taking mainly *written* texts as the primary focus here. Written documents exist in huge numbers in our society, both of a private or personal kind and in the form of what Hakim (1987: 36) refers to as 'administrative records':

> Vast quantities of information are collated and recorded by organizations and individuals for their own purposes, well beyond the data collected by social scientists purely for research purposes.

Indeed, both the proliferation of written records, and communication through writing more generally, are widely seen as major features of modern society. Some scholars would go so far as to regard them as *the* defining attribute of Western industrial culture, whether because of the (arguably) central role of print in our modern consciousness or through the development of modern bureaucracy, with its reliance on written rules and administrative records (for some of the arguments on this, see Goody, 1986; Finnegan, 1988). Something of the variety of documentary sources can be judged from Box 6.1.

Box 6.1 *Summary of types of source for the contemporary and recent UK*

Standard and official sources

- Works of reference, e.g. *Whitaker's Almanack, Statesman's Year Book, Annual Abstract of Statistics, The Times Index, Keesing's Contemporary Archives, Who's Who, Annual Register of World Events*
- Government reports including (a) parliamentary papers (i.e. all papers ordered by or laid before either House of Parliament and papers printed by command of the government, including reports of Royal Commissions); and (b) non-command papers (e.g. reports of departmental committees)
- Statistical records, including the Census and the Registrar-General's Reports (the decennial Census, and the annual Registrar-General's Statistical Review of England and Wales and Annual Report of the Registrar-General for Scotland). For further examples see Box 5.1 in the previous chapter
- Annual and special reports, local and unofficial, including reports by local Medical Officers of Health, and reports of companies, societies, schools, universities, political parties, trade unions, etc.
- Parliamentary debates (*Hansard*)
- Documents on foreign policy issued by, or with the cooperation of, the Foreign Office

Cabinet and other papers

- Cabinet records (because of the '30-year rule' these cannot be consulted for the most recent period)
- Other government documents (the same difficulty applies)
- Private papers, e.g. private papers of politicians (many deposited in libraries throughout the country), trade unions or political parties

Memoirs, diaries and biographies

(These may be particularly useful for the period for which government records are closed by the '30-year rule')

- Biographies and autobiographies
- Diaries (not very many available)
- Memoirs (available in abundance: a sometimes informative but hazardous source to use)

Letters, contemporary writing

- Current affairs, including works by journalists as well as by social scientists
- Social surveys, including public opinion polls
- Novels, poetry, plays (imaginative writing provides source material of a particular kind, more useful for answering some kinds of question than others)
- Newspapers and other periodicals

Box 6.1   *(Continued)*

Images, sound and objects

- Film
- Photographs, maps and pictures
- Sound and video recordings (including audio and video cassettes; also programmes currently going out via radio and television and the records of these – if preserved – in the archives)
- Interviews, tape-recorded and other
- Museums and their contents
- History on the ground: townscapes, landscapes, aerial photographs

Computerized records

- Any one or more of the above stored or distributed electronically (e.g. the BBC 'Domesday' interactive video-disc; statistical records stored as computer databases)

Source: derived from Mowatt, 1971

Not all sources follow the traditional model of written documents: printed text is not the only medium for reproducing words. Modern technologies have made possible the storage and dissemination of sights and sounds other than traditional verbal texts: in radio, for example, film or photographs, and other categories listed under 'Images, sound and objects' in Box 6.1. Varieties of documentary sources include:

- *Medium*: for example, papyrus, parchment, stone, tape, cassette, micro-film/ fiche, electronic.
- *Form*: usually words/text and figures, but also other related forms: graphic, picto-rial, audio, video and material; and all of these forms expressed in digital tech-nology (as discussed in Chapter 5).

These other (non-written) forms and media are now common enough to be given the label of 'documentary'.

A final point is that, where researchers rely on documentary sources for their data, their methods have to be evaluated in rather a different way from that applied to research based on interviews, observation or experiment. Researchers using documentary sources

> have to compile their own *post hoc* account of the procedures and methods used to compile … the records on which a study is based. This account replaces the usual methodological report on how data were specially collected in other types of study. (Hakim, 1987: 41)

Therefore, to understand – and so be able to produce a critique of – the method-ological procedures in document-based research, we need to explore further some-thing of the nature of documents and how they are compiled: how they come into being. Some of the basic principles at work here are considered in the rest of this chapter. (Further treatment of more specialist and advanced techniques for textual analysis is given later in the book.)

Some Initial Distinctions

Let us start by looking at some distinctions both between different types of documentary sources and between different ways of using them. Both distinctions have their uses. They also, as we will see, have their limitations – and limitations which, in their turn, can be illuminating.

Primary Versus Secondary Sources

When considering how researchers use documentary sources to collect and analyze evidence, one of the most commonly invoked distinctions is between 'primary' and 'secondary' sources. Historians and others conventionally regard as primary sources those that were written (or otherwise came into being) by the people directly involved and at a time contemporary or near contemporary with the period being investigated. Primary sources, in other words, form the basic and original material for providing the researcher's raw evidence. Secondary sources, by contrast, are those that discuss the period studied but are brought into being at some time after it, or otherwise somewhat removed from the actual events. Secondary sources copy, interpret or judge material to be found in primary sources. Thus, the Magna Carta would be a primary source for the history of thirteenth-century England, while an account of thirteenth-century politics by a twentieth-century historian would be a secondary source. Both can be useful – but they are different. There are many possible controversies over detailed definition here, but by and large the distinction between primary and secondary material is widely accepted as a fundamental one, defined in terms of the 'contemporaneity' of the source and closeness to the origin of the data. True research, it is often implied, should ideally involve acquaintance with all the relevant primary and secondary sources for the topic being studied, but with particular emphasis on the primary sources – the basic and original data for study.

It is true that this distinction can be pressed too far and ultimately (as will become clear in later sections of this chapter) breaks down. But at one level it can be very helpful for assessing others' usage of documentary sources in their research. A report which purports to be based on detailed evidence about some complex question, but in fact depends only on consulting secondary accounts without ever getting to grips with the primary sources, could certainly be open to criticism. Examples might be drawing conclusions about a company's financial standing from a speculative newspaper comment (secondary) rather than its detailed balance sheets, or deducing the family structure of a particular town in, say 1881, not by studying such sources as the 1881 Census Enumerators' books (primary), but by generalizing from twentieth-century secondary accounts. General matters outside the researcher's main topic of interest are, reasonably enough, not usually followed up in primary sources. Time and cost constraints play a part here, as so often, in limiting the researcher's scope. Similarly, primary sources would not need to be researched for matters of common and agreed knowledge (like, say, the date of the establishment of the European Common Market). They would not need to be researched, that is, unless that topic itself became a matter of controversy, turning on some fine point of interpretation, or the researcher wanted to counter conventional wisdom. In such cases, it is not uncommon to 'go back to the original sources' precisely so as to issue a well-founded challenge.

Each case, then, must be taken according to its specific circumstances. But, in general, asking about the *nature* of the sources used to obtain the information for the research is one key question to pursue in assessing a piece of research. And one of the central aspects of this is whether the researcher made use of primary or of secondary sources and how far such a choice can be judged the appropriate one.

'Direct' and 'Indirect' Uses

One way of approaching a given source is to seek information directly from the factual content contained in it. Thus a university's published annual report will give information about numbers of students, staff, departments or courses, its library resources, its future plans and so on – useful information for someone researching on such topics. Similarly, a newspaper report, a biography, or a column in *Hansard* will provide direct information about certain events or situations which could be essential for answering questions to which a researcher needs the answers. The same could be applied to just about any other documentary source you could think of: parliamentary papers, the Census, diaries, letters, broadcasts, advertisements, organizational records. All of these could, on appropriate occasions, be the source of direct information.

Activity 6.1 (pause for a moment)

Does the statement above raise any problems?

You will probably have identified the fundamental problem here even before I asked you – the problem, that is, of whether you can trust the overt message in the source. The *Hansard* speech, the newspaper account, the advertisement, even the 'authoritative' biography, might all have their own hidden agendas and select or 'twist' the evidence to fit their own purposes.

So, if we cannot trust the overt content, does this then mean that the source is useless? This is where the *indirect* use of sources comes in. The glossy public relations leaflet for a firm or a university might not – to put it baldly – state 'the truth, the whole truth, and nothing but the truth'. But the *gloss* put on the message can itself convey indirect information about, say, the ideals aimed at, the standard terminology used in a particular place or period, the kinds of subterfuges engaged in, or the sort of images thought likely to appeal to the intended market. Similarly, even the most self-indulgent and flagrantly non-factual autobiography might tell you something unintentionally about, say, the author's perspective, motivations, personality or imagined audience, or about the social context in which she or he was writing. In other words, a great deal of information can often be gained from a source *indirectly,* even when a *direct* approach employing a (perhaps simplified) model of information-transfer in terms of literal truth is likely to be less successful.

As with the primary/secondary distinction, the direct/indirect distinction becomes more complex the more closely you look at actual source usage, and ultimately it too breaks down. It is a useful one to start out from, however, and the 'indirect' use of sources is particularly worth bearing in mind in the following section.

How Documentary Sources Come into Being

Faced with written or numerical records, it is easy to forget that these sources do not just arise automatically through some natural process. They may look authoritative, as if they could not have been produced in any other way. But, in effect, all these sources are the results of human activity. They are produced by human beings acting in particular circumstances and within the constraints of particular social, historical or administrative conditions.

Often these sources rest on a series of human decisions. An individual decides to write a diary or memoir, a committee agrees to issue a report, a sociologist decides to work on a book about drug addicts, a political party decides to publish an election manifesto, or a business organization to issue an annual report (this may be as much a result of a taken-for-granted routine as of a single once-and-for-all decision, but a decision in some sense is involved). This may be followed by further decisions: that the diary (or memoir) will be, for example, indiscreet or hard-hitting, that the report will stress one aspect of the situation more than another, that the sociological study will concentrate on one particular locality, that the manifesto or the annual statement will play up certain issues and factors and play down or even suppress others. All these decisions will obviously affect the nature of the source as it comes into existence. It can equally be affected by what could be called 'unconscious decisions'. The diarists may (not admitted even to themselves) be really writing with an eye to later publication and so be representing events, personalities and even inner feelings in the light of this; the committee may, without members themselves fully realizing it, form part of a general reaction within the organization against the increasing influence of some special group and be directed as much to countering that influence as to stating isolated recommendations; the sociologist may turn the research direction to fit the interests of those who control research funds or the accepted wisdom of the moment among established academic colleagues; the details in the party manifesto may result from a compromise between several opposing factions; and so on.

In all these cases a series of choices has been made – at least in the sense that the result *might* have been otherwise. The resultant source can thus often be better assessed if one can discover the kind of process by which it came into being. We can in this way learn more about the author's circumstances, and (perhaps) about the influences on him or her by other individuals or groups, who may sometimes bear more responsibility than at first appears. If some account has come into existence through rumour rather than concrete evidence, this too is relevant. Or some particular source might be a forgery – if so, it is essential for someone using the source to know this. The cautions about statistical sources made earlier could equally well have been brought in here: to assess them effectively we need to know how they were collected and by whom. So, too, we can bring in the whole process of exactly how material on a particular subject has been gathered. Knowing how a source came into being may be directly relevant both for understanding *who* was responsible for it (and thus the kind of interpretation likely to be involved) and for assessing its reliability.

There is a further aspect too. This is a matter of the *audience* or purpose towards which a particular source is directed. A political speech may be prepared and delivered to stir up the party faithful and have more comments about what *ought* to be so than descriptions of actual situations; reports in particular newspapers may be directed to a readership which demands, or is thought to demand, personalized and dramatic stories rather than dispassionate analysis in depth; scholarly books and articles are often directed to a readership consisting of academic colleagues and competitors. Who the supposed audience is and the extent to which the creator of the account/speech/report shares the audience's preconceptions are likely to affect both what is said and what is left unsaid – once again, this is essential background information for an assessment of the source.

How material is presented is also likely to be affected by the audience the author has in mind. Certain styles of presentation have become accepted as appropriate for particular types of publication: in other words, the style gives yet another clue to the nature of the source, and hence what you can expect from it. Academic articles, for example, can adopt a number of different formats, but they are commonly expressed in relatively dispassionate language ('is' rather than 'ought' statements predominate, with critical discussion of the central concepts), relate explicitly the content of the article to work by other scholars, pursue a coherent argument and conclude on a general or theoretical point. Political memoirs, on the other hand, generally use a more chatty and personal style, giving a vivid picture of events and the author's contribution to them, rather than reaching any general conclusion. Newspaper styles vary considerably according to readership and editorial policy, but once again – as, too, in television – there tends to be an emphasis on personalization and the glamour of unusual or striking events. Statistical tables, by contrast, especially in official publications, have their own appropriate style of presentation: impersonal, starkly quantitative and unlikely to be chatty. Thus, although the distinction we looked at above, between primary and secondary sources, is indeed a useful one, *no* source is really primary in the literal and ultimate sense of giving the plain, unvarnished facts. There is always some element of production and shaping, some process by which the source came into being.

Further, we can now go back again to the 'direct' and 'indirect' uses of sources. When we grasp the many complexities behind the creation of sources, it seems too simple just to contrast the 'surface' message of a document with all the indirect or implicit meanings that could be drawn from it. For, as will become even clearer in a later discussion, most, perhaps all, texts contain a series of meanings and functions. These depend on both the viewpoint of the creator (or creators – for sometimes there are multiple strands even at the most simple level) and that of anyone reading or hearing it. Texts are typically multi-functional and multi-vocal, and which elements one picks out of these is seldom a simple direct/indirect alternative, but a matter of judgement and interpretation.

There is also the simple but extremely important point that what counts as primary (or secondary) or as direct (or indirect) depends crucially on the *purpose* of the reader – or the researcher. Once again, the role of documentary sources (like so many others) turns out to be relative, rather than absolute.

The implication of all this for assessing researchers' use of written sources as data must by now be obvious. Sources have to be *interpreted* not just consulted. And one fundamental criterion for how sensibly the sources are thus interpreted in the research you are assessing is precisely what the researcher has used them for, and how far he or she *has* taken account of how they came into being: by whom, under what circumstances and constraints, with what motives and assumptions, and how selected. To ignore all these aspects and merely take the sources at face value is, admittedly, more disastrous in some cases than others. But it is *always* a question to be asked about any use of written sources as data.

Further Questions to Ask

Thinking about how sources have come into being will lead to other related questions to ask when assessing the use of documentary sources as data. Among these are the following:

(1) *Has the researcher made use of the existing sources relevant and appropriate for his or her research topic?* Given the wealth of existing sources indicated above – verbal, numerical, audio-visual, electronic – this is a sensible question to ask in assessing any piece of research. Sometimes, of course, there are *no* relevant sources – or problems about access, quality or their specific nature make their use less appropriate than data gathered directly by the researcher. But often they *are* available and their use would save time, money and trouble – and, in some cases, (arguably) lead to more accurate or insightful results.

This is partly a matter of the overall design of the research and of the initial 'literature search'. But it also affects the data-collection phase (in so far as this can be separated as a specific stage): collecting and analyzing the information needed for the researcher's final conclusions. 'Not knowing, or not consulting, the relevant sources' is an effective and not uncommon criticism of someone's research.

(2) *How far has the researcher taken account of any 'twisting' or selection of the facts in the sources used?* This is a simple question in one way – it is an *obvious* consideration to raise, after all. But, in another way, it can prove an elusive question, one extremely hard to elucidate. Deliberate falsification, forgery or explicit propaganda is perhaps relatively straightforward to detect, even if sometimes missed in practice by naive or uninformed researchers. More difficult to assess is the less conscious shaping of what is represented in written reports. Whatever form this takes, there is bound to be some social filtering, possibly because they are produced by interested parties to suit their own views and preconceptions, dictated by particular administrative needs and arrangements, influenced by currently dominant models, theories or interpretations among scholars, and so on. It is worth remembering that a source purporting to represent generally held views or an 'objective assessment' of the situation sometimes expresses only the views of a minority or of a particular interest group. Indeed, it is not uncommon for people to speak rhetorically of the common good rather than of their own specific interests. They rightly consider they will in this way get a better hearing for their case, as well as sometimes being sincerely convinced that their own and the general interest coincide.

Besides such cases, there is always the possibility that what are assumed to be the views of 'the public' are in fact no more than those of the rich, educated or powerful. Marx put this point with particular clarity and force when he wrote:

> The ideas of the ruling class are, in every age, the ruling ideas: i.e. the class which is the dominant *material* force in society is at the same time its dominant *intellectual* force. The class which has the means of material production at its disposal, has control at the same time over the means of mental production, so that in consequence the ideas of those who lack the means of mental production are, in general, subject to it. (Marx, *German Ideology*, transl. in Bottomore and Rubel, 1963: 63)

One need not agree with the details of Marx's analysis (or even with his use of the concept of 'class') to appreciate the point being made here.

Bias or selectivity need not be deliberate or ill motivated to be pervasive in sources. Indeed, 'bias' may not even be the correct term here, suggesting as it does a concept of some absolute and asocial correspondence with the 'bare facts' which could be reached if we could only get through the misleading veil of 'bias'. There are many philosophical controversies over the nature of 'truth', but one common position among many social scientists would now certainly be that *all* human formulations are inevitably shaped by the social and cultural contexts in which they are created, and by the individuals or collectivities who create them. It does not follow that they are necessarily 'false' in some simplified sense, nor that they are valueless. But it does mean that interpretation, rather than an automatic 'reading off' of the results, is needed in analyzing any human-constructed formulation, written, spoken or gestured.

(3) *What kind of selection has the researcher made in her or his use of the sources and on what principles?* Sometimes the amount of source material potentially relevant to a particular issue is huge and *some* selectivity is necessary; it will also, of course, depend on the aims and parameters of the research. But with documentary, as with any other sources, *how* the selection is made is crucial. Written sources sometimes come in relatively measurable units. If so, similar sampling techniques to those discussed in Chapter 2 might well, depending on the nature of the enquiry, be appropriate. Many, however, do not, in which case has the researcher adopted other principles to ensure a fair and representative coverage of the questions to be investigated? Either way there are still problems. How can you test whether or not the treatment has been representative without knowing the full list of possible sources from which the selection has been made? And what counts as 'fair' or 'representative' may depend on one's viewpoint. A similar question could be asked, not just of the researcher's conscious or unconscious selection among the sources, but also of the picture conveyed by those sources themselves.

The above assumes that sources *are* in existence and that the researcher's use of them can be judged by how far he or she takes advantage of their availability. But there is also the further problem that sources do not just 'exist' in some natural state for the researcher to 'sample'. They are preserved selectively and, once again, in a social context. Quite apart from the accidents of time, some written sources are more likely to be lost than others – depending among other things on their content, medium or location – and further selectivity in their preservation is imposed by, for example, changing academic or political fortunes. There is also the possibility of direct censorship, secrecy and confidentiality, particularly if there is something in the sources perceived as to someone's discredit, and of denial of access by those controlling the sources. It can never just be assumed, without checking, that to consult just the available documentary sources provides a fair coverage.

(4) *How far does a source which describes a particular incident or case reflect the general situation?* This is a relatively straightforward question, though it can also lead into some more detailed points like the usefulness or otherwise of 'case studies'. Often one has to go to other sources besides the original one studied to answer the question. Can the account also be taken as true of other kinds of people and situations? It may be that there is no explicit claim in the account that what is described there also applies to other cases, but there may be an *implication* that it does – and this is sometimes all the more effective from *not* being explicitly stated.

It is often worth bearing in mind here the common tendency for the news media to highlight the flamboyant and the unusual rather than the humdrum and ordinary, and to personalize events rather than fill in the overall social background. So when a researcher is using documentary sources to gather information, how far does he or she appear to be alive to these possible distorting effects, and to have taken account of them?

(5) *Is the source concerned with recommendations, ideals or what ought to be done?* If so, it does not necessarily provide any evidence about what *is* done or is so in practice, but it is often tempting for researchers using such sources to leap to this mistaken conclusion.

Explicitly normative statements (i.e. those which clearly state that something *ought* to be done) are relatively easy to recognize and criticize. But, in other cases, what are really normative statements about what *ought* to be are often expressed in language more suited to describing what *is*. When it is a question of policy statements it is often hard to sort out just how far the statement is merely an empty ideal for propaganda purposes and how far a guiding principle for practice (with perhaps certain unavoidable exceptions). However, difficult to answer as it is, this is often a question worth asking, and a researcher who seems not to have considered such issues could certainly be criticized as naïve.

(6) *How relevant is the context of the source?* The particular points described or emphasized in the source may need to be interpreted in the light of the historical context in which the source arose: the particular crisis in which the author was involved, the political state of play, the nature of public opinion at the time – in fact, all the background factors which influence how both the author and the intended audience would understand the words in the context in which they were originally said or written. Taken out of context, this original meaning may be misunderstood. Similarly, the context in which particular administrative records were compiled or the constraints under which the compilers acted are all part of the background which a critical researcher has to consider.

(7) *With statistical sources: what were the assumptions according to which the statistics were collected and presented?* Statistical records, too, are not just self-evident facts of nature. They have to be collected, interpreted and presented. In so doing, a number of assumptions must inevitably be made about, for instance, what is a suitable sample, what categories are to be counted, how they are to be defined, the questions used to get at data, and so on.

One particularly important set of assumptions are those that shape the basic categories employed: what the statistics are in effect *about*. In statistics referring to 'the crime rate', for example, what is the category 'crime' assumed to mean? If it is 'crimes known to the police', that will result in one figure; if 'people prosecuted', in another (lesser) figure; if 'persons found guilty', yet another (lesser still). For this reason, always look carefully at the *title* of tables and figures cited by researchers.

Here, too, some considerable background knowledge of the subject is often near-essential for evaluating a researcher's use of the figures. This enables one to look at the assumptions behind statistical sources on the subject more critically and knowledgeably. Knowing how they were collected, by whom and in what circumstances, is one unavoidable precondition for interpreting statistics. So, too, may be some grasp of the ways in which new categories or definitions can be introduced, such as those in the definitions of 'employment' or 'poverty' in the UK in the 1980s discussed in the previous chapter.

(8) *And, finally, having taken all the previous factors into account, do you consider that the researcher has reached a reasonable interpretation of the meaning of the sources?* This central question is seldom a simple one to answer. But it has to be faced. For, irrespective of all the care we take in considering the background, counting the units, analyzing the contents, in the end few or no humanly created sources are just transparent purveyors of clear-cut and objective 'truth'. Interpretation is always needed, not only by those constructing the documents, but also by those intended and unintended audiences who consult them.

This is more complex because of the multi-layered nature of meaning, something of which we are nowadays becoming increasingly aware. A document – whether the transcript of a speech, a government paper, a personal diary or a set of business records – may be perceived in one way by one reader, in another by others. The interpretations may vary as between different interested parties, historical periods and geographical cultures – and this without any of these interpretations necessarily being 'wrong' (some may well be, of course). And it is always a possibility that a source which it would be misleading to interpret as evidence for one purpose (interpreting a firm's publicity handout as providing the facts about its actual financial standing) may well be an excellent source if interpreted as evidence for, say, the current conventions in the public relations industry and the sorts of values thought likely to appeal to its targeted readership. This recalls the difference which Arthur Marwick (1977: 63) neatly makes between the 'witting' and 'unwitting' evidence provided by sources. *Which* of these is considered, for what purposes, and in what mix, is also a matter of interpretation.

Conclusion

The sources of evidence discussed in this chapter are inevitably historical in nature. But that is not the crucial characteristic from the point of view of the social researcher. The evidence on which the social sciences is based always relates to past human behaviour. The crucial distinction is between the evidence which social researchers have arranged to be collected with a particular purpose in mind, and the evidence from other sources which has not usually been brought into existence with the social scientist's research purpose in mind.

(Continued)

(Conclusion continued)

A most useful distinction to make in approaching the use of sources of information is that mentioned above between *wittingly* and *unwittingly* gathered evidence. Where the social scientist arranges for evidence to be collected, that evidence is wittingly gathered with the purpose of the study in mind. But where other sources are used, the first question that the researcher must ask is whether the evidence came into existence in order to serve the same or similar purposes to the study being made.

In many cases, the answer will be positive; for example, where a study replicates an earlier study or one made of a different population. However, much of the evidence of value to the social scientist will have come into existence for quite different purposes. In other words, it provides unwitting evidence. The second question the researcher must ask is about the nature of the purpose which led to the evidence being created. Why was the letter written? What was the purpose of collecting the statistic? Who took the photograph, and why did he or she take it?

A difference in *purpose* may not reduce the *value* of the evidence. But it is important to know the collection purpose in order to be able to interpret the evidence properly and to assess its value. Nearly all the points made in this chapter stem from asking such questions about the ways in which the evidence which may be useful for social research was created.

Key Terms

Administrative records   records, in written form or in figures, produced as a by-product of the operation of an institution, firm or department.

Direct use   interrogation of records for their factual content.

Form   mode of presentation – e.g. words/text, pictures, audio.

Indirect use   interrogation of records for their unwitting content – what they betray about the writer, for example – or as examples of a form of presentation (e.g. as typical advertisements of a given period).

Medium   the physical carrier of the content – e.g. paper, stone, microfiche.

Primary sources   documents providing raw data for the researcher.

Secondary sources documents providing information *about* primary sources.

Unwitting evidence   *see* Indirect Use.

Further Reading

Becker, H.S. (ed.) (1981) *Exploring Society Photographically,* Chicago, Northwestern University Press.

Finnegan, R. (1992) *Oral Traditions and the Verbal Arts: a Guide to Research Practices,* London, Routledge.

Hakim, C. (1987) *Research Design: Strategies and Choices in the Design of Social Research,* ch. 4, London, Unwin Hyman.

Kitson Clark, G. (1967) *The Critical Historian: Guide for Research Students Working on Historical Subjects,* New York, Garland.
Plummer, K. (1983) *Documents of Life,* London, Allen and Unwin.

Research Proposal Activity 6

This chapter has focused on the use of documentary (and other) sources. In designing a research proposal you could usefully consider the following questions:

I   What primary and secondary sources are available on the topic at the centre of the research proposal?
2   What assessments can be made regarding the validity of these sources? Who produced them, when, how and for whom?
3   How valuable are such sources for the formulation of your research questions, the overall design of the research, aspects of data collection and/or as triangulation on the validity of conclusions derived from first-hand research?
4   Is the research question such that documents are the only means by which it can be investigated?

PART III

DATA ANALYSIS

7

Preparing Numerical Data

Betty Swift

This chapter is about a process that receives scant attention in many research reports: namely, the process of transforming 'raw' data into variables that can be analyzed to produce the information found in the results sections of such reports. In other words, we shall be looking at the extent to which the data on which research arguments are based are not 'found in the world', but are *constructed* by the researcher(s). This is not to say that data are false or fictional: all our knowledge of the world is constructed because it all depends crucially, not just on perception, but on *interpretation* of what we experience. As readers of research, however, we need to remind ourselves of the extent to which interpretation and manipulation take place even before data are analyzed. In this chapter we shall be considering mainly quantitative data – data expressed in numbers and counts – because numbers give the strongest impression of factual accuracy and do not appear to bear the marks of interpretation. The degree of interpretation involved in qualitative research is more obvious to the reader and is discussed elsewhere in the book.

With the exception of highly structured data which are to be analyzed in a pre-specified way, the process of 'preparing' data always involves exploration of their characteristics and structure. This is the stage at which the researcher 'tunes into' the meaning and messages in his or her data and builds up an appreciation of the nuances and structure and the possibilities for analysis. The appreciation includes recognition of errors and omissions, as well as the development of a deepening understanding of the comparisons and other possibilities for analysis that are likely to be productive. Even for an experienced researcher, every occasion of 'taking a first look at the data' is one in which there are novel things to be appreciated and new possibilities for developing his or her methodologies and ideas.

What is under discussion here is that part of the analysis that is largely invisible in the final report: the tidying up and recategorization which precedes the main data analysis. You will seldom be able to examine what goes on at this stage in any detail when you read research reports, but you need a strong awareness of it in order not to be seduced by the 'facts' with which you are presented; many, if not all, of the findings follow this stage of the research process and are therefore, at least in part, a construction of the coding and manipulation process.

Establishing the Nature of the Problem

The rest of this chapter is, in effect, a large-scale role-play in which I am inviting you to participate. In my job in the Institute of Educational Technology, the Open University's 'in-house' research unit, I am continually being approached by all kinds of people – 'management', course teams, fellow lecturers who have been doing research, research students, administrators, outside agencies – for help with data. They have data which they have collected, acquired or inherited from a predecessor, and they want to know what to do with them – how to get them into the best shape for analysis in order to answer their research questions. From this point in the chapter, I want you to put yourself in my sandals and see what you would do if you were in my job, or sitting next to me, when such questions arise.

A consultation begins, of course, with a request. The 'presenting problem' may be at any level of generality and address any stage of the process of preparing the data for analysis. It may be a contained problem, involving just one small part of the process of dealing with data. For example, the researcher might just want to discuss the problem of categorizing answers to a particular open-ended question: for instance, 'What have you found particularly excellent about studying with this University?' In this case, all that may be needed is a session with the researcher, involving inspection of a sample of the data, together with discussion of possible options for categorizing and coding the data in the light of his or her objectives. This might be followed up, perhaps, by later discussions of problems arising in the client's initial attempts to categorize the answers to the question. In many cases, however, problems which appear to be quite contained none the less require that we build up knowledge about the data and the project as a whole. Without the requisite knowledge, we might make suggestions which are all right in principle but inappropriate or not possible given the resources and time available:

1 Decisions about what to do with data require an understanding of the particular characteristics of the data, based on information about how they have been collected as well as their content and the nature of the sample.

2 They also require an understanding of the desired 'outcomes' of the research. Information on outcomes is needed because, in making what we hope will be optimum decisions, we shall be continually (a) checking back to see in what ways we are constrained by the design decisions (including compromises that had to be made); and (b) looking ahead to the data analysis to optimize the possibilities for achieving the research objectives.

3 Beyond this, it is useful to have in mind the kind of report that is required. For example, for an academic paper it might be appropriate to work towards transformation

of the raw data into scales that summarize the data prior to hypothesis testing. For many audiences, it is more appropriate to keep quite close to the original data so that readers can see the relationship between the original questions and the results.

Activity 7.1 (10 minutes)

Think back to what you have learnt so far in this book about research design and data collection. What information might we need to understand before we can begin to discuss what to do with the data produced by any enquiry?

Draw up a list of the broad areas in which we might need information. Write your answers down in the form of questions to which we would want answers.

The four basic questions I would ask in response to this are given below; but note that each one is a beginning question only, in that it leads on to further questions like the ones listed beneath the first question. I would continue with these and similar subsidiary questions until I had obtained the information needed to confirm with the client the nature of the problem. Only at that point could we discuss issues and procedures related to doing something appropriate with the data.

1 What is the nature of the data that have been collected?

- What was the method of data collection?
- Are the data basically structured, or will they require structuring, e.g. categorizing, prior to data analysis?
- How many cases are there; who or what are they; and how were they selected?
- How were the data recorded and in what form are they at present?

2 What kind of analysis of the data is planned?
3 What are the research objectives; and what kind of report is planned?
4 What is the time-scale and what resources are available for data handling and analysis?

Let us ask the first question and see what kind of answers we get.

Question 1: what is the nature of the data that have been collected?

Here are some replies from various hypothetical clients: most of these replies are from real situations, but the details have been changed to preserve anonymity:

 A: It's information to help with the development of a social science course. I've got 250 questionnaires from a random sample of students who've taken the predecessor course in its last two years. The data relate to reactions to the old course and to features the students would like in the new course. I need to put the data on computer and talk through the appropriate data analysis.
 B: I've got some tapes of interviews with patients, doctors and nursing staff in two local hospitals. They ask about views on the existing facilities and needs. I want to build up a picture of the facilities and the main gaps in provision in the two hospitals.

C: I've got some data from a data bank and I want to do some secondary analysis. They come from interviews with staff and clients in various voluntary organizations. I want to see how client satisfaction relates to the type and size of organization. I also want to test some hypotheses about gender. I think client satisfaction will be different according to whether the voluntary sector worker and the client are the same gender or different genders. Most of the information I need is there, but I need a bit of help in checking it out and constructing the scales I need.

D: Other members of a working party and I have collected a lot of information in order to look at equal opportunities in our town. We've got some national and local statistics, records of what has been said in the Council, interviews with ten local employers and also a small survey on attitudes collected from people living on one of the estates. We think some new initiatives would help a lot – and there are grants going. The information we have collected might be used to support an application. What is the next step in analyzing the information?

E: They are data collected from students attending a residential weekend at Reading and I have been asked to analyze them. I got the questionnaires and put the info in a database on my PC. Now I've had a look at the first results I'm not very happy. For example, the figures for the number of hours spent on the first Project look a bit odd – the average number of hours is far too high. And there are lots of other oddities; there are only 60 women in the sample yet I've got about 85 answers to the questions that only the women were supposed to answer. How should I go about sorting it all out?

F: I'm interested in developmental education and I've got some interview data from two year-groups in my school. I've also got their exam grades in various subjects. The aim is to look at children's knowledge of various countries and attitudes to people in those countries by age group and stage of cognitive development. I'm interested at this stage in getting a picture of how the attitudinal information hangs together. If possible I would like to make up some scales that would be stronger measures of the concepts I'm interested in than the individual questions.

G: I've been interested for quite some time in trade unions and I've collected quite a lot of information about six unions. I've got some data from the archives on how they developed, membership, decision-making structure, the policies they've voted for at TUC conferences, and strikes. I've also got access to some interview data from members of the six unions. I want to look at factors related to 'militancy'.

The answers to Question 1 from our hypothetical clients *A* to *G* give us 'hooks' into the essential information that we need in order to establish the nature of the data that have been collected. However, as is the case with all broad, open-ended questions, the information we need about the formal characteristics of the data as collected is mixed up with other pieces of information about different aspects of the research: for example, the research objectives. These latter details supply us with important information about goals, but the options concerning what can be done with data all relate to the formal characteristics of the data, not to the research objectives.

As the client gave his or her first answer to Question 1, I would normally be jotting down a list of keywords, such as 'structured questionnaire' and 'postal survey', from the answer. I would be particularly keen at this stage to form a clear picture of:

1 The method(s) of data collection.
2 The type of questions that had been asked of informants or that had guided the data collection.

Also, I would be keen to know:

3 Details of the cases: who or what they comprised and the number of cases.
4 The method of recording the data and the current form of these data: for example, raw data recorded on a questionnaire, edited data on a computer file, etc.

All these pieces of information would guide the next steps in handling the data. Other information, such as details of how the sampling of cases had been done and the subgroups, would be important pieces of information but would only become essential later. For example, in the case of raw data we would make sure, at the data preparation stage, that we recorded membership of particular subgroups that were needed for analysis purposes. At the analysis stage it might be very important to know just how the cases had been sampled and how many cases there were in each subgroup, but the information would not be essential for the first steps in doing something with the data.

Prior Structure, Method of Recording and Sample Size

Let us take a closer look at methods of data collection and their implications for the extent to which data are already structured at the point when we try to do something with them. How they were recorded and how many cases we have will also shape our decisions.

Prior Structure

Box 7.1 indicates various methods of data collection which produce different types of data that require different handling strategies. It contains two main groups of data: data collected from informants (items 1 and 2) and data secured from other sources (items 3 and 4). The first group is amenable to researcher control during data collection, but for the second the data are limited by what is available.

Box 7.1   *Methods of data collection*

1   Tests
2   Questionnaires and interviews
3   Direct observation: of individuals, groups, communities or events, for example
4   (a) Trace records: that is, indicators of some variable that have been left behind (e.g. contents of household, amount of pavement wear, proportion of 'gentrified' houses in the street)
    (b) Archive documents: running records (e.g. Census data, hospital admission statistics, court reports); episodic records from private and institutional sources (e.g. sales catalogues, published accounts, committee papers, correspondence, diaries, speeches, newspaper reports)

Source: based on a classification in Runkel and McGrath (1972)

Information about the method of data collection gives clues as to the likelihood of the data being already highly structured – a very important feature as this indicates the operations needed to handle the data. In a highly structured data set, a great deal will already have been determined. In contrast, with highly unstructured data, the major task of the data handling is to determine both the variables that are to be abstracted from the raw data and the appropriate answer categories. It may even be that the research problem and any hypotheses are to be decided in the light of the content and the clues to underlying variables that are suggested by the data.

The method of data collection also points to the likelihood of the data being complete in terms of there being the same information for all the cases (at least, in principle). Where the data have been specially collected – for example, using tests, questionnaires and interview schedules – the likelihood is that we will have information for most cases on most variables. Where the data represent observations of naturally occurring events, or are the product of searches for traces of past events or archive searches, the likelihood of incomplete data increases.

The implication of the latter is that handling the data may involve bridging gaps in the evidence when we attempt to categorize, scale or structure the data. For example, we might have to decide that quite disparate 'events' and possessions were indicators of the relative wealth of households; that is, there might be no *single* indicator of wealth for all cases in the data set, so we might have to assess it on a *range* of evidence. Occasionally, it may not be possible to establish 'common ground' for comparing cases: the responses are very different from each other, or there is a great deal of missing information, and not the same missing information for each case. If you are in this situation, probably all you can recommend is that the cases be presented individually, as 'case studies', rather than shaping them up for comparison. Mostly, however, it is possible to 'work over' the data so that some kind of valid comparison can be made.

Tests usually imply data that are highly structured. The stimuli or the questions are presented in a given order and with specific instructions which set the framework for measuring 'performance'. The data are scores which are either produced directly by some calibrated instrument or derived from the 'raw data' according to given rules. Usually, norms are available which indicate the meaning of given scores in terms of the performance of a general population and subgroups of the population. (It can be a problem at the data interpretation stage to decide the extent to which the norms for the populations on which the scores were standardized are appropriate to one's own sample.)

Test data clearly include scores on variables such as height and weight, and scores in exams. They arguably also include scores on standard personality inventories. The latter are based on questions to which there is no right answer, but the sum of answers to particular questions is used as a measure of standard dimensions of personality: for example, introversion/extroversion. Test data can even include scores on such tests as the 'Draw-a-Man' test, in which a child draws a person and a trained interpreter then analyzes various elements in the drawing, and the relationship between elements, according to a set of rules, and gives a numerical score to the child's stage of cognitive development.

Data from tests will generally be expressed as numbers on an interval or ratio scale – 'real numbers' with which you can do arithmetic and calculate means. There are four distinct scales of measurement, each with its own properties:

1 *Ratio scales,* where the intervals between adjacent numbers mean the same up and down the scale, and multiplication can be carried out (e.g. an increase of one

mile per hour means the same whether it is an increase from 30 mph or from 60 mph, and 60 mph is twice 30 mph).

2   *Interval scales,* where the intervals mean the same up and down the scale but multiplication is not meaningful (e.g. an increase of 1 degree means the same additional heat up and down the scale, but 80 degrees Celsius is not twice 40 degrees Celsius in terms of heat delivered).

3   *Ordinal scales* are ordered, but the intervals are not constant (an example would be educational qualifications: GCSE, 'A' level, diploma, degree).

4   In *nominal scales* the numbers are just labels for discrete items, and no ordering is implied.

Sometimes it will be necessary to degrade the numbers by recoding to a less powerful type of scale (ordinal or even nominal); this will be discussed later in the chapter. It is worth noting, however, that in principle *anything* can be measured at least at the nominal level (e.g. as 'present' or 'absent', coded 1 or 0).

Tests are one special case of the general class of structured *questionnaires* (or *interview schedules,* or *observational schedules*). The distinguishing feature that separates questionnaires or schedules from other types of data-collection method is that they ask exactly the same questions of all informants, and in the same order. Thus they produce data that can be treated in the same way for all cases – converted into scores or categorized according to rules set out in a coding frame. The result is a score or value for each informant on each of the variables that are under investigation – at least in principle, though there can be missing data. In other words, questionnaires produce data that are amenable to easy quantification.

The questions asked can be divided into two types: 'closed' questions and 'open-ended' questions:

1   *Closed questions* specify a task and also the range of possible responses to it. The respondent is forced to choose from one of a set of numbered options (although one of these might be 'don't know' or 'cannot decide'). Numbers (codes) may be assigned to the possible answers on the questionnaire itself, or they may be written in 'in the office' when the questionnaire is returned, but the range and meaning of the numbers is decided in advance. These questions are relatively unproblematic at the pre-analysis stage: the numbers can be entered directly into the database.

2   *Open-ended questions* pose a question or specify a 'task' just as closed questions do, but the informant has the freedom to answer in his or her own way rather than in terms of the researcher's predefined answer categories. Open-ended questions can, in principle, be reduced to numerical scores in the same way as any other questionnaire item. (In Chapter 10 you will be introduced to an alternative way of looking at open-ended questions, but for the purposes of this chapter we will refer only to this specific form of measurement.)

Some points to note:

•   In the case of closed questions, the data reflect the researcher's prior structuring of the 'universe'. In contrast, open-ended questions identify a topic and task but the respondent has freedom to select what is relevant.

- When open-ended questions are asked of all informants – for example, through a questionnaire or during an interview – the answers can be transformed into variables for which there are values for all cases. These values can be treated quantitatively to produce statistics, just as with closed questions.
- Pre-coding of the data is possible with closed questions, but the information from open-ended questions has to be structured and transformed into a form suitable for statistical and other analyses. This is probably carried out after all the data have been collected.
- Some apparently open-ended questions in interviews may be treated just like closed questions in self-completion questionnaires. The interviewer may have a list of previously determined codes for those answers that are of interest. Instead of writing down the informant's words, the interviewer rings a numerical code to indicate which one of a predetermined set of answers has been given.

As you are aware, not all research proceeds by asking people questions. For example, data may also be gathered by *direct observation*. Sometimes observation is carried out purely to form an understanding of what is going on, with no intention of analyzing frequencies of occurrence (though even here a few relevant numbers can improve a report). It is also possible, however, to carry out an *observational survey*, using a structured form of data collection to count and/or measure relevant aspects of what is being observed: the number of cars passing a given point, the extent of aggressive behaviour in a school playground, the number of references to women as 'girls' in a given kind of text, for instance. In this case, most of what we have said about questionnaires applies also to observation. 'Structured observation' generally proceeds by recording data in predetermined categories, but there could, in principle, be the equivalent of open-ended questions as well – descriptive notes, written in the field, to be coded into categories in the office.

Finally, we measure the past by inference from *traces* in the physical environment – for example, assessing the flow of traffic through a doorway by measuring the degree to which the step has been worn away – or from *archive* data, by using numbers collected at the time or making our own counts of relevant features from records. The degree of structure in the data collected by these methods will vary a great deal according to component sub-sets of data and how they were collected. Some sets of data may be highly structured and, indeed, pre-processed; for example, data from a survey archive which have been processed for other analysis purposes, or data which largely comprise published statistics (sets of company accounts and sales records). Sometimes, however, the data will show very little structure: the records may have been drawn from many sources and there may be a lot of missing information. Archive source materials and trace records are also likely to contain material that is irrelevant to the purposes of the study. A major task at the data-processing stage is, therefore, that of bringing some order to the assembled materials. It could involve sorting the materials that are pertinent to the enquiry from those that are not; organizing the former in some order; abstracting and summarizing relevant data; and, in general, preparing the materials in such a way that the process of investigating relevant data can be carried out efficiently.

Method of Recording

In the case of questionnaires and similar pre-coded documents, typically all the information is recorded on the questionnaire itself, either by the informant or an interviewer or (later) by a coder. The coder codes the open-ended questions and enters the appropriate code in the relevant place on the questionnaire. The numbers representing the data are then keyed into a computer.

Sometimes the process is even more automated. In the case of some telephone interviews, everything is computer controlled: the dialling; the presentation of the appropriate question on a screen for the interviewer to read out; and, at the end of the process, there is 'real-time' recording of the interviewer's codes for answers so that up-to-date results are always available. A survey of television viewing which used a machine plugged into the television to record when the television was on and what channel was showing is another example.

Where topics are researched by identification and retrieval of existing records, researchers have no control over the medium in which the information has been recorded: they must take the data as they come. Typically, they will photocopy documents when they can and, when this is not possible, abstract information in the form of précis, quotations, tables, graphs or whatever seems most suitable for making a personal record of these data. Inevitably, there will be diversity in the format of the information assembled and, as already noted, there is likely to be a high proportion of missing information. The first task at the data-processing stage will be to bring order to the raw data by, perhaps, working out an appropriate filing system for the various records that will allow ready access when needed.

Sample Size

When we considered the information we needed in order to be able to advise on data handling, the number of cases, and their nature, came quite high on the list of priorities. This most basic information alerts us to the kinds of comparison that will be possible, and hence whether any initial data handling should be geared towards transformation of the data into a form suitable for case history-type analysis or for statistical analysis. Let us take a brief look at the surface implications of the following sources of information:

- 20 students attending a course induction meeting
- 600 secondary school students
- 250 companies participating in a CBI survey
- Six trade unions
- Our village

'Our village' is probably a case history. What we are likely to have is detailed information about one location over time, and this lends itself most readily to 'telling the story' rather than to 'presenting the figures'. However, if appropriate data have been collected, it might be possible to locate the village in some greater space through relating its features to national statistics and comparative information secured in studies of other villages.

In the case of the six trade unions and the 20 students at the induction meeting, some primitive counting and some comparisons of the data for given variables might be possible, but testing for statistical significance (see Chapter 9) would be inappropriate because the number of cases is too small. It would therefore not be worth the trouble of coding the open-ended questions, as we do in the case of questionnaire data for large numbers of cases.

The data sets comprising information for 250 companies and information from or relating to the 600 students open up the possibilities for treating the data quantitatively, undertaking subgroup analysis and, if appropriate, doing tests of statistical significance. But we would be alerted to possible trouble ahead if we had been told that the company data had been collected through open-ended questions. This would point to the possibility that huge resources might need to be committed if all the data had to be coded into variables suitable for statistical analysis.

Getting the Data into Shape for Analysis

The 'preparation' stage of an analysis involves devising a good form in which to reproduce the data so that they (a) provide a fair summary of what has been studied and (b) can readily be analyzed to answer the researcher's questions. Key phrases which arise from these objectives are 'error reduction/minimization', 'data representation', 'data transformation' and 'data reduction'. In this section we will be considering these phrases or 'concepts' in the context of handling the data that have been collected. In this case, 'handling' means shaping the raw data so that they are transformed into variables to enable us to inspect or analyze them more readily.

Think of the situation that might apply at the end of the data-collection process. There could be bundles of questionnaires, notes or tapes of interviews, perhaps videos and, in the case of archive materials, folders containing copies of original documents, sets of notes containing abstracts, and possibly more. What are we aiming to do and how do we begin? In many kinds of social research, the objective is to structure the records in such a way that the data become elements in a data matrix. This might sound alien and off-putting, but in fact it is quite simple. People have been constructing data matrices from the time of the earliest records, and you have probably been doing it yourself for years.

Basically, a data matrix comprises a grid of rows and columns. Traditionally, the rows represent cases, the columns represent variables and the entries are the data. If you were planning a holiday and wanted to put the information from the brochures and the various comments from travel agents and friends in some order, you might construct a data matrix like the one shown in Box 7.2.

Box 7.2   *A matrix of holiday information*

Destination	No. of nights	Accommodation	Food	Price
Brest	7	Single	Half	High
Quimper	7	Single	Full	High
Huelgoat	7	Single	Self-catering	Medium
St Brieuc	5	Single	Self-catering	Medium
Rennes	7	Single	Half	Medium
Val-Andre	7	Single	Half	Low
La Rochelle	6	Shared	Half	Medium
Perpignon	12	Shared	Self-catering	Low

By organizing the data on holidays in this way, we can analyze them relatively easily. Clearly, however, there are likely to be more items of data collected in research projects than in the case of our holiday example. Where there are many cases and fairly complete records for each case, it is usual to code all the data that come in so that they can be held in a parsimonious format with numbers and letters (called 'alphanumerics') representing them. In this instance, the data matrix might look like that shown in Box 7.3.

Box 7.3 *A research data matrix*

A10156M1197012253722B51195741188221   .   .   .   3
A10478F311205432126328   263141322510   .   .   .   3
Z10530F4132331413261195A734118   270   .   .   .   2

There is one major difference between the data matrix in Box 7.3 and that representing data about holiday destinations in Box 7.2. Given the information that it is a data matrix, we are pretty confident that the rows represent cases and the columns variables, but we lack the information to interpret it. Therefore, we cannot draw up the instructions for processing it, even though it is obvious that the values can be counted and the cases divided up into groups. In the case of the variables, individual columns (digits) might represent discrete variables, but they could equally well be a representation of data such as age, which might require two columns to represent the full data collected. It is clear that, unless the data matrix records the raw data in a way that we can recognize (e.g. 'male', 'female'), a set of instructions must have been drawn up for transforming the data into codes and for identifying the location of all the variables. This set of instructions is called the *coding frame*. A coding frame always includes three pieces of information for each variable:

1   A reference back to the source data (e.g. Q12(b) or 'age of informant').
2   A list which comprises the codes and their associated symbols.
3   An identification of the column location of the variable within the matrix.

Box 7.4 is an example of a coding frame.

Box 7.4 *An example of a coding frame*

Column   *Variables/codes*

1   Location of sample

          1   Hospital
          2   Rest home
          3   Own home

(Continued)

Box 7.4 *(Continued)*

2–4	Case number (3 digits)
5–6	Age (2 digits)

7	Gender (M or F)
8	Are you able to move around your house without help?

    0 No answer
    1 Yes
    2 With some difficulty
    3 With great difficulty
    4 No

9   What help do you receive to move around your house?

    0 No information
    1 None
    2 Aids (e.g. stick)
    3 Personal help

    (Note: if 2 and 3 are indicated, code as 3)

10   Are you able to move around outside the house without personal help?

    0 No answer
    1 Yes
    2 Garden, but not beyond
    3 Garden, but with great difficulty
    4 No
    9 'Don't want to go out', and other refusals to answer

Given this coding frame, we could read off the data for individual cases, just as we could read the data in the matrix for holidays. Secondly, we could give all the instructions needed for (a) naming the variables and the categories so that they can be recognized by a computer and also printed out on tables; and (b) writing a specification for analyzing the variables: counting the data, dividing the cases into groups and analyzing according to group membership, relating variables to each other, and so on.

Data matrices like the one described above are clearly best suited to machine analysis, in that much of the meaning of the data is not obvious. But the same concepts apply to matrices held on paper, with 'hand counting' of the frequency of particular codes.

However, as I pointed out at the beginning of the chapter, data are constructed by the researcher, not just 'found', and the coding frame is one of the major means by which this construction takes place. Whether the codes are established beforehand (i.e. the questions pre-coded), or whether the coding frame is 'derived from the data' (in the case of open-ended questions or unstructured interviews coded after data collection),

the outcome is the result of a series of decisions taken by the res
researcher may try to minimize error and to represent the views and c
of the sample faithfully, but in practice this means that it is the research
mines what shall count as error and what is acceptable as a faithful re
In the next section we look at some of these decisions and how they are taken.

Getting the Pre-coding Right

This topic may seem on the surface to be quite trivial compared with the important
decisions that researchers have to make about the coverage and structure of their
questionnaires and the questions asked of informants. Naturally, researchers focus
on these decisions and sometimes pay scant attention to the technicalities of getting
the pre-coding right. As consultants to researchers who come to ask what to do with
their data, we would see the consternation of clients who had got it wrong. Instead
of proceeding smoothly to the interesting task of analyzing the data, scarce resources
of time and money might be needed to put things right – and time would be lost.

The particular advantages of pre-coding are that it cuts the time and costs of data
handling and also one source of error: that is, error introduced at the coding stage.
Especially in the case of large-scale surveys, the ideal is to have a questionnaire that
requires little more than clerical checking for respondent errors (e.g. an answer
circled instead of its code, or too many codes circled) and, if required, coding of
open-ended questions before the questionnaires are passed on to the people who will
key the data into a computer file. The task of these operators is to key for each case
(respondent) a sequence of letters and numbers (the codes) in the given column locations, so pre-coding involves the allocation of column numbers as well as answer
codes for each variable.

Clearly, problems arise when insufficient columns have been allocated to hold the
data for each question. An example is age: only one column might have been allocated for this variable, but the data require two columns. Worse, a badly worded
question might result in many informants circling several answers between which
we cannot discriminate and therefore want to record in full; and a deceptively simple
open-ended question can generate replies that require an unexpectedly large number
of columns to record. All of this is supposed to be ironed out by pilot studies of the
design and coding of the questionnaire, but mistakes still slip through.

Coding Open-ended Questions

Many questionnaires and other documents contain open-ended questions. To transform the raw data from these questions into a form in which we can analyze them efficiently requires a lot of effort and thought in the initial stages of handling the data. In
the case of open-ended questions in pre-coded questionnaires, provision will have
been made in the pre-coding for codes derived from the written-in answers, but we
shall need to prepare a code list for these later. If we decide to go ahead and code the
written-in information, the checking and coding phase which precedes any data keying is the obvious time to do this – coding at a later stage and inserting the codes into
a data matrix is tedious, and sometimes substantial computer skills are needed to
merge the new data with an existing data matrix. Thus we face an important decision:

to code the open-ended information or to analyze it by hand-listing the data for inspection, then quoting comments that are typical or of special interest in the report.

If it is *essential* for the project that we code open-ended questions (for example, if we need to report the frequencies of the answers or to relate the answers to the open-ended questions to other variables), then there is no option. We have to find the time and human resources to draw up a coding frame and code the answers on the questionnaires prior to data keying. If time presses – for example, a report has been promised in the near future in which the major interest will be in the closed questions – we might decide that the best course is not to have the open-ended data coded and keyed in, but to treat them by other means as best we can.

If there is any doubt about whether to code, then we must get more information. In this case it would mean selecting a stack of questionnaires – possibly 50 or so – and taking a look at the raw data. We will be interested in the *kind* of answers written in and the *numbers* of informants who have written something in the space on the questionnaire. The cases (questionnaires) may be picked out for inspection in a variety of ways. They could be (a) picked at random from the various batches as they came into the office; (b) sampled more systematically on the basis of the groups represented in the survey; or (c) chosen in a way that might ensure that the diversity in the answers was as great as possible. For example, we might want to represent both men and women and both younger and older people.

The initial inspection might just involve opening up the questionnaires at the relevant page, reading the answers for the sample and forming an impression about whether the answers were of sufficient interest and diversity to warrant coding. A better variant of this quick inspection might be to stack the questionnaires in piles according to our impressions of which answers to a given question were of the same kind. We might then go through each pile a second and perhaps a third time, re-sorting as necessary, with the aim of ending up with as small a number of piles as possible, with a reasonable set of questionnaires in each pile, and with the answers in each pile representing a particular category of response. It would be important that the piles differed from each other in some significant way, not in some trivial respect. They should represent answer categories that were of interest in relation to the research objectives. Finally, there should be only a small number of answers that we could not classify. At this stage we would have the basis for our initial coding frame for the particular open-ended question. In the light of this initial coding, either we might decide to go ahead with coding the questions, or we might make a decision not to go ahead, on the grounds that the categories were not sufficiently interesting to warrant investing the resource and time needed to do the coding.

A different approach is to invest in typing out the responses or keying them into a document on a computer. This involves a greater initial investment of time, but the record is permanent and allows sorting and re-sorting (e.g. through 'cutting' and 'pasting') until we feel we have got it right. It also allows the various concepts that the respondents may have given in the answer to a question to be split up and allocated to different categories. Even if a decision is made not to code, we have a useful set of keyed-in answers that can be used for illustrative purposes and extended, if need be, by adding further answers from a larger sample of the questionnaires.

Given that the decision is to code, we would then draw up a coding frame using the same principles that guided the assignment of codes to the closed questions; that is, a unique value for each category. Typically, we would set this out in the format given in Box 7.5. Note that this format contains all the information needed for someone else to carry out the task of coding the data. It also contains all the labelling information needed to identify the question to which the data refer and the location of the variable in a data matrix.

The next stage might be trial coding on a larger sample, or we could go straight on to the task of coding all the questionnaires. In either case, we might find answers that could not be coded. If relatively few, they might be coded as 'other'. If substantial in number and representing new themes, we might well want to modify the coding frame. This might be done through the addition of further categories or it might require abandoning the existing frame and starting again. Whenever the modifications are other than trivial, it is good practice to go back over all the coded questionnaires and check that the code that has been assigned still applies.

Box 7.5 *A coding frame with examples of typical answers*

Col. 20 *Why did you decide to study at a University? (1st reason)*

0	No answer
1	Job/career reasons (get better job; start new career; re-enter paid employment)
2	Personal development (develop wider perspectives; become more confident; develop new interests)
3	Subject-related reasons (interest in maths; want to gain skills in computing; learn more about social sciences)
4	To get degree or other qualification (to get a degree; gain credits for BPS recognition; HSW diploma; Advanced Diploma in Criminology, etc.)
9	Other answers

Col. 21 *Why did you decide to study at a University? (2nd reason)*

Codes as for Column 20.

Activity 7.2 (allow about 30 minutes)

The Appendix to this chapter is an extract from a report I wrote on the reactions of teachers to a pack of learning materials that they had used (Swift, 1991a). The materials had been devised to help teachers like themselves make full use of their teacher placement in business and industry. The extract selected relates to the additional comments that the teachers made at the end of the questionnaire. The answers are responses to a very general invitation: 'If you would like to say anything about teacher placements in general or your own placement, please feel free to write in.'

You should now draw up a coding frame – or to get as far into this task as possible in the time you have available.

Note: You might like to work in pencil, working through the list several times to identify the comments that seem similar. As you work, write a code against those you have identified as belonging together. Keep a list of the codes: this list is your trial coding frame. An alternative strategy is to use a highlighter, but that is not as easy to change as pencil.

Having tried out your skills and experienced some of the problems of coding data, we can now go on to consider data collected in a situation where the questions are not as standardized as the ones you have been considering. But first we might note that not all coding operations require the drawing up of a new coding frame. An example is coding information on occupations. In this case, the initial task of identifying categories has been done by a variety of organizations that have devised coding frames to suit their particular requirements. Thus, there are coding frames such as those used in coding Census data which try to reflect the ways in which occupations group together, and there are coding schemes that are more concerned to measure social status. Researchers generally choose the coding scheme that best fits their purposes and then proceed to code their own data in terms of the published coding frame. Where this strategy is used, of course, the research data can be compared with other published data.

Coding Data from Unstructured Interviews

The first step in appreciating the potentialities in the information that has been collected is to become thoroughly acquainted with it. Let us imagine we are engaged in this task. If the information was recorded in the form of notes, we would read through these, perhaps several times, and make further notes identifying things that seem of particular importance, or add annotations to particular passages. If audio or video tapes are available, the first step would be to listen to or view them, replaying sections as needed. As we listen or view, we might jot down brief notes on ideas that form in the mind about themes and meanings, perhaps identifying variables that might be derived from the data.

The second step with audio tapes might be to transcribe the interview data: listening and note-taking is not always enough. We might need to have the raw data in a 'hard copy' form that we can manipulate according to the system that suits us best. My method involves making copies of the transcribed data so as not to lose them in their original format. I then split up the records into what seem to me the basic elements or concepts that have been expressed, or I use a highlighter to mark what I see as variables and as categories within variables. (It is more difficult to transcribe video recording; systems do exist for transcribing the action on videos, but they tend either to simplify what is going on very grossly indeed, into a very few theory-derived categories, or to require a great deal of work to transcribe a very short sequence of video.)

What the variables are is not always clear, especially when there has been no interview agenda and the interviews have elicited diverse information. In such cases,

I might split up the verbatim records into elements that I could group and sort rather than try to treat individual interviews one by one. (I would take care, though, to label each of the elements with a number or mnemonic for the person who made the comment and with the question number, if applicable, so that I had the information to hand.) I would then, as my first strategy, sort the elements according to a theme or topic that had to be looked at because it was central to the objectives of the research or the research hypotheses, setting aside those that seemed to have no bearing on the topic. This process would continue until I felt fairly confident that I had identified the set of variables that I needed and could measure, and had also identified some of the main categories of each variable. This step completed, I would then proceed to construct a coding frame following the steps indicated for coding information on discrete questions.

There are at least three ways of thinking about data that are much more common in this kind of data analysis than in the coding of responses to a single open-ended question. These are:

1   Thinking about what the variables comprise and the boundaries between variables.
2   Thinking about the meaning of any new and unexpected categories that have emerged from the data and the extent to which they could help understanding of the topic. Stimulated by the data in front of us, we might identify variables and categories that *potentially* exist, that are hinted at by the data but cannot be explored properly because we do not have much information. This might lead to a new project in which we would explore the issues in a different way with an appropriate sample of people, to test this new insight and to see whether the potential new variables or categories emerge. In my case, I might represent the idea in a list of statements in a survey I would carry out later. I could then see whether the respondents recognized the idea and 'owned it', in the sense that their responses were meaningful and informative when related to other variables.
3   Thinking about meanings and, possibly, about causal relations.

For example, suppose we carried out interviews with employers who sponsored students at a particular university, with the aim of finding out the employers' views on the quality and relevance of the university's courses and on the institution as a whole. Our first focus would probably be on what they said about the university. We might start by looking at the data for the following overall groups of employers who are:

• Happy with courses/provision and experiencing no problems in relating to the institution.
• Happy with courses/provision but experiencing problems in relating to the institution.
• Critical of courses/provision but experiencing no problems in relating to the institution.
• Critical of courses/provision and experiencing problems in relating to the institution.

At a more detailed level, we would be able to identify a variety of aspects of happiness and unhappiness in relation to the university's offerings and the university as an organization, and these data might provide a basis for variables and categories. But suppose we had a sense of unease. For example, the categories with which we had ended up might not give us much insight into the research question, or the statements within each category might be an uneasy mix of generalities and very precise appreciations and criticisms. Also, interviews with some employers might have become focused on issues which scarcely emerged in other interviews.

Possibly we should start again, this time focusing on an employer's own organization rather than on the university. It might be that the positive and negative reactions to the university, and specific criticisms, made more sense when viewed in terms of the constraints and systems within the employer's organization. For example, criticisms of the courses might relate not to inadequacies in provision but to an employer's inability to make use of relevant courses, and the same might be true at the level of the university as an institution. From this new perspective, even if the data were partial because the focus of the interview had been on the university rather than on the employer's organization, the beginnings of a model might emerge that made sense and was informative about the research problem.

In summary, a systematic approach helps the task of drawing up a coding frame for the diverse data from unstructured interviews. Normally, this starts with getting acquainted with the data from each interview and proceeds to a search for similarities across interviews in terms of the variables under investigation. Given openness on the part of the researcher to the less obvious messages in the data, perhaps clearly expressed in only one or two comments, new perspectives on the research problem may be formed and become a basis for further codes or new research. (The same applies in respect of good open-ended questions in questionnaire-based studies.) As Erickson and Nosanchuck (1983: 5) remarked in the context of exploring data:

> You never look for *the* interpretation of a complex data set, or *the* way of analysing it, because there are always lots of interpretations and lots of approaches depending on what you are interested in. There are many good answers to different questions, not just one right answer as in the detective story.

Three Approaches to Coding

So far, I have talked about the process of drawing up a coding frame as if a good solution will naturally emerge if we have the right raw material. This is seldom the case: variables and categories are constructs and are not just 'out there' with their own independent existence. This applies as much to closed questions, and lists of items within closed questions, as to the coding of less-structured interview material. In the case of some closed questions, however, a topic may have been so thoroughly explored that the categories seem self-evident to the researcher and informant.

Drawing up a coding frame is governed by the *approach* the researcher takes in respect of data in general in terms of what the data signify and useful ways of understanding them. I find it helpful to group the approaches in three ways.

(1) A researcher may view the data (e.g. the words that have been said) as expressing in their surface content – what is 'out there'. In this case, the researcher's main concern will be to produce a set of codes that reduce the data to their essentials, with the codes reflecting the surface meaning of the raw data as faithfully as possible, independently of any views that the researcher may have about underlying variables and meanings. We can call this the *representational* approach.

(2) The researcher may view the data as having additional and implicit meanings that come from the fact that they are *anchored in,* and are dependent on, the data-gathering

context. Thus, what is relevant will have been communicated to informants through information about the enquiry and, indirectly, through the questions or the interview agenda. According to this perspective, in order to maximize the usefulness for the particular project, the pre-codes and also the categories derived from the open-ended data should be aligned with the research context, or 'anchored in the appropriate external reality', as well as in the words said. For example, in investigating employers' happiness or unhappiness with the university, we might want to do this within a framework comprising types of formal and informal university/employer interactions to which the university commits resources. So our variables might include brochures, other mailings, enquiry services, 'road shows', visits to employers, transactions about fees, and so on. The words given by the informants could also be 'interpreted' to produce codes on more than one dimension relating to the context. For instance, (a) *nature of contact*: informal versus formal contacts, initial contact versus continuing contacts; (b) *initiator of contact*: university versus employer. When this approach is taken, the coding frame takes into account 'facts' in the situation, rather than treating the data individually as though they are context-free. This creates a bridge to the 'world outside the research'. In cases in which the research involves recommendations, it may open up the path to action.

(3) The researcher may view the data as having a variety of meanings according to the theoretical perspective from which they are approached. This view has some similarities with Approach 2, but both are distinctive from the 'representational' perspective of Approach 1. In this case, the data do not have just one meaning, which refers to some 'reality' approachable by analysis of the surface meaning of the words. For example, a data set might contain data on illnesses and minor upsets that the informants had experienced during the year. A researcher taking the 'representational' approach (Approach 1) might classify them according to the various types of illness. In contrast, a researcher taking the *hypothesis-guided* approach (Approach 3) might use the raw data and other apparently quite disparate material to create and/or investigate variables that were defined in terms of his or her theoretical perspectives and research purposes. The illness data might be used as an indicator of a particular kind of stress or of ageing or of a reaction to a traumatic event. The coding frame would specify how mentions of particular illnesses, or ill health versus good health, were to be coded. However, the coding frame would be one based on the researcher's views and hypotheses rather than on the surface meanings of the set of written-in answers.

Activity 7.3 (allow 30 minutes)

A survey that I carried out (Swift, 1991b) for the Open University School of Management during the first presentation of a dissertation module on the MBA included the following question:

> *what experience of research/investigation had you had before doing your MBA dissertation?*

There were seven pre-coded categories, listed below, plus an 'other' category. (The percentages refer to frequencies of response in the survey.)

1 Little or no previous experience of research	28
2 Evaluated research projects/proposals in my capacity as a manager	32
3 Commissioned one or more substantial pieces of research	16
4 Carried out desk (literature-based) research	35
5 Carried out database and similar research work	19
6 Carried out one *or* more substantial research project(s) at work	24
7 Completed a dissertation/thesis as part of a degree/qualification	52
8 Other research experience *(please specify below)*	8

Here is a sample of the responses in the 'other' category:

1 'Consultancy work'
2 'Clinical trials'
3 'Biochemistry PhD 20 years; scientific research'
4 'Research paper for Dip. NEBSS'
5 'Technical research and development not management research'
6 'Taught research at university – supervised and examined postgraduate research students'
7 (a) 'Scientific research'
   (b) 'Experience with short research problems relating to the use of drugs in patients, i.e. practice research'
8 'My job as an investigator involves examining documents and interviewing people to establish the cause of some failure, therefore there is an element of fact finding on research'

Now try your hand at constructing three different coding frames:

1 A frame that reflects the essentials of the surface content of the 'other' answers (Approach 1 above).
2 A frame that also takes account of and is 'anchored in' the nature of the research project (Approach 2 above).
3 A more 'theoretical' or 'hypothesis-guided' coding frame (Approach 3 above).

You will find my answers at the end of the chapter.

Notes and hints

1 The number of codes in each of your coding frames may be quite small, if that is all that is required.
2 In the case of your 'anchored' and 'hypothesis-guided' coding frames, there may well be categories that are not represented by this small sample of data. Indeed, this is very likely for the 'hypothesis-guided' coding frame; that is, you will want the frame to be able to reflect important concepts, if only by showing that they did not occur among the responses.
3 For the 'anchored' frame, you may wish to consider the concept of relevance to the task the student faces.
4 For the 'hypothesis-guided' frame you may want to think about what kinds of previous experience are most likely to be useful for the task of preparing an MBA dissertation.

To reiterate, data are not just something that exist, there to be collected and reported on. Rather, they are constructs. They are created through the questions asked of informants, the questions that guide record searches, and so on – and also through the processes of data collection, recording, coding or other representation. This does not mean, however, that all data are false. One of the things that researchers take most seriously is that they should not build bias into their data by imposing on them structures (codes) that are not applicable. At the stage of coding open-ended questions (and in drawing up the categories that will be pre-coded), this means being involved actively in thinking about how the topic might best be mapped in terms of variables and categories.

Correcting Errors

Thinking back to the beginning of the chapter, you will remember that, as consultants, we were concerned to find out about the nature of the data, and how they had been collected and recorded, for two reasons:

1   To guide the decisions we made about handling the information collected so that it was transformed into data that we could analyze.
2   To ensure quality through the reduction of error and bias. This has two aspects:

    (a)   correction, if possible, of errors and biases in the data
    (b)   minimization of the error and bias that could be introduced during handling of the data

Let us look at the first phase of handling questionnaires and similar structured records before keying into the computer. Can you think of two sources of error in the replies to questionnaires that might be identified and possibly corrected before data keying? The major sources of error that can be identified in the questionnaire-checking process are:

1   Those introduced by the researcher through the wording of the questions and erroneous pre-coding and coding.
2   Those introduced by the respondent in completing the questionnaire. These might involve 'errors' in interpreting the question, and (in the case of self-administered questionnaires) failure to record the answer according to instructions. Where the questionnaire is interviewer-administered, the recording and coding errors of the interviewer would also fall into this category.

Where appropriate – in other words, where the changes can be made without altering the informant's clear intentions – the errors are corrected at the data-checking stage. If an error has been made that cannot be corrected and would lead to erroneous statistics if left in, the answer is either crossed out or a note made that it is to be corrected during data analysis by either recoding or collapsing of categories.

Many respondent/interviewer errors are obvious and can be corrected immediately by the coder: such errors might include ticks by codes rather than circling of the numerical code and entry of a single digit where two are required (e.g. forgetting to insert a leading zero for the number of hours spent on a task – writing '9', for instance, instead of '09' – even though asked to do so). Omitted answers are also fairly obvious – where a respondent has simply failed to answer part of the questionnaire, or has failed to follow the 'routing' (e.g. instructions to answer certain questions if the answer to a previous one was 'yes', or to move on to another part of the questionnaire) – and are generally dealt with by insertion of a 'missing value' code or by leaving the column(s) blank and treating blanks as missing values at the analysis stage. Sometimes missing information can be filled in at this stage if the answer to a question is present somewhere else in a questionnaire. For example, if the 'head of household' occupation is not filled in, but we have the respondent's occupation and know that the respondent is 'head of household', then the information can simply be transferred.

More difficult to correct are errors involving the provision by the respondent (or interviewer) of inappropriate information. Where the respondent is recorded as having no children, for example, but children's ages have been filled in, we might have to exercise judgement as to whether we code the respondent as having children, or delete the answers about children's ages, or code this whole sequence of values as 'missing information' because we do not feel confident enough to make a decision. Multiple answers (several choices circled) on a question where only one was required are also a problem – for example, if several course components were coded as 'the most useful'. Here it may be possible to make a decision on behalf of the respondent if the purpose of the survey is limited: for example, if we were only really interested in how useful students found the statistics teaching, and students have listed both this and something else as the most useful components, then we might ignore that other component. In other cases, it would probably be necessary, again, to code the question as 'missing information' because the answers that have been given cannot be interpreted within the structure of the question or the questionnaire as a whole.

Errors which originate with the researcher and the design of the questionnaire are often the most difficult to correct. Occasionally, the solution will be easy: for example, where the coding frame does not allow the correct number of columns for the data, it is not difficult to change the coding frame after data collection has taken place by making use of spare columns. Less can be done when questions have been asked wrongly, however: important items omitted from lists of pre-coded categories; inadequate instructions given on how to answer a question; ambiguities in a question; or poor routing instructions so that respondents are not directed to the questions that they ought to be answering. Sometimes something can be salvaged. Where there is an open-ended component to the question (for example, an 'others' category in a list or a 'why is that?' question), it may be possible to deduce what the answer ought to be. Sometimes the information obtained from badly designed questions is still usable, but the researcher has to keep in mind that the question was ambiguous or the instructions unclear and therefore caution is called for in interpreting the results. Sometimes, however, questions have simply to be omitted from the analysis as uninterpretable.

Data Manipulation During Analysis

Coping with Missing Values

I have noted above that, where data are missing or uninterpretable, we can often do no better than to record the item as 'missing' for the case. Missing values are, of course, no problem when we have planned that they shall be missing: in instances where a question is answered only by those in paid employment, for example, and therefore is not answered by anyone who is *not* in paid employment. Where values are missing for other reasons, however, they can be a problem. It is important, when reporting on the analysis of data, to state in any tables the number (and proportion) of missing cases, so that the reader can get some idea of how representative the analyzed cases are likely to be of the whole sample. (When there is a substantial number of missing cases, it might be even better to describe them: are they typical or untypical of the sample as a whole, and thus is the fact that their answers are not available likely to bias the conclusions? For example, if you were analyzing data on views of childbirth and most of the 'missing values' were women, and it further turned out that the women were more likely to be working class than middle class, you might be hesitant about generalizing very far from your results.)

Sometimes it is possible to infer what a value must be from the values on other variables – before analysis, as we discussed in the last section, or once data are keyed in. For example, if we know that someone is employed as a teacher and has very recently started paid employment, we shall probably not do violence to the facts if we code him or her as earning the average starting salary of teachers, even if 'earnings' is a missing value on the questionnaire. A more sophisticated form of inference is possible on some computer packages, which amounts to taking an informed guess as to the value of a missing variable on the basis of several other variables which are highly correlated with it. For example, if we know someone's age, occupation and educational background, and in the sample as a whole these three variables are highly correlated with income, then we might be able to substitute an estimate of income for a missing value. We would not want to do this when a large number of cases have missing values, however; it would change the nature of the variable from 'income' to 'estimated income'. The alternative – and normal – practice is to leave 'missing value' cases out of the analysis, but to report on their number and, preferably, their nature, in order to show whether there are enough of them, and they are sufficiently non-random, to invalidate the conclusions of the analysis.

Re-coding Variables

We have already talked about re-coding some cases to deal with errors or missing values. Sometimes it is necessary to re-code the data file as a whole when preparing it for analysis. If you are planning to run off tables, for example, and some of your variables are continuous ones (for example, age in months), you will need to re-code these variables at least temporarily into bands such that the tables will have a reasonably small number of rows and columns. If you are comparing groups, you may need to re-code some cases, at least temporarily, so that similar cases all fall into the same group (or so that certain rare kinds of case all carry a code which you can use to tell the computer to exclude them from the analysis). For certain kinds of statistical analysis (correlation, for example), it may be necessary to re-code values so that the variables have the right mathematical properties for the analysis. Sometimes, also, we re-code for 'theoretical' reasons, adding values of a variable together into a smaller set of categories in order to make better sense of them; for example, in a survey comparing the experience of English and Continental holidays, we may as well add 'France' and 'Germany' together into a code meaning 'Continental' – and we would certainly want to add rare destinations such as Luxembourg into this category.

Activity 7.4 (5 minutes)

In the *People in Society* survey, a national Open University survey of class location and class attitudes carried out by students on Open University methods courses (see Abbott and Sapsford, 1987a), one measure of educational achievement was coded as follows:

Qualifications attained:

1 None
2 To GCSE/'O' level
3 To 'A' level
4 Above 'A' level but less than degree
5 Degree or higher
6 Other

How might you need to reshape this variable for different kinds of analysis? Think about this, and then see my answer at the end of the chapter.

An extension of such re-coding is to construct new variables, summarizing two or more pieces of information which the questionnaire has collected into one new value for purposes of analysis. We might, for example, have asked (a) whether the informant is in paid employment; (b) if so, how many hours he or she is supposed to work; and (c) whether overtime is normally worked, and, if so, how much. From this we could construct a single variable of 'hours worked in paid employment'. It would take a value of zero if the respondent was not in paid employment. If the respondent *was* in paid employment, and overtime was not normally worked, then the variable would be equal to the hours that he or she was supposed to work. If overtime *were* normal, we would want to add on the number of hours of overtime normally worked. This sounds complicated, but most statistical packages can cope with it. It involves arithmetical operations (new variable = old variable *A* plus old variable *B*) and some logical branching (if variable *A* has this value, add such and such to the new variable). Competent statistical packages can certainly do both.

The construction of scale scores from test answers is a case of 'creating new variables'. What happens is that we take the answers to a large number of questions – intelligence test tasks, for example, or personality/attitude items – and add them up or combine them according to some more complicated pattern in order to obtain a single score of the underlying supposed trait or ability. Composite measurement – summarizing several variables with a single index – is another example. In a study of health and deprivation in Plymouth (Abbott, 1988; Abbott and Sapsford, 1994), for example, four different Census items were combined to give a single and more interpretable 'Index of Material Deprivation', and another set of Census and health statistics were combined into an 'Index of Health Status'.

Activity 7.5 (5 minutes)

In the *People in Society* survey, one of the questions asked was 'age at which left full-time education'. Some researchers might find this variable of interest in its own right, as representing years of experience of a particular type of stimulus situation. Others, however, would find it more interesting to know how long people stayed on at school *beyond the date when they could legally leave,* using the concept as a measure, not of years of experience, but of commitment to education expressed by staying on instead of leaving (and presumably looking for a job). For a recent sample, we could deal with this simply by re-coding: people leaving school at 16 or less would be classed as having no years of post-compulsory experience, and one year for every year after the age of 16 would be scored for those who remained at school. Unfortunately, the school-leaving age has been raised twice since 1950, from 14 to 15 and then to 16.

Given that the survey also collected information about the age of the respondents, and that we would know in which year a given sample was surveyed, how would you go about constructing a variable of 'years of post-compulsory schooling'? My answer is at the end of the chapter.

Finally, most good computer analysis packages will let you 'weight' cases to change the balance of your sample. Suppose, for example, you had a sample which was three-quarters men from a population which you knew consisted of equal numbers of men and women. If we just generalize from the sample to the population, men's opinions would be grossly over-represented, which would matter for anything in which the genders tended to differ. We can fix this by counting each woman as two cases (*weighting* her by a factor of 2) and each man as only two-thirds of a case (*weighting* him by a factor of 0.67). Then, as you can see, the sample will behave as if the right number of each gender had been obtained.

Conclusion

You now realize (if you did not realize it before) the amount of manipulation and the number of decisions that may be necessary before raw data can be analyzed, and you see why we speak in this book of data being *constructed.* Most of this process is invisible to the reader of research; if it were all reported, research papers would be extraordinarily long and extraordinarily tedious to read. You need to be and remain aware, however, of the possibilities for the introduction of bias which exists during this initial pre-analysis stage where researchers are 'working over' the data to try to give a true picture of what their survey shows.

However, you should not leave this chapter with the idea that most research results are falsified and merely the result of the researcher's data

(Continued)

(Conclusion continued)

manipulation. The majority of data sets are re-coded, re-weighted and 'manipulated' or otherwise 'reinterpreted' in a parsimonious way during data handling and coding. If the design of the research is sound and has no major flaws, results can flow from the data as defined in the precoding and coding frames, with restructuring being confined to a limited amount of re-coding and collapsing of variables. This restructuring is mainly undertaken when it will clarify underlying structures and the relationships among variables, *or* permit comparisons to be made with the findings of other researchers or national statistics, *or* allow exploration of interesting ideas which emerge in the course of data analysis or, perhaps, testing of new theory. A variety of constraints, such as limited resources (research assistance, money and personal time) and the need to produce results in the form of papers or reports to deadlines, each impose natural limitations on the amount of data manipulation that can be carried out. The most important limiting factor, however, follows from the motivation for engaging in research at all: why build biases into the research and be anything other than meticulous in the treatment of hard-won data when the object is to contribute to knowledge or understanding of a field or problem?

Key Terms

Archive data   data collected at some other time and stored – often official statistics or surveys.

Case   one example of what is being surveyed – a person, or a town, or a school.

Coding   the numerical (or alphanumeric) representation of data; turning data into numbers (or names) for analysis.

- *Representational*: reproducing the frequency of different responses in the words of the answers.
- *Anchored*: analyzed in terms of categories which reflect meanings in the social world being surveyed.
- *Hypothesis-driven*: analyzed in terms of categories which reflect the research question(s).

Data   information – raw (as received) or processed (*coded* – see above).

Data matrix   an array of data; traditionally, cases are represented by rows and variables by columns in the array.

Field coding   coding at the time of data collection, on the basis of predetermined rules.

Levels of measurement

- *ratio*: a scale where the intervals between adjacent whole numbers are equal and there is a true zero so that a number twice as large does represent a quantity twice as large.

> *(Key Terms continued)*
>
> – *interval*: a scale where the intervals between adjacent whole numbers are equal but there is no true zero and so a number twice as large does represent a quantity twice as large; examples would be temperature measured in degrees Fahrenheit or Celsius.
> – *Ordinal*: a scale where the ordering of the values represents an ordering in the outside world but the gaps between adjacent ranks may not be equal.
> – *Nominal*: a variable with discrete values which are not in any order or numerical relationship; the labels only name the values, even if they are numbers.
>
> **Office coding**   coding after data collection, on rules derived from the research hypotheses and/or preliminary examination of the data.
> **Pre-coding**   recording the answer as one of a predetermined list of values, without needing to use any further judgement rule.
> **Trace records**   (or 'traces'): measurements of the physical signs of an activity, not involving asking questions.
> **Variable**   a piece of data collected about each case.

Further Reading

de Vaus, D.A. (1991) *Surveys in Social Research,* 3rd edn, ch. 14, London, UCL Press.
Erikson, B.H. and Nosanchuck, T.A. (1977) *Understanding Data,* Milton Keynes, Open University Press.
Oppenheim, A.N. (1992) *Questionnaire Design, Interviewing and Attitude Measurement,* ch. 14, London, Pinter.

Answers to Activities

Activity 7.3

You cannot, of course, do much with such a small sample of responses, but here are some possible frames:

1 *Representative (of the areas of research)*

Code	Content	Responses
0	No answer	
1	Science-orientated	3, 5, 7(a)
2	Business/management	1, 4
3	Medical	2, 7(b)
4	Academic	6
5	Other	8

2 *Anchored (in the fact that it is a dissertation that was being undertaken)*

Code	Content	Responses
0	No answer	
1	Not relating to a thesis/dissertation	1, 2, 5, 7(b), 8

2	Relevant to a thesis/dissertation	3, 4, 6
3	Not classifiable	7(a)

3 For the *hypothesis-guided or theoretical frame,* I thought about what I know about MBA dissertations – that they involve research into business or management. So:

Code	Content	Responses
0	No answer	
1	Relevant by reason of content or field of study	1, 8
2	Relevant in that a thesis or dissertation was prepared	3, 4
3	Relevant in *both* senses (none in this sample)	
4	Relevant in *neither* sense	2, 5, 7(a), 7(b)

Activity 7.4

For purposes of tabular analysis, it might be sufficient to use the variable as it stands, provided that numbers were reasonably large in all categories. Alternatively, for some purposes you might want to dichotomize: to split the cases into two categories with respect to this variable. This would be quite simple if what was of interest was whether those surveyed had any qualifications at all: you could split the cases into 'none' (code 1) and 'some' (codes 2–6). If you split them anywhere else, you have problems with code 6 'other' because you do not know at what level these 'others' could reasonably be counted. You would probably have to miss them out by declaring them 'missing values' for the purpose of this part of the analysis. You would certainly have to do so for correlational analysis, unless you could think of some good reason for combining them with one of the other categories, because their numerical value (6) places them higher even than a degree, and this is unlikely to reflect the true state of affairs. (Correlational analysis is discussed at length in Chapters 8 and 9.)

Activity 7.5

Given the respondent's current age in years, the year in which the sample was collected and a knowledge of the dates on which the school-leaving age was raised, the problem can be tackled by simple arithmetic and a little logic:

1 Current year minus current age = year of birth.
2 Year of birth plus 14 = year in which the respondent could have left school if the minimum leaving age was 14.
3 If that year is before the leaving age was raised to 15, then years of post-compulsory schooling = age at which left school minus 14.
4 If it is after this, but before the leaving age was raised to 16, then it equals this value minus 1.
5 If it was after the leaving age was raised to 16, it equals the value calculated at stage 3 minus 2.

There is one further problem, however: that it is possible to score a larger number on this new variable if you left school when it was permissible to do so at 14 than if you left school when you could not do so until 16. Given that the highest category of the 'age at which left school' variable was '18+', someone who left school at 14 could score up to 4, while someone who left at 16 but stayed in full-time education to the age of 21 (to the end of a degree, for instance) could score only 2. It is necessary, therefore, to re-code the new variable into only three categories: 0, 1 and 2 +. Otherwise there would be a spurious correlation with age (see Chapter 9).

Thus we can see that what looks simple (I hope) in principle may none the less work out as quite complicated in practice. This is why I describe analysis and data preparation as an art rather than a science: they require a good deal of sensitive imagination.

Appendix

Extract from B. Swift (1991a) *Teachers into Business and Industry: the Views of Users of the Pack,* Milton Keynes, The Open University Institute of Educational Technology, Student Research Centre Report No. 56, pp. 21–7.

Teachers' Comments on their Placement

Two in three of the teachers are well satisfied with what they have gained through their placement: 27 per cent felt they had achieved their objectives almost entirely, and 46 per cent said this was so to quite a large extent. A further 24 per cent said that they had/would achieve them to some extent. Only 4 per cent reported that they had achieved less than they had hoped.

Many teachers used the space at the end of the questionnaire to comment on their placement. The comments give a flavour of the experience of placements and provide useful information and insights. Some identify things that have helped to make the experience particularly useful and others identify problems. This section concludes, therefore, with a sample of the teachers' comments on their experience.

> I found it extremely valuable. I made excellent contacts, and as a result have had several meetings with P&O personnel, and as a result agreed on a project which is mutually beneficial.

> Teacher placement should be an integral part of a teacher's professional development and every teacher should experience industry at least every three years. Personally, I would like to undertake a teacher placement every year.

> I thoroughly enjoyed my placement, and personally learned a lot and gained a lot of experience, but no one else has been interested in my school, so I have not had the opportunity to pass on my knowledge and experience. I felt that the management skills were very important. I would like to complete the OU, but unfortunately I will have to pay for this privilege myself and due to heavy family commitments I cannot afford this.

> Having now completed teacher placement, I would feel better equipped to do it again, and this time gain more from it. It was a very unknown quantity, and I wasn't sure what to expect or what was expected.

> An excellent idea which should be broadened. I found it very rewarding and helpful. A fulfilling and profitable experience for both myself and the company. It has led to a much greater awareness of the aims and challenges of both sectors, points of mutual interest, and a mutual appreciation of the quality produced by both.

> Very useful for preparing 14–16-year-old pupils of varying abilities for their own work experience, and for their choice of employment suitable for their skills and interests.

The placement was extremely illuminating and I gained much from it that is difficult to verbalize, but has been of use to me personally in school.

Excellent idea, but there must be ways of facilitating knowledge/experience gained through the placement being disseminated to others 'back at base'. It seems all too often that lecturers and teachers go back full of ideas and enthusiasm, but there is no means of capitalizing on this.

They are a very useful way of finding out something about industry, but (1) I would have liked to experience more than one industry, and (2) I found it difficult to make the most of the experience and keep my teaching commitment going, and therefore the pack has not yet been much use.

The most rewarding thing was seeing how my pupils were getting on in the outside world.

Extremely useful experience: personal development, to help students in teaching: sharing of information with colleagues: updating of business philosophy.

I feel that more time could be set aside for follow-up placements or follow-up work and, for teachers involved, some recognizable remuneration for the work involved. Placements seem to highlight the gap which exists between industry and education, and there is a need for far more liaison between the two.

In my own case, I was the first in my school to have taken up a teacher placement. The results have been slow, but over twelve months I can see a pattern emerging and changes in style at school happening.

My placement was important to me. The school was not interested in the outcomes, except in the possibility of financial benefits.

An excellent idea, but it is increasingly difficult to get out of school due to cash limitations on supply cover. Many people in industry may have an out of date idea of present ideas in education – more input here may be useful. We would have liked employees to visit school.

I was not impressed by the organization of the teacher placement. I do not feel that my needs were really considered, but an easy option was chosen. The company were extremely accommodating, but I feel they also considered the placement not entirely appropriate and were sorry they could not do more.

They should be well arranged and given more support from school management. I was refused time off for the placement this academic year. The unions should insist – no refusals.

Will not work unless senior management use ideas and experience gained. This has been obvious from an adviser teacher viewpoint.

Research Proposal Activity 7

This chapter has outlined ways of transforming data so that they can be analyzed in relation to research aims and objectives. In planning research and in preparing a research proposal, it is important from the outset to anticipate the form of analysis that is intended. In turn, it is important to ensure from the earliest possible moment that the form in which the data will be collected render them amenable to the analysis intended. The worst possible situation in which you can find yourself, towards the end of a project, is having data structured in a fashion that is inappropriate to the intended analysis strategy. Therefore, you should anticipate data transformations and data analysis in designing a research strategy. Do so by considering the following questions:

1 What variables are to be included in your study and how is each to be measured?
2 How many cases will be included and how will they be selected?
3 How do you wish the data to be structured?
4 Will the data be structured at the point of collection (for example, by the use of closed questions) or will they be coded at some later stage (for example, by deriving a coding frame from a sample of the data and applying it subsequently to the full set)?
5 Is the way in which data are to be structured appropriate to the intended form of analysis (for example, does it meet the assumptions of the proposed statistical tests about levels of measurement)?
6 Is the form of data manipulation and analysis appropriate to the form of output (article, report, book, thesis) which is intended, and will it yield information appropriate to the intended audience?
7 Do you have the resources and time to carry out the intended data manipulations?

8

Extracting and Presenting Statistics

Roger Sapsford

This chapter covers the presentation of figures in reports of research: tables and graphs. It looks at how we demonstrate differences or associations between variables and begins the book's coverage of statistical control – making allowance for the effects of a third variable.

The Right Figure for the Job

According to the 1981 Census, there were approximately 49,154,700 people in England and Wales on Census night, of whom some 23,873,400 were men. The figures are impressive, but they do not tell us very much. More information is *conveyed*, paradoxically, by sacrificing precision and simplifying the total figure: '49 million' is a more usable concept than '49,154,700'. In terms of components, proportions and percentages are often more useful than absolute numbers; it is more useful to know that 48.5 per cent ('just under half') were male than to know the number in millions. Actual numbers may be useful for planning purposes, but percentages are more interpretable and lend themselves more easily to useful comparison. The art of presenting numerical data lies in giving the figures that will convey the desired information in an easily readable form, while still giving enough information for the reader to check the figures and draw conclusions from them other than those presented by the author.

Depending on the audience for the paper or report, different kinds of presentation will be appropriate. Sometimes we *are* interested in actual numbers, particularly if we have to plan a service; people who plan school provision are less interested in whether the local population of children is going up or down, for example, than in *how many* children will need school places in five years' time. More often, however, a description or a theoretical argument is better served by quoting a summary figure (a mean or median, for example, or a correlation) or a comparative figure (a mean or a percentage compared with the mean or percentage for another interesting group or for the population as a whole). The reader of a report or paper is entitled to expect the figures that are most appropriate for the argument being made or the description being given. In addition, he or she is entitled to expect sufficient additional detail for the conclusions to be checkable and for obviously relevant further calculations to be feasible. Precisely what is needed will, of course, depend on the target audience of the presentation: planners have different needs from academics, who in turn have different needs from policy-makers and the informed general public. However, many presentations of 'applied' research, including most research reports published in journals, will reach all three of these audiences. It is therefore incumbent on the writer(s) to demonstrate the size of 'the problem', to locate it in a relevant context or contexts, to provide enough detail for other researchers to test the conclusions, but to do so in such a way that the main conclusions remain accessible and the evidence is interpretable.

A number of statistical and other technical terms are used in this chapter. Most of them you will have encountered elsewhere, but sometimes they will have been mentioned only in passing. For definitions of key terms see the end of the chapter

Frequencies

One of several local area studies which used Census, birth and mortality statistics to build composite indicators of 'material deprivation' and 'health status' was carried out in the Plymouth Health District (Abbott, 1988; Abbott and Sapsford, 1994). It showed that the two were substantially correlated (but less so in rural areas). The 'unit of analysis' was the Census ward: the analysis correlated the level of material deprivation in a ward with the level of health status in the same ward, across the whole of the Plymouth Health Authority District (which included the City of Plymouth itself, a range of small towns and rural areas in south-west Devon, and a narrow band of more remote rural wards in east Cornwall).

In this section we shall be concentrating on the deprivation data. Table 8.1 is taken from Abbott (1988) and lists the wards in order of their score on the composite indicator of material deprivation (highest numbers indicating greatest degree of deprivation). We can see that the first ten or so wards have high positive scores, indicating that they are among the most deprived, while the last seven on the list have substantial negative scores, indicating relative affluence. We can also see that the departure from zero (the average, neither deprived or affluent) is greater in the direction of deprivation than of affluence; St Peter's, the most deprived ward, scores much higher in a positive direction than the most affluent ward, Wembury, scores in a negative direction.

This is probably the simplest of all the ways of presenting data: to list them in some interpretable order. The table does not convey much to the sociological reader, but it was of interest to 'professional' readers of the original report – doctors, health visitors, social workers and the like – who were interested to see where their area ranked in the distribution of deprivation. The research was 'commissioned' in a sense, by the Community Health Council, and the results were intended to inform practice and policy as well as to add something to the sociology of health; the findings have since been used as a basis for funding inner-city initiatives.

Table 8.1   *Ranked Material Deprivation Index scores for the wards of the Plymouth Health Authority District*

Rank	Name	Score	Rank	Name	Score
1	St Peter's	4.16	43	Charterlands	−0.15
2	Ham	3.32	45.5	Dobswall	−0.18
3	Keyham	2.30	45.5	Saltash	−0.25
4	Budshead	2.25	47	St Dominic	−0.25
5	Sutton	2.09	48	Callington	−0.27
6	Southway	1.79	49	Estover	−0.28
7	St Budeaux	1.75	50	Brixton	−0.29
8	Honicknowle	1.65	51	Menheniot	−0.30
9	Efford	1.53	52	Thrushel	−0.34
10	Maker with Rame	1.01	53	Walkham	−0.36
11.5	Drake	0.96	54.5	Compton	−0.40
11.5	Mount Gould	0.96	54.5	Shevioc	−0.40
13	Lydford	0.94	56	Thurlstone	−0.41
14	Stoke	0.63	57	Lyner	−0.42
15	Erne Valley	0.49	58	Cornwood	−0.50
16	Launceston North	0.44	59.5	Garrabrook	−0.53
17.5	Lansallas	0.32	59.5	Newton and Noss	−0.53
17.5	Looe	0.32	61	Mary Tavy	−0.54
19	Morval	0.31	62	North Petherwine	−0.56
20	Lanteglos	0.29	63	Chilsworthy	−0.60
21	Liskeard	0.28	64	Stokeclimsland	−0.61
22.5	Gunnislake	0.27	65	Milton Ford	−0.63
22.5	Kingsbridge	0.27	66.5	Stokenham	−0.64
24	Sparkwell	0.16	66.5	Modbury	−0.64
25	Millbrook	0.11	68	Tavistock North	−0.65
26	Calstock	0.08	69	Ugborough	−0.66
27	St Neot	0.06	70	Saltstone	−0.69
28	Bickleigh	0.03	71	St Ive	−0.72
29	Trelawney (Plym.)	0.01	73	Marlborough	−0.86
30.5	Trelawney (Comw.)	0.00	73	Tavistock South	−0.86
30.5	South Brent	0.00	73	Landrake	−0.86
32	Eggbuckland	−0.01	75	Yealmpton	−0.90
34	Altarnum	−0.02	76	Avonleigh	−0.91
34	Bere Ferris	−0.02	77	South Petherwine	−0.93
34	Ottery	−0.02	78	Plymstock Radford	−0.95
36.5	St Veep	−0.05	79	Ivybridge	−1.05
36.5	Launceston South	−0.05	80	Plympton Erle	−1.17
38	Salcombe	−0.06	81	Buckland	
39.5	Tamarside	−0.09		Monachorum	−1.18
39.5	St Cleer	−0.09	82	Plymstock	
41	Downderry	−0.13		Dunstone	−1.19
43	Torpoint	−0.15	83	Burrator	−1.31
43	St Germans	−0.15	84	Plympton St Mary	−1.61
			85	Wembury	−1.71

Source: Abbott, 1988, Table 4.1.

High positive scores denote poor health status and high negative scores good health status. Where two or more areas have identical scores, they have been allocated the average of the rank positions all of them would have occupied.

One form of graphic presentation might be to display the Census wards not in terms of geographical location but by their location on a variable of interest. Figure 8.1 (from the 1988 report) shows how the wards of the Plymouth Health Authority District 'stack' in terms of the material deprivation indicator (with the values of the indicator grouped to cut down the number of 'bars'). Again, this was of interest to professionals and administrators because it shows in graphic form where their particular areas are to be found along the dimension of deprivation. It also illustrates the shape of the 'distribution': taller bars in the middle, growing shorter as we move outwards in either direction, but with more wards at the extreme of the 'high deprivation' end than at the other end.

Figure 8.1 shows much the same information as Table 8.1 – which wards are extremely different from the mean, and in which direction – but it shows it in a form more readily assimilated. It is a complex display, however, both to read and to prepare. For most purposes something similar can be done without displaying the names of the wards but using a *bar graph* or *histogram.* Figure 8.2 illustrates what this would look like for the same set of data. It shows the shape of the deprivation variable as something like a normal distribution: tall stacks of cases in the middle of the range, sloping off into smaller stacks as we get towards the extremes in either direction. Also, it illustrates the point, made in the reports, that the distribution is not symmetrical (the technical term is 'skewed'). There are more Census wards far from the mean at the materially deprived end of the variable than at the materially advantaged end, and the worst stand out further from the mean; the very deprived wards' scores are more extreme in the direction of deprivation than the affluent wards' scores are in the direction of affluence.

Figure 8.3 illustrates the same data display as a *line graph,* treating the variable as a continuously varying one rather than stacking cases by grouped values. Again the underlying shape is quite apparent: the largest number of cases at zero or not far from it, sloping away to very small numbers at the extremes, but with too many cases towards the extreme at the right to make the distribution quite a normal one.

Note that in Figures 8.2 and 8.3 the apparent extremity of the skew is partly a question of how the figure is produced: you can make it seem more extreme by increasing the size of the vertical axis, or less extreme by spreading the horizontal axis. For example, in Figure 8.4 the two graphs both use the data illustrated in Figure 8.3, but in the one on the left the scale has been manipulated to produce something more akin to a straight line, while in the one on the right the scaling is arranged to produce more marked 'peaks' in the line. The same kind of thing can be done with bar graphs. The temptation is to think of these variants as 'cheating', but the fact is that there is no right way of drawing a graph; you scale it so that it makes the point you want it to make. For this reason you should treat the graphic presentations you come across in published reports as illustrations of points, not proof of them; the proof – if proof is possible – lies in the data themselves, not in how they are drawn.

Finally, of course, we shall need the actual numbers if we are to be able to do more than just look at the data. Numbers are needed for planning purposes, and also for further analysis; we can draw more detailed conclusions from numbers than from most forms of graphical presentation. Table 8.2 is a *frequency distribution* of the Material Deprivation Index scores, in arbitrary units of 0.5 standard deviations (normalized scores). It shows, of course, a similar pattern to the graphic presentations:

<−1.01	−1.00 to −0.51	−0.50 to −0.01	0.00 to 0.49	0.50 to 0.99	1.00 to 1.99	2.00 to 2.99	3.00 to 3.99	4.00+
		Eggbuckland						
		Launceston S						
		Downderry						
		St Germans						
		Charterlands						
		St Dominic						
		Callington						
	Newton & Noss	Menheniot						
	N Petherwine	Thurlstone						
	S Petherwine	Altarnum	Erne Valley					
	Mary Tavy	Bere Ferris	Launceston N					
	Chilsworthy	Ottery	Lansallas					
	Stokeclimsland	St Veep	Looe					
	Milton Ford	Salcombe	Morval					
	Stokenham	Tamarside	Lanteglos					
	Modbury	St Cleer	Liskeard					
	Tavistock N	Dobswall	Gunnislake					
	Tavistock S	Torpoint	Kingsbridge					
	Ugborough	Saltash	Sparkwell					
	Saltstone	Estover	Millbrook			Southway		
Ivybridge	St Ive	Brixton	Calstock			St Budeaux	Keyham	
Plympton E	Marlborough	Thrushel	St Neot	Drake		Honicknowle	Budshead	
Buckland M	Landrake	Walkham	Bickleigh	Mt Gould		Efford	Sutton	Ham	St Peter's
Plymst. D	Yealmpton	Compton	Trelawney (P)	Lydford		Maker/Rame			
Burrator	Avonleigh	Shevioc	Trelawney (C)					
Plymp. St M	Garrabrook	Lyner						
Wembury	Plymst. R	Cornwood	S Brent	Stoke				
Score:								
<−1.01	−1.00 to −0.51	−0.50 to −0.01	0.00 to 0.49	0.50 to 0.99	1.00 to 1.99	2.00 to 2.99	3.00 to 3.99	4.00+

Figure 8.1 Distribution of wards of the Plymouth Health Authority District on the Material Deprivation Index (Abbott, 1988, Figure 2)

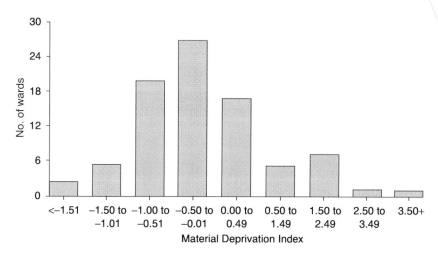

Figure 8.2   *Bar graph of Material Deprivation Index scores*

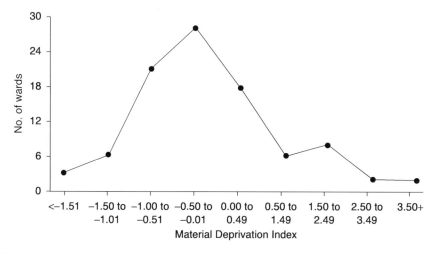

Figure 8.3   *Line graph of Material Deprivation Index scores*

the majority of cases clustered around zero, and a longer 'tail' at the high end of the distribution than the low end.

An important point about the presentation of numbers, incidentally, is that you should *never* 'let the figures speak for themselves'. Wherever a table is presented, there should also be at least a sentence or so saying what you think the table demonstrates. A research presentation is a reasoned argument in which the author's job is to take the reader through, step by step, from the initial premises to the final conclusions. This holds even for what we would normally call 'descriptive statistics'. The annual *Social Trends,* for example, reports on the year's statistics and sets them in the context of past years by means of tables and graphs, but it also explains in

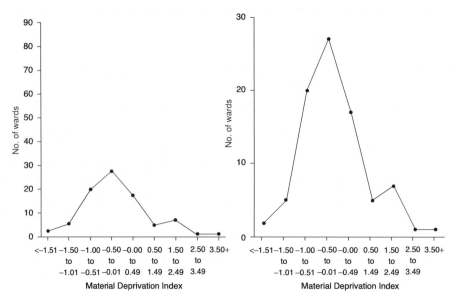

Figure 8.4   *Effects of varying scale on a line graph*

Table 8.2   *Material Deprivation Index scores in the
Plymouth Health Authority District: raw data*

Score[a]	No. of wards
<–1.51	2
–1.50 to –1.01	5
–1.00 to –0.51	20
–0.50 to –0.01	27
0.00 to 0.49	17
0.50 to 0.99	4
1.00 to 1.49	1
1.50 to 1.99	4
2.00 to 2.49	3
2.50 to 2.99	–
3.00 to 3.49	1
3.50 to 3.99	–
4.00+	1
Total	85

[a]A low score denotes affluence and a high score deprivation.

Source: Derived from Table 9.1 (Abbott, 1988)

words what the statisticians see the figures as meaning. (This does not hold for publications such as the volumes of Census statistics which simply present tables for a
county or administrative area; these are not research reports, however, but the comparatively raw material out of which research reports might be written.)

Activity 8.1 (5 minutes)

In itself, Table 8.2 is not very informative for the average reader. What other figures would you like to see here?

As a minimum, we would normally display percentages in each category; readers are entitled to be told what percentage of the total each figure constitutes, without having to work it out for themselves. For some purposes, it might also be useful to show *cumulative* percentages, so that the reader can see at a glance what percentage of cases have a given score *or a lower one*). Table 8.3 remedies these omissions.

You can also present percentages graphically, using bar graphs or (to show visually how the different percentages add up to the total) in a pie chart, in which the total number of cases are represented as a circle and each percentage is shown as a sector of the circle (or 'slice of the pie'). Figure 8.5, for example, illustrates a fictional political constituency in which 42 per cent of the voters chose the Conservative Party, 43 per cent the Labour Party, and the rest other parties.

Activity 8.2 (allow 30 minutes)

You get a better grasp of data analysis by doing it yourself than by reading about it. Using the Plymouth data set provided in the Appendix, try producing a frequency table like Table 8.3 for the score on the Health Index. My version is at the end of the chapter.

Table 8.3 *Material Deprivation Index scores in the Plymouth Health Authority District: percentages*

Score	No. of wards	%	Cumulative %
<−1.51	2	2.4	2.4
−1.50 to −1.01	5	5.9	8.2
−1.00 to −0.51	20	23.5	31.8
−0.50 to −0.01	27	31.8	63.5
0.00 to 0.49	17	20.0	83.5
0.50 to 0.99	4	4.7	88.2
1.00 to 1.49	1	1.2	89.4
1.50 to 1.99	4	4.7	94.1
2.00 to 2.49	3	3.5	97.6
2.50 to 2.99	–	–	97.6
3.00 to 3.49	1	1.2	98.8
3.50 to 3.99	–	–	98.8
4.00+	1	1.2	100.0
Total	85	100.0	

Percentages may not add exactly to a hundred because of rounding errors; 25.04 would be expressed to one decimal place as 25.0, but four of them would add up to 100.16, which would round to 100.2. The same may happen with the cumulative percentages in the final column; you will notice, for example, that the first two percentages appear to add up to 8.3, but the true total is 8.2.

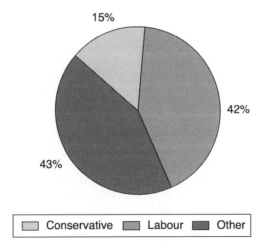

Figure 8.5   *Pie chart showing share of votes in a fictional constituency*

Two-way Distributions

Frequency distributions show you how many cases fall in each band of a variable, but they cannot tell you anything about the relationship between variables. For this, we need to be able to *compare* the values on one variable with the values for the same cases on the other. Comparing health status with material deprivation, for example, we could show the relationship by drawing maps of the incidence of each and comparing the two maps, seeing which wards scored highly on both variables and which on neither, and so exploring the extent of *correlation*: the extent to which either variable predicts the other. We could demonstrate it on a single map by using clever graphics; for example, marking wards high on one variable with slanting lines in one direction, wards high on the other variable by lines slanting in the other direction, and seeing which wards finished up decorated with a cross-hatch pattern. It can be shown more directly using a tabular presentation, however: using each of the dimensions of a two-dimensional array to stand for one of the variables, and placing cases in some way within the two-way table thus defined.

The most straightforward way, using the Plymouth example, is to name the wards in each cell of a table defined by the two variables, and this is what we did in the 1988 report (see Table 8.4). This is a useful form of presentation for professionals who want to see where their particular area falls in terms of the two variables. More generally useful, however, is a table where numbers replace the names (Table 8.5). We can usually do without knowing which particular cases fall where, and the results are much easier to read if tabulated numerically; this is the only sensible way of proceeding if you have more than a relatively small number of cases.

As with Table 8.3, percentages are a useful aid to the reader. For this reason, two more tables have been produced: Table 8.6 shows percentages by rows (showing what percentage of each category of health status falls in each of the Material Deprivation Index categories) and Table 8.7 shows percentages by columns (showing

Table 8.4 Location of Plymouth wards by Material Deprivation Index and Health Index

Health Index	Material Deprivation Index							
	<-1.00	-1.00 to -0.51	-0.51 to -0.16	-0.15 to 0.14	0.15 to 0.49	0.50 to 0.99	1.00 to 1.99	2.00+
<-1.00	Burrator Wembury	Yealmpton Tavistock S Buckland M	Cornwood St Dominic S Petherwine Newton & Noss Garrabrook	Tamarside Salcombe Compton		Lydford		
-1.00 to -0.51	Plymst. D	Stokeclimsland Mary Tavy	Brixton Thurleston	Altarnum Charterlands Ottery	Lanteglos Erne Valley Sparkwell Looe Morval			
-0.50 to -0.21	Ivybridge	Milton Ford Saltstone Landrake Marlborough	Walkham	St Veep Bere Ferris	Lansallas Kingsbridge Gunnislake			
-0.20 to 0.19	Plymp. St M	Chilsworthy Stokenham St Ive	Lyner Menheniot Thrushel	S Brent Bickleigh Downderry Launceston S	Launceston N		Maker/Rame	
0.20 to 0.49		Plymst R Modbury Tavistock N Avonleigh	Estover Dobswall Callington	St Germans Trelawney (C) Torpoint St Neot	Liskeard	Mt Gould		

(Continued)

Table 8.4 (Continued)

Health Index	Material Deprivation Index							
	<−1.00	−1.00 to −0.51	−0.51 to −0.16	−0.15 to 0.14	0.15 to 0.49	0.50 to 0.99	1.00 to 1.99	2.00+
0.50 to 0.99		N Petherwine	Saltash Shevioc	Trelawney (P) Eggbuckland Calstock St Cleer		Drake	Southway	
1.00 to 1.99	Plympton E	Ugborough		Millbrook		Stoke	Honicknowle Efford St Budeaux	Sutton
2.00+								Keyham Budshead Ham St Peter's

Source: Abbott, 1988

Table 8.5   *Location of wards by Material Deprivation Index and Health Index: raw numbers*

		Material Deprivation Index							
Health Index	<−1.00	−1.00 to −0.51	−0.50 to −0.16	−0.15 to 0.14	0.15 to 0.49	0.50 to 0.99	1.00 to 1.99	2.00+	Total
<−1.00	3	5	3	2	–	1	–	–	14
−1.00 to −0.51	1	2	2	3	5	–	–	–	13
−0.50 to −0.21	1	4	1	2	3	–	–	–	11
−0.20 to 0.19	1	3	3	4	1	–	1	–	13
0.20 to 0.49	–	4	3	4	1	1	–	–	13
0.50 to 0.99	–	1	2	4	–	1	1	–	9
1.00 to 1.99	1	1	–	1	–	1	3	1	8
2.00+	–	–	–	–	–	–	–	4	4
Total	7	20	14	20	10	4	5	5	85

Source: Abbott, 1988, Table 26

what percentage of each Material Deprivation Index category falls within each category of health status). The two kinds of percentages are useful for different purposes. In this case we use row percentages (Table 8.6, p. 196) to compare material deprivation categories: we can see at a glance, for instance, that most of the low Health Index scores fall in the first three columns, and all the highest scores in the last column. Table 8.7, similarly, is useful for comparing Health Index categories.

If the two variables are *correlated* – related in such a way that the score on one of them predicts the score on the other at better than a chance level – then we should expect the large percentage figures to 'move' diagonally across the table as we scan down (Table 8.6) or across (Table 8.7, p. 197). In other words, low scores should predict low scores – the largest percentages should be high in the columns at the left-hand side of the table – and as we move across the mean of the distribution and out to the other extreme the large percentages should 'move' towards the middle of the row or column and then away in the other direction. This does indeed appear to be the case in these tables. In Table 8.6 we can see a degree of correlation: by and large, the larger percentages are in the lowest deprivation categories in the first two columns, around the middle (with some variation) in the middle of the table, and towards the bottom of the table as we reach the right-hand columns. Table 8.7 shows the same.

Activity 8.3 (5 minutes)

Look at the two tables and make sure you see what I mean, scanning *down* Table 8.6, row by row, to see where the large concentrations of cases, in percentage terms, fall in each row, and doing a similar scan *across* Table 8.7, column by column.

Table 8.6 *Location of wards by Material Deprivation Index and Health Index: row percentages*

Health Index		<-1.00	-1.00 to -0.51	-0.50 to -0.16	-0.15 to 0.14	0.15 to 0.49	0.50 to 0.99	1.00 to 1.99	2.00+	Total no.
				Material Deprivation Index						
<-1.00	(%)	21	36	21	14	–	7	–	–	14
-1.00 to -0.51	(%)	8	15	15	23	38	–	–	–	13
-0.50 to -0.21	(%)	9	36	9	18	27	–	–	–	11
-0.20 to 0.19	(%)	8	23	23	31	8	–	8	–	13
0.20 to 0.49	(%)	–	31	23	31	8	8	–	–	13
0.50 to 0.99	(%)	–	11	22	44	–	11	11	–	9
1.00 to 1.99	(%)	12	12	–	12	–	12	38	12	8
2.00+	(%)	–	–	–	–	–	–	–	100	4
Total	(%)	8	24	16	24	12	5	6	6	85

Source: Abbott, 1988, Table 26

Table 8.7 *Location of wards by Material Deprivation Index and Health Index: column percentages*

Health Index	<-1.00 (%)	-1.00 to -0.51 (%)	-0.50 to -0.16 (%)	-0.15 to 0.14 (%)	0.15 to 0.49 (%)	0.50 to 0.99 (%)	1.00 to 1.99 (%)	2.00+ (%)	Total
			Material Deprivation Index						
<-1.00	43	25	21	10	–	25	–	–	16
-1.00 to -0.51	14	10	14	15	50	–	–	–	15
-0.50 to -0.21	14	20	7	10	30	–	–	–	13
-0.20 to 0.19	14	15	21	20	10	–	20	–	15
0.20 to 0.49	–	20	21	20	10	25	–	–	15
0.50 to 0.99	–	5	14	20		25	20	–	11
1.00 to 1.99	14	5	–	5	–	25	60	20	9
2.00+	–	–	–	–	–	–	–	80	5
Total	7	20	14	20	10	4	5	5	85

Source: Abbott, 1988, Table 26

Two-way distributions can also be presented in a number of ways using bar graphs (see Figures 8.6–8.8). Figure 8.6 preserves information about the absolute numbers – the height of each bar increases with increased totals on the variable along the bottom – and shows how those numbers are 'shared out' in each bar according to the categories of the other variable. Figure 8.7 does the same but loses information on absolute numbers in favour of percentages; all the bars are the same height, which makes it easier to see where a category of the other variable becomes proportionally more or less common. Figure 8.8, which compares the incidence of certain major diseases between a 'bad' inner-city ward and an affluent country area, shows how a similar job can be done by stacking the bars side by side. Which is the most appropriate to use will depend on the point you want to make. Line graphs can also be used in similar ways.

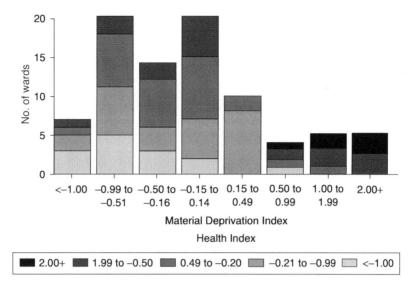

Figure 8.6 *Health Index by Material Deprivation Index*

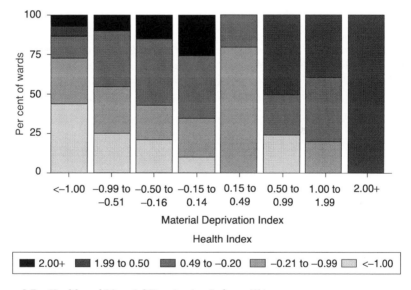

Figure 8.7 *Health and Material Deprivation Indexes (%)*

Incidentally, tables do not have to record just figures or percentages adding up to a total. The tabular format can be a very good way of presenting a range of information in compact and interpretable form. Table 8.8 (see p. 200), for instance, compares the best and the worst wards in London and in Plymouth on four 'deprivation' variables. The figures in the body of the table are not percentages of the column or row, but the percentage of people or households in each ward who fulfil the conditions of each variable.

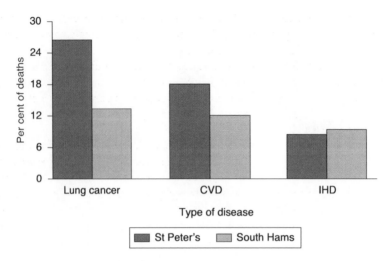

Figure 8.8 *Deaths from lung cancer, cerebrovascular disease (CVD) and ischaemic heart disease (IHD) in St Peter's and South Hams*

Activity 8.4 (allow 30 minutes)

By way of practice, use the Plymouth data set in the Appendix to construct a tabulation of the Material Deprivation Index by the Health Index. What may be inferred from it? My answers are at the end of the chapter.

Introducing a Third Variable

As a reader of a report or article, you can be faced with a table or some other way of presenting figures and find the point that it makes quite convincing. None the less, there may be more for the writer to do in order to make a convincing case and/or to make the most of the available data. Quite often two variables are related, but allowance needs to be made for some third variable (or more than one). The reader needs to know that some obvious explanation has been considered, and to see evidence that it may be rejected. Otherwise, he or she may not be in a position to accept the writer's arguments.

1   There may, for example, be *spurious correlation* between two variables because both are related to a third: in other words, the causal relationship is with the third variable, not between the two under examination. The example of this most beloved of statisticians is a series of Dutch statistics showing a positive correlation between the number of storks nesting in a series of springs and the number of human babies born at that time. (Both were related to the state of the weather some nine months previously!)

2   A third variable may simply be *more important,* in causal terms, than the explanation being put forward. For example, many attempts have been made to identify parents likely to be violent to their children in terms of their psychological characteristics. However, far more of the variance in behaviour seems to be contributed by their material circumstances: poverty, unemployment, overcrowding, lack of resources, etc. This tends to mean that any effect of psychological variables is, simply, swamped by the large effect of material circumstances.

3   There may be an *interaction effect* between the supposed cause and some third variable. For example, the likelihood of reaching a senior management position is (currently) related, among other things, to gender and to the social class of origin. Either alone shows some correlation with the thing to be explained, but both together are enormously more predictive. Moreover, the effect of class differs by gender: in many studies the class of eventual job is more affected by class of origin than level of education for boys, but somewhat less so for girls.

There are sophisticated statistical techniques for dealing with such questions. However, a fair amount can be done, simply, through tables. We will look at examples of each of the effects listed above, mostly using 'made-up' figures (because it is easier to make the point if the figures are specifically designed to make it) and tries to suggest to you what to look out for when reading this kind of analysis. The basis of the technique involves splitting a table into two sub-tables to show the effect of the third variable.

As a case of *spurious correlation,* let us consider a fictional study of the use of flashing lights to ameliorate toothache. Over a period of months, a dental receptionist is instructed to send one patient out of two to the dentist for examination in the normal way, turning them over to the dentist if he or she is there, or waiting with the patient until the dentist arrives. On the other hand, alternate patients are conducted by the receptionist to a special room where he or she settles them in a chair and switches on stroboscopic lights, explaining this as a new therapy for pain; then, after five minutes, the receptionist takes them to the dentist. (Sometimes the receptionist is not able to stay with them, if another patient arrives during the five minutes.) At the end of each treatment, the patients report on the degree of pain they were feeling on arrival at the dentist. Table 8.9 shows the results of the study. (As you can see, the allocation to treatment or control does not work out perfectly even in fictional studies! We have 440 'treatment' cases, whereas the design should have yielded 500.)

The first block of the table is looking for the main effects of treatment (i.e. irrespective of the receptionist's presence or absence), and it suggests that there is quite a respectable effect: only a third of the treatment cases report severe pain, compared with nearly 60 per cent of the control cases. The two blocks on the right, however, separate out cases with whom the receptionist stayed (most of the 'treatment' cases, but also nearly a fifth of the control cases) from those with whom she or he did not stay (approximately four-fifths of the control cases, but also 40 people in the treatment group). From these figures, we can see that the apparent effect of the treatment is almost certainly spurious, and that the determining factor is whether the receptionist stays with the patient. Alternatively, we might have found – with slightly different figures – that most of the effect was contributed by the receptionist staying with the patient, but that there was still a small effect of the treatment even when this

Table 8.8   *Deprivation indicators: Greater London Council Area and Plymouth Health Authority District*

Wards	Unemployed adults (%)	Overcrowded households (%)	Households not owner-occupied (%)	Households with no car (%)
Worst				
GLC				
Tower Hamlets, Spitalfields	22	28	97	80
Tower Hamlets, St Mary	20	17	95	74
Brent, Carlton	22	10	98	77
Kensington & Chelsea, Golborne	19	13	93	74
Tower Hamlets, Shadwell	17	14	98	71
Plymouth Health Authority				
Plymouth City, St Peter's	19	6	84	68
Plymouth City, Ham	17	8	55	52
Plymouth City, Keyham	14	5	52	56
Plymouth City, Budshead	14	3	76	51
Plymouth City, Sutton	14	3	60	59
Best				
GLC				
Bromley, Biggin Hill	3	2	10	8
Sutton, Woodcote	5	1	15	7
Sutton, S. Cheam	3	1	9	11
Croydon, Selsdon	3	1	7	14
Havering, W. Cranham	3	1	4	12
Plymouth Health Authority				
Plymouth City, Plymstock Radford	7	2	22	29
South Hams, Ivybridge	5	2	23	19
Plymouth City, Plympton Erle	6	1	22	20
Plymouth City, Plymstock Dunstone	6	1	20	21
Plymouth City, Plympton St Mary	5	1	10	18

The table compares the best and the worst five wards overall, in each district.

Source: Abbott, 1988, Table 1

effect was controlled for. In other words, there could be a genuine effect of the treatment, but swamped by the effect of a more important variable.

Our example of a third variable being *more important* comes from *Rival Hypotheses* by Huck (1979), an intriguing collection of research studies and alternative ways of interpreting results. Huck's example is a study of women students' halls of residence, in a period when some still imposed a time by which students were required to be back in hall, while others had relaxed this requirement. Huck looked specifically at a college of 787 women, 371 of whom were required to observe 'dormitory hours', while the rest had parental permission to ignore the closing hours. Scores on academic tests were compared at the end of the first academic term. Obviously, there was a risk that the two groups differed on initial academic ability, given that allocation to one group or the other was not random, but the researchers allowed for this in their statistical analyses. After initial ability had been controlled in this

Table 8.9   *The effects of light therapy in dentistry (fictional data)*

Degree of pain	Total patients (%)	Effect of 'treatment'		Receptionist stayed		Receptionist did not stay	
		Treatment (%)	None (%)	Treatment (%)	None (%)	Treatment (%)	None (%)
Severe	48	34	59	30	32	70	65
Mild	52	66	41	70	68	30	35
Total	1,000	440	560	400	100	40	460

Table 8.10   *The pay-off of education by gender*

Education	Total		Male		Female	
	Low	High	Low	High	Low	High
'O' level or less (%)	62.9	37.1	44.2	55.8	82.3	17.7
Higher than 'O' level (%)	31.2	68.8	15.9	84.1	46.8	53.2
n	4,632		2,307		2,325	

Source: Open University's *People in Society* Survey, responses for 1980–4

manner, there was no difference between the two groups in their performance at the end of the first term. The researchers conclude that time restriction has no effect on academic performance. As Huck points out, however, it is very likely that the girls whose parents did not relax the restrictions were ones considered likely to perform badly if not supervised, and that the reason their initial academic performance (based on high-school grades) was as good as the others was because their parents had supervised their hours while they were at high school. In other words, there could well be a genuine difference between the two groups in likelihood of gaining good academic grades, but it is suppressed by the limitations imposed on their social lives.

For an example of an *interaction effect,* we can turn to some real results on the pay-off of education in terms of salary, by gender. Table 8.10 shows data from the 1980–4 responses to the Open University's *People in Society* Survey (see Abbott and Sapsford, 1987a). Among other things, the survey recorded gender, whether or not the respondents were in full-time employment, how much they were earning, and their educational qualifications. In Table 8.10 the level of earnings has been dichotomized at the overall mean into 'low' and 'high', and educational qualifications have been dichotomized into 'O level or less' or 'higher than O level'.

Overall, there is a marked association, as you would expect, between level of education and amount earned: nearly two-thirds of people with lower-level qualifications fall in the low-wage column, but less than a third of those with higher qualifications. Looking at males and females separately, we find a similar pattern, with a much larger proportion of the less-educated than of the more-educated earning low wages.

We can also see that the overall level of earnings is markedly lower for females than for males. Thus we have identified two main effects. The dependent variable (earnings) is predicted separately by two independent variables: level of qualifications and gender. However, we have also noted an interaction effect – an effect of one of the independent variables on the other, changing the extent to which it predicts the dependent variable. In this case, the relationship of qualifications to earnings is not the same for men as for women; there is an interaction between gender and qualifications in the prediction of earnings.

Activity 8.5 (allow up to 1 hour)

Now try your hand at three-way analysis, verifying a point made in Abbott et al. (1992) about the predictability of health status from material deprivation in urban and rural areas. In Activity 8.4 you prepared a table of health *v.* material deprivation overall. Now, using the Plymouth data set in the Appendix, construct tables of the relationship between the two separately for rural and urban areas. My answers are at the end of the chapter.

Postscript: the Element of Chance

Finally, we should note in reading other people's data or in presenting our own that the observed difference between two groups may not necessarily be due to a real difference between them; it may be a product of the way in which the figures were collected. When looking at trends in population size since 1861 from the Census, for example, we need to be very sure that the figures were collected in the same way from decade to decade. Further error is likely to be introduced where the figures are samples from larger populations, as they usually are, because a sample represents its population only within a margin of error, even if properly drawn. As we saw in Chapter 2, even the best of samples is not necessarily a perfect representation of its population; it just stands as high (and precisely estimable) a chance of being so as possible. You have already met the concept of sampling error in Chapter 2, and in Chapters 9 and 10 you will learn how to capitalize on it to calculate the *statistical significance* of differences. For now, let us merely note that we cannot have great confidence in any of the differences between groups which have been illustrated in this chapter. We have not tested whether they are big enough, in relation to their sampling errors, to be unlikely to have come about by chance alone.

Key Terms

Bar graph *see* graph
Cell percentages *see* percentages
Column percentages *see* percentages
Correlation the systematic linear relationship of two variables. We talk about two variables being *positively correlated* when high values on one variable predict high values on another, and low values predict low values. *Negative correlation* is the opposite: high values on one predict low values an the other, and vice versa. Two variables are said to be uncorrelated – to exhibit *zero correlation* – when the values on one variable do not at all predict the values on the other

- *correlation coefficient* a summary of the amount of correlation between two variables. Correlation coefficients are constructed to take the value of +1 if there is perfect positive correlation, –1 if there is perfect negative correlation, 0 when there is no correlation, and values in between where some degree of correlation exists but not perfect correlation. (This last situation will normally *be* the case in social science research)
- *spurious correlation* said to occur where two variables are correlated, but not because one has an effect on the other; the effect is due to the fact that both are correlated with a third variable

Effect in statistical jargon, an *effect* is a proportion of variance explained by a variable or by error. More colloquially, we speak of 'an effect' when we have shown a relationship *between* one or more independent variable(s) and the dependent variable

- *main effect* the effect of an independent variable, over and above the effects of any other variables
- *interaction effect* the effect of two variables in combination, over and above their main effects. The effect is shown by the relationship between two variables being of a different degree for different levels of a third variable. For example, ability to run fast might well be attributable to age, weight and the interaction between them: the effect of weight on running speed might be different for children than for adults

Error term the amount of variance still unexplained after all the variables have been taken into account: taken as due to (a) other variables, (b) sampling error, and (c) measurement error
Graph a graphical presentation of data. The main variants are:

- *bar graph or histogram* a graph which presents figures as bars whose height is proportional to what is being measured. Strictly speaking, the term *bar graph* should be used where the variable being measured has natural discrete categories (e.g. male, female), and *histogram* where data presented are continuous scores aggregated into categories (e.g. age in 5-year bands)
- *histogram* see Bar graph, above

(Continued)

(Key Terms Continued)

– *line graph* a graph which presents data as a line whose points are
   defined by the two variables which form the vertical and horizontal
   axes; for example, a plot of height against weight in a population
– *pie chart* a graph where the total is illustrated as a circle or 'pie', and
   figures are shown as segments of the circle ('slices of the pie'), and
   values are shown

Index a summary variable relating all scores to a comparison point.
One common form of indexing is to set one data point (e.g. a year) equal to
100 and express all other data points as percentages of it. Another is to set
the mean equal to zero and express all other points as deviations from it

Indicator where a quantity cannot be measured directly, an *indicator*
is a variable which is measured that can plausibly be argued to be highly
correlated with the desired quantity. For example, scores on intelligence
tests are indicators of intelligence; the height of mercury in a thermo-
meter is an indicator of temperature

Interaction effect *see* Effect

Line graph *see* Graph

Main effect *see* Effect

Mean the arithmetical average of a set of figures, obtained by adding
them all together and dividing by the number of cases

Median another form of average, the mid-point of a distribution. This
may or may not be close to the mean, depending on whether the distribution is a symmetrical one

Normal curve a distribution of events occurring randomly, with the
largest single number of cases at the mean, large numbers of cases close
to the mean, and progressively fewer cases as we move further away
from the mean

Percentages figures expressed as though their total were 100

– *cell percentages* on a table, cell percentages add up to the total of
   the table: the figure in each cell is divided by the overall total and mul-
   tiplied by 100
– *column percentages* percentages based on the totals of the *columns*
   of a table (down the page)
– *row percentages* percentages based on the totals of the *rows* of a
   table (across the page)

Pie chart *see* Graph

Proportion figures expressed as though their total were 1.00

row percentages *see* percentages

Spurious correlation *see* Correlation

Suppressor variable a variable which has the effect of suppressing the
visibility of another variable's effects. For example, mode of transport
would suppress the relationship of fitness to speed of travel: bicycles go
so much faster than walking that even an unfit cyclist should be able to go
faster than a fit walker

Further Reading

Marsh, C. (1988) *Exploring Data: an introduction to data analysis for social scientists*, Cambridge, Polity.
Antonius, R. (2003) *Interpreting Quantitative Data with SPSS*, London, Sage.
Brace, N. et al. (2000) *SPSS for Psychologists*, Basingstoke, Macmillan.
Bryman, A. and Cramer, D. (1997) *Quantitative Data Analysis with SPSS for Windows*, London, Routledge.
Coakes, S.J. and Stted, L.G. (2003) *SPSS without Anguish*, Milton (Australia), Wiley.
Huff, D. (1981) *How to Lie with Statistics*, Harmondsworth, Penguin.

Answers to Activities

Activity 8.2

The frequency distribution of the Health Index should look something like Table 8.11.

Table 8.11   *Distribution of Health Index in the Plymouth study*

Score	No. of wards	%	Cumulative %
<−1.51	4	4.7	4.7
−1.50 to −1.01	10	11.8	16.5
−1.00 to −0.51	13	15.3	31.8
−0.50 to −0.01	17	20.0	51.8
0.00 to 0.49	20	23.5	75.3
0.50 to 0.99	9	10.6	85.9
1.00 to 1.99	8	9.4	95.3
2.00+	4	4.7	100.0
Total	85	100	

Activity 8.4

The table might look like Table 8.12.

Table 8.12   *Health and Material Deprivation Index in the Plymouth study*

Material Deprivation Index	Health Index			
	<−1 (%)	−0.99 to −0.01 (%)	0.00 to 0.99 (%)	1.00+ (%)
<−1.00	21	7	3	8
−0.99 to −0.01	71	60	62	8
0.00 to 0.99	7	33	28	17
1.00+	−	−	7	67
Total *(n)*	14	30	29	12

Table 8.13 *Health, material deprivation and type of area*

	Health Index			
	Urban		Rural	
Material Deprivation Index	Zero or Negative (%)	Positive (%)	Zero or Negative (%)	Positive (%)
Negative	78	36	74	75
Zero or positive	22	64	26	25

Percentages the other way, or even the raw figures, would have shown much the same in this case. We can see that the correlation is by no means perfect – there is a spread up and down each column – but the tendency of high values to go with high ones and low values with low ones is quite clear.

Activity 8.5

The overall pattern is given in Table 8.12, in the answers to Activity 8.4 above. Splitting the figures by rural and urban areas, we get Table 8.13. (Numbers were so small in some columns that I have added adjacent columns together to give a better base for percentages, turning each block of the table into a dichotomy.)

Even a table as crude as Table 8.13 shows very clearly that there is a strong relationship in urban areas but virtually none in rural areas. So, splitting the original table by a third variable, in this case presenting separate tables for the urban and the rural wards, enables a hidden relationship to emerge.

Research Proposal Activity 8

It is usually not advisable to prescribe the strategy of data analysis completely and right from the start; you will need scope, as the project develops, to pursue the avenues that turn out to be fruitful. However, you do need to address the following at the planning stage:

1 How are data to be presented? In tables? Graphically?
2 What dependent and independent variables will the analysis probably require, and for what 'third variables' might it be necessary to control?
3 When your data are recorded, will they be in a form suitable for the proposed analysis and mode of presentation?

Appendix: Data-set

Health and Material Deprivation in the Plymouth Health Area

Ward name	Urban/ rural	Depriv. index	Health index	Ward name	Urban/ rural	Depriv. index	Health Index
St Peter's	U	4.2	3.3	Charterlands	U	−0.2	−0.8
Ham	U	3.3	2.0	Dobswall	R	−0.2	0.4
Keyham	U	2.3	2.4	Saltash	U	−0.2	0.9
Budshead	U	2.2	2.2	St Dominic	R	−0.2	−1.0
Sutton	U	2.1	1.7	Callington	U	−0.3	0.3
Southway	U	1.8	0.8	Estover	U	−0.3	0.5
St Budeaux	U	1.8	1.3	Brixton	R	−0.3	−0.6
Honicknowle	U	1.6	1.8	Menheniot	R	−0.3	0.0
Efford	U	1.5	1.4	Thrushel	R	−0.3	0.0
Maker/Rame	R	1.0	0.2	Walkham	R	−0.4	−0.5
Drake	U	1.0	0.7	Compton	U	−0.4	−1.0
Mt Gould	U	1.0	0.4	Shevioc	R	−0.4	1.0
Lydford	R	0.9	−1.4	Thurleston	R	−0.4	−0.9
Stoke	U	0.6	1.3	Lyner	R	−0.4	0.1
Erne Valley	R	0.5	−0.9	Cornwood	R	−0.5	−1.6
Launceston N	U	0.4	−0.2	Garrabrook	R	−0.5	−1.7
Lansallas	R	0.3	−0.3	Newton & Noss	R	−0.5	−1.6
Looe	R	0.4	−1.0	Mary Tavy	R	−0.5	−0.8
Morval	R	0.3	−0.9	N Petherwine	R	−0.6	0.5
Lanteglos	R	0.3	−0.7	Chilsworthy	R	−0.6	0.2
Liskeard	U	0.3	0.4	Stokeclimsland	R	−0.6	−0.7
Gunnislake	R	0.3	−0.4	Milton Ford	R	−0.6	−0.2
Kingsbridge	U	0.3	−0.3	Stokenham	R	−0.6	0.0
Sparkwell	R	0.2	−0.9	Modbury	R	−0.6	0.4
Millbrook	U	0.1	1.0	Tavistock N	U	−0.7	0.3
Calstock	R	0.1	0.6	Ugborough	R	−0.7	1.2
St Neot	R	0.1	0.2	Saltstone	R	−0.7	−0.4
Bickleigh	R	0.0	0.0	St Ive	R	−0.7	−0.1
Trelawney (P)	U	0.0	1.0	Marlborough	R	−0.9	−0.5
Trelawney (C)	R	0.0	0.4	Tavistock S	U	−0.9	−1.1
S Brent	U	0.0	0.1	Landrake	R	−0.9	−0.4
Eggbuckland	U	0.0	1.0	Yealmpton	U	−0.9	−1.0
Altarnum	R	0.0	−0.6	Avonleigh	R	−0.9	0.3
Bere Ferris	R	0.0	−0.4	S Petherwine	R	−0.9	−1.3
Ottery	R	0.0	−0.8	Plymstock			
St Veep	R	0.0	−0.3	Radford	U	−1.0	0.4
Launceston S	U	0.0	0.1	Ivybridge	U	−1.0	−0.2
Salcombe	U	−0.1	−1.7	Plympton Erle	U	−1.2	1.1
Tamarside	R	−0.1	−1.3	Buckland			
St Cleer	R	−0.1	0.5	Monachorum	R	−1.2	−1.4
Downderry	R	−0.1	−0.1	Plymstock			
Torpoint	U	−0.2	0.3	Dunstone	U	−1.2	−0.7
St Germans	R	−0.2	0.5	Burrator	R	−1.3	−1.3
				Plympton			
				St Mary	U	−1.6	0.1
				Wembury	R	−1.7	−1.3

9

Statistical Techniques

Judith Calder and Roger Sapsford

In the previous chapter we looked at how figures are laid out – in tables and graphs, for example – so that the reader can easily grasp the points that the author is trying to make and observe any differences between groups or associations between variables which may be important for the argument of the report. At the end of the chapter it was pointed out, however, that an observed difference or association in a sample does not prove that such a difference or association exists in the population which the sample represents. The sample you picked could be very different from the population by chance alone (which is called *sampling error* – see Chapter 2). This chapter takes statistical skills a stage further by looking at some of the methods that have been evolved for checking the likelihood that a result observed in a sample really *does* represent what the population is like.

After working through this chapter you should not only be in a position to read and understand a wider range of research papers and reports and understand the arguments better, but you should also be able to tell when conclusions may be suspect because of the inappropriate use of a particular form of analysis.

We are working on the assumption that you will have what most sensible researchers secure for themselves: access to a statistical package on a computer. We have therefore not talked about how you work out the statistics for yourself or, generally, given the statistical formulae which underlie them.

Different Kinds of Data

Data can be categorized into two types. Some data, such as time, temperature and length, are examples of data which are *continuous*; that is, they can take values *between* whole numbers (someone can be 36.33 years old, for example). Other data are only meaningful as whole numbers. In spite of the predilection of newspapers for such families, you cannot have 2.4 children, for example! Data like these are known as *discrete* data.

The amount of information which data may give can vary considerably, and we can also categorize them by the kind of information they yield and the kind of calculation that can be done with them. In the previous chapter you were introduced to four *levels of measurement*. *Nominal data* give the least information, recording merely the name of the group or category to which an individual or item belongs. *Ordinal data* indicate the rank order in which items are placed but give no indication of distance between ranks. The fact that a child may be the second child in a family reveals nothing about distance in age from the older sibling. Rating scales which use classifications like 'very important', 'fairly important', 'not very important', 'not at all important' produce ordinal data. In contrast, with *interval data* there are equal intervals or equal distances between each of the measures on the scale. However, with interval data there is no *absolute* zero point, and so it is not possible to divide or to multiply one score by another. Measurements of temperature are an example of interval data, where a temperature of 40°C cannot be divided by a temperature of 20°C to claim that 40°C represents twice as much heat as 20°C. There is what is *called* a zero, at 0°C, but this is merely a point of reference against which other temperature measures can be set. Finally, where we have *ratio data,* we can draw conclusions about the *relative* size or worth of the data (hence the term 'ratio'). For example, a person's income, regardless of the units in which it is measured, can be expressed as a ratio of someone else's. So, for example, we can say that people earning £30,000 have twice as much as people earning £15,000.

It will be apparent that it can sometimes be quite difficult to identify correctly the type of data being investigated. Statisticians have pointed out that, strictly speaking, although data such as intelligence, aptitude and personality tests have numerical scores attached to them, they are only ordinal data – there is no real or absolute zero, nor any guarantee that the values are equidistant. One way of dealing with data that are difficult to 'type' correctly is through the use of *models*. Scientists use models of weather systems to study the relationships between different factors in order to understand better what the contributory factors are. In the same way, statisticians produce statistical models based on their current understanding of a problem. When they do not quite work as expected, they modify some of their assumptions. If the assumption of an interval scale does not work, then further analyses can be carried out on the assumption of an ordinal scale. Over the years, reviews of the statistical evidence suggest that the assumption of equality of equal intervals within rating scales is justified. But where such assumptions are made, there is always the *possibility* of misinterpretation of the data. The important point is to be clear always that there are different types of data, and that this will affect the type of analyses that can be used on them.

Approaches to Analysis

Looking at Variables

We have been discussing the fact that the level and type of data you are dealing with can have a considerable influence on the type of analysis you are able to undertake. A number of other criteria also play a key role in determining the approach used for

Table 9.1　*Subject totals and means by retention interval for age, grade and contact in a study of memory*

RI (months)	Subject totals		Age at retrieval		Grade		Contact	
	n	%	m	s.d	m	s.d	m	s.d.
3	33	8.8	39.6	8.1	2.5	0.834	1.88	0.331
15	37	9.9	39.8	8.9	2.5	0.650	1.65	0.484
27	35	9.4	45.5	10.1	2.7	1.01	1.57	0.502
39	25	6.7	46.7	11.1	2.8	0.913	1.60	0.500
41	42	11.3	46.8	9.4	2.8	0.881	1.69	0.468
53	48	12.9	48.5	10.1	2.5	0.849	1.60	0.494
65	28	7.5	52.9	8.7	2.8	0.803	1.68	0.476
77	27	7.2	54.4	11.6	3.0	0.898	1.78	0.424
89	27	7.2	55.7	10.0	2.9	0.759	1.63	0.492
101	23	6.2	52.6	10.7	2.4	0.988	1.57	0.507
113	18	4.8	53.3	11.9	2.8	0.707	1.89	0.323
125	30	8.1	58.9	9.6	2.4	0.817	1.63	0.490

RI, retention interval; *n*, total number; m, mean; s.d., standard deviation.
Contact refers to ratings of contact with course material with the exception of research methods.

Note: the authors draw the attention of readers to the fact that 'the spacing of RIs is not equal, and this is because testing was conducted in two waves some months apart'.

Source: Conway et al., 1991, p. 398, Table 1

the analysis: for example, the amount and type of units of analysis, the number of variables, the research design, the sample design and sample size, and, most importantly, the research question(s).

In general, one of the key points that must be established as early as possible is which of the variables are seen as being dependent and which independent. A variable is termed *independent* if, for a particular research question, it is hypothesized as being the cause or origin of some effect on a *dependent* variable. For example, if we hypothesize that a person's income is affected by his or her gender, then, for this research question, income would be the dependent variable and gender the independent variable. The independent variable is always the antecedent and the dependent variable the consequent. It would never be hypothesized that someone's gender was in some way influenced by their income, for example!

Now look at Table 9.1, reproduced from Conway et al. (1991), which is a report from a research project on age and retention of undergraduate learning (m and s.d. are used as the symbols for the mean and standard deviation – explained later in the chapter). The data in the table, clearly, are already summarized. The RI column (RI stands for retention interval) shows how long it was between the student studying the course and being tested, while going down the next column (*n* for total number) we can see how many former students last studied the psychology course 3 months ago, 15 months ago, 27 months ago, and so on. The information about the retention intervals of the former students has been *grouped* into frequencies for each of the retention intervals, so the researchers are here dealing with only 12 measures rather than the 373 they started with. The rest of the table similarly summarizes information about the former students. Reading across the table this time, you can see that for the

33 students who last studied psychology 3 months prior to testing, their mean age (m) at the time of the study was 39.6 years, and the standard deviation (s.d.) about the mean age for that group of 33 people was 8.1 years. Moving further along the same line, we read that the mean grade for their psychology courses achieved by this group of former students was 2.5 (remember that 2 is the code for an upper second and 3 the code for a lower second class degree) with a standard deviation of 0.834, and, further along, that the mean contact level for this group was 1.88. Again, this score can only be interpreted if you know that contact was coded either as 1 for a considerable amount of post-course contact with psychology, or 2 for only a little or no further contact with the field after completing the course. These statistics, then, are *describing* the data which have been collected.

Two Types of Statistics

In Table 9.1 no hypotheses are being tested nor inferences drawn about a wider population. Such statistics, which focus on the description of data presented, are known as *descriptive statistics*. In contrast, *inferential statistics* are used in order to draw conclusions about a wider population from sample data and to examine differences, similarities and relationships between different variables. There are two aspects to inferential statistics.

1 The first concerns the making of inferences about populations from data drawn from samples. For example, if 29 per cent of our *sample* listen to a certain radio programme, then we use that information to make an inference about the percentage of our *population* who listen to that radio programme. Statistical techniques are used to estimate the range within which the population parameters are likely to lie, given the sample statistics. (See Chapter 2.)
2 The second aspect comes from the testing of hypotheses or the study of relationships. Here the emphasis is on hypotheses about the data being studied. In the research reported, we shall see that the researchers have tested a number of hypotheses about the relationship between age, retention interval and amount and quality of recall. Statistical techniques are used to assess how likely it is that the observed difference or relationship could arise by chance alone if the same difference was not to be found in the population from which the sample was drawn.

Descriptive Measures

In Table 9.1 several different kinds of descriptive statistics were used. We saw frequency scores, percentages, means and standard deviations referred to. You have met most of these already, but let us just spend a moment looking at each one in turn.

First, the *frequency scores* for the retention intervals can be plotted as a graph. When the points are joined together, we have a *distribution* of retention interval frequencies from 3 months to 125 months (see Figure 9.1). To summarize and describe the distribution in Figure 9.1, two pieces of information are needed. First, we need information about what is called the *central tendency* in order to see where the central values or 'typical' values are located. Secondly, we need information about the *variability* or spread among the values of the variable.

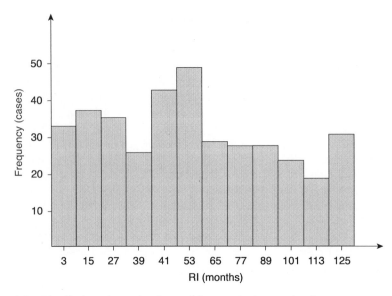

Figure 9.1   *Distribution of retention interval frequencies in a study of memory*

Measures of Central Tendency

You will recall that the three measures of central tendency are the mean, the median and the mode. The *mean* is simply the average of all the data. The *median* is the middle value of the ordered data, i.e. when the data are arranged from the smallest up to the largest, or vice versa. The *mode* is the value which is most common in the data set. If the distribution is a normal distribution, the mean, median and mode will be the same. If the distribution is *skewed* – if it is not symmetrical – they will have different values.

Measures of Spread

As Figure 9.2 shows, however, it is quite possible to have two distributions with the same mean, but with very different distributions of values. The spread, or the variability, of the distribution for (b) is much greater than that for (a). A second piece of information is therefore needed to summarize and describe a distribution: namely, some measure of its spread or variability. The simplest measure for doing this is to look at the *range* of the data scores or measures. In the research reported, the retention interval ranges from 3 months to 125 months, a range of 122 months. This figure gives quite a good indication of the actual spread of the data because the frequencies are relatively even. However, if we were looking at the age of the former students, and there was one very elderly person of, say, 90 years, with everyone else being under the age of 65 years, then the range of ages would not be a good indicator of spread because of the distortion introduced by the extreme case. (These extreme cases are often referred to as *outliers*.) Any extreme cases will mean that the range over-estimates the spread of the data. The *interquartile range,* which looks only at the middle 50 per cent of the distribution, is a better indicator, and it is frequently used as an indicator in economics.

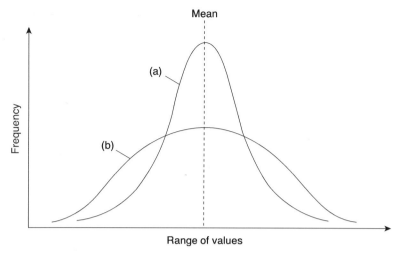

Figure 9.2   *Low variability (a) and high variability (b)*

However, the most useful and most powerful indicator of spread is the *standard deviation*. This is the square root of the *variance*, which in turn is calculated by taking all the deviations of data points from the reference point (in this case the mean), squaring them and dividing by the number of items. The variance is what is to be explained in statistics – the amount of variation in the sample; we look to see whether less variation is shown if we 'take out' the effects of other variables – in other words, whether the variation is not random but shows some kind of pattern.

You will recall from Chapter 2 that the standard deviation will be small where the data cluster closely around the mean, and where the standard deviation is large, it is because the data are spread out. So, in Figure 9.2, for example, (b) will have a larger standard deviation than (a).

Activity 9.1 (5 minutes)

Look at the 'age at retrieval' column in Table 9.1 and identify which RI groups have the greatest differences in the spread of ages as measured by the standard deviations of their mean ages.

Measures of Location

In social and economic research, the different variables which comprise a data set are often measured in different units: for example, time, attitude ratings, income and occupation. In the research under discussion, the units used were months and years (RI and age), and grades and rating scores (interest). In order to make comparisons between distributions using different measures, the measurements have to be transformed in order that they can all be located on one common scale. Even simple operations like addition or multiplication are not possible on data which are not comparable because they are measured in different units. One common way of achieving this is to use *percentages,* as we saw in Chapter 8.

Another way of handling this issue is through the use of units based on standard deviations, known as *standard scores* or *z-scores.* Remember that the standard deviation measures the spread of a group of data, such as scores, by examining the distance of the individual scores from the mean. The z-score simply transforms each score into the number of standard deviations or fractions of standard deviations it is away from the mean. A key feature of z is that, by transforming any measure from a distribution into a z-score, it is possible to say how likely it is that a particular z-score will lie between certain limits or how far from the mean an observation is located. This means that, where researchers have to deal with estimates of population data or with sample data, they are able to assign probabilities through the use of z. Thus z transformations form one of the basic building blocks in inferential statistics.

Inferential Statistics

Descriptive statistics are the most widely used measures in research reports and papers. We have discussed the three major measures of central tendency, measures of variability and measures of location used in descriptive statistics. Each of them summarizes the set of data it is describing in a different way. They also underpin what we are going to say about *inferential* statistics.

Earlier in the chapter you were briefly introduced to the two aspects of inferential statistics: hypothesis testing, and estimation of population parameters from sample data. As you will see in the next section, the same measure or test is often used for both purposes. Remember that inferential statistics are about generalizing from the evidence available. Researchers can either generalize from the sample to the population, as you saw in Chapter 2, or they can test hypotheses about relationships or differences in the population, using the data from the sample. Either way, because the results are based on samples, they will be subject to sampling error. With either type of conclusion, inferential statistics enables you to say with what level of uncertainty the findings should be treated.

Types of Error

Not surprisingly, a hypothesis has to be expressed in statistical terms before it can be tested. But it always has to be tested against some alternative. In fact, you can never actually prove statistically that a hypothesis is right. You can only show either that it should be rejected or that it should not be rejected. (Hence the difficulty of proving statistically that there is a causal relationship between lung cancer and smoking, or between radiation and childhood leukaemia.) The actual formulation of the hypothesis is therefore very important.

Suppose a large institution has an equal opportunities target for its staffing profile. Their aim is 5 per cent of employees who could be classified as people with physical

Table 9.2 *Types of error*

Real situation	Conclusion drawn from test	
	Reject H_0	Do not reject H_0
H_0 true	Type 1 error $P = \alpha$	Correct
H_0 false	Correct[a]	Type 2 error $P = \beta$

[a] The probability of achieving the appropriate conclusion when the null hypothesis H_0 is false, that is, of correctly rejecting H_0 when it is false, is known as the *power* of a statistical test. This term is used frequently in research and statistical literature.

disabilities. The question is whether this target has been attained or whether further action needs to be taken to achieve it. A small sample study involving 140 staff is carried out which gives a figure of 2.7 per cent of staff who could be categorized as people with physical disabilities. The sample data suggest that the target has not been reached. However, it might be argued that the figure of 2.7 per cent of staff has emerged by chance because of the particular sample which was selected, and that the target figure for the staff as a whole had actually been reached. For this sort of problem, two hypotheses have to be presented. The researchers form what is known as the *null* hypothesis (written as H_0), which says that the target has been reached. That is, they propose there is no significant difference between the sample figure and the target figure. The *alternative* hypothesis H_a is that the target has not been reached. The null hypothesis is always the one which is actually tested. The researchers can then show either that the null hypothesis should be rejected and that therefore there is a likelihood that the target has not been reached, or that the null hypothesis is not rejected and that therefore it is likely that the target *has* been reached.

When researchers are drawing conclusions from a sample, there is the danger of two different types of incorrect conclusions being drawn from the evidence available. The null hypothesis may be rejected when it is true (so in the example above, scarce resources may be spent unnecessarily in continuing to try to reach the target) or the null hypothesis may not be rejected when in fact it is false (i.e. it is assumed that the target has been reached when in fact it has not).

These two types of error are referred to as Type 1 and Type 2 errors. Whenever a hypothesis is being tested, the probability that either of these errors will occur can be calculated. The probability of a Type 1 error, i.e. rejecting H_0 when it is true, is written as α. The probability of a Type 2 error, i.e. not rejecting H_0 when it is false, is written as β. Table 9.2 shows a summary of the situation.

Alpha (α), the Type 1 error, is also known as the *significance level*. In order to carry out a test on the hypothesis, researchers have to decide what level they wish to set α at. The job of the hypothesis test then is to calculate the probability that the test statistic lies within a range which is fixed by the level the researchers selected for α (see Figure 9.3). The shaded *area* in Figure 9.3 shows the significance level α.

If the test statistic is found to lie outside the range set, then H_0 would be rejected. *But,* in reality, one of two things could have occurred. Either H_0 was outside the limits

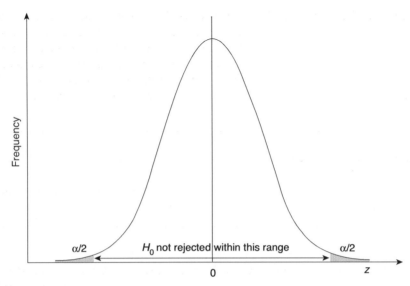

Figure 9.3 *Standard normal distribution: each shaded area represents $\alpha/2$*

because H_0 was actually false, or it was actually true but was outside because the test involves the use of sample data, and sample estimates will always carry a small but known probability of being an extreme measure. This, you will now recognize, would be a Type 1 error. Similarly, if the statistic falls inside the limits, then the null hypothesis would not be rejected. However, here there is still a possibility that H_0 is actually false and that the statistic fell within these limits by chance. This would be a Type 2 error. (Note that for the Type 2 error, the term 'not rejected' rather than 'accepted' is used. The distinction between the terms 'not rejecting' and 'accepting' a hypothesis is an important one in research.)

So how is α determined? At the beginning of the example, it was explained that the job of the hypothesis test is to calculate the probability that the null hypothesis H_0 can safely be rejected, and what counts as 'safe' is determined by the level the researchers selected for α. If α is minimized, then β is maximized. Conversely, if β is minimized, then α is maximized. The issue of whether researchers should minimize the Type 1 error or the Type 2 error depends very much on the problem being investigated. In some instances, a Type 2 error can have very serious effects. For example, say the null hypothesis H_0 was that the attempted suicide rate was not increasing. Then α would be the probability of rejecting H_0 when it was true. That is, the data suggested that an increase had occurred when this was not the case (= Type 1 error). And β would be the probability that the test suggested that there had not been an increase when in fact there had been one (= Type 2 error).

Clearly, in dealing with such issues, the aim of researchers analyzing the data would be to minimize as far as possible the probability of Type 2 errors. In contrast, other situations could be such that the researchers would want to minimize the probability of Type 1 errors. If there is no reason to expect any differences between the effects of either type of error, then α is usually fixed at 0.05. An α of 0.05 means that there are five chances in 100 of making a Type 1 error, with H_0 being wrongly rejected when it is true. Similarly, an α of 0.001 means there is only one chance in 1,000 of making a Type 1 error. Unfortunately, the smaller α is made, the larger the probability of a Type 2 error. By convention, researchers tend to set α equal to 0.05 (one chance in 20 of a Type 1 error) or the more stringent 0.01 (one chance in 100), but where it is to be set must depend on the nature of the research problem.

Activity 9.2 (5 minutes)

Think of an example where the null hypothesis was such that researchers would want to minimize the possibility of Type 1 errors.

You may have remarked by now that there is no reference to either α or β in most research papers. The reason is that a measure called the *observed significance level* or *P value* is normally used to indicate the exact point at which H_0 is either rejected or not rejected. Again, the decision to reject or not to reject H_0 may be made by the researchers on the basis of the chosen value for α. If the P value is less than α, then H_0 is rejected. If the P value is greater than or equal to α, then H_0 is not rejected. So, for example, if α has been set at 0.05, and P is calculated to be 0.15, then H_0 would not be rejected. Alternatively, rather than choosing a specific value for α, what often happens is that where $P < 0.01$ then H_0 is rejected, and where $P > 0.05$ then H_0 is not rejected. If P lies between 0.01 and 0.05, then the results are usually considered to be inconclusive.

Chi-square

In Chapter 8 you looked at the use of tables to show differences between groups or associations between variables in samples, but it was pointed out that the differences may not be representative of the population under examination, but a product of sampling error. In other words, it is always possible to draw a sample that is utterly unrepresentative of the population, but if random methods are used correctly (see Chapter 2) the probability of doing so should be small. Inferential statistics can be used on tabular data, as well as on other kinds of data, to check the likelihood of having obtained a spurious result through sampling error.

In a paper on the effects of age on long-term memory, which we have already discussed, Gillian Cohen and her colleagues (1992b) presented tables designed to reveal whether there was any association between age and the grade students received on their courses, age and how interesting they found them, and age and retention interval (RI): how long had elapsed between learning the material and being re-tested on it. The statistical significance of the results was described as follows:

By χ^2 the distribution of age groups is significantly different for all these variables: RI (χ^2 (10) = 98.42, $P < 0.0001$); grade (χ^2 (6) = 18.40, $P < 0.005$); and interest (χ^2 (4) = 10.90, $P < 0.02$) (Cohen et al., 1992b: 156).

If you are a new reader of academic journals, the first word of advice on how to handle this piece of information is: don't panic! This statement is merely a succinct summary of some of the test results expressed in statistical terms. By unpacking the statement and examining each piece of information, we can interpret what the researchers are reporting about what the data reveals.

The χ^2 referred to in the paper is sometimes written as *chi-square* (pronounced 'chi-square' as if it rhymed with 'why-square'), and is a key test used to establish whether or not the two variables of the contingency table (or cross-tabulation) are independent of each other. For example, if there is no association between age and grade, then you would expect the proportion of elderly former students who got high grades to be similar to the proportion of young former students getting high grades. The null hypothesis being tested, then, is that the frequencies or proportions found in the cells of the contingency table are what you would expect to find if there was no association. The chi-square test itself is based on the differences between the actual observed frequencies and the frequencies which would be expected if the null hypothesis were true.

Let us look at the extract we looked at above laid out slightly differently.

By χ^2 the distribution of age groups is significantly different for all these variables:

RI (χ^2 (10) = 98.42, $P < 0.0001$);
grade (χ^2 (6) = 18.40, $P < 0.005$); and
interest (χ^2 (4) = 10.90, $P < 0.02$). (Cohen et al., 1992b: 156)

In this extract, we are given three figures for the chi-square values of each of three tables. These figures measure the differences between the frequencies that actually emerged or were observed in the research and the frequencies expected by chance. In order to interpret them we need to look at the rest of the information.

The number in parentheses after χ^2 in the extract refers to *degrees of freedom*. (In this chapter's text we normally use the initials *df.*) This term simply means the number of independent terms in the table: that is, the opportunity for variation in the content of the cells, given that the row and column totals are fixed. For example, a 2 × 2 table (see Table 9.3) has only one degree of freedom. This is because once we know the row and column totals, only *one* figure in the body of the table is free to vary and we can work out all the rest by subtraction (i.e. the cells which are shaded). So only one figure in the table can come as any surprise. You can test this for yourself by putting your own figures into cell α and into the row and column totals, and working out what the shaded cells should be. Consider the example given in Table 9.4. As you can see, any number less than 20 could have been chosen for the first cell, but once that number is fixed (at 15 in the example) there is no choice about what the empty cells should contain. The easy way to calculate degrees of freedom, if you need to do so, is to multiply the number of rows minus 1 by the number of columns minus 1.

Let us now consider the final part of the jigsaw. Returning to the extract from Cohen et al. (1992b), consider the χ^2 value for the retention interval of 98.42. You know that P is the term for the *observed level of significance* that can be attached to the result. In our example the statement that P is less than 0.0001 (expressed as $P < 0.0001$) means that, if the null hypothesis that there is no association is not rejected, the probability that a chi-square value of at least that level occurring purely

Table 9.3 *Degrees of freedom for a 2 × 2 table*

		Variable 1		
		1	2	Total
Variable 2	1	a	b	$a + b$
	2	c	d	$c + d$
Total		$a + c$	$b + d$	$a + b + c + d$

Table 9.4 *Degrees of freedom: a second example*

		Variable 1		
		1	2	Total
Variable 2	1	15		20
	2			
Total		30	40	70

by chance is less than 0.0001, which, put another way, is less than one in 10,000. The researchers, not surprisingly, therefore concluded that the null hypothesis should be rejected.

The smaller P is, the more significant (in the statistical sense) the finding is and the less likely it is to have occurred by chance. It is always possible to draw a random sample from a population and pick an untypical one by chance, and so to produce findings for the sample which do not hold for the population. What the statistical test does is to assess the probability of having done so. Because the probability level in this particular instance is so small, it is highly unlikely that such a value for chi-square could have occurred by chance: there is less than one chance of it in 10,000. Therefore, the hypothesis that the two variables are independent for this particular set of data – that there is no relationship between them – is rejected, and we describe the findings as *statistically significant*.

Putting all this another way, you can think of it as a kind of 'model-fitting'. What we are trying to do is to see how well our data correspond to the null hypothesis that the two variables are *not* associated in the population – that knowing the value of one does not help you to predict the value of the other.

It should be noted that the finding of an association between variables does not necessarily imply causality. For example, a study which examined parents' smoking habits and children's behaviour was reported in the national press as having found an association between the number of cigarettes smoked by mothers and the incidence of bad behaviour in children. From this association, it would not be at all clear whether the bad behaviour drove the mothers to smoke more, or whether the sight of mothers smoking drove the children into rebellion – or even, as we shall see later, whether the association was not a direct one at all, but the result – for both mothers and children – of an association with some other variable, such as poverty or family stress.

z *and* t *tests*

There are various techniques that can be used to test different types of hypothesis. We have already looked at the chi-square test. In this section, we will look briefly at two other commonly used tests, z and t tests, followed by a look at F tests in the next section.

One of the simplest hypotheses which researchers wish to examine is the difference between two means. Consider, for instance, if researchers at a university wished to compare the mean examination scores for students who had studied the recommended prerequisites for a given course and for students who had not. The question they would need to address would be whether the difference between the two means could have arisen by chance, or was it a 'real' – that is, statistically significant – difference. One standard way of testing whether the difference between two means is significant or not is through the use of either the z test or Student's t test. Remember that we have already discussed how z-scores use standard deviations to transform measures into standard deviation units. A similar approach is used with the z test, which is so called because the difference between two means is converted into standard deviation units.

This statistic has an approximately normal distribution which, you may recall, means that we can identify the likelihood of the null hypothesis: that the two means are equal. Unfortunately, if either of the two samples is smaller than 30, then the z statistic no longer approximates a normal distribution. Instead, the t statistic is used (this is often referred to as Student's t). In practice, with large samples, there are no differences between the z distribution and the t distribution. To use the t statistic, however, you must take into account the degrees of freedom involved as its value is affected by the sample size. Both z and t tests are for use with variables measured on an interval or ratio scale. The test itself, whether z or t is used, allows the researcher to calculate the probability of a difference of that size or larger occurring if the means were equal in the population from which the sample was drawn. The statistically significant difference would be one which resulted in a test value with an observed probability P of, say, < 0.05, in which case H_0 would be rejected.

We have been discussing z and t tests for *any* differences between pairs of means, whether they represented increases or decreases. These are termed *two-tailed* tests. However, it should be noted that if we had good reason to suppose that the variation had to be all in one direction – the aeroplane can either stand still or go forward, but it cannot go backwards – then a *one-tailed* test might be used. This merely means that the significance level α would need to be divided by 2 (making it even less likely that differences between sample means occur by chance), so a test value yielding a two-tailed P of 0.05 would give a one-tailed P of 0.025 (remember the shaded areas in Table 9.3).

Let us look briefly at an example for interpreting t and z. The stages the researchers would have to go through in order to test their hypothesis would include:

1   Setting up the null hypothesis.
2   Deciding on the most appropriate test to assess that hypothesis.

3 Calculating the result of the test.
4 Setting the probability level α.
5 Comparing the probability of obtaining the test result against the α level.
6 Deciding whether to accept or reject the null hypothesis.

Suppose that researchers were investigating gender differences in examination results. In a small study of marks achieved by students in a particular examination, they reported that the analysis of the marks achieved by men and women in the study were:

for 16 women: mean marks = 17.5, standard deviation = 3
for 16 men: mean marks = 15.0, standard deviation = 4

1 The null hypothesis H_0 is that the mean for women = mean for men.
2 Because n_1 and n_2 (sample sizes) are each less than 30, the researchers use Student's t test to test their hypothesis. We are also interested in differences in *either* direction so we will be using a two-tailed t test.
3 The result for the t test on the data is $t = 2$. The degrees of freedom are:

$$n_1 + n_2 - 2 = 16 + 16 - 2 = 30 \; df$$

4 We decide that the probability level α should be set at 5 per cent, i.e. $\alpha = 0.05$.
5 Reading a table of t values, we find that at the 30 df level the probability of t being greater than $1.697 = 0.10$, and the probability of t being greater than $2.042 = 0.05$. Since we have calculated that $t = 2$, the probability of it occurring by chance is less than 0.10 (10 per cent) but greater than 0.05 (5 per cent).
6 Since we had previously decided to set α at 5 per cent, and we know that the probability of $t = 2$ is greater than 5 per cent, then the difference is *not* significant and we do not reject the null hypothesis (though the researchers would undoubtedly comment on the narrow margin of rejection and the fact that the samples were so small).

Activity 9.3 (5 minutes)

In the example above the researchers were investigating whether there were *any* differences between exam results achieved by men and women. Suppose, however, that they wanted to investigate whether women achieved higher exam results than men.

1 What sort of test would be needed?
2 What would be the effect on how P is interpreted?

Analysis of Variance

While z and t tests are useful for examining single differences, there can be problems when a whole set of differences is to be examined. A significance test looks at how likely it is that a given result is due to sampling error rather than representing a real

Table 9.5   *Mean percentage correct response, by age, in a study of memory*

Test	Young	Middle	Elderly	Chance[a]	F [b]
Name recognition	71	66	66	50	6.12
Concept recognition	72	69	68	50	5.32
Fact verification (gen.)	67	65	65	50	n.s.
Fact verification (spec.)	71	65	64	50	7.19
Grouping	43	36	34	17	4.70
Cued recall names	37	29	27	0	n.s.
Cued recall concepts	42	32	24	0	11.73
Experimental design	76	77	74	50	n.s.

[a]The 'Chance' column indicates the score achievable by picking answers at random.
[b]All F values are significant at $P < 0.001$.
n.s., not significant.

Source: Cohen et al., 1992b, Table 2

difference, and by convention we reject the null hypothesis of 'no difference' if the likelihood of this is as low as 0.05 – one chance in 20. This means, however, that if we do 20 tests we are very likely indeed to be making at least one Type 1 error. We therefore need a way of testing the significance of patterning in a whole set of differences, all at the same time. One such procedure is known as *one-way analysis of variance*.

The two pieces of information needed to describe a distribution – namely, a measure of the central tendency, such as the mean, and a measure of the spread, such as the standard deviation or variance – play a key role when it comes to drawing conclusions about a population from the results obtained through hypothesis testing. We can use information about the variance of each of the samples when examining the means of several different populations for any significant differences. The total variance of the data in all the samples is split into two parts: that due to the variance *between* the samples and that due to the variance *within* the samples. This is in effect the principle underlying analysis of variance. The ratio of these two parts of the total variance is known as F. If the calculated value of F is found to be significant, then it is assumed that the differences between the means are also significant.

When testing the means of different groups, the variance s^2 will comprise two parts:

1   The variation of the means between groups, the measure of which is the *between-groups sum of squared deviations*.
2   The variability of the measures within each group, the measure of which is the *within-groups sum of squared deviations* (also sometimes called the error sum of squares).

The null hypothesis being tested is that the means of all the groups are equal, i.e. that any differences between means are not significant. The test used for this is the F test – the ratio of mean squared deviation between groups to mean squared deviation within groups.

In Table 9.5, taken from the study of age and memory which has been the 'running example' in this chapter, the mean of the test scores achieved by respondents in each of three age groups are given for each of the eight tests used. The question being investigated is whether the differences identified in the mean test scores between the people in each age group are attributable to chance, or whether they represent real differences between the groups. In other words, is age a significant factor in students' test performance? If it is, then the mean scores for different age groups will not be equal. The null hypothesis H_0, in other words, is that the populations from which the samples have been drawn all have equal means – that any differences there are between the sample mean scores for each age group are likely to have arisen by chance. The test for this hypothesis is the F test.

If the null hypothesis of equal means is not rejected, then the expected ratio of the two parts of the total variance will be $F = 1$. In Table 9.5 three F values are identified as 'n.s.', 'not significant'. In other words, differences in sample means do not suggest that there are differences between age groups in the larger population for those particular tests. The calculated values for F for the other listed test means range from 4.70 to 11.73. The given P level is < 0.001; this means that the probability of obtaining just by chance an F value at least as large as the ones calculated is less than 0.001, i.e. less than one in 1,000. In other words, the F values suggest strongly that there are real differences between the means of the different age groups. The question then arises for each of the tests as to which of the means of the three age groups do differ significantly from each other.

It is after having found significant values of F that pairs of means should be tested. At this point, while we know there are significant differences somewhere between the group means, we do not know which of the groups are the ones which differ significantly from each other. Cohen et al. (1992b) reported that they tested individual pairs of scores using a procedure called Fisher's LSD test, one of a number of techniques devised for this purpose. Multiple comparison tests such as this have been devised in such a way as to minimize the chance of either Type 1 or Type 2 errors. It is clearly good practice to carry out a preliminary analysis of variance in this way so that the significant F ratios can be identified through the analysis of all the groups, before comparing individual pairs of means. By doing so, we do just a single test to find out whether there is sufficient variance between groups to explain, before trying to locate where it lies.

The next step in analysis reported in Cohen et al. (1992b) is the *two-way analysis of variance*. This is used for data which are grouped using two variables rather than just the one (age) used for the one-way analysis of variance (ANOVA). The two variables used in the reading are age and retention interval.

Again, the total variance is being split into its component parts. However, this time, because the effects of two independent variables are being investigated, the possibility of each of them affecting the other, as well as there being a possible association between each of the independent variables and the dependent variable, must be taken into account. In the particular example in Cohen et al. (1992b), we already know that there is some interaction between these two variables as the correlation between them has already been shown to be significant (we will be discussing correlation in the next section). If we carried out the same procedure as for one-way analysis of variance, and a significant difference were found, we would have no way of knowing whether this was due to differences between the age groups, the retention intervals, or to both of them. This is called a *confounded* effect. In order to take account of the joint effects of the two independent variables acting together, an additional variance component is included in the formula. This means that F ratios then have to be calculated for the interaction as well as for separate contributions which each of the two independent variables may make (known as *main effects*).

Suppose, for example, that we were interested in examining the effects of gender and height on promotion. There would be three sets of hypotheses which could be tested using a two-way design:

H_{01}:   gender is not a factor in promotion

H_{02}:   height is not a factor in promotion

H_{03}:   the interaction between height and gender is not a factor in promotion

There will be a number of possible degrees of freedom, depending on which hypothesis is being tested. In addition, because we are dealing with the ratio of two parts of the total variance when we use the F test, we will be handling two sets of degrees of freedom when we come to interpret the F statistic: the set arising from the factor whose effect is being tested (V_1) and the set arising from the unexplained variation (V_2). If you look at a table of F values, you will see how the values of F are determined by the degrees of freedom V_1 and V_2. For example, suppose we have a computed F statistic of $F = 2.59$. If we have set $\alpha = 0.05$, and we know our degrees of freedom are $V_1 = 3$ and $V_2 = 28$, then we can read from the table that $F(3,28)$ for $\alpha = 0.05$ is 2.95. This is sometimes written in research journals as $F_{0.05,3,28} = 2.95$. Comparing the two figures, we can see that our computed $F = 2.59 < 2.95$, so we would not reject our H_0.

Activity 9.4 (15 minutes)

Read the following extract:

Main effects of RI were significant for name recognition ($F(5,355) = 9.07$, $P < 0.001$); concept recognition ($F(5,355) = 18.57$, $P < 0.001$); fact verification specific ($F(5,355) = 2.41$, $P < 0.05$); grouping ($F(5,355) = 6.30$, $P < 0.001$); cued recall of names ($F(5,355) = 3.95$, $P < 0.001$); and for cued recall of concepts ($F(5,355) = 6.95$, $P < 0.001$). (Cohen et al., 1992b: 158)

Explain what this extract is saying. Our answer is at the end of the chapter.

Analysis of variance can be used with even more independent variables. The techniques are more complex and varied but the principles are the same. The strength of ANOVA is that it relies on the additive properties of sample variances. However, three criteria must be met to check the appropriateness of analysis of variance for specific data sets:

1   All observations should be independent of each other; that is, no individual should appear twice in the data set.
2   The populations from which the samples are drawn should be normally distributed.
3   The groups should have the same within-groups variance (because the estimate of the population within-groups variance will be biased if the variances differ widely).

The great strength of this technique is that it can deal with all types of data: nominal, ordinal, interval and ratio. However, the *dependent* variable must be interval level while the independent variables are treated as nominal variables. Its great weakness is that, in its simplest form, it requires all the groups to be the same size. This is not a problem in experimental research, where equal-sized groups can generally be arranged, but in survey analysis it is rarely the case that groups to be compared are of equal size. There are forms of analysis of variance which can cope with this, but for the most part their use is valid only under very restricted circumstances, so analysis of variance as a technique is not much used in survey analysis. However, the *principles* underlying analysis of variance also underlie several other important analysis techniques, and understanding them is therefore as important for survey researchers as for experimenters.

Measuring Association

Correlation Coefficients

Finally, in this chapter, let us look at measures of *association* – ways of expressing the strength of a relationship in a single figure. As you saw earlier, there are several measures of association based on chi-square. All assume only that the variables are nominal. You will sometimes see examples of researchers using χ^2 with ordinal and other types of data. This is perfectly valid statistically, but information about the data is being lost where this occurs because chi-square only identifies the existence of an association and not its type or strength. The additional information which ordinal, interval and ratio variables hold can be used to give us a better idea of the strength and type of association between them. Of particular importance here is the form of association known as *correlation*. A correlation is simply the association between two variables. If a high value on one variable is associated with a high value on another (for example, height and age in children), they are said to be *positively* correlated. If a high value on one variable is associated with a lower value on the other, then they are said to be *negatively* correlated (for example age and energy!).

The index or statistic most commonly used to indicate the *strength* of the association between these two variables is the *correlation coefficient* (*r*). Just as the mean and variance give a useful summary description of one distribution, the correlation coefficient gives a useful summary description of the association between any two distributions. Pearson's product moment correlation coefficient *r* can take values from +1 to –1, by which means it indicates how close to linearity the association is. 'Linear' is just the statistical term for a straight line, so a linear correlation means that the measures for the pair of variables being investigated together form a straight line when plotted on a graph.

Various forms of correlation coefficient have been developed for different types of variables. For interval or ratio data such as test scores, Pearson's *r* is the most widely used. For ranked ordinal or non-normal interval data, the most frequently used measure is Spearman's rank order correlation coefficient r_s.

So how is *r* interpreted? A value of 1 would indicate a perfect association. This would be a highly unlikely result and would be the cause of concern and questioning if it occurred. Far more likely are correlations around the 0.1, 0.2 level which would be taken to indicate no association. A correlation of $r = 0.8$ would indicate a strong association. However if, for example, it was reported that two variables had an r of 0.3, then the interpretation would be less clear and would depend on whether or not r was found to be statistically significant. Like all other statistics, if the aim of getting the correlation coefficient in a sample is to test hypotheses about an unknown population correlation coefficient ρ (rho, pronounced roe), then the correlation coefficient r must be tested for statistical significance. The null hypothesis, H_0, being tested would be that in the population the correlation coefficient is zero; in other words, that there was no correlation between the two variables. Checking the statistical significance of r is simply a matter of looking up the value of r for the appropriate number of degrees of freedom $(n - 2)$ in a table of critical values. Alternatively, the significance of r may be calculated by using t.

Thus, for any value of the correlation coefficient calculated from a sample, the likelihood that there is a positive linear correlation can be tested using the t test in the usual way with $df = n - 2$.

Simple Linear Regression

We have already seen that, if it is possible to construct a straight line through data points on a scattergram, we can use the information it gives us about the relationship between the two variables in order to estimate or predict the behaviour of one variable from the other. Using the computational power of a computer, it is possible to fit a prediction line to the data very rigorously and precisely.

The convention is that the dependent variable is usually shown on the vertical (or Y) axis, and the independent (or explanatory) variable is shown on the X axis. Consider the data from the research on age and memory. We might expect that at a given time those people who have only been away from the course for a relatively short time – that is, those with only a short retention interval – would have more accurate recall of aspects of the course than those who finished the course some years earlier. If we plotted the test results, data on the Y axis, and the retention interval on the X axis, as a scattergram, we might expect to see a positive correlation in the form of a linear association. However, it is equally clear that any attempt to draw a straight line through the data points on the scattergram would leave many of the points near rather than actually on the line. It is therefore necessary to make sure that a line is drawn which minimizes the distances of the data points from the line, by drawing the *line of best fit*. Figure 9.4 illustrates three such lines: a perfect fit, a good fit and a poor fit to the data set (because the data points are *not* randomly scattered about the line so the average distance of the data points from the line will not be zero as they would be with a good fit). Even though there is a fair degree of variability with the good fit, the average distance of the data points from the line *do* add up to zero. In other words, the line is positioned in such a way as to achieve the least variation possible among the residuals. This line is called the *linear regression line*.

Having computed the regression line, we now need a measure of how *good* a fit it is. That is how much residual variance is left after we subtract the variance explained by the regression. This measure, in fact, is provided by r, the correlation coefficient.

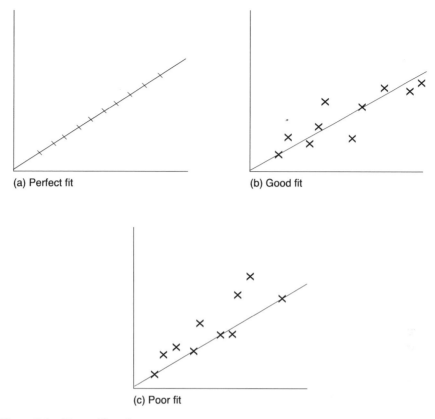

(a) Perfect fit

(b) Good fit

(c) Poor fit

Figure 9.4   *Lines of best fit*

As we saw above, the correlation coefficient expresses the extent to which the data points cluster about the regression line (see Figure 9.5).

The nearer the data points are to the line, the higher the correlation. So when regression analysis is used, a correlation coefficient is cited as an estimate of how much of the variance is explained by the analysis. Squaring the correlation coefficient gives us the proportion of the variance explained in the dependent variable; so, for example, a correlation of $r = 0.7$ explains 0.49 of the variance (49 per cent).

Multivariate Statistics

The chapter has concentrated mainly on 'zero-order' results so far: the direct relationship between one or more independent variables, one at a time, and a dependent variable. When a result is accepted as statistically significant as the result of a zero-order test, however, this does not mean that a causal relationship has been established; there is still important work to do, making the argument secure. If I can show a significant relationship between, say, height and intelligence, it does not mean that

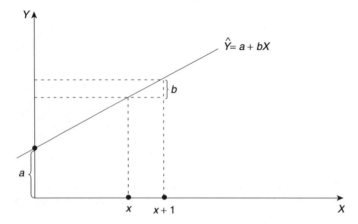

Figure 9.5   *Linear regression line and the regression coefficient*

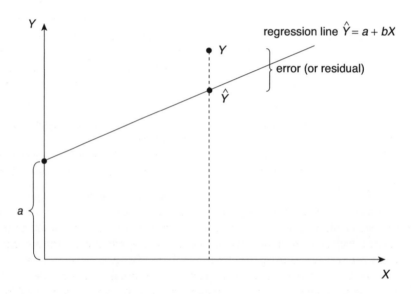

Figure 9.6   *Linear regression line showing the residual*

either necessarily has a causal effect on the other. Much more likely is that both are a product of some third factor: in this case probably level of nutrition as a child and in the womb, which in turn is likely to be a product of parental affluence. Thus, establishing whether an apparently causal or predictive relationship is statistically significant is only the first stage of the argument; we still have to establish that it is *this* independent variable, and not some other which is also associated, that produces the effect. Some of this work is done by the design of the study (see Chapter 1). Some, however, can be done during statistical analysis.

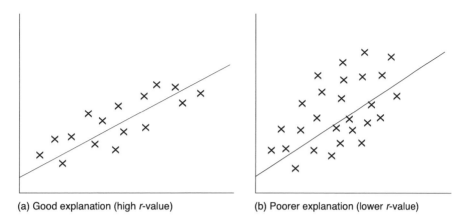

(a) Good explanation (high *r*-value)   (b) Poorer explanation (lower *r*-value)

Figure 9.7   *Correlation as a measure of variance explained*

The normal research question in social research *needs* a multivariate approach; few research problems are so neatly circumscribed that we can identify and test a single cause or influence. Many research papers look at a number of possible influences on the dependent variable to be explained. Some just examine these influences one at a time, to show whether each bears a significant relationship to the dependent variable, but this does not tell the reader a great deal. We really need to know:

1   Which of the influences are strong and which are weak.
2   To what extent the different independent variables are *independent* influences (or, conversely, how much their influence overlaps).
3   Whether there are *interaction effects* (whether the influence of two or more variables together is different from what would be predicted of any one solely by itself).

Another reason why we might want to involve more than one potential independent variable in our analysis is that experiments are relatively rare in social and educational research. In a true experiment, it is possible to select groups that are arguably identical on everything except the 'treatment' variable – by matching or by random allocation. In 'real world' research, we are more often comparing groups that differ in a number of respects as well as the one which is of interest to us. Lacking the design controls of experimental studies, we therefore need multivariate analysis techniques for the statistical control of these 'unwanted' differences (see Chapter 1). In other words, we need to show:

1   Whether the effects of extraneous variables are larger than those of the influence(s) we are studying.
2   Whether they are *confounded* with them (that is, inseparately correlated with them).
3   Whether they *interact* with them.

There are broadly two 'families' of multivariate techniques: the analysis of variance family and the regression family. Each 'family' is illustrated below by discussing one or two members in some detail and then covering more briefly other variants which you might well encounter in research papers. The two 'families' aim to perform very similar tasks – and indeed they are closely related mathematically, for the most part – but they have different strengths and weaknesses. Both aim to establish which of the variables have the strongest effects, and generally to estimate the proportion of the variance in the dependent variable which is 'explained' by each independent variable. Regression techniques concentrate on linear relationships and are weaker at exploring interaction effects. Analysis of variance techniques are strong on exploring interaction effects but do not provide such precise predictions of linear causal factors. In this section of the chapter we look briefly at a range of the most common multivariate techniques.

Analysis of Variance and Related Techniques

Tabular Techniques

At the risk of seeming deliberately paradoxical, we might count the use of tabular analysis and χ^2 as a member of the analysis of variance family: the simplest member, but showing a family resemblance to its more grown-up siblings. Thinking back, you may recall how, like analysis of variance, χ^2 is a 'model-fitting' technique; it tests the null hypothesis that the observed pattern in a table could plausibly be written off as a chance sample from a population in which the pattern would not be observed. In other words, χ^2 tests the hypothesis of random distribution between columns and rows of tables in the same way that analysis of variance tests the null hypothesis of random distribution between groups.

Chi-square enables you to say that an observed association is significant – that the observed association has a low probability of occurring by chance alone. Thus the first stage in a multivariate tabular analysis would be to tabulate each independent variable separately against the dependent variable and compute χ^2 for each table. This would enable you, perhaps, to discard some variables as not showing a significant relationship with the dependent variable. If all your tables have the same degrees of freedom you can also compute ϕ for 2×2 tables, or some other coefficient of association for tables of a different size, and compare these. This will tell you which of the independent variables has the strongest effect (the largest χ^2).

You can take tabular analysis further, and use it to explore for interaction effects and confounded extraneous variables, by partitioning your tables by a third variable. The following extended example is based on an analysis of the 'pay-off' of educational qualifications in terms of wages earned (see also Chapter 8). The data came from the 1980–4 responses to the Open University's People in Society survey. (Note that the χ^2 values reproduced here were calculated from the original raw numbers, of course, not the percentages shown in the tables.)

Table 9.6, in its first block, looks at the relationship of educational qualifications to current income. There is a significant and reasonably strong relationship ($\phi = 0.32$, and ϕ tends to underestimate association). Looking at the 'total' block of the table, about two-thirds of people with few or no qualifications have 'low' incomes (defined as 'below the median' for the total sample), and about two-thirds of people with higher qualifications have 'high' incomes. In the other two blocks of the table we look separately at males and females – we 'control for gender' – and see that the

Table 9.6   *Wages and educational qualifications, in total and by gender*

	Total		Male		Female	
Education	Low wages	High wages	Low wages	High wages	Low wages	High wages
'O' level or less (%)	17.7	62.9	37.1	44.2	55.8	82.3
More than 'O' level	53.2	31.2	68.8	15.9	84.1	46.8
	$n = 4,632$		$n = 2,307$		$n = 2,325$	
	$\chi^2 = 472.02$		$\chi^2 = 220.81$		$\chi^2 = 324.70$	
	$df = 2, P < 0.0001$		$df = 2, P < 0.0001$		$df = 2, P < 0.0001$	
	$\phi = 0.32$		$\phi = 0.31$		$\phi = 0.37$	

Table 9.7   *Wages and educational level by gender and job status*

	Male: full-time (%)		Male: not full-time (%)		Female: full-time (%)		Female: not full-time (%)	
Education	Low wages	High wages	Low wages	High wages	Low wages	High wages	Low wages	High wages
'O' level or less	35.3	64.7	86.4	13.6	66.2	33.8	94.0	6.0
More than 'O' level	11.4	88.6	76.5	23.5	27.4	72.6	85.3	14.7
	$n = 2,028$		$n = 279$		$n = 1,223$		$n = 1,102$	
	$\chi^2 = 164.21$		$\chi^2 = 3.34$		$\chi^2 = 182.37$		$\chi^2 = 21.60$	
	$df = 1, F < 0.0001$		$df = 1,$ n.s.		$df = 1, P < 0.0001$		$df = 1, P < 0.0001$	
	$\phi = 0.28$		$\phi = 0.11$		$\phi = 0.39$		$\phi = 0.14$	

relationship holds good for both. Women more often have lower incomes than men –
substantially more women than men appear in the first column of their respective
blocks – but within that constraint the relationship holds. So far, therefore, we have
a two-factor explanation of wage levels: women earn less than men, but for both education brings rewards. (If the χ^2 in the male and female blocks of the table had both
been non-significant, we should have concluded that gender, not educational level,
was the determining factor. If they had come out as of very different sizes, we should
have concluded that there was an interaction effect at work, the size of the relationship being affected by the value on the 'gender' variable.)

Table 9.7 splits each half of the sample by whether or not they are in full-time
work. For men, as we can see, this makes a crucial difference; there are relatively
few men not in full-time work, and among them there is no statistically significant
association of education with wages. For women, there are also fairly marked differences, but even in the 'not' category the sample is large enough that a relatively
low association comes out as statistically significant. Even among women with part-
time jobs, therefore, education has some tendency to be associated with higher
income. There is clearly an interaction between educational level and being in full-
or part-time work, however, and the latter is a confounded variable which is distorting the analysis.

Table 9.8   *Wages and educational level by gender: full-time workers*

Education	Total		Male		Female	
	Low wages	High wages	Low wages	High wages	Low wages	High wages
'O' level or less (%)	46.9	53.1	35.3	64.7	66.2	33.8
More than 'O' level (%)	17.5	82.5	11.4	88.6	27.4	72.6
	$n = 3,251$		$n = 2,028$		$n = 1,223$	
	$\chi^2 = 461.55$		$\chi^2 = 164.21$		$\chi^2 = 182.37$	
	$df = 1, P < 0.0001$		$df = 1, P < 0.0001$		$df = 1, P < 0.0001$	
	$\phi = 0.38$		$\phi = 0.28$		$\phi = 0.39$	

Table 9.8 shows the effects of removing the part-timers from the analysis. As in Table 9.6, we find a significant and reasonably strong relationship for both sexes, though again women tend overall to earn less than men; the lower apparent level of women's wages was not just due to the larger proportion of them working part-time or not at all. We may also note an interaction effect, however: the association is substantially higher for women than for men. This is in line with other research on women's work, suggesting that the level of women's jobs is better predicted by initial qualifications than men's because men receive more 'promotion on the job'.

From this example, then, you can see how tabular analysis, conceptually the simplest of the multivariate analyses, can deliver quite a lot of what we need. It can tell us which variables relate significantly to the criterion (the dependent variable), which relationships are stronger than others and even whether there are interaction effects. The estimate of strength of relationship is only a rough one, however, and tabular analysis cannot estimate at all the proportion of variance explained by interaction effects. For this we need more sensitive and precise techniques.

More on Analysis of Variance

The best known of such techniques is *analysis of variance* itself. As we saw earlier, one-way analysis of variance can be extended into two-way analysis of variance, and it can be extended again to include multiple independent variables. With one-way ANOVA, the hypothesis tested is that, for one particular variable, the means of all the groups are equal; that is, that the populations from which the groups are drawn have equal means. For example, different age groups scored equally well on a factual recall test. With two-way ANOVA, we saw how two factors are explored, by looking at an example of the effects of both height and gender on promotion. As we saw, the major difference between one-way and two-way analyses was that we now had to consider not just the effects of each individual factor, but also the possible *interaction* effects. Look at the following extract from Cohen et al. (1992b), on their research into age and memory:

> Two-way analyses of variance were also performed for each test with age and RI as between-subjects factors. Age was grouped into young, middle-aged and elderly, and RI was grouped into two-year intervals. Main effects of RI were significant for name recognition ($F (5,355) = 9.07, P < 0.001$); concept recognition ($F (5,355) = 18.57, P < 0.001$); fact verification specific ($F (5,355) = 2.41, P < 0.05$); grouping ($F (5,355) = 6.30, P < 0.001$); cued recall of names ($F (5,355) = 3.95, P < 0.001$); and for cued recall of concepts ($F(5,355) = 6.95, P < 0.001$). The effects of RI were not significant in the test of fact

verification general nor in the test of experimental design. The main effect of age was significant only in two of the tests, fact verification specific (F (2,355) = 3.05, $P < 0.05$) and, marginally, in cued recall of concepts (F (2,355) = 2.41, $P < 0.09$). The interaction of age % RI did not approach significance in any of the tests. It is clear that the age differences which emerged from the one-way analyses of variance are much less evident when RI is included as a factor and this is due to the fact that, as shown in Table 1a, age and RI are highly correlated. (Cohen et al., 1992b: 157–8)

Here you will see that a series of eight two-way analyses of variance were carried out – one for each of the individual tests. In each computation, the test score was the dependent variable, with age and the retention interval as the two independent variables. Remember, that with *two* independent variables being investigated, there are *three* null hypotheses.

H_{01}:   *retention interval is not a factor in the test score achieved*

H_{02}:   *age is not a factor in the test score achieved*

H_{03}:   *the interaction between age and retention interval is not a factor in the test score achieved*

The extract above summarizes the results of the two-way analyses of variance that tested this set of hypotheses for each of the eight tests the sample were asked to complete. The main effects of the retention interval (H_{01}) were reported first. (The layout has been changed slightly for ease of comprehension.)

Main effects of RI were significant for

name recognition (F (5,355) = 9.07, $P < 0.001$);

concept recognition (F (5,355) = 18.57, $P < 0.001$);

fact verification specific (F (5,355) = 2.41, $P < 0.05$);

grouping (F (5,355) = 6.30, $P < 0.001$);

cued recall of names (F (5,355) = 3.95, $P < 0.001$); and for cued recall of concepts (F (5,355) = 6.95, $P < 0.001$).

The effects of RI were not significant in the test of fact verification general nor in the test of experimental design. (Cohen et al., 1992b: 157–8)

The paragraph then goes on to report the main effects of age (H_{02}) and then the interaction effects (H_{03}). The concluding comment illustrates the importance of the two-way design, and one of its advantages over the simple one-way design. The one-way ANOVA, which was used first to study the effect of age on test scores, had suggested that age could be a factor in achievement on some types of test. However, as the researchers pointed out, age was highly correlated with the retention interval. In other words, the older students were also those with the longest gap since they had studied. The two-way ANOVA showed both that there was no interaction effect and that age appeared to be a less important factor than retention interval.

The analysis of variance approach can be used in much more complex ways in situations where researchers want to examine the effects of more than two independent variables at a time, or where they want to examine the effects on several dependent variables at the same time. In this latter situation, they would be using a modified form of analysis of variance, termed multivariate analysis of variance, or MANOVA for short. These forms of analysis are relatively uncommon, in that the underlying statistical assumptions about the data which the techniques make grow more demanding – and the interpretation of the results also becomes more difficult.

Regression Techniques

The techniques discussed above enable us to explore the effects of more than one independent variable on a dependent variable, or (which is the same thing) to control statistically for the effects of extraneous variables. They have the advantage that they allow us to explore interaction effects as well as main effects in a fairly straightforward manner. Their weakness, however, is that they are cumbersome to use and/or difficult to interpret when the number of independent variables grows beyond about three or four. A second family of techniques, based around notions of correlation and regression, has been devised to overcome this problem.

You may recall that simple linear regression is a way of examining the extent to which one variable can be predicted from another. Multiple regression is a simple extension of the idea of linear regression to allow us to predict one variable from a combination of several others. The aim of researchers in using it is usually to try to develop a model (in the form of an equation) which can use information about a set of independent variables to predict the dependent variable as accurately as possible (Figure 9.8). The more of the variation in the dependent variable which the regression equation can explain, the more accurate will be the predictions. Unfortunately, in practice, there is usually a substantial amount of variance which is unaccounted for by regression models. This is termed the residual or the error variance.

The 'zero-order' effect of each variable – its effect by itself, ignoring the effects of other variables – is given by the correlation coefficient r. Remember that squaring r yields the proportion of variance explained for a pair of variables. If the independent variables being examined as predictor variables were entirely independent of each other, we could just add the proportions together to obtain total proportion of variance explained. However, if the variables are correlated not just with the dependent variable but with each other as well, this means that we would be counting some of the variance explained twice or even more if we just add the proportions together (see shaded areas in Figure 9.9). In other words, the total explained variance is less than the sum of the proportions. This point is shown visually in Figure 9.9, where the circles are the proportion of variance explained by each variable by itself.

What multiple regression does is to assess the total proportion of variance explained by all the variables together, taking their correlation into account. The regression equation for predicting the amount of knowledge a student had retained, using a single independent variable such as age, would be, for example:

$$\text{amount retained} = a + b \, (\text{age}) + \text{error.}$$

For all four variables, the multiple regression equation would be:

$$\text{amount retained} = a + b_1 \, (\text{age}) + b_2 \, (\text{grade}) + b_3 \, (\text{RI}) + b_4 \, (\text{interest}) + \text{error}$$

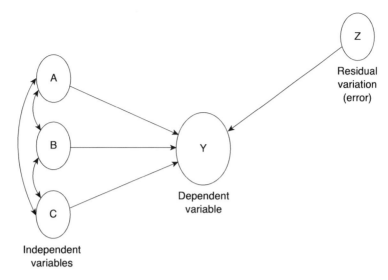

Figure 9.8   *A model of multiple regression*

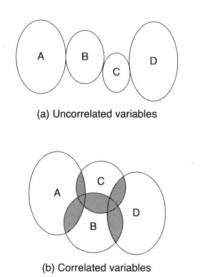

(a) Uncorrelated variables

(b) Correlated variables

Figure 9.9   *Proportions of variance explained*

The results are not presented as an equation, however, but as a series of summary statistics.

1   The overall prediction yields R, a multiple correlation coefficient. R^2, the coefficient of determination, is the proportion of variance explained overall. (R is used instead of r because we are dealing with *multiple* correlation rather than simple correlation between *pairs* of variables.)

2   The significance of R^2 will be tested, using an F-statistic, to see whether the overall level of prediction allows the rejection of the null hypothesis of no overall association.

3   Some computer programs will also test, again using the F-statistic, whether R is a significantly better predictor than the largest of the zero-order r values – in other words, whether anything is gained by adding in the extra independent variables.

4   For each variable, a beta coefficient should be supplied (β_1, β_1, etc.). These are derived from the regression coefficients (b_1, b_2, etc.) by standardizing them (converting to z-scores), and they are also referred to as *standardized partial regression coefficients*. They estimate the independent contribution of each variable to the prediction, controlling for overlap with all the other variables in the equation. The larger this is, the larger the effect of that particular independent variable on the dependent variable.

5   Finally, this estimate is tested for significance (generally using Student's t test). If the t is *not* significant, the prediction would be just as good if that variable were left out of the equation.

Therefore, a straightforward multiple regression analysis yields an overall estimate of variance explained (R^2), a test of its significance (the F test), a test of whether each variable is contributing significantly (the t test), and possibly an estimate of each variable's *independent* effect (the β coefficients).

Dummy variables

We have said all along that regression and correlation techniques are designed for numbers at the ratio level of measurement, may be used for interval or perhaps even ordinal data, but can never be used with nominal data. In general this is true. You could not, for example, use a variable of 'voting preference' (coded 1 = Labour, 2 = Conservative, 3 = other) in a regression equation, because the numbers do not mean anything – they are just labels. There is one exception to the rule, however: dichotomous data can be used in regression equations. A dichotomy is a variable with two values (for example, gender: 1 = male, 2 = female). Although this is interpreted as a nominal variable – 'female' could not be said to be twice 'male' – it behaves like a ratio variable. The mean is interpretable – if a group has a mean gender score of 1.67, it is two-thirds female and one-third male – and so are the standard deviation and variance.

That being so, you can enter any variable as an independent variable in a regression equation and represent it as a dichotomy (or more than one). We might do this by re-coding. In the example above, for instance, 'voting preference' might be represented as Labour (1) *v.* Conservative (2), leaving out the 'others' altogether. Or, depending on the hypothesis to be tested, you might re-code it as major parties (codes 1 and 2) *v.* others (code 3). However, if you wish to preserve all the information, what you can do is to enter it as a series of *dummy variables* (dichotomies), thus:

Dummy 1: Labour (code 1) v. *others (codes 2, 3)*
Dummy 2: Conservative (code 2) v. *others (codes 1, 3).*

This preserves all the information:

> *if old code was 1, Dummy 1 is coded 1 and Dummy 2 is coded 0*
> *if old code was 2, Dummy 1 is coded 0 and Dummy 2 is coded 1*
> *if old code was 3, Dummy 1 is coded 0 and Dummy 2 is coded 0.*

It is not good practice to use a dichotomy as a dependent variable, however. Regression tries to build a continuous prediction line, minimizing residual deviation from it and finishing up with a random distribution of deviations along the line. With a dichotomy as a dependent variable this process can never be very successful because the dependent variable can take only one of two values, not the continuous distribution which the prediction equation assumes. You will find analyses in the research literature which use a dichotomy as an independent variable (particularly in the literature on social class) but it is not good practice – a different kind of analysis is needed.

Further Multivariate Approaches

A range of other multivariate techniques may be used where they fit the nature of the data better or are more interpretable than the 'battery' outlined above.

Log-linear Analysis

In situations where the research problem involves categorical data – either where the researcher wishes to identify relationships between variables, and what their effect is on each other, or where a predictive model is wanted – then the analysis is likely to involve a technique known as *log-linear analysis*.

Researchers construct a multivariate contingency table, then investigate the relationship between the variables, treating *all* the variables used in the table as independent variables, with the dependent variables being the *number of cases* located in each cell of the contingency table. The linear model which is developed as a result of this analysis enables cell frequencies to be predicted. The better the model, the closer the predicted or expected frequency is to the observed frequency. The distinctive feature of this particular technique, and the one which gives the technique its name, is that the natural logs of the cell frequencies are used in the construction of the linear model.

With log-linear analysis, all the variables are treated as independent variables, with the cell frequencies being the dependent variables (that is, the variable which is predicted by the other variables). However, other techniques, such as logistic regression, enable log-linear analysis to be used to examine the relationship between independent variables and a dependent dichotomous variable.

Discriminant Function Analysis

Discriminant function analysis can be used both to predict the group to which a person or 'case' might belong, on the basis of a set of characteristics which that person or case holds, and to identify which variables are most powerful in distinguishing between the members of different groups. Take, for example, juvenile crime. Researchers may have drawn together a range of socioeconomic information about a sample of youngsters – some of whom may be persistent offenders, others who may be first offenders, and a third group with no known convictions. Discriminant analysis could be used by the researchers to identify which of the socioeconomic data they held was most useful in discriminating between members of the three different groups. They could also devise a model in the form of an equation, using the data they held to enable them to predict the group membership for other youngsters. This form of analysis clearly has many applications. It has been used in credit risk work, psychological testing, investigating effects of medical treatment, researching sentencing practices and studying voting intentions.

The direction of causation can run either way in this analysis. If group membership is seen as being dependent on the variables, then the analysis is very closely related to multiple regression, except that the dependent variable (the groups) is a nominal variable. If the values of the discriminating variables are seen as being dependent on the group to which the case or individual belongs, then the analysis can be seen as closely associated with analysis of variance.

The output which will be reported includes:

- A statistic assessing the significance of the prediction – whether using the independent variables to predict in which category each case should fall improves the prediction at all over chance. The most commonly used statistic is Wilks' λ (lambda), which counts in the opposite direction from most of the statistics we have considered in this chapter: a value of 1 means no difference from chance, and a value of 0 means perfect prediction.
- An indication of which variables contributed to the prediction and by how much.
- A 'hits and misses' table, tabulating actual category against predicted category and giving the percentage correctly classified by the prediction equation.

There are statistical assumptions that must be met, such as that the discriminating variables must be interval level and that groups are drawn from populations with normal distributions on the discriminating variables.

Logistic regression

One relatively new technique which makes fewer statistical demands on the data is logistic regression, for dependent variables which take only two values. The equation which can be constructed from the output gives a statistic which is the estimated probability of an event. Normally, if the probability is less than 0.05, then the event is predicted not to occur.

Key Terms

Analysis of variance   a statistical technique for comparing the means of more than two groups. In its multivariate form it assesses the influence on a continuous variable of two or more nominal independent variables, separately, and of their interaction.

Chi-square (χ^2) a test of association between nominal variables.

Confounded variables   independent variables which are highly correlated and whose effects cannot be distinguished. More loosely, extraneous variables whose unwanted effects cannot be controlled statistically.

(Key Terms continued)

Continuous variables   variables which can take any value, not just integers or categories. The latter are called *discrete* variables.

Correlation coefficient   an index of the extent to which the values of one variable can be predicted from the values of another. The main forms are the Pearson Product Moment Coefficient (r), used for interval or ratio data, and the Spearman Rank-Order Coefficient (ρ), used for ordinal data.

Degrees of freedom   the extent to which values in e.g. a table can *not* be calculated from the marginal totals alone.

Dependent variable   one whose variation is to be explained by variation in one or more independent variables.

Discrete variables   *see* Continuous variables.

Discriminant function analysis   a form of multivariate analysis in which independent variables are continuous but the dependent variable is nominal. The analysis predicts probability of inclusion in one of the categories rather than others

Dummy variables   the representation of a nominal variable as a series of dichotomies – 'yes' or 'no' on each value of the original variable – in order that the nominal variable may be used in analyses which normally demand continuous variables.

F-test   a test of significance used in regression and analysis of variance – the ratio of correct prediction to error, or the ratio of mean variation between groups to mean variation within groups.

Hypothesis   the term is often used loosely, but its strict meaning is a proposition derived from a model or body of theory. Hypotheses are tested as crucial tests of the validity of the theory

Independent variable   a variable posited as having an influence or causal effect on a dependent variable.

Interaction   *see* Main effect.

Interquartile range   a measure of spread – the distance between the value a quarter of the way up the distribution and a value three quarters of the way up. (This is better than the range for many purposes because it is not affected by outliers).

Interval variables   numbers whose integers represent equal intervals, so that they can be added together, but where there is no true zero and so multiplication is not possible. An example would be temperature on the Fahrenheit or Centigrade scales, where doubling the temperature does not represent twice the absolute amount of heat, because the zero is an arbitrary point.

Logistic regression   a form of regression in which the independent variables are continuous variables but the dependent variable is a dichotomy.

Log-linear analysis   a multivariate method of modelling associations in nominal data.

Main effect   in analysis of variance or regression, the independent effect of a supposed causal factor (as opposed to *interactions*, which are the joint or overlapping effects of variables).

(Continued)

(Key Terms continued)

Median   a measure of central tendency – the value of the middle of the distribution.

Mode   a crude measure of central tendency – the largest category.

Nominal variables   numbers used as labels, without arithmetical properties. An example would be 'town of birth' with the towns assigned numeric labels.

Non-sampling error   *see* Sampling error.

Null hypothesis   the model which asserts that the difference or association observed in a sample could be due to sampling error and therefore not necessarily represent a real difference or association in the population. This is what we seek to falsify by inferential statistical testing.

Ordinal variables   variables where data are ranked but the ranks do not necessarily correspond to equal intervals. An example would be position in class on an arithmetic test (as opposed to the actual score on the test).

Outliers   extreme values, not typical of the rest of the distribution, which sometimes need to be removed in order to reveal the shape of the main part of the distribution.

Percentages   a form of standardization which allows unequal samples to be compared easily – the number per hundred cases.

Range   the spread of the distribution, from the lowest value to the highest.

Ratio variables   variables where intervals are equal and there is a true zero, so that a number twice as large does represent a quantity twice as large. Examples would be age, distance from a fixed point in miles, number of questions right on a test.

Regression   a statistical technique for predicting a continuous dependent variable from one or more continuous (and/or dummy) independent variables.

Sampling error   the probability of drawing an unrepresentative sample by random methods. All other sources of error (including, paradoxically, bias in sampling) are considered *non*-sampling errors.

Scattergram   a graph representing individual data items as points on two axes, demonstrating the shape of any relationship between the axes.

Significance   a difference or association is said to be statistically significant when the likelihood of it being due to sampling error (occurring by chance alone in a sample drawn from a population where the difference or association does not hold) is less than an agreed level. By convention we generally take the 5%, 1% and 0.1% levels as cut-off points here.

Skew   the extent to which a distribution departs from normality – the extent to which it is not symmetrical.

Standard deviation   a measure of spread in a distribution – the location, relative to the mean, in terms of standardized units devised so that about two thirds of the data points in a normal distribution lie within plus or minus one standard deviation and about 95 per cent lie within plus or minus two.

Statistical significance   *see* Significance.

(Key Terms continued)

t-test   *see* z-test.
Variance   the total variability in a distribution. Technically, the mean of squared deviations from the mean.
  z-scores   a form of standardization – the values of variables are expressed as deviations from the mean in standard deviation units.
  z-test   a test of the difference between the means of two groups, based on the normal distribution. The *t*-test, which has the same function, is now preferred to this because it is less affected by small samples.

Further Reading

Marsh, C. (1988) *Exploring Data: an introduction to data analysis for social scientists,* Cambridge, Polity.

Antonius, R. (2003) *Interpreting Quantitative Data with SPSS,* London, Sage.

Brace, N. et al. (2000) *SPSS for Psychologists,* Basingstoke, Macmillan.

Bryman, A. and Cramer, D. (1997) *Quantitative Data Analysis with SPSS for Windows,* London, Routledge.

Coakes, S.J. and Stted, L.G. (2003). *SPSS without Anguish,* Milton (Australia), Wiley.

Roberts, M. J. and Russo, R. (1999a) *A Student's Guide to Analysis of Variance,* London, Routledge.

Roberts, M. J. and Russo, R. (1999b) *Quantitative Applications in the Social Sciences,* Sage University Paper Series, Newbury Park, Sage.

This series of methodological works provides introductory explanations and demonstrations of data analysis techniques applicable to the social sciences.

Answer to Activity 9.4

The form of the statistics indicates that the extract summarizes the results of an analysis of variance. Retention interval (RI) is being examined as a possible causal influence on a series of variables: concept recognition, fact verification, and so on. Remember that F is the ratio of the estimated variance based on the variation in means *between* the different groups and the estimated variance based on the variation of the measure *within* groups. The P value of each F gives the likelihood of a particular measure of F for the two given degrees of freedom occurring by chance. So the first part of the extract, 'Main effects of RI were significant for name recognition $(F (5,355) = 9.07, P < 0.001)$' is saying that the likelihood of getting a figure of 9.07 for F with 5 and 355 degrees of freedom is less than one in a thousand. Similarly, the next part of the extract is saying that the likelihood of an F value of this size for concept recognition is also less than one in a thousand. All the variables listed in the extract have F values which are seen as unlikely to have arisen by chance for the particular number of degrees of freedom given.

Research Proposal Activity 9

The analysis of quantitative data typically takes place towards the end of a research project. Nevertheless, it is important to anticipate from the outset the type you are likely to carry out. In doing so, it is important to consider the following:

1 What is the sample size, what are the units of analysis and how many variables are involved?
2 At what level is each variable measured – nominal, ordinal, interval or ratio? How will this influence the kind of statistics you might use?
3 What are the basic research questions and how will these influence the type of analysis to be carried out? For example,

   (a) is the intended analysis likely to be purely descriptive and, if so, what descriptive statistics will be used (and will these be appropriate to the level at which variables are measured); and/or
   (b) is the intended analysis likely to require inferential statistics to make inferences to a population from a sample or to test hypotheses about relationships between variables (and, if so, what kind of analysis is likely to be most appropriate to the aims of the study and the type of data collected)?

4 Will a multivariate approach be necessary? (Remember that 'multivariate analysis' can be as little as splitting a two-variable table by a third variable – for example, controlling for the effect of gender.)

   (a) Is the research problem such that there is more than one independent variable and, if so, is it necessary to know which of the independent variables have strong influences on a dependent variable and which have weak influences?
   (b) Is it necessary to know whether there is interaction between independent variables in relation to the effects on the dependent variables; in other words, to know the extent to which the explanatory variables act independently of each other in producing the effect?
   (c) Is it necessary to examine the effects of variables extraneous to the set included in the research hypotheses – statistical control?

5 Taking account of the above questions, what form(s) of statistical analysis should be employed?
6 Are the data and the way in which they are to be recorded adequate for this form of analysis?

10

Analysis of Unstructured Data

David Boulton and Martyn Hammersley

In this chapter we shall look at some of the problems involved and techniques used in analyzing unstructured data. This kind of data is central to qualitative research. Indeed, 'qualitative data' and 'unstructured data' are often treated as synonyms, although unstructured data are also used outside qualitative research (Chapter 7 outlines some of the ways in which survey researchers handle such data). We shall concentrate here on the strategies used by qualitative researchers, but this does not imply any sharp distinction between quantitative and qualitative forms of analysis.

What we mean by 'unstructured data' is data that are not already coded in terms of the researcher's analytical categories. Such data consist mainly, but not exclusively, of written texts of various sorts: published and unpublished documents (including official government reports, personal diaries, letters, minutes of meetings, and so on), as well as field note descriptions written by researchers and transcripts of audio or video recordings. These kinds of data contrast with structured data, which include, for example, tallies recording respondents' choices from pre-specified answers or the observed frequencies of various predefined sorts of activity. The structuring of data can take two forms:

1 It may result from the physical control of responses, as in experiments or structured questionnaires, where people are effectively forced to choose one or other response by the researcher.
2 It may be produced by the application of a set of categories to 'unconstrained' behaviour, as in the case of systematic observation or the coding of free responses to questionnaire items in terms of a pre-established coding scheme.

What is distinctive about unstructured data is that they involve neither of these forms of structuring.

It is important not to be misled by the term 'unstructured', however. It does not mean that the data lack *all* structure. All data are structured in some ways. For instance, documents will be structured by the concerns and intentions of the writer. When we analyze documents we usually want to know how they were shaped by the writer's intended audience, since this may well affect what inferences we can reasonably draw from what is written. For example, when the data are observational field notes, we must consider the possibility of reactivity, of how the researcher may have affected what was observed, as well as how he or she decided to select and describe what is portrayed. With interview data, it is necessary to remember that the questions asked are likely to have influenced the answers given.

There has been much argument about the relative value of unstructured and structured data, and some have viewed them as underpinned by different epistemological paradigms. While we recognize that qualitative research is often associated with methodological and epistemological arguments that are different from those espoused by most quantitative methodologists, and while we accept the value of some of those assumptions, we do not think it is helpful to see qualitative and quantitative research as based on clearly distinct and incompatible paradigms. Thus, we do not regard the use of structured and unstructured data as representing a commitment on the part of researchers to different research paradigms. We view both sorts of data as having varying advantages and disadvantages for particular research purposes. Which should be used depends in large part on the goals of the research, and the circumstances in which these are to be pursued; and often the two sorts of data may need to be combined. It should be noted, though, that this is by no means the only or even the predominant view about this issue among social scientists. There is much disagreement, even among qualitative researchers, about what the relationship is or should be between qualitative and quantitative research (see, for example, Smith and Heshusius, 1986; Bryman, 1988; Walker and Evers, 1988; Hammersley, 1992, ch. 9).

Complementary Perspectives of Reader and Researcher

In assessing the validity of claims and evidence found in research reports based on unstructured data, two considerations are important:

1 *Plausibility*: the extent to which a claim seems likely to be true given its relationship to what we and others currently take to be knowledge that is beyond reasonable doubt.
2 *Credibility*: whether the claim is of a kind that, given what we know about how the research was carried out, we can judge it to be very likely to be true.

Where a claim is neither sufficiently plausible nor credible to be accepted, we must look at the evidence offered in support of it (if there is any). And when we do so we must be concerned with the plausibility and credibility of the evidence itself and the strength of its relationship to the claim it is intended to support.

In assessing the plausibility and credibility of the claims and evidence presented in a research report, we are in effect engaging in a dialogue with the writer of that report. Of course, it is a dialogue in which one side (that of the researcher) is only imagined by the reader, although on some occasions it may turn into a real dialogue: for example, in the case of a book review to which the author replies.

It is important to recognize that a similar dialogue, again with one side largely imaginary, takes place in *doing* research. In framing research questions, selecting cases, gathering and interpreting data, the researcher constantly has an audience, indeed perhaps several audiences, in mind. So, in the course of their work, researchers continually ask themselves whether their interpretations of data are sufficiently plausible and credible, and what other data may be necessary to check and support these interpretations. Their answers to these questions will be shaped by their anticipations of how particular sorts of audience will react to their interpretations. Of course, there is an important difference between the dialogues in which readers and researchers engage. Whereas the reader starts with the main claims presented by an author and, as and when necessary, moves to what evidence is given in support of them, the researcher begins with data (and, of course, with a lot more than is ever likely to appear in the research report) and must move, somehow, from those data to some major claims. However, despite coming from different ends, as it were, the analytical work of reader and researcher is similar in character. To some degree, in order to understand a piece of research, one has to reconstruct the activity of the researcher, to imagine what he or she was trying to do and how that task was tackled; though, of course, how far this is possible will depend on the information available about the research process.

In this chapter we shall look in some detail at the process of analyzing unstructured data. This should enable you to get a clearer sense of what is involved in qualitative data analysis and also, perhaps, make more effective the dialogue you engage in when you read texts employing this sort of analysis.

Types of Qualitative Data

Some research is largely *descriptive* in character: for example, involving the production of a narrative account of some series of events. It is rare for a whole research report to take this form, but there are some examples that come close to this. A striking one is Susan Krieger's account of the life of a radio station. Here is her summary of the study:

> The study was begun in 1972 and consisted of eleven months of interviewing persons involved with the station, obtaining documentary evidence from them and from other sources, visiting the station, and listening to it. The next two years were spent in writing a text which described a process of cooptation in the life of the station over the years 1967–72. The station had been closely associated with the Summer of Love in San Francisco in 1967. It was thought to have been the first hard rock 'hippy' radio station in the country. In the five years since, it had become increasingly commercial, professional, and successful, and was frequently criticised for having sold out to the establishment. (Krieger, 1979:167–8)

Sometimes, qualitative research produces narratives which document the course of the research project itself, rather than a sequence of events independent of the researcher. Furthermore, it is quite common to find so-called 'reflexive accounts' or 'natural histories' of particular studies written by researchers. One of the first and best known is Whyte's account of his research on various aspects of the Italian-American community of Boston's North End in the 1940s (Whyte, 1981; see also Boelen, 1992; Whyte, 1992). Such reflexive accounts of the research process may, of course, be an important source of information relevant to the assessment of studies' findings. (You will find lists of reflexive accounts of research in Hammersley and Atkinson, 1983; Walford, 1987).

There are other sorts of largely descriptive research. Some is focused on the way in which discourse (verbal interaction or written text) is patterned (see Potter and Wetherell, 1987). Discourse analysis is becoming increasingly common in sociology and social psychology, and in other areas too, and it takes a variety of forms. It may be concerned with mundane features of everyday life; for example, with the way that turn-taking is organized in conversations. Other work is concerned with presuppositions built into what is said or written by some individual or group. For example, Schegloff (1971) looks in detail at the process of giving directions to those unable to find their way. He notes how the character of the directions given is context-sensitive: it is affected, for instance, by the location in which the directions are being given and by the geographical knowledge that the recipient is assumed already to have. Other discourse analytical work focuses on more controversial areas. Thus, Billig (1991) has looked at the way that different 'ideologies' come into conflict in discourse surrounding, for example, medicine and social work.

Another distinctive form of largely descriptive qualitative research, this time in cultural anthropology, is devoted to documenting the array of concepts used by a particular group to deal with some aspect of their experience. This approach is sometimes referred to as 'ethnosemantics'. Ethnosemantics is directed towards producing a detailed account of the array of concepts used by a particular group of people to make sense of their environment. Much qualitative research takes this as part of its focus: qualitative researchers often place great emphasis on the importance of understanding the perspectives of the people they are studying. However, normally they seek to do this simply by listening for the categories that people use in informal talk or interviews, rather than by using the rather more structured elicitation devices favoured by ethnosemanticists. Equally important, they generally do not restrict themselves to the description of people's perspectives, being also concerned with the causes and consequences of these. And, often, they do not draw a sharp distinction between description, explanation and theory development, so that much qualitative research seems to be aimed at producing all three kinds of product simultaneously (Hammersley, 1992, ch. 1).

The Process of Analysis

In this section we shall look at what is actually involved in doing qualitative analysis, focusing on what is the most commonly used set of procedures, often referred to as 'grounded theorizing'. A common concern in qualitative data analysis, and especially in grounded theorizing, is the identification of the perspectives of various groups of people involved in a setting, the documentation of the problems that they face in their lives, and the description of the strategies that they have developed to deal with those problems. This provides a general framework for the analysis, but the substance must come from the data.

Data Preparation

Data are rarely obtained in an immediately analyzable form: usually they must be prepared before analysis can begin. The need for data preparation is most obvious with audio and video recordings. While listening to or watching a recording is a good way to familiarize oneself with the data, for the purposes of analysis it is usually necessary to transcribe recordings, or at least to produce a summary and index of what is on them – a task which is, of course, quite time-consuming.

There is a variety of conventions in terms of which audio recordings can be transcribed, and which set of conventions is appropriate depends partly on the purposes of the research. For example, where detailed analysis of the process of discourse will be involved, pauses may need to be timed, overlaps in talk between one speaker and another clearly marked, as well as other verbal (and perhaps even non-verbal) features of the talk included. By contrast, the transcripts normally used by qualitative researchers, who are not so closely concerned with discourse features, contain much less detail and are often imprecise in the linguistic sense.

How detailed a transcription needs to be, and what does and does not need to be included, then, are matters of judgement that depend on the purposes of the research (see Box 10.1; and Ochs, 1979). But the form of transcription will also partly depend, of course, on the amount of information that a recording supplies. Obviously, video recordings supply much more information than audio recordings, and special forms of transcription have been developed for handling these (see, for example, Goodwin, 1981). Also important is the quality of the recording, and this will depend on the nature of what is recorded as well as on the recording equipment. Clearly, in the case of an audio recording, the more speakers involved, and the more background noise, the more difficult it is to get adequate recording quality. Similarly, with video recordings, the more crowded the setting, and the more movement there is, the more difficult it may be to see what is going on.

In assessing a study that draws on transcriptions and provides a transcription scheme, a useful question to ask is whether the scheme used is appropriate, given the sort of data collected and the purposes of the research. Does it include all the relevant information that seems likely to have been available, given the nature of the recordings? On the other hand, does it provide too much detail, thereby making it more difficult to assess the evidential status of the data presented in the report? Does it seem likely to be accurate in the relevant respects?

Box 10.1 *Two records of an interaction*

Below we reproduce two extracts from notes that purport to recapture the same interaction. They are recognizably 'about' the same people and the same events. By the same token, neither lays any claim to completeness. The first obviously compresses things to an extreme extent, and the second summarizes some things, and explicitly acknowledges that some parts of the conversation are missing altogether:

1   The teacher told his colleagues in the staff room about the wonders of a progressive school he had been to visit the day before. He was attacked from all sides. As I walked up with him to his classroom he

(Continued)

Box 10.1 *(Continued)*

continued talking of how the behaviour of the pupils at X had been marvellous. We reached his room. I waited outside, having decided to watch what happened in the hall in the build up to the morning assembly. He went into his classroom and immediately began shouting at his class. He was taking it out on them for not being like the pupils at X.

2 *[Walker gives an enthusiastic account of X to his colleagues in the staff room. There is an aggressive reaction.]*

Graves: Projects are not education, just cutting out things.

Walker: Oh no, they don't allow that, there's a strict check on progress.

Holton: The more I hear of this the more wishy-washy it sounds.

[...]

Walker: There's a craft resources area and pupils go and do some dress-making or woodwork when they want to, when it fits into their project.

Holton: You need six weeks' basic teaching in woodwork or metalwork.

[...]

Holton: How can an immature child of that age do a project?

Walker: Those children were self-controlled and well-behaved.

[...]

Holton: Sounds like utopia.

Dixon: Gimmicky.

Walker: There's no vandalism. They've had the books four years and they've been used a lot and I could see the pupils were using them, but they looked new, the teacher had told them that if they damaged the books she would have to replace them herself.

[...]

Holton: Sounds like those kids don't need teaching.

(Walker and I go up to his room: he continues his praise for X. When we reach his room I wait outside to watch the hall as the build up for the morning assembly begins. He enters his room and immediately begins shouting. The thought crosses my mind that the contrast between the pupils at X he has been describing and defending to his colleagues and the 'behaviour' of his own pupils may be a reason for his shouting at the class, but, of course, I don't know what was going on in the classroom).

( ) = observer descriptions.

[...] = omission of parts of conversation in record.

(Hammersley, 1980)

The second version is much more concrete in its treatment of the events; indeed, much of the time the speech of the actors themselves is preserved. We can inspect the notes with a fair assurance that we are gaining information on how the participants themselves described things, who said what to whom, and so on. When we compress and summarize we do not simply lose 'interersting' detail and 'local colour', we lose vital information. (Hammersley and Atkinson, 1983: 152–3)

The need for the preparation of data is not restricted to audio and video recordings. Field notes are often written initially in jotted form and then written out, and filled in, later. There are variations in format and style between researchers in the writing of field notes, just as there are in the transcription of audio and video recordings. In general, though, the aim is to make the notes as concrete as possible, minimizing the amount of questionable inference involved. This emphasis on concrete description in field notes does not mean, of course, that researchers are uninterested in how the events they observe and record might be interpreted. Indeed, any interpretations that the researcher thinks of in the course of observation, or while writing up the field notes, are usually noted. But care is taken to avoid those interpretations structuring the data recording itself, since they may turn out to be wrong. And, usually, such interpretations are distinguished typographically from the field notes proper; for example, by being put into brackets.

Also included in field notes may be the researcher's personal feelings about what has been observed or about her or his own role. Once again, these will usually be recorded in a way that marks them off from the observational record. Apart from its value in indicating possible sources of bias in the data, reflection by the researcher on her or his own experience in the setting may also facilitate the process of understanding the people being studied. Bogdan and Taylor (1975) illustrate this (in Box 10.2) from their studies of a hospital for people with learning difficulties (the 'state institution') and a job training agency.

It is unusual for field notes to be presented extensively in their original form in research reports. Normally, only brief extracts are given, frequently edited and tidied up. However, it is worth remembering that field notes are the raw material from which the evidence provided in many qualitative research reports comes. In assessing those reports, we need to be aware of the contingencies of field-note writing (the selectivity involved, the fact that often there is considerable reliance on memory in filling out jotted notes), and of the filtering process that has taken place between the original field notes and the data presented as evidence in research reports.

Even in the case of documents, data preparation may be necessary before analysis can begin; for example, translation from a different language may be required. It may also be necessary to collect contextual information and to add this to documentary material, indicating, for instance, who produced the material and in what circumstances, what any obscure references in the text mean, and so on.

Box 10.2   *Reflexive analysis*

What you feel may be what your subjects feel or may have felt in the past. Your first impressions may be the same ones that others have had. You should use your feelings, beliefs, preconceptions, and prejudices to help you develop hypotheses. The following comments are excerpted from field notes in the state institution study.

(Continued)

Box 10.2   *(Continued)*

I feel quite bored and depressed on the ward tonight. I wonder if this has anything to do with the fact that there are one two attendants work-ing now. With one two attendants on, there are fewer diversions and less bantering. Perhaps this is why the attendants always complain about there not being enough of them. After all, there is never more work here than enough to occupy two attendants' time so it's not the fact that they can't get their work done that bothers them. Although I don't show it, I tense up when the residents approach me when they are covered with food or excrement. Maybe this is what the attendants feel and why they often treat the residents as lepers.

In the following excerpt from the job training study conducted by one of the authors, the observer reflects upon one of his first encounters with a trainee after having spent the initial stages of the research with staff members:

I approached the two trainees who were working on assembling the radio. The male trainee looked up. I said 'Hi.' He said, 'Hi' and went back to doing what he had been doing. I said, 'Have you built that (the radio) right from scratch?' (After I said this I thought that that was a dumb thing to say or perhaps a very revealing thing to say. Thinking back over the phrase, it came across as perhaps condescending. Asking if he had built it right from scratch might imply that I thought he didn't have the ability. He didn't react in that way but maybe that's the way people think of the 'hard core' unemployed out at the center. Doing well is treated with surprise rather than as standard procedure. Perhaps rather than expecting that they are going to produce and treating them as if they are going to produce, you treat doing well as a special event.)

The observer thus gained a possible insight into staff members' defini-tions of trainees through a reflection on his own remark. (Bogdan and Taylor, 1975: 67)

Starting the Analysis

The most obvious difference between analyzing unstructured and structured data is that, whereas the latter come ready coded, the former do not. In other words, struc-tured data are collected in a form whose relevance to the focus of the enquiry is obvi-ous (at least if the data-collection procedures have been designed properly), so that what can and should be done with the data is, to a large extent, a matter of follow-ing rules about what sorts of analysis are appropriate given the nature of the data and the purposes of the research. This is not the case with unstructured data, and this is no minor practical consideration for the researcher. The most common question asked by researchers carrying out qualitative data analysis for the first time, and the one that is most difficult to answer, is: now I've got the data, what do I do with them? The reason it is difficult to answer this question is that there is no set of rules, no simple recipe, that one can follow with unstructured data which will always be appropriate and guarantee good results. The task is not just the assignment of data to categories; the categories themselves have to be developed at the same time. In fact, what is involved is a process of mutual fitting between data and categories. There is, then, an essential element of creativity involved, and this is one reason why different researchers working with the same data may produce rather different analyses. Having said this, there are certain general steps that are typically followed in grounded theorizing and the forms of qualitative data analysis analogous to it.

An essential first step is a close reading of the data. This involves looking carefully at the data with a view to identifying aspects of them that may be significant. It is worth emphasizing that grounded theorizing is usually associated with research that is exploratory or discovery-orientated; for example, ethnographic, participant observation and life-history work. Here, the process of analysis is not confined to a particular stage of the research; it begins at the start of data collection and continues in more or less formal ways through to the completion of the research report. Thus, Howard Becker, a well-known exponent of qualitative method, comments that in participant observation research 'analysis is carried on sequentially, important parts of the analysis being made while the researcher is still gathering his data', and he notes that one of the consequences of this is that 'further data gathering takes its direction from provisional analyses' (Becker, 1970: 26–7). This contrasts sharply with research that begins with a set of hypotheses and proceeds to test these. Indeed, such research would normally collect structured data. One of the implications of the exploratory character of qualitative research is that the focus of enquiry is clarified over the course of data collection and analysis. Furthermore, the analytical categories used to make sense of the data (which in the case of hypothesis-testing research are supplied by the hypotheses and the theory lying behind them) have to be developed in the process of data analysis. Indeed, developing such categories is the central task in grounded theorizing.

Usually, the initial close reading of data necessary for this sort of analysis focuses on a sub-sample of the data. This data sample may be chosen haphazardly on the basis of what is most convenient, or those data which look most promising may be selected. Eventually, all the relevant data will be analyzed: it is simply a matter of finding a place to start. Reading through the data, the researcher notes down topics or categories to which the data relate and which are relevant to the research focus, or are in some other way interesting or surprising. Annotations are usually made in the margins of the data record, specifying the categories. Also, the researcher is on the look-out for recurrences that may indicate patterns, whether these are typical sequences of events in a setting, or preoccupations around which a particular group's or individual's view of the world revolves.

A next step is often the gathering together of segments of data from different parts of the data record that are relevant to some category. This distinguishes grounded theorizing from other forms of qualitative data analysis. Some qualitative researchers do not segment and compare data in this way. This is particularly true of those who are concerned with analyzing processes of social interaction as in conversation or discourse analysis. For them, segmenting the data and comparing the segments would lose much that is relevant, notably details about the way in which one utterance relates to those before and after it (for instance, the relationship between the interviewer's questions and the informant's answers, how the informant builds on or refers back to things he or she has said earlier). Here again, the strategies employed depend on the purposes of the research, and the costs and benefits of each strategy must be borne in mind.

The categories produced in the course of coding the data may come from a variety of sources. They may arise from some of the ideas that originally sparked off the research or that set the framework for it, or from more general background knowledge. Perhaps the data seem to confirm the researcher's expectations. But equally, if not more significantly, perhaps they do not. Categories may also arise from the data themselves, in the sense that the people studied may use concepts that seem particularly significant for understanding their behaviour. Good advice that is often given to those engaging in grounded theorizing for the first time is to look out for 'insider' terms: words and abbreviations that are distinctive to the world that the informant inhabits, and which may appear strange to outsiders. Often these can tell us something about the distinctive ways in which the people we are studying view the world. A classic example is to be found in the study of students in a state medical school in the USA, carried out by Becker and colleagues (1961). The researchers found that the students used the word 'crock' to describe some patients. For the students a 'crock' was a patient who did not seem to have an identifiable illness and, as a result, did not constitute a useful case from which the students could learn about the diagnosis and treatment of known illnesses. What the use of that concept suggested was that the students had an instrumental attitude towards patients, viewing them in terms of the opportunities they offered for learning relevant knowledge and skills, rather than primarily as people in need of help. And, indeed, Becker et al., went on to argue that the process of medical education tends to involve a transformation of students' attitudes from the altruism with which they enter medical school towards a more 'professional' orientation.

At the beginning, researchers seek to generate as many categories as possible, not worrying what the relevance of those categories might be to their intended goal. This reflects the creative, exploratory character of the process. Of course, how unconstrained this process of category development should be depends on the purposes of the research and the time constraints under which the researcher is operating. However, generating as many categories as possible is sound advice in many circumstances because it may enable the researcher to see features of the data, or of what the data refer to, that might be overlooked with a more focused approach. Such discoveries can guide the subsequent analysis in two ways. First, they may reveal that there is some doubt about one or more of the assumptions with which the researcher began the analysis. For instance, perhaps the people described are not primarily concerned with what the researcher expected them to be concerned with. Secondly, it can suggest a quite different focus for the research, one that the researcher judges to be more interesting or significant. (Again, whether or not a researcher can change the research focus, and to what degree, will depend on the constraints under which he or she is working.)

The aim of this sort of initial analysis of unstructured data, then, is to generate categories, each of which collects together several segments of data, some of which look promising as a basis for organizing the analysis and, eventually, the research report. This concern with categories that group many of the data together arises because researchers are usually concerned with stable characteristics or recurrent patterns, not just with what happened at particular points in time, though we noted above that this is not *always* true. The categories may vary in character too, of course. Some may be relatively banal, others may be rather less obvious and more interesting. Research is judged not only in terms of its validity but also in terms of its relevance, and one element of this is the extent to which it tells us something new. It follows from this that any novel or theoretically interesting categories that emerge are especially welcome to a researcher. That said, it is rare for such categories to appear immediately or to predominate; and sometimes what appear to be banal categories turn out not to be so at all, while apparently interesting ones prove inapplicable. So, grounded theorizing almost always starts from relatively obvious categories. The goal initially is simply to get a general descriptive sense of the content of the data and how analysis of it might be pursued. Box 10.3 provides an example of the identification of categories.

The next step in qualitative data analysis of the kind discussed by Strauss and Corbin (1990) is to compare and contrast all the items of data that have been assigned to the same category. Glaser and Strauss (1967) refer to this stage as the 'constant comparative method'. The aim of this is to clarify what the categories that have emerged mean, as well as to identify sub-categories and relations among categories. In the process, these categories may be developed and some data segments may be reassigned as a result. It is then necessary to go through the data sample again in case any data segments not previously identified as relevant have been overlooked (this is frequently the case). After this, further data samples will be analyzed, perhaps producing new developments in the categories, and these will, of course, make it necessary to re-code previously coded data. What is involved here, then, is an iterative process of analysis that generates categories and interpretations of the data in terms of these categories. And, over time, at least some of the categories will come to be integrated into a network of relationships. These will usually form the core of the main claims of the resulting research report(s).

A number of elaborations of these general principles can be noted. First, in the early stages of analysis, it is possible that not all data are assigned to categories; in other words, the categorization may not be exhaustive. For some purposes exhaustive categorization is needed, but not for all. Also, categories which are developed may not be mutually exclusive; in other words, sometimes the same segment of data may be listed under more than one heading. It may sometimes be necessary to develop categories that are mutually exclusive, but to seek to do so is not typical of the sort of analysis characteristic of grounded theorizing. Further, the allocation of data to categories may not be very rigorous in the first instance; the categories may not be clearly defined with specific criteria indicating the sort of data which should and should not be included. The goal of grounded theorizing is to facilitate the more rigorous definition of categories *through the process of analysis,* rather than specifying at the beginning of the research process (as is typical in quantitative, hypothesis-testing research) what categories are appropriate and how they are to be defined.

Box 10.3 *Labelling phenomena*

Concepts are the basic units of analysis in the grounded theory method. One can count 'raw' data, but one can't relate or talk about them easily. Therefore, conceptualizing data becomes the first step in analysis. By breaking down and conceptualizing, we mean taking apart an observation, a sentence, a paragraph, and giving each discrete incident, idea or event a name, something that stands for or represents a phenomenon. Just how do we do this? We ask questions about each one. What is this? What does it represent? We compare incident with incident as we go along so that similar phenomena can be given the same name. Otherwise, we would wind up with too many names and very confused!

Let's stop here and take an example. Suppose you are in a fairly expensive but popular restaurant. The restaurant is built on three levels. On the first level is a bar, on the second a small dining area, and on the third the main dining area and the kitchen. The kitchen is open, so you can see what is going on. Wine, liqueurs, and appropriate glasses in which to serve them, are also available on this third level. While waiting for your dinner, you notice a lady in red. She appears to be just standing there in the kitchen, but your common sense tells you that a restaurant wouldn't pay a lady in red just to stand there, especially in a busy kitchen. Your curiosity is piqued, so you decide to do an inductive analysis to see if you can determine just what her job is. (Once a grounded theorist, always a grounded theorist.)

You notice that she is intently looking around the kitchen area, *a work site*, focusing here and then there, taking a mental note of what is going on. You ask yourself, what is she doing here? Then you label it *watching*. Watching what? *Kitchen work*. Next, someone comes up and asks her a question. She answers. This act is different than watching, so you code it as *information passing*. She seems to notice everything. You call this *attentiveness*.

Our lady in red walks up to someone and tells him something. Since this incident also involves information that is passed on, you also label it, *information passing*. Although standing in the midst of all this activity, she doesn't seem to disrupt it. To describe this phenomenon you use the term *unintrusiveness*. She turns and walks quickly and quietly, *efficiency*, into the dining area, and proceeds to *watch*, the activity here also.

She seems to be keeping track of everyone and everything, *monitoring*. But monitoring what? Being an astute observer, you notice that she is monitoring the quality of the service, how the waiter interacts and responds to the customer; the *timing of service*, how much transpires between seating a customer, their ordering, the delivery of food; and customer *response and satisfaction* with the service.

A waiter comes with an order for a large party, she moves in to help him, *providing assistance*. The woman looks like she knows what she is doing and is competent at it, *experienced*. She walks over to a wall near the kitchen and looks at what appears to be a schedule, *information gathering*. The *maître d'* comes down and they talk for a few moments and look around the room for empty tables and judge at what point in the meal the seated customers seem to be: the two are *conferring*.

> **Box 10.3** *(Continued)*
>
> This example should be sufficient for you to comprehend what we mean by labelling phenomena. It is not unusual for beginning researchers to summarize rather than *conceptualize* data. That is, they merely repeat briefly the gist of the phrase or sentence, but still in a descriptive way. For instance, instead of using a term such as 'conferring' to describe the last incident, they might say something like 'sat and talked to the *maître d''.* Or, use terms such as: 'read the schedule', 'moved to the dining room', and 'didn't disrupt'. To invent such phrases doesn't give you a concept to work with. You can see just from this initial coding session that conceptually it is more effective to work with a term such as 'information gathering' rather than 'reading the schedule', because one might be able to label ten different happenings or events as *information gathering* – her asking a question of one of the chefs, checking on the number of clean glasses, calling a supplier, and so forth. (Strauss and Corbin, 1990: 63–5)

Secondly, there is a question about how much of the surrounding context should be included in data extracts. For example, in the case of interview data, should one always include the questions asked by the interviewer? These are matters of judgement: some context will be necessary to make the extract intelligible, but the longer each data extract is, the more cumbersome the analysis becomes.

Thirdly, even when working with a relatively small amount of data – from just four or five interviews, say – there can be practical problems involved in grounded theorizing. Using a word processor to copy, file and print out segments of data relevant to particular categories is certainly a lot easier than copying segments of data by hand or cutting and sticking segments onto cards (methods commonly used in the past) but it is still time-consuming. As a result, a number of computer programmes have been developed especially for carrying out this sort of analysis (see Tesch, 1990; Fielding and Lee, 1991; Dey, 1992).

Fourthly, an important question is how far any given analysis should be pursued. With a small amount of data it is often difficult to go beyond the description of a few key themes. A larger amount of data may allow greater development of understanding of the perspectives and behaviour of the people being studied, especially in terms of looking for relationships among categories. Also, where observational data are available it may be possible to look at the relationship between what informants say they do and what they actually seem to do. Strauss and Corbin (1990) provide a clear account of one direction that this further analysis can take, involving the development of a dense and well-integrated theory. Another is towards providing the basis for quantitative analysis, but this requires the development of the categorization into mutually exclusive types that can form the basis for counting instances or even developing scales. Which of these directions is most appropriate depends on the purpose of the research and the nature of the data.

Finally, much of the discussion above has been concerned with analysis of a single case, devoted to describing or explaining some of the features of that case. However, qualitative research often involves collecting data on several cases. Sometimes the data will be pooled and the sort of analysis described here will be applied to the whole corpus. At other times, separate analyses will be carried out on each case – perhaps to develop and test theoretical ideas through systematic comparison of strategically selected cases. Equally, sometimes the categories developed in one case will be applied to another simply to illuminate similarities and differences.

Reflexivity and the Assessment of Validity

The process of data analysis produces the main claims that form the core of research reports. And in qualitative research the evidence that is presented by the researcher in support of claims will be a selection from the segments of data collected together as relevant to the categories that form part of those claims. However, of course, claims are not assessed only in terms of the evidence offered in support of them but also in terms of credibility, against the background of information about how the research was carried out and the likelihood of error that this implies. Such consider-ations should also be taken into account by the researcher engaging in qualitative data analysis. In deciding what are and are not reasonable inferences to be made on the basis of her or his data, the researcher must consider the likelihood of errors of various kinds. For instance, does it seem likely that the data may have been shaped by the presence of the researcher in such a fashion as to lead to misleading conclu-sions? This is the problem of reactivity again. Were the people observed 'putting on a show' or 'maintaining a front' for the observer? Did the informant simply tell the researcher what he or she thought the researcher wanted to hear? Similarly, how complex and uncertain in validity are the judgements likely to have been that pro-duced the data? Was the observer or informant in a position to be able to observe and record accurately what happened? Were the phenomena being described of a kind that anyone would probably be able to recognize and agree on, or were they more problematic? Equally, is there any indication that the observer or the informant could have been biased, consciously or unconsciously selecting evidence to support one outcome rather than another? As readers, we need to look for the extent to which the researcher seems to have been aware of potential sources of error, and what he or she did to counter these, as well as considering them for ourselves.

Consideration of the process of research and its possible implications for the validity of the main claims and conclusions of a study is one part of what is some-times referred to as *reflexivity* (Hammersley and Atkinson, 1983). What is proposed is that the researcher should be a reflective practitioner, continually thinking about the process of research and especially about her or his own role in it, and the impli-cations of this for the analysis. As we noted earlier, qualitative researchers usually record in their field notes their interpretations of and feelings about what they observe and about their role. And this process of reflection is often continued throughout the whole process of the research.

An equally important aspect of reflexivity is that the process of data collection and analysis should be made sufficiently explicit for a reader to make a reasonable assessment of the credibility of the findings. Of course, the information about the research that we have available to us as readers will always be quite limited. It will also vary a great deal between research reports. Not surprisingly, book-length reports tend to provide more information than do articles. However, sometimes we are able to track down other reports arising from the same piece of research and these may give us extra information. Furthermore, occasionally a reflexive account or natural history of the research will be available and this may provide very useful background information on which to assess the claims made by the researcher.

Researchers may sometimes provide reports of attempts at respondent validation and triangulation. These are useful further sources of information, especially where the claims made are very controversial. Indeed, evidence of this kind may occasionally be crucial for the assessment of the findings of qualitative research. However, such evidence, like evidence of other kinds, is never absolutely conclusive. It must be interpreted and assessed, and there is usually scope for conflicting judgements about it.

Conclusion

In this chapter we have looked at some of the strategies used by qualitative researchers for analyzing unstructured data. We concentrated in particular on the kind of qualitative data analysis that has been codified by Glaser and Strauss (1967) as grounded theorizing, since this represents probably the most common approach in use today. We have only been able to provide an outline here of what is involved in this sort of analysis. However, it gives a sense of the sort of analytical work that underlies qualitative research reports, and this provides a basis for assessing the claims made in such reports.

Key Terms

Constant comparative method   the comparison and contrasting of data segments within a thematic category, leading perhaps to reassignment of segments and/or re-scrutiny of the original texts.

Ethnography   studies which attempt to describe a social context, in the first instance, in the terms used and understood by its members.

Ethnosemantics   studies which attempt to establish the array of concepts used by a group to make sense of their environment.

Field notes   factual records of what went on in a research setting – insofar as this is possible even in theory – and, separately, notes of the personal feelings and interpretations of the researcher.

Grounded theorization   the attempt to render thematic analysis rigorously through the process of analysis itself rather than through prior specification of categories.

Reflexive analysis   reflection by researchers on their own feelings and behaviour in a research setting; more broadly, consideration of effects of

(Continued)

(Key Terms continued)

the researcher, the research process and the concrete events encountered on the nature of the data produced.

Respondent validation evaluation by respondents of the data or the interpretation of them.

Triangulation bringing more than one method or source of data to bear in the same context.

Unstructured data in this context, data which are not pre-coded (but may well be structured by the rules of conversation, the demands of the situation and the prompting of the researcher).

Further Reading

Many introductions to qualitative or ethnographic social research include some discussion of qualitative data analysis. See, for example:

Hammersley, M. and Atkinson, P. (1983) *Ethnography: Principles in Practice*, London, Tavistock.
Lofland, J. and Lofland, L. (1984) *Analysing Social Settings*, Belmont, CA, Wadsworth.

There are also some books devoted entirely to this subject. See, for instance:

Strauss, A. and Corbin, J. (1990) *Basics of Qualitative Research: Grounded Theory Procedures and Techniques*, Newbury Park, CA, Sage.
This is the best of the books on grounded theorizing as regards how to do it. The initial chapters provide a very straightforward introduction.

Strauss, A. (1987) *Qualitative Analysis for Social Scientists*, New York, Cambridge University Press.
This book represents the same approach as that of Strauss and Corbin (1990) above, but is more advanced and more demanding to follow.

Glaser, B.G. and Strauss, A. (1967) *The Discovery of Grounded Theory*, Chicago, IL, Aldine.
This is the original book on grounded theorizing. It has since been superseded by the above, but it indicates something of the original motivation for this approach.

On the use of microcomputers in handling qualitative data, see:

Tesch, R. (1990) *Qualitative Research: Analysis Types and Software Tools*, Lewes, Falmer Press.
Fielding, N.G. and Lee, R.M. (eds) (1991) *Using Computers in Qualitative Research*, London, Sage.
Dey, I. (1992) *Qualitative Data Analysis*, London, Routledge.
This also serves as an introduction to qualitative data analysis.

Research Proposal Activity 10

This chapter has been concerned with the analysis of unstructured data. Such analysis does not follow strict protocols. Indeed, this is one of its strengths. Also, it is often a continuous process of developing and refining categories by moving backwards and forwards between the output of the analysis and the data themselves, and indeed between the output of analysis and fresh fieldwork to generate new data in order to refine categories further. For this reason, it is difficult to anticipate what strategy of analysis will be appropriate when formulating a research proposal.

Nevertheless, it is useful to address the following questions:

1 In what form are the data?
2 What form of data preparation will be required? (For example, will a transcription of audio or video materials be necessary and, if so, what transcription procedures need to be adopted? Alternatively, if the data are in the form of field notes, will these require development, contextualization and/or editing?)
3 Have sufficient time and/or resources been allowed for the analysis process and the data preparation?
4 What procedures will be used for data analysis? Will some form of coding be used and, if so, how will the analytical categories be developed (for example, from a subset of data and/or from ideas which sparked off the research)?
5 What factors can be anticipated which may affect the validity of inferences drawn from the data (for example, reactivity)?
6 What should be included in the reflexive account of the research?

11

Discourse Research

Roger Sapsford

This chapter introduces conceptions of discourse in sociology and social psychology and the kinds of research perspectives and techniques that build on them.

Ideology and Discourse

Ideology

One sense of the term 'ideology', now relatively uncommon, aims purely to describe the symbolic content of a culture and has no critical overtones (Kaplan and Manners, 1972; Geuss, 1981, Ch. 1). In the more 'politicized' sense that we associated with the work of Karl Marx, however, an ideology might be characterized very simply as a set of propositions that are taken as defining what life is like and how one should act within it – that describe what we take for granted about it and define how we should feel and act – that purport to define the interests of one group but in fact work in the interests of another and more powerful group. For example:

- The protestant work ethic, which defines men's lives in terms of the paid employment they perform, makes work a (*the?*) desirable goal, considers someone who does not or cannot work as having little or no value and considers work as something people naturally want to do and as rewarding in its own right. Tied up with this is a view of the world as defined in money terms – rewards and even necessities have to be paid for – and in terms of competition for resource – some do better than others, by their ability and their hard work.
- The domestic division of labour, writ large upon society, in which men are responsible for resourcing and governing families and women are responsible for maintaining the home and family life, providing meals and caring for the health and well being of their husbands and children. Tied up with this are propositions such as 'a woman's place is in the home' and 'children must come first'.

The first of these is true of our age – I subscribe to it myself! – but it is also curiously useful for those who own factories and commercial institutions and need to buy labour on a far from free market. It reinforces and reproduces a power distribution based on ownership. The second reinforces a power distribution based on gender and is curiously convenient for men, individually and as a group, for the organization of heavy industry, which requires the servicing of male workers, and for a state organization which needs and plans for the reproduction of industrial/commercial relations into the next generation.

Activity 11.1 (5–10 minutes)

The last paragraph described itself as 'very simple'. Spend a few minutes thinking and making notes on the ways in which it is *too* simple.

The formulation above is too simple, in the first place, because it characterized ideology as a set of propositions. While I suspect an ideology *could* always be expressed in words, it does not have to be so expressed in order to have force – it is not a set of learned verbal statements – as Althusser (e.g. 1971) has shown us; people learn from their lived experience. In the London of the sixties and seventies, for example – the beginnings of the comprehensive schools in British education – the dominant rhetoric and belief to which children were exposed was that anyone who was able and worked hard could succeed, irrespective of parental class; this was an era whose political correctness was meritocratic. At the same time, those whose parents had received more help in the home – both in material terms, having access to books, educational toys, trips abroad, etc., which were not available to working-class children, and in terms of cultural and educational 'capital', having parents who could help them with their homework and who understood the school system and how to work it. Despite their best efforts, therefore, working-class children tended to do worse at school than middle-class ones, and the consequences for many working-class boys have been well illustrated by Willis (1977): a counterformation of identity as tough, competitive, 'hard' and despising deskwork and book learning. This amounted to reproducing the existing class system, through lessons learned by children from their own experience in schools which were trying hard to promote the exact opposite. In other words, ideologies are often latent, expressed in institutions and behaviours, rather than explicitly formulated (Lane, 1960 – and see also Billig, 1988).

A second point is that the formulation suggests conspiracy – that ideology is imposed by owners on workers. This may sometimes be true to some extent, but it conjures up a picture of industrialists meeting at annual conferences to determine this year's ideology. More plausible is an account in terms of dominant ('hegemonic') values that are learned by experience and precept in upper- and middle-class as well as working-class childhood. A third is that accounts in terms of ideology have a strong tendency to overstate the degree to which ideologies are hegemonic: if ideologies had the degree of dominance which they are generally ascribed, it is difficult to see how we could escape them sufficiently to write accounts such as this one!

A final point is that the concept of ideology includes an explicit truth-claim – that you are deceived by ideology, while I see through this to the truth. Unfortunately, there is absolutely no way to establish the validity of this claim.

Discourse

The concept of discourse was developed by writers such as Michel Foucault (e.g. 1970, 1972, 1982) as an extension of the concept of ideology and to overcome the last two of the problems outlined above. To the extent that an ideology may be characterized as a set of propositions, a discourse may be characterized as a set of rules – rules for determining truth (epistemology) and rules for declaring the objects about which it is sensible and meaningful to speak (ontogeny). Discourses create the 'conditions of possibility' for beliefs about the world – they provide the elements or objects which are to be described and set the rules by which actions are to be warranted/justified/excused. Foucault himself 'specialized' in identifying turning-points – periods in which one way of conceptualizing a segment of the social world changed, rendering both the old and the new conceptions visible by their contrast. Notable examples would be the birth of rehabilitation as a penal policy and the notion of criminals as a reclaimable resource (Foucault, 1977), the birth of modern clinical concepts in medicine (Foucault, 1973) and the birth of modern conceptions of sexuality (and, particularly, homosexuality) as a characterological property of individuals (Foucault, 1990).

An important aspect of discursive theory and research is its emphasis on debate, conflict and resistance – the availability and use of *different* discourses within which a given area of social life *could* be constituted and the use of one rather than another to establish or reproduce a power gradient.

> Words are about the world but they also form the world as they represent it. ... [As people speak] a formulation of the world comes into existence. ... As accounts and discourses become available and widely shared, they become social realities to be reckoned with ... The account enters the discursive economy to be circulated, exchanged, stifled, marginalised or, perhaps, comes to dominate over other possible accounts and thus marked as the 'definitive truth'. (Wetherell, 2001: 16)

(See also Billig et al., 1988; Billig, 1991.) Another way of conceptualizing this is to think about narratives and the variety of stories we tell about ourselves and the world, to others and to ourselves:

> ... as members of a culture we are rarely original. Rather ... we have to draw on accepted and conventional images, ideas and modes of talking about ourselves and others. ... Discourse researchers often focus on the kinds of stories people tell. They look at the way these stories are formed, the genres of storytelling they draw upon ... and the ways in which stories construct identities and events. (Wetherell, 2001: 23)

See also Gergen (2001).

What discourse research cannot do, and does not try to do, is to establish causal connections. What underlies a social constructionist position is a view of events which seldom leads to accounts in terms of linear causation. Instead, what is sought is relationships between events (taking ways of coming to understand and name social objects as one kind of event). Kendall and Wickham (1999) talk about 'contingencies' in this context, to emphasize that the account will always be in terms of what *happens/happened* to be the case, not what *must/had to be* the case. Events, actions, becoming subjected to a given discursive formation, taking up and using a discursive formation to one's advantage (consciously or unwittingly) have a history once they have happened, but other things *could* have happened, giving a different history. A chain of events will make sense in terms of internal consistency, logic, purpose, function, and that sense in turn will become a link in other chains of events, but the sense is imposed *post hoc*, not implicit and inevitable in the first links of the chain.

> When we say that ... events are contingent, this is not the same thing as saying that anything could have happened or did happen. Of course, there were definite pressures at work ... The point that Foucault regularly makes, however, is that so often our much-cherished advances are the quite accidental result of some apparently unrelated change. ... To draw up a list of contingencies ... certainly involves ... a knowledge of some facts ... but it does not require an exercise in artificially designating some items on the list to be primary. (Kendall and Wickham, 1999: 6–7).

Concepts of discourse and ideology have profound consequences for research, from its very beginnings in problem selection and research design, because not one but two forms of reflexivity are required:

> There are two types of reflexivity: personal reflexivity and epistemological reflexivity. *Personal reflexivity* involves reflecting upon the ways in which our own values ... and social identities have shaped the research. *Epistemological reflexivity* requires us to engage with questions such as: How has the research question defined and limited what can be 'found'? (Willig, 2001: 10)

In *Discourse Theory and Practice* Margaret Wetherell distinguishes three domains of discourse research and theory: the study of social interaction, the study of minds, selves and sense-making, and the study of culture and social relations (Wetherell et al., 2001a: 5) and six traditions of research which are brought to bear on them. In this chapter I shall adopt a simpler division into two kinds of discourse research: *structural* studies (broadly embracing culture, social relations and identity) and investigations of discourse *processes* (broadly embracing social interaction, sense-making and how identities are established). Both express a *social constructionist* perspective:

> Social constructionism draws attention to the fact that human experience, including perception, is mediated historically, culturally and linguistically. That is, what we perceive and experience is never a direct reflection of environmental conditions but must be understood as a specific reading of those conditions. ... Research from a social constructionist perspective is concerned with identifying the various ways of constructing social reality that are available in a culture, to explore the conditions of their use and to trace their implications for human experience and social practice. (Willig, 2001: 7)

Structural analysis looks at *what* the 'various ways' are, in a given context, and process analysis at *how* they are used.

The 'problem of truth' discussed above in relation to ideology is solved in discourse by dissolving the notion of absolute truth altogether. 'True' comes to mean 'provable or justifiable within a given discourse' – as the accepted output of what discursive rules produce:

> 'Truth' is to be understood as a system of ordered procedures for the production, regulation, distribution, circulation and operation of statements. 'Truth' is linked in a circular relation

with systems of power which produce and sustain it, and to effects of power which it induces and which extend it. (Foucault, in Rabinow, 1984: 74)

This raises equal and opposite problems, however, because there is no 'super-discourse' to adjudicate truth claims *between* discourses. The tensions between a realist and a relativist position in social constructionism are beyond the scope of this book; the reader will find the article by Wetherell and Stills (1998) a good place to begin considering them.

Discursive Structures

The main focus in structural discourse analysis is on the repertoire of discursive resources – what is available in a given culture, to people in a given position, and what shapes them. In Foucault's own work and in many sociological applications of the approach there is also a concern with the historical development of discourses, seen as recognizable regularities in signification which have an origin – there is a time after which they appear to become dominant or 'normal' and before which they yield place to some other form of conceptualization – and which develop and change over time and with use. Foucault (1977) looks, for example, at the birth of prisons as *reformatories* and the, at least partial, replacement of a lurid punitive style aimed at deterrence of others by a more private and technical process aimed at the reclamation of the offender himself. This process is linked, in this and other work, with a wide range of social strategies based in an understanding of the population as a resource for industry, agriculture and the army – exploitable, capable of development, seen often as in decline and in need of revitalization and better management – which also informs the collection of population statistics, the provision of universal education, the growth of physical and mental health facilities and public health works, the birth and development of the health visiting movement in the United Kingdom and the characterization and forms of control of the poor, the unemployed and the unemployable. Donzelot (1979) looks at the development of the modern nuclear family, together with the housing that contains it, the wage structures and employment practices which sustain it and render it 'normal', the practices and responsibilities of childrearing which create the modern 'mother' role, the influence of medicine on mothering and the monitoring of child welfare, the control of juvenile delinquency, the rise of psychology and psychiatry as experts in mothering and in delinquency and the changing functions of the law and the courts with regard to children.

Following Parker (1992) and Willig (2001) to some extent, we may identify three or four steps or stages that a typical piece of structural discourse research would follow:

1 The selection of text and identification of discourses – coherent bodies of 'statements'. Discourse research is typically driven explicitly by theory in a way that would be much less true of ethnographic or phenomenological qualitative research, and so one typically has a discourse or discourses already identified or 'previsioned' when starting the research. Texts will be selected to make useful descriptions and contrasts in terms of its/their application and modification. At

the level of policy we may be exploring government publications, newspaper 'editorial' and 'news' accounts, academic writings, perhaps textbooks for the training of professionals, perhaps professional accounts of practice (e.g. case records, court proceedings, prison files). At the level of public experience and 'collective representation' we may be contrasting these with interviews with a spread of people from a relevant public, with novels, with media presentations and advertising, with school textbooks, with diaries and autobiographies, and so on. Anything which conveys and encapsulates meaning could be a relevant source:

> speech, writing, non-verbal behaviour, Braille, Morse code, semaphore, runes, advertisements, fashion systems, stained glass, architecture, tarot cards and bus tickets. (Parker, 1972: 7)

(Due note will be taken of the origin and function of the texts, of course, in the process of interpreting them.) The process continues with the identification of discourses by gathering or coding relevant segments together thematically, as one would in ethnographic analysis. At this stage it will be necessary to put prior theory to some extent aside, in that one's understanding of the provisioned discourses may be modified by what clearly 'belongs together' in the text and that other regularities may emerge as competing or parallel discursive formations. Concepts of 'normalization' will be important in delineating discourses – paying attention to what is taken for granted as 'normal' or 'proper' and what can be said within a discursive formation and even justified but is seen as in need of justification.

2 Action orientation, positioning and contestation. This stage will involve extracting and elaborating the rules which constitute a given discourse – rules of truth and rules for the delineation of objects. We shall be looking at what is allowable in the production of statements, what kinds of statements cannot be made and what the 'spaces' are for the production of new statements. Of particular interest will be those areas where more than one discursive formation appears to be being brought to bear. One will identify, internally from the text and externally from other sources and from analysis of the situation, what function the different discourses appear to perform, what is gained or avoided by constructing an object in a particular way and by whom, what subject positions are assigned to or taken by the actual or logical participants in the debate or conversation. There will be a concern with 'discursive practice' here: what lines of action or argument are opened up or closed down by the adoption of one discursive position rather than another: in other words, what is the power gradient embodied in the discourse?

3 Subjectivity. What is the nature of the self and its social world, as seen from a given discursive position? What are the consequences, for oneself and for others?

4 Resistance. This embodies a range of questions about identity and subjectivity, but from a different perspective. What counter-measures are taken by those whose role and nature a dominant or normalizing discourse tends to define? Are they re-mobilizing previously dominant discursive forms, or colonizing and changing a currently dominant one, or pitting one currently accepted discursive formation against another (arguing about agenda-setting)? Or are they living within the definitional space of the discourse, but subverting it by following the outward forms without internalizing the prescribed subjectivity, or following it in public while maintaining a different way of defining the situation in private?

Another important point to make is that texts do not stand alone but are always related to other texts. We have what Fairclough (1992) calls 'manifest intertextuality' (the explicit reference to another source for an expression or a story-line – as I am doing here in citing Fairclough – or explicit echoes of a well-known story line – as when young lovers are 'summarized' by reference to *Romeo and Juliet*). In a broader sense there is also what Fairclough calls 'interdiscursivity' – the implicit location of a current account or narrative within its genre or 'order of discourse' (Fairclough) or the 'archive' (Foucault) – the entire corpus of currently available discursive characterizations of the event or situation. While innovation is certainly possible, we do a lot of our thinking and characterization by explicit or implicit reference to previous accounts, and it is this which gives discourses their coherence and relative stability.

Although this is not a necessary part of its theoretical apparatus, structural analysis of discourse tends towards a sociological determinism, in which people are constituted by the discursive regimes to which they are subject.

> Foucauldian Discourse Analysis draws attention to the power of discourse to construct its objects, including the human subject itself. The availability of subject positions constrain what can be said, done and felt by individuals. (Willig, 2001: 122)

This places it in a dialectical relationship with process accounts (below); both are needed in order to reflect the full complexity of a social constructionist perspective on the relation of agency and structure in human life.

Discourse Processes

The 'process' side of discourse analysis emerges at least in part from the 'turn to language' in social psychology from the 1950s onward. A 'cognitivism' which saw language as merely a description of internal states (and external ones as mediated through the processes of perception) has increasingly been supplanted by a social constructionism in which the real nature of the social world depends on our understanding of it (rather than the other way around), in that it is our understanding of the world that will determine how we act within it and therefore what reaction we get from it.

The focus of process analysis is on how participants *use* the elements of discursive repertoires, to what end and with what effects. The focus tends to be on positioning, on managing 'stake', on strategies for claiming or disclaiming. We are reading text, not for the attitudes or beliefs it expresses, but for the ways in which elements are deployed and conversational 'moves' made to establish the position of one or more of the participants, and the success of such strategies.

> Discursive psychologists have argued that social psychologists have underestimated the centrality of *conflict* in social life, along with the importance people place on issues of stake and interest. An analysis of rhetoric highlights the point that people's versions of actions, features of the world, of their own mental life, are usually designed to counter real or potential alternatives and are part of ongoing arguments, debates and dialogues ... In doing so, they are participating in and developing the collective and communal forms of life which make up their culture. (Potter, 1996: 152)

It may be argued (see Willig, 2001: 92) that the ideal material for process analysis is naturally occurring talk. Conversations and pronouncements in familiar settings – the home, the office, the factory, the football ground, the public house – exhibit the performatory character outlined above. Formal interviews, on the other hand, have discursive rules of their own and may display different rules and different 'objects', differently used, from the discourses of normal social conversation. A frequent compromise is the group interview or group discussion, deliberately encouraged to 'run its own course' rather than closely steered by the researcher.

Analysis proceeds thematically.

- Discourses which might potentially figure in the exchanges will already have been identified, and the use of these yields initial themes for the analysis. (Others will emerge, however, during the experience of data collection or during analysis.)
- All relevant items are identified and coded or filed – being sure to include *all* potentially relevant material, and including what was contributed by the interviewer(s) in an interview/group interview study; their positioning will have to be included in the analysis, because it affects that of the other participants.
- Discursive repertoires will be constructed – sets of statements/ references that appear consistent, in the light of the discourses already identified. (It will not be surprising to find variability – that individuals bring more than one discursive repertoire to bear on the same topic, or even that these are sometimes in conflict, see, for example, the accounts of Maori culture described by Potter and Wetherell (1995) or the conflicting histories of the royal family described by Billig (1997).)
- Uses of elements of these repertoires will then be examined, within and between subjects, and what they imply for the positioning of subjects vis-à-vis each other and the credibility of narratives about self and others will be teased out. This is sometimes called 'rhetorical analysis' – the analysis of what ideas are *used for* and what function they play in concrete social interactions.
- The analyst will generally try to identify coherent strategies and relate them to the exigencies of the participants' lives. What is of interest is content rather than form or underlying process, however. Unlike, for example, some kinds of role analysis or analysis of group processes, what is said is what forms the focus of analysis, not the manner of its saying or a supposed group process or individual attitude of which it is the expression. Thus, analysis of racism looks at people's actual practices of discrimination, not at group boundary maintenance or racist attitudes or authoritarian personality (Potter and Wetherell, 1995: 82).

Looking for resistance and how it is conducted and for variant interpretation and use is an important part of much process analysis, as it is with structural analysis:

What I have said so far implies interpreters that are compliant in the sense of fitting in with the positions set up for them in texts. But not all interpreters are compliant, some are, of course, … resistant. Interpreters are … more than discourse subjects in particular discourse processes; they are also social subjects with particular accumulated social experiences, and with resources variously oriented to the multiple dimensions of social life, and these variables affect the ways they go about interpreting particular texts. … [but] the capacity for critical reading … is not distributed equally among all interpreters in all interpretative environments. (Fairclough, 1992: 136)

The existence of multiple and conflicting discursive positions for a given subject is an important point to bear in mind:

> The obvious psychological interest in dilemmas is to analyse the psychological state of the decision-maker. ... Our concern, by contrast, is to show how ordinary life, which seems far removed from the dramas of wolves and precipices, is shaped by dilemmatic qualities. It will be suggested that the mentality of the ordinary person, not placed in the dramatic situation of choosing between precipice and wolf, nevertheless contains the conflicting themes which surface so vividly in the dilemmatic situation per se. (Billig et al., 1998: 9)

Connell (1987) suggests that identity and personality themselves are social practices and are usefully seen as 'projects', in which the individual develops an identity from a number of sources, including collective understandings and representations about their particular social locations as middle- or working-class, Black or Asian or white, male or female, older or younger, etc. He or she has also to reconcile the conflicting logics of different discursive environments – home, school, work, etc. The continuity of identity, in this view, is something to be seen as *made* or forged by the individual, not something to be taken for granted. (See also Davies and Harré, 1990.)

Process accounts tend to privilege agency over structure in that they focus on actions and strategies more than on limitations and pressures. A prime focus is on accountability and on people's orientation towards their own interests and their stake in maintaining or enhancing their position. (As Willig points out (2001: 102), this orientation is largely taken for granted as natural, normal and inevitable; taking it as the basis for analysis is not seen as in need of justification.) However, the relationship is portrayed as dialectical and displays a dialectical understanding of the relationship between received culture and personal ideation:

> Individuals incorporate the narratives of their culture and their incorporations of these narratives construct their self-understanding – external cultural narratives become a set of personalised voices and positions. (Wetherell, 1996a: 224)

The same point is made about intertextuality – that we take up existing conceptions but rework and personalize them before returning them to the 'archive':

> Our speech ... is filled with others' words, varying degrees of otherness and varying degrees of 'our-own-ness', varying degrees of awareness and detachment. These words of others carry with them their own expression, their own evaluative tone, which we assimilate, rework and re-accentuate. (Bakhtin, 1986: 89)

Conclusion

'Critical analysis' is the analysis of text to expose (mostly ideological) presupposition, in the light of the purposes for which it was constructed and the social location of its authors and distributors. 'Discourse analysis' goes beyond this to consider the 'rules of the language game', which is the form of conceptual life expressed in a text or series of utterances or actions – what counts as a valid argument and what count as meaningful objects of discussion. Sociological discourse analysis is concerned mostly

(Conclusion continued)

with what might be termed 'structures of discourse' – coherent, historically developing ways of conceptualizing the social world or a significant part of it – and the ways in which they embody, reproduce and/or modify power relations. Some psychological discourse analysis has been more concerned with the processes by which people and groups *use* discourses to establish themselves in a 'social location' or confirm/change the location of others.

Structural discourse tends towards determinism, describing how we are constituted by the meanings about us. Psychological discourse analysis tends more towards an 'agency' perspective. Both remain aware of the dialectical relationship between being constituted by discourse and using and changing discourse. Both are also aware of the possibilities for resistance, of the variability of the forms in which a given discourse may be expressed and of the implicit or explicit conflict of discourses within the whole body of ways of thought and expression which are available to us.

Analysis of discourse usually proceeds by identifying and coding statements and grouping them thematically into coherent repertoires that express an underlying discourse. Depending on the purpose of the analysis, the next steps will involve looking for change over time, conflict between discourses, the functions they perform, the relationships, freedoms and relative status they accord their participants and objects, the social locations they confer and how people use them to position themselves and others, enduring strategies and temporary or enduring and implicit or explicit resistance.

Key Terms

Agency   the voluntary/deliberate actions of people, groups or institutions, or the perspective which focuses on actions as deliberate and purposeful.

Archive   a term Foucault uses for the whole body of meanings currently available in a society or culture.

Collective representation   a shared way of viewing (and explaining the nature of) a phenomenon or object.

Critical analysis   the study of text to uncover presuppositions, taking into account its authorship and the circumstances of and reasons for its production.

Determinism   a focus on causes or antecedents of actions, which in its extreme form denies validity to accounts in terms of agency.

Discourse   the rules that define a section of social reality and the objects which it may meaningfully be said to cover. More loosely, a set of

(Continued)

(Key Terms continued)

taken-for-granted ways of characterizing a portion of the social world – in which sense the term is readily confused with 'ideology'. Discourses are not seen as fixed and static, but as developing and changing over time and with use.

Epistemology   the nature of truth, the rules for what shall count as true.

Hegemonic   dominant, ruling – usually used of the power of an ideology or discourse to define social reality.

Ideology   a set of (false) beliefs about or definitions of an area of social life, defining what is to be valued and taken for granted. Mostly the term implies that these beliefs/definitions serve the interests of a more powerful group than the one to which the ideology directly applies.

Intertextuality   the extent to which and the ways in which one text depends on, refers to, or is contained within another.

Ontogeny   the definition of objects of discourse; labels for what can meaningfully be described in a given context.

Positioning   establishment of identity in relation to another's, generally expressing duties, rights and power relations or relations of influence.

Reflexivity   consideration of (a) the extent to which one's own presuppositions and those of others structure the production of particular texts (personal reflexivity) and (b) the extent to which discursive structures determine what may be discussed and concluded (epistemological reflexivity).

Repertoire   a coherent set of ways of discussing and defining the world which lie within a single discourse but do not necessarily exhaust its possibilities; the selection from possible discursive propositions that is actually used by a person, group or institution.

Social constructionism   an account of the meaning of social life and social objects which looks to history, social relations and social structures for their explanation.

Structure   in the senses in which the term is used in this chapter, (a) a discursive form as described 'cross-sectionally' at a given moment of time or (b) a coherent pattern of rights, duties and resources (and the corresponding social institutions) which defines a power inequality.

Further Reading

Kendall, G. and Wickham, G. (1999) *Using Foucault's Methods*, London, Sage.
Fairclough, N. (1992) *Discourse and Social Change*, Cambridge, Polity.

Kendall and Wickham are more accepting of Foucault's methods, while Fairclough is more critical and attempts to develop them.

For an introductory account of discourse as process see several of the chapter in

Wetherell, M. (Ed.) (1996) *Identities, Groups and Social Issues*, London, Sage.

Research Proposal Activity 11

1 Does your research question revolve around historically and socially constructed/shared frameworks of meaning – ideologies, discourses? How are these to be identified? What elements are 'previsioned', from your reading so far, and what else do you propose to read in order to form your ideas and your grasp of historical process?
2 Are you interested predominantly in underlying structures of thought or in how these structures are applied in social interaction?
3 How will you obtain 'text' for study? What does this text represent?
4 How will you identify multiple discourses, contestation, resistance? Does an interest in these aspects of discursive practice modify or extend your decisions about what to sample?
5 Even if discourse is not the main focus of your research, ought you be applying some level of discursive analysis to the literature and other sources that you are using?

12

Documents and Critical Research

Victor Jupp

This chapter is concerned with the use of documents in social research. The range of documents upon which social scientists have drawn includes diaries, letters, essays, personal notes, biographies and autobiographies, institutional memoranda and reports, and governmental pronouncements as in Green Papers, White Papers and Acts of Parliament. This list might give the impression that such researchers are exclusively concerned with non-quantitative (sometimes called qualitative) documentary sources. However, this is not necessarily the case; they are also interested in the way in which quantitative data are collected, assembled and analyzed in order to reach conclusions.

Throughout this book a range of analytical strategies has been introduced. Some of these are structured and formal (as, say, in the analysis of experimental data) and others are less so; some strategies are founded on the principles of statistical analysis, whereas others follow the traditions and practices of qualitative research. Analytical strategies associated with structured and less structured data, and with quantitative and qualitative analyzes, have found expression within the documentary tradition. Although these strands will all be represented in this chapter, the main emphasis will be upon *critical analysis* of documents. The chapter brings together a distinct methodological approach – the *critical* – with particular forms of data – *documents*. (It should be recognized, however, that critical research is not exclusive to, and extends beyond, the use of documents.)

It is important to distinguish 'criticism', in its everyday usage, and 'critical analysis' as used by social scientists. The former usually refers to an evaluation which is negative, censorious or fault-finding. Critical analysis in social science involves an examination of the assumptions that underpin any account (say, in a document) and a consideration of what other possible aspects are concealed or ruled out. It can also involve moving beyond the documents themselves to encompass a critical analysis of the institutional and social structures within which such documents are produced. For example, Anne Worrall's *Offending Women* (1990) is concerned with the assumptions about femininity that are found in probation reports about women offenders which are produced, and acted upon, in the criminal justice system in the UK. As with criticism in its everyday usage, critical analyzes can involve being censorious or fault-finding, perhaps in terms of rejecting in-built assumptions of documents or seeking to overturn institutions or systems within which they are produced. However, this is not a necessary part of critical analysis.

In contrast with some other sections of the book, this chapter makes much greater reference to theoretical approaches. This is because the critical analysis of text makes much more obvious and explicit use of theoretical concepts and ideas than other approaches (for example, survey research, which can often collect data without explicit reference to theory). Indeed, the distinction between theorizing and empirical research is not one that is readily accepted by those who engage in critical analysis.

Documents, Texts and Discourse

This chapter adopts the distinction between 'document', the medium on which the message is stored, and 'text', the message that is conveyed through the symbols which constitute writing. Documents can have a number of features. For example, they may be made up exclusively of written words, or they may include statistics, as in a survey research report. Documents may refer to particular individuals, as with school records and reports about pupils, or may concern more 'macro' issues, as with one of Her Majesty's Inspectorate Reports on the physical state of schools. Further, documents may refer to contemporary events and issues, as in the case of newspaper reporting of a prison riot, for example, or they may relate to past events and issues, as in a nineteenth-century report on conditions in British prisons. Finally, documents may have been produced for purposes other than social research but none the less be of interest to researchers, in which case they are sometimes termed unobtrusive measures (Webb et al., 1966): 'An unobtrusive measure of observation is any method of observation that directly removes the observer from the set of interactions or events being studied' (Denzin, 1978: 256).

One rationale for the use of such measures is the belief that the effects of the observer on the data are reduced, thereby improving internal validity. Unobtrusive measures can derive from a number of sources, such as simple observations of behaviour without the individuals concerned knowing, or physical traces of behaviour left behind by individuals, and can also include documents. An example of the latter would be institutional memoranda, produced as a normal part of bureaucratic functioning but to which the social scientist can gain access in order to study key aspects of institutional processes. Punch (1979b, 1985), for example, has outlined the use of police organizational records to study corruption among officers working in a red-light district of Amsterdam. The problem with the use of unobtrusive measures to study a sensitive issue such as police corruption is that access is vigorously denied by those who have an interest in doing so.

In other instances, documents may be solicited deliberately and explicitly by social researchers and may even be produced by them, in which case they cannot be treated as unobtrusive measures. This is the case with many life histories and also with detailed interviews which are recorded and transcribed by social scientists for subsequent analysis.

There is one further term which deserves consideration in this section, namely *discourse*. The dictionary definition of 'discourse' refers to talk, conversation and dissertation. Within social science, it takes on a wider meaning as a result of its close association with a particular theoretical and methodological position, namely *discourse analysis* (see also below). As with documents and texts, discourses are concerned with communication. However, as Worrall points out, discourse goes much further 'to embrace all aspects of a communication – not only its content, but its author (who says it?), its authority (on what grounds?), its audience (to whom?), its objective (in order to achieve what?)' (Worrall, 1990: 8).

'Discourse' encompasses ideas, statements or knowledge that are dominant at a particular time among particular sets of people (for example, 'expert professionals') and which are held in relation to other sets of individuals (for example, patients or offenders). Such knowledge, ideas and statements provide explanations of what is problematic about the patients or offenders, why it is problematic and what should be done about it. In providing authority for some explanations, other forms of explanation are excluded. Implicit in the use of such knowledge is the application of power. In some instances, discourses may be viewed as imposed by professionals on clients but this is not necessarily the case. Discourses really come into their own when the client, for whatever reason and by whatever means, shares the professional's analysis of the problem and the means of addressing it. As indicated earlier, discourse involves all forms of communication, including talk and conversation. In the latter, however, it is not restricted exclusively to verbalized propositions, but can include ways of seeing, categorizing and reacting to the social world in everyday practices, such as policing practices. Its relevance to this chapter is that discourse can also be expressed in text through the medium of documents.

Types of Document

A wide range of documents has been used in social research, including the following.

Life histories   The life history is similar to a biography or autobiography and is a means by which an individual provides a written record of his or her own life in his or her own terms. It can include a descriptive summary of life-events and experiences and also an account of the social world from the subject's point of view. There is no concern with whether the account is 'right' or 'wrong'; if a subject sees the world in a particular way then that way is, for that person, 'right'. The examination of social perspectives and images is often a forerunner to the analysis of social actions, the assumption being that actions are underpinned by the way in which the social world is interpreted by actors.

Life histories may be written by the subject or by a second party, often a social scientist. A major landmark in the development of life history as a method was Thomas and Znaniecki's *The Polish Peasant in Europe and America,* Volume 1 of which comprises a 300-page life history of a Polish emigré to Chicago in the early part of the twentieth century (Thomas and Znaniecki, 1958, first published in 1918–20). It provides an account, not only of life in an American city at that time, but also of the way in which it was experienced by the immigrant. Following Thomas and Znaniecki's work, the life history became an important element in what was known as the Chicago School of Sociology of the 1930s, which focused especially on the problems of urban life.

The diary   Diaries have been used by both psychologists and sociologists but for different types of analysis. For example, the psychologist Allport focused on diaries as the prime means of uncovering the dynamics, structure and functioning of mental life (Allport, 1942). Luria (1972) used diaries, among other accounts, to explore the experience of brain damage, leading to short-term memory loss. The sociologist Oscar Lewis (1959) used diaries to assemble data about the economy, life-style and daily activities of individuals in poor Mexican families. More recently, the diary has been used to gain insights into physical conditions and constraints of imprisonment, and individuals' subjective experiences, reactions and responses to them, as, for example, in Boyle's chronicle of his life in a number of Scottish prisons (Boyle, 1984). In a more formal sense, diaries can be used as part of survey methods, as in the National Food Survey, in which families are asked to list their food intake over a period of one week.

Newspapers and magazines   The use of newspapers has been central in what is usually referred to as media analysis. Media analysis has several interests, one of which is an examination of the way in which stereotypes of categories of people or types of action are created, reinforced and amplified with wide-ranging consequences for those people and actions. For example, newspapers have been used to examine the portrayal of 'folk devils' such as 'mods' and 'rockers' (Cohen, 1972), and the creation and career of the label and stereotype of the 'mugger' in the British press (Hall et al., 1978).

Letters   Along with a life history, the analysis of letters played a central part in Thomas and Znaniecki's *The Polish Peasant in Europe and America* (1958). For example, the authors were able to gain access to letters sent by emigrés to relatives in Poland, which they used to gain insight into the experiences of assimilation into American culture. The problem with the use of letters in social research is that they have a tendency not to be very focused, though where they are they can be a valuable source of unsolicited data. This is the case, for example, with letters written on a specific issue to newspapers, which can be used to identify differing and sometimes conflicting political viewpoints in relation to that issue.

Stories, essays and other writings   Researchers can make use of essays or other writings which are already in existence or can solicit such writings as part of their research design. For example, analysis of children's writings has been used to explore their experience of home, family and social relations (Steedman, 1982), whereas Cohen and Taylor's (1972) examination of the subjective experiences of imprisonment and strategies of psychological survival among long-term prisoners was in part founded on an analysis of essays and poems on topics suggested by Cohen and Taylor themselves. This strategy was consistent with the qualitative, naturalistic and discovery-based methodological approach, directed at uncovering the subjective experiences of prisoners, and it was also appropriate on practical grounds in so far as Cohen and Taylor gained access to the prison and to prisoners in their role as part-time visiting lecturers. As such, they were in an ideal position to solicit essays and other writings for research purposes.

Official documents and records   A great many official documents and records on a wide range of topics are available for analysis. An important part of government activity relates to the production of official documents as, for instance, forerunners to legislation (as in the case of Green Papers and White Papers), as part of the regular review of activities of Departments of State or institutions under government control (as with reports of Select Committees of the House of Commons), or as part of official investigations into the running of affairs (as in the case of some Royal Commissions). Official documents provide valuable data for the analysis of official definitions of what is defined as problematic, what is viewed as the explanation of the problem, and what is deemed to be the preferred solution. In this way, analysis of such documents provides an important element in the critical analysis of texts.

Apart from documents at a societal or macro level, there are other official documents at an institutional or micro level which can be just as important to the disposal and destiny of individuals. These are organizational records which define what is, or is not, problematic about individuals, which put forward explanations for behaviour and actions and which record decisions relating to outcomes. Of course, such individual records are not necessarily separate from official documents operating at a societal level in so far as there is often a close connection between the formulation of concepts, explanations and solutions at one level and such formulation and application at another. Official records from a variety of settings have been examined. For example, Kitsuse and Cicourel (1963), working within an *interpretative* approach, analyzed pupils' records to make assertions about the labels and stereotypes assigned by teachers, and about the consequences of these. Anne Worrall (1990), working within the *critical* approach, examined the discourses of solicitors, magistrates, psychiatrists and probation officers, and the consequences these have for the disposal of women offenders.

Research reports   Finally, documents of particular interest to us in a book on research methods are reports of social science research written by academics and other researchers (perhaps government-sponsored researchers). The position taken in this chapter is that such reports should not be treated as objective, accurate statements of 'fact', but as documents which require examination and challenge in terms of what they define as problematic, the way in which such problems are operationalized, the forms of explanation put forward and the policy implications which flow from them. A critical analysis of particular research reports is important in instances where such reports have a high profile or hold an influential position in the public domain.

Box 12.1 *A classification of documents*

		Authorship		
		Personal	Official	
			Private	State
	Closed	1	5	9
Access	Restricted	2	6	10
	Open-archival	3	7	11
	Open-published	4	8	12

Source: Scott, 1990: 14

A Typology of Documents

Scott (1990) has produced a typology of documents based on two main criteria: authorship and access (see Box 12.1). 'Authorship' refers to the origins of documents and under this heading he distinguishes 'personal' documents from 'official' ones (which have their source in bureaucracies). Official documents are further subdivided into 'state' and 'private' (non-state: for example, business annual reports and accounts). The second criterion, 'access', refers to the availability of documents to individuals other than the authors. 'Closed' documents are available only to a limited number of insiders, usually those who produce them; 'restricted' documents are available on an occasional basis provided permission has been granted; 'open-archival' documents are those documents which are stored in archives and are available to those who know of them and know how to access them; 'open-published' documents are the most accessible of all and are in general circulation.

Such classifications can be useful in themselves. However, for Scott (1990) the usefulness of a classification based on the criteria he suggests is that it poses four key questions pertaining to the validity of particular documentary sources. Who has and has not authored a document, and the degree to which a document is accessible or withheld, influences its *authenticity* (whether it is original and genuine), its *credibility* (whether it is accurate), its *representativeness* (whether it is representative of the totality of documents of its class) and its *meaning* (what it is intended to say).

Critical Social Research

Harvey (1990: 1) distinguishes critical social research as follows:

> Critical social research is underpinned by a critical-dialectical perspective which attempts to dig beneath the surface of historically specific oppressive social structures. This is contrasted with positivistic concerns to discover the factors that cause observed phenomena or to build grand theoretical edifices and with phenomenological attempts to interpret the meanings of social actors or attempt close analysis of symbolic processes.

This quotation reveals some of the differences between critical research and, on the one hand, *positivism* (which is often, but not exclusively, associated with quantitative research such as surveys, experimentation and content analysis) and, on the other hand, *phenomenology*, which is roughly equivalent to what we have termed the interpretative tradition (and often, but not exclusively, associated with ethnographic research). The differences that are highlighted are as follows: first, positivism emphasizes explanations cast in causal terms, whereas critical research does not; secondly, while both interpretative and critical perspectives are concerned with social meanings, the former places emphasis on how these are generated in small-scale interactions, whereas the latter seeks to analyze them critically in terms of structural inequalities in society (for example, class, race or gender inequalities).

Within the social sciences, the critical tradition owes much to Marx or to reworkings of Marx by other writers. Critical research which is influenced by this source is concerned with social structural inequalities founded on class inequalities. The work of the American sociologist, C. Wright Mills, was influenced by the Marxist tradition but was less explicitly class-based in directing its attention at bureaucratization in mass society and at the concentration of power in a power elite (see especially Mills, 1956). During the 1970s, the critical tradition received impetus from the rise of Black movements and from feminism. This led to the examination of structures founded on race and gender inequalities.

There are variations within the critical tradition. Nevertheless, a number of central assumptions are discernible. First, *prevailing knowledge* (for example, that provided in official documents such as reports of Royal Commissions) is viewed as being structured by existing sets of social relations which constitute social structure. Secondly, this structure is seen as oppressive in so far as there is an unequal relation between groups within it and in so far as one or more groups exercise power over others. Thirdly, the inequality, power and oppression are rooted in class, race or gender or some combination of these. Fourthly, the aim of critical analysis is not to take prevailing knowledge for granted or to treat it as some 'truth', but to trace back such knowledge to structural inequalities at particular intersections in history. In doing so, it is considered important to examine the role of ideology in the maintenance of oppression and control and also the way in which social processes and social institutions operate to legitimate that which is treated as knowledge. Ultimately, the aim of critical research and analysis is to confront prevailing knowledge – and the structures which underpin it – by providing an alternative reading and understanding of it.

A final point relates to *emancipation*. For Fay (1987), for example, it is not sufficient that critical research enlightens oppressed groups by providing an analysis of the root causes of such oppression. Such enlightenment should lead to emancipation:

> By offering this complex set of analyses to the relevant group at the appropriate time in the appropriate setting, a social theory can legitimately hope not only to explain a social order but to do so in such a way that this order is overthrown. (Fay, 1987, in Hammersley, 1993: 36)

The twin concepts of 'deconstruction' and 'reconstruction' are central to much critical research. *Deconstruction* is the process by which prevailing knowledge, or any construct within it, is broken down into its essential elements. This can involve the collection of empirical data and the examination of such data in relation to the abstract constructs that constitute knowledge. *Reconstruction* involves the rebuilding of a construct in terms of the oppressive social structural arrangements which underpin it and sustain it.

An example is required in order to illustrate what is otherwise an abstract set of prescriptions for analysis. We can take the construct 'housework', which can be deconstructed or broken down in terms of a set of activities and tasks which are viewed within prevailing knowledge as constituting its essence (for example, washing dishes, ironing clothes). The process of reconstruction involves an examination of this construct in terms of wider structural arrangements, especially gender inequalities in society. It may also provide an analysis in terms of class (e.g. a study of working-class housewives) and class and race (e.g. a study of Black working-class housewives). Such reconstruction views 'housework' not as a set of activities, such as washing dishes, making beds and so forth, but as an exploitative relationship within a social structure with patterned inequalities and oppressions.

Critical Analysis of Documents

Critical analysis is explicitly theoretical. However, empirical work has been and is carried out, including social surveys, detailed interviews, social history research, participant observation and, of course, the analysis of documents. (For examples of the use of each of these in critical research, see Harvey, 1990.) The contribution which the analysis of documents can make within the critical research tradition is outlined by Jupp and Norris (1993). Their exposition is based upon 'discourse analysis', an important development within the critical paradigm, stemming from the work of the French social theorist Michel Foucault. In general terms, *discourse analysis* has a number of features. One key assumption is that discourse is social, which indicates that words and their meanings depend on where they are used, by whom and to whom. Consequently, their meaning can vary according to social and institutional settings and there is, therefore, no such thing as a universal discourse. Secondly, there can be different discourses which may be in conflict with one another. Thirdly, as well as being in conflict, discourses may be viewed as being arranged in a hierarchy: the notions of conflict and of hierarchy link closely with the exercise of power. The concept of power is vital to discourse analysis via the theoretical connection between the production of discourses and the exercise of power. The two are very closely interwoven and, in some theoretical formulations, are viewed as one and the same.

Box 12.2 *A discourse-analytic research agenda*

1 What public and/or institutional discourses are important in terms of knowledge of what is 'right' and what is 'wrong'?
2 In what kinds of documents and texts do such discourses appear?
3 Who writes or speaks these discourses and whom do they represent or purport to represent?
4 What is the intended audience of such writing or speech?
5 What does a critical reading of these documents uncover in terms of:

(Continued)

Box 12.2   *(Continued)*

   (a)   what is defined as 'right' and 'wrong' and therefore what is seen
         as problematic;
   (b)   what explanation is offered for what is seen as problematic;
   (c)   what, therefore, is seen as the solution?

6   What does a critical reading of these documents tell us about

   (a)   what is *not* seen as problematic;
   (b)   which explanations are rejected or omitted;
   (c)   which solutions are not preferred.

7   What alternative discourses exist?
8   How do these relate to 'internal differentiation' within and between
    semi-autonomous realms of control?
9   What does a critical reading of these alternative discourses tell us?
10 Is there evidence of negotiation with, or resistance to, dominant
    discourses?
11 What is the relationship between the discourses and social conflict,
    social struggle, hierarchies of credibility, order and control and, most
    of all, the exercise of power?
12 Are discourses, knowledge and power pervasive or reducible to
    class, class conflict and struggles refracted through one source, the
    state?

Source: Jupp and Norris, 1993: 50

The Foucauldian approach to discourse analysis is distinctive on a number of
counts, including the position that discourse and power are one and the same:
'Power produces knowledge, they imply one another: a site where power is exer-
cised is also a place at which knowledge is produced' (Smart, 1989: 65). What is
more, Foucault's position is that there is not one focus of knowledge and power (the
state) but several:

> His viewpoint is that strategies of power and social regulation are pervasive and that the
> state is only one of several points of control. This is an important divergence from
> Marxist analysis. For Foucault there are many semi-autonomous realms in society, where
> the state has little influence, but where power and control is exercised. In this way
> Foucault's notion of the pervasiveness of loci of regulation and control encourages
> research about discourses in a range of institutional settings. (Jupp and Norris, 1993, in
> Hammersley, 1993: 49)

The ways in which research may be carried out in such settings are laid out in the
'research agenda' suggested by Jupp and Norris (see Box 12.2). The 'agenda' brings
together questions which typically would be asked in a critical analysis of documents, especially with reference to discourse analysis. It is unlikely that any given
analysis will deal with all these questions; rather, it will tend to focus on some to the
exclusion of others.

Critical analysis, and discourse analysis in particular, has a tendency towards the theoretical. It is appropriate, especially in a book concerned with social research methods, to consider how an abstract set of ideas and concepts can be converted into a programme for research. This will be done in the following sections via a number of case studies, each of which uses different types of documents and represents a different selection of research questions, from the above agenda, with which to address the documents.

The first case study is of a fictitious research proposal to carry out discourse analysis on what – using Scott's typology (Box 12.1) – can be called 'state' documents which are 'open-published'; that is, they are in general circulation. This case study is especially useful because it shows how a particular theoretical system can be turned into a programme of research. The second case study shows the end product of a critical analysis of an open state document. It illustrates the conclusion that one social scientist, Mike Fitzgerald, reached after a critical 'reading' of a report on prisons. The third case study is based on institutional records and transcripts of detailed interviews with professionals in the criminal justice system to examine decision-making regarding the disposal of women offenders. The final case study involves a different form of document, a report of survey findings produced by social researchers. This case study illustrates the difference between a critical analysis of text and a 'technical' evaluation of research design and the findings derived from it.

Case Study 1: A Proposal for Critical Analysis

Activity 12.1 (allow 30 minutes)

You should now read Box 12.3, an example of a research proposal based on critical analysis of a text. Write notes on these questions:

1   Which, if any, of the research questions included in the agenda outlined earlier are represented in the proposal?
2   What method of enquiry is advocated?

The research proposal puts the analysis of the report of the Woolf Inquiry at its centre. In doing so, it enlists theoretical ideas from Foucault, particularly the viewpoint that society comprises an array of discourses which express and produce moral norms defining what are 'right' explanations and techniques of control. The report of the Woolf Inquiry is one such official discourse relating to prisons. It provided official definitions of what is wrong with prisons, why these problems exist and how they should be solved. (The precise recommendations are not reproduced here: for a useful summary and commentary consult Sparks, 1992.) The theoretical ideas derived from Foucault generate research questions to be asked of the Report at two levels.

Box 12.3   *A research proposal*

Introduction
The transformation of a sequence of events into what becomes defined as a deep-seated 'social problem' is often marked by the setting up of a public inquiry. The theoretical analyzes and moral perspective of such inquiries play a large part in determining public perception of 'normality' and 'dangerousness'. In 1990 serious rioting took place in Strangeways Prison, Manchester. The government of the day commissioned Lord Justice Woolf to conduct inquiries into the rioting. Woolf decided to adopt a broad interpretation of his terms of reference to address wider issues which the disturbances raised (for example, physical conditions in prisons, the use of local prisons to keep individuals on remand, the extent of overcrowding). The Report of the Woolf Commission was published in 1991 (Woolf, 1991).

Research questions
Two sets of important questions can be asked about the Woolf Report, or, indeed, any other official report. First, we can try to ascertain the nature of the official discourse it represents:

- How does Woolf define the *problems* of prisons in the 1990s?
- What range of *explanations* does he consider?
- What does he propose as the *control solution*?

Secondly, and more generally, we could investigate the role of such public 'voices' as Woolf's, perhaps by comparing the Report with other official or quasi-official reports. For example, in relation to crime and criminal justice, we could undertake 'readings' of the Scarman Report on the Brixton disorders of 1981 (Scarman, 1981) or of the Taylor Report on the Hillsborough disaster (Taylor, 1990). However, we need not restrict ourselves to this area of concern. Instead, we can investigate a wide range of official reports (on health, education and housing). The important questions to ask are:

- What is the *audience* addressed by these official reports and for whom do they speak?
- What *influence* do reports of this kind have on what happens in agencies of social control?

Theoretical frameworks
Much of the interest today in official discourses stems from the influence of Michel Foucault on social science. Foucault envisages society not as something 'out there' which causes, and is in turn reacted upon by, certain kinds of knowledge or social policy. Rather, 'society' comprises an array of *discourses* which exhibit and produce moral norms, theoretical explanations and techniques of social control. These three aspects of social regulation are, in Foucault's view, quite inseparable. So, the first three research questions listed aim to try to establish the various components of official discourse about problems in prisons and the overall moral climate such discourse creates.

Box 12.3 *(Continued)*

The second set of questions gets us to think about who is represented in public discourse of this kind. On whose behalf does Woolf speak: the liberal professions, the ruling class, the Establishment? And whom is he addressing: the moral majority, the British public, the respectable white male citizen? It is important to recognize here that, for Foucault, these 'subjects', on both sides, are not concrete individuals or groups existing *outside* the field of the discourse itself. Rather, they are 'ideal' positions which are produced in and through such discourses, serving as powerful moral regulators. The last questions further reflect Foucault's view that official discourse is only *one* type among others, and that the social priorities established in any given discourse may well be undercut or qualified by those established in other discourses (such as those of the media or the police).

Methods of enquiry
This project involved 'reading' and reflecting upon Woolf and similar official reports, looking closely at the way in which language is used, and at the values involved, so as to produce the typical 'subject' of the discourse. Reports embody certain types of theory or knowledge – which may be embodied in policy and institutions – about what or who is the problem, about what is the explanation and about what is the 'correct' solution.

Considerations of power are deep-embedded in such theory and knowledge. The purpose of 'reading' is to apprehend such theory, knowledge and power. This type of approach does not accept a distinction between the 'theoretical' and the 'empirical' modes of investigation.

First of all, one set of questions is asked of the document itself. These questions are concerned with what is defined as problematic (and, by implication, what is not defined as problematic); the explanations or theories that are provided (and, by implication, the explanations that are omitted or rejected); the solutions that are offered (and, by implication, the solutions that are rejected). These are typical of questions 5 and 6 of the research agenda given in Box 12.2.

A second set of questions relates not to the document itself but to the 'subjects' on either side, asking *on whose behalf* the report speaks and *to whom* it speaks. These are close to questions 3 and 4 of the research agenda. Note that, in contrast to an interpretative approach, the focus in the approach advocated in this proposal is not upon the actual person who wrote the report, nor is it upon the actual people who read it. Rather, it is upon 'ideal' positions that are produced in and through such discourses, serving as powerful regulators.

With regard to methods of enquiry, the position adopted is in complete contrast to that of positivist content analysis of documents (which is similar to the analysis of survey data). There is no reference to formal protocol of categorization, coding and counting of words, themes, headlines or column inches. Rather, the project involves 'reading' and 'reflecting' and is founded upon an approach that does not accept that there are two separate yet interrelated activities of theorizing and empirical research carried out by two different kinds of people: theorists and research technicians.

Case Study 2: Critical Analysis of a Public Document

The second case study is based on an article entitled 'The telephone rings: long-term imprisonment', by Mike Fitzgerald (1987), which represents a critical analysis of a public document about prisons: the Report of the Control Review Committee. Fitzgerald focuses on a number of official reviews, inquiries and policy papers that have followed disorders in prisons, with a view to uncovering the principles of penal policy that underpin their recommendations. In terms of the typology outlined earlier, the documents can be classified as official state open published.

In his consideration of the Report of the Control Review Committee, in particular, Fitzgerald focuses on three main areas that make up what he calls the 'general orientation' of the Report. This general orientation, and its three sub-areas, constitute the object of analysis. First, he is concerned with the concepts that the Committee employs to define that which it sees as problematic, and he then goes on to deconstruct some of these concepts to see how they themselves are defined. For example, he notes that 'control' is central to the Committee's conceptualization and also that control is defined in terms of the control of the prisoners themselves, instead of in terms of problems in the Prison Service. In short, this form of analysis asks why certain kinds of concepts, defined in certain ways, are placed on the public agenda.

Secondly, he is concerned with the kinds of solution that emerge from the Committee's thinking. As he points out, such solutions are largely in terms of new prison designs to increase security and control and not in other terms, such as improving prisoner-staff relations. The preferred solution does not stand in isolation but flows directly from the way in which the Committee conceptualizes what is seen as being problematic in the prison system.

Thirdly, Fitzgerald analyzes the implicit theory of management that underpins both the conceptualization of the problem and the preferred solution and its implementation. As Fitzgerald argues, he is not against management *per se* but questions the rigid hierarchical theory of management that dominates the thinking of the Committee.

At this point it is appropriate to summarize some of the key features of the critical approach to documents in the light of Fitzgerald's analysis of the Report of the Control Review Committee.

1 The sources of data are often, but not always, official texts which are important at a macro level in so far as they put forward conceptualizations regarding, in this case, the prison system, although they could refer to any other element of the social system.

2 The method does not exhibit the formal protocols of quantitative content analysis (categorizing, coding, counting), but is a critical reading of texts aimed at uncovering how problems are defined, what explanations are put forward and what is seen as the preferred solution. It also seeks to bring to the surface that which is rejected in the text and that which does not even appear: what is *not* seen as problematic, what explanations are not considered, and what are not the preferred solutions. In other words, the analysis is concerned with how official documents frame the public agenda.

3 Fitzgerald is not solely concerned with analyzing the definitions, explanations and solutions put forward in official documents, but seeks to challenge them and

suggests alternative proposals and viewpoints. In this sense, the methodological approach is not exclusively a critical reading of the text, but is also a challenge to the text.

4   The paper is concerned solely with the 'communication'; that is, with the text. It could have gone beyond this by examining the 'senders' and the 'recipients'. Had it done so it would not have been concerned with the identity of individual authors or with the meanings they bring to the text as someone from the interpretative tradition would be, but with the section of society for whom the document speaks, and with the consequences for the prison system and its inhabitants.

Case Study 3: Critical Analysis of Decision-making

The next example, also within the critical tradition, is slightly different from the preceding two case studies, in so far as it is not concerned with macro state-originated documents. Rather, it involves transcripts of detailed interviews with 'experts' within the criminal justice system and institutional records. What is more, it is not solely concerned with one discourse, namely that represented in official state reports on prisons, but with a multiplicity of interacting discourses which have consequences for the decisions made regarding women who offend.

Anne Worrall's *Offending Women* (1990) is concerned with the ways in which female offenders experience different treatment from that experienced by male offenders. She examines how this situation occurs and is perpetuated, and also charts the implications for women offenders. This is done by analyzing the discourse surrounding women's deviancy. This discourse is accessed by interviews with professionals in criminal justice and welfare agencies – probation officers, magistrates, solicitors, psychiatrists – as well as women offenders themselves. The transcripts of such interviews represent documents appropriate for critical analysis. In addition, Worrall had access to case records of offenders made available by probation officers.

The position taken by Worrall eschews social science which, on the one hand, is concerned with the search for universal properties and causes and, on the other hand, is solely concerned with social meanings. She is not interested in questions of what is the 'truth', but rather with 'the relationship between those who claim to know the "truth" and those about whom they claim to know it' (Worrall, 1990: 6). In turn, this relates to the question, 'What is it that endows certain individuals to have such knowledge and to apply it?' These are the hallmarks of critical analyzes in general and of discourse analysis in particular.

The relationship between power and knowledge is vital to such analyzes. Worrall's viewpoint is that knowledge does not of itself give power. Rather, those who have power have the authority to know. In this context, such people are magistrates, probation officers, solicitors and psychiatrists. Power is not reducible to one source, class (as Marxist analyzes would have it), but exists in all social relations. In this case, it exists in the relations between women offenders and those who make decisions about them, and also in the relations between such decision-makers themselves. Within this analysis, the exercise of power is not the naked oppression of one group by another but the production and subtle application of coherent 'knowledge' about other individuals which has consequences for what happens to these individuals (for example, Social Inquiry Reports, written by probation officers about offenders, which can influence decisions taken about such offenders). This is discourse as discussed in the section on 'Documents, Texts and Discourse'.

Discourses have implications for practice in terms of programmes, technologies and strategies: that is, coherent sets of explanation and solutions, ways of implementing these solutions and strategies of intervention. The discussion of discourse analysis (see 'Critical Analysis of Documents' above) indicated that there can be differing and competing discourses. In this respect, Worrall suggests that the power of the offender lies in the ability to resist, and even refuse, the coherent and homogeneous discourse of 'experts': 'By demonstrating the existence of heterogeneity and contradiction, the speaking subject is helping to keep open the space within which knowledge is produced' (Worrall, 1990: 10). In the main, however, women offenders remain markedly non-resistant and 'muted'.

The methodological approach is one of a case study of detailed interviews with magistrates, probation officers, psychiatrists and solicitors and of institutional records and reports. It has no claims to randomness or representativeness (as, for instance, a social survey would) and it seeks to generalize via theorizing rather than by reference to probability theory (again, as a survey would): 'The adoption of this particular mode of theorizing women's experiences calls for a method of research which rejects notions of generalizability through probability in favour of generalization through theoretical production' (1990: 12). As with the first case study, there is rejection of the viewpoint that there are two distinct activities, theorizing and empirical enquiry.

The main conclusion of Worrall's work is that women are 'muted' within the criminal justice system by being subject to the multiple discourses of the 'experts' who are authorized to present coherent knowledge concerning problems, explanations and solutions and who deny legitimacy to the discourses of the women themselves. Worrall's analysis involves deconstructing the discourses of the 'experts'. Despite the power and authority of such discourses, offenders develop means of resisting them by exploiting construction within them:

> Yet, while much of the women's resistance is individualistic, inconsistent and, in some, self-destructive, it has the important effect of undermining the authority of official discourses and keeping open the possibility of the creation of new knowledge about them – both as women and as law-breakers. (Worrall, 1990: 163)

The contribution which this case study makes to the discussion of critical analysis is that, in comparison with the other examples, it shows that there can be a *multiplicity* of discourses, that these can operate in *subtle* ways, that there can be *resistance* to prevailing discourses, and that outcomes have a good deal to do with the positions of particular discourses in the *hierarchy of legitimacy and authority*.

Case Study 4: Critical Analysis of a Research Report

The final case study relates to the critical analysis of a research report. This is done to emphasize that such reports are themselves documents and as such are not immune from critical analysis. It is also done to emphasize that social science research reports are social constructions with their own in-built assumptions about what is problematic and why.

Almost any output from social science research would be appropriate by way of illustration. Here the selection is from the Cambridge Study of Delinquency Development, a prospective longitudinal study of 411 males in the London Borough of Camberwell, started in 1961. At the time when they were selected for inclusion in the sample the target males were eight years old.

The primary aim of the programme of research was to describe the development of delinquency in inner-city males and to investigate how far delinquent and criminal behaviour can be predicted in advance. In addition, the researchers wanted to explain why certain individuals continue offending into adulthood. The sample members were interviewed at various points of time from the age of eight up until their thirties. About one fifth of the sample had been convicted of criminal offences as juveniles. These members differed significantly from the remainder of the sample on many counts: for example, on a scale of anti-social behaviour. Over one third of the sample had been convicted of a criminal offence by the time they were 32 years old. Those who were convicted as juveniles tended to be the persistent offenders at a later age. Six variables about which data were collected over the period of the survey are suggested by the researchers as predictors of delinquency: poverty, poor parenting, family deviance, social problems, hyperactivity (plus impulsivity and attention deficiency), and anti-social behaviour. There have been many outputs from the Cambridge Study. One summary of findings is provided in Farrington (1989).

Activity 12.2 (15 minutes)

Chapters 1 and 2 of this book cover various aspects of survey sampling. (Indeed, the Cambridge Study is outlined in Chapter 1 as an example of a longitudinal study.) In using the principles addressed in these chapters, either to plan survey research or to assess research reports, one would be led to what can be called a *technical evaluation*. This involves asking the fundamental question: 'What would fellow researchers and policy-makers ask of the research design of any study in order to gain an assessment of the validity of the findings derived from it?' Look back over these chapters and consider what features of the research design of the Cambridge Study you would address in order to assess its validity. (If possible, refer to the summary presented by Farrington, 1989.)

Typically, a technical evaluation would be concerned to examine the representativeness of the sample and the validity of making generalizations from the sample to wider populations. The survey involved a sample of 411 working-class, predominantly white boys. This makes generalizability to girls, to the middle class and to ethnic minority groups questionable. A second question to be asked in a technical evaluation relates to sample attrition or drop-out, which is especially relevant to a longitudinal study requiring long-term commitment on the part of sample members and detailed procedures to ensure that they can be traced and contacted. Two aspects are particularly important: the size of the drop-out can seriously deplete the sample, and the drop-out may affect the representativeness of the sample in so far as the drop-outs and those who are difficult to trace may have distinctive features and experiences which correlate with delinquency. Other aspects to consider in a technical evaluation include the possibility of fading relevance (the issues addressed at the beginning of a longitudinal study may have little relevance at the end), expectancy effects (the sample members may become so accustomed to the themes of the study that they answer questions in the ways which they believe are expected of them), and causal inference (the researchers may make fallacious inferences regarding causality on the basis of correlational evidence).

Activity 12.3 (15 minutes)

The reason that attention has been paid to matters to be addressed in a technical evaluation is that it facilitates comparison with matters to be addressed in a critical analysis. Reflect back over this chapter and consider what questions should be asked in carrying out a critical analysis of what you know about the Cambridge Study.

The sophistication of such a critical analysis will obviously depend on the level of knowledge of the Cambridge Study and of criminology in general. However, at an elementary level, a number of key points can be made. For example, the agenda presented in Box 12.2 provides a starting point, and within that agenda questions 5 and 6 are especially crucial. Question 5 concerns what is seen as problematic, and what is seen as the solution. In the Cambridge Study, the central problem is conceptualized in terms of delinquent behaviour and subsequent criminal behaviour in adulthood in modern British society. Farrington (1989) describes those engaging in such behaviour as working-class males who are typically characterized by tattoos, heavy drinking, heavy smoking, drug-taking and fighting. The explanation is in terms of the six predictors mentioned above about which the researchers collected data throughout the study. The solutions are based upon using the six predictors to identify those who are likely to offend, followed by intervention in their lives in order to influence what are seen as the causal agents, thereby diverting individuals from potential criminal careers. Some of the 'solutions' that have emanated from this kind of analysis, although not necessarily directly from the researchers themselves, have included education and guidance for parenthood, pre-school education for children of disadvantaged parents and family support programmes for so-called 'problem families'.

Asking question 6 in the research agenda – what is *not* asked in the research – gives a critical edge to the analysis. This is not to be critical of the authors as individuals or as researchers; rather, it is to question what is missing in order to uncover and clarify the assumptions built into the discourse of the research report. With regard to the Cambridge Study, what is not identified as problematic is the range of other types of criminal activity typically associated with white-collar and corporate crime; the people who are not seen as problematic are middle-class men who wear suits, drink wine and work in key financial institutions; and the kinds of explanation that are not assembled are those in terms of crime as an outcome of power, opportunity and structural inequalities in society. Instead, the explanation emphasizes individual and familial variables, which is consistent with the dominant discourse about crime and other forms of behaviour in the 1990s.

Conclusion

Critical research is not confined to the analysis of documents (see, for example, Harvey, 1990). However, the focus in this chapter has been on critical analysis of documents, especially in terms of documents as media for discourses. The four case studies have illustrated a range of key points regarding such analysis. For example, it can involve official public documents addressing macro issues, or it can involve institutional or personal documents influencing the disposal of individuals at a micro level. Critical analysis is characterized by not taking for granted what is being said in a document and what is often assumed to be 'knowledge'.

There are no formal protocols to the strategy of analysis, as there are, say, in the design of an experiment or a survey. Instead, critical analysis involves uncovering what is being treated as knowledge – often by addressing what is *not* being treated as knowledge – and examining the consequences of such knowledge. Critical analysis is different from technical evaluation, and as such asks different questions from those asked by other styles of research. In all of these senses, critical researchers go about their business in different ways from those employed by other researchers.

Key Terms

Critical analysis   examining the assumptions that underpin an account, and probably the institutions and social structures within which it was produced and/or is being used.

Deconstruction   breaking down a prevailing knowledge into its essential elements.

Discourse   (here) ideas, statements or knowledge dominant at a particular time among a particular set of people.

Reconstruction   rebuilding a construct to emphasize or to overcome underlying oppressive elements.

Further Reading

Fairclough, N. (1992) *Discourse and Social Change*, Cambridge, Polity.
Garland, D. and Young, P. (eds) *The Power to Punish*, Aldershot, Gower.
Harvey, L. (1990) *Critical Social Research*, London, Unwin Hyman.

Research Proposal Activity 12

Documents can be used in a variety of ways in social research. For example, an examination of documents is central to a literature search and evaluation, culminating in the formulating of research problems, questions and hypotheses. With regard to research design, especially survey research design, a reading of relevant documents can give insights into how a population ought to be defined, in terms of the significant groups or sub-groups to be included, and how the sample should be selected, perhaps in terms of appropriate stratification factors to use. Documents can also be used to suggest topics to be covered in questionnaires, and to help in the formulation of questions in ways that are understandable by informants.

In such instances, documents are being used as *resources* in research. This chapter, however, has been concerned with documents as *objects* of research. A research proposal concerned with the critical analysis of documents as objects of research should address the following questions:

1 What documents are central to the research problem?
2 How can these be characterized in terms of what Scott (1990) calls 'access' and 'authorship', and what are the implications in terms of authenticity, credibility, representativeness and meaning?
3 Are the documents and their features appropriate for critical analysis (for example, in terms of representing discourses)?
4 What questions should be asked of these documents in order to map the central features of such discourses (for example, what is seen as problematic by the authors of the document, what explanations do they provide and what solutions)?

PART IV

CONCLUSION

13

Ethics, Politics and Research

Pamela Abbott and Roger Sapsford

The evaluation and planning of research is, of course, concerned with the 'technical' questions that have formed the main bulk of this book. Beyond these, however, there is another important aspect of research evaluation: looking at the ethics and politics of particular research programmes and of the research process as a whole. In many ways, this chapter ought to have come first in the book, underlying as it does all the decisions we make about research. It is placed here, however, because we need to understand the technicalities of research in its social context before we can fully consider their political and ethical impact.

We need to look at ways in which what is taken for granted in our ordinary lives is also taken for granted in research (often thereby supporting one side of a 'political' issue at the expense of another) and how we can perhaps start to overcome our own 'cultural blinkers'. We need to look also at the relationship of researchers to the 'subjects' of the research and their interests and to the needs and interests of the wider society. When considering questions of 'harm to subjects', we need to bear in mind that research is embedded in people's real lives and it is *not* just the subjects of research who may be harmed, but those of whom they are taken as representative or typical, or even people who are not part of the research in any sense at all. This is less likely to be the case in the social sciences than, say, applied physics or environmental science, but we need to be aware that the possibility of harm exists. Careful consideration needs to be given to the ways in which anyone whose interests are touched by the research might be harmed by it or by the dissemination of its conclusions.

Much of this chapter is about the ethical and political issues which appear in research to be technical ones: the ways in which the choice of measuring instruments and the selection of samples express assumptions which may not be neutral in respect of power relationships. Our examples are mostly drawn from fields where complex concepts are expressed in complex measuring instruments – intelligence, achievement and personality. The points we want to make about them, however, also hold true for much simpler concepts, and for concepts used in participant observation and 'unstructured' interviewing, as much as for the sort of highly structured research which calls for measuring instruments to be constructed. Ultimately, all research stands or falls by the way in which the researcher conceptualizes the field of study: in the design of the study, in the way that measures are defined and measuring instruments constructed, in how the data are coded or clustered or segmented for analysis and in the decisions the researcher makes about what it is important to report and what sense to make of it.

In the next section we look, not at the measurements themselves, but at some of the purposes to which widely used measuring instruments have been put and at what kind of theory underlies them or is implicit in them. We look at the use of intelligence tests for purposes that would now be regarded as racist – or at least discriminatory in a pejorative sense – to declare some people unfit to be citizens, and indeed to exclude immigrants of certain nationalities. We look at the use of concepts of intelligence and achievement, and the whole paraphernalia of measurement that goes with them, to help reproduce a particular type of social order and a set of taken-for-granted beliefs about the world. We look, in other words, at researchers in their social context and the role of research ideas in maintaining and interpreting that context.

Finally, we look briefly at the suggestions sometimes now made that ideological perspectives are reproduced, not just by what we measure or how we measure it, but by the overall 'style' in which we conduct research and what it takes for granted about the nature of the social world. Questions are raised about the normal relationship of researchers to the researched, about the ownership of data and about the status of knowledge and expertise. In other words, we look at the *politics of* research. The fact that we normally take the answers to these questions for granted makes them no easier to answer once the questions have been raised and made explicit.

Nationally and internationally there is a growing concern about providing guidelines and codes of conduct for the practice of research involving human subjects in the health, behavioural and social sciences. Most of the professional social science associations in the UK, for example, have professional codes of conduct which members are expected to follow. Broadly, these voluntary codes or guidelines encompass the conduct of all research practice, whether or not human subjects are involved in research. While on the one hand such codes are welcomed as providing guides and some degree of confidence in the ways research is conceptualized, carried out and the findings reported and used, there is some concern about the possible loss of academic freedom and that important areas of social life may be excluded from research. While the codes are voluntary, compliance with them is at least to some extent secured through a variety of mechanisms. These include the peer/expert review of research proposals, academic journal articles and proposals for books, as well as the requirements that employers may place on employees. More specifically, proposals often have to get ethical approval before research can begin (see below).

The European Union is funding a project – RESPECT (www. respectproject.org) – to develop a voluntary code of practice covering the conduct of socio-economic research, with the aim of ensuring that there are common standards of research practice within the European Research Area that are transparent and universally agreed. The RESPECT Code is based on three main principles:

1   upholding scientific standards
2   compliance with the law
3   avoidance of social and personal harm.

It recognizes that the elements and principles of the code may come into tension or even conflict and that judgements and compromises may have to be made. All researchers should consider these three areas explicitly when they are designing, carrying out and reporting on research findings. However, there are not always right and wrong answers, and, ultimately, value judgements may have to be made. The key thing is that decisions should be defensible.

Ethics and Research

Research ethics has become an area of much greater concern in recent years, with many universities and research funders requiring that research receives ethical approval before it is carried out. Many professional associations have guidelines for members on research ethics, and these are generally available on their web sites. The guidelines issued by the Social Research Association are very detailed and have a guide to useful links as well as a list of references (www.the-sra.org.uk). All research that involves NHS patients in the UK has to gain approval from Local/Regional Medical Ethics committees, and the Department of Health Research Governance Framework will require that all research involving human subjects carried out on NHS premises, in social care settings or otherwise involving NHS patients, social care clients and/or employees, shall gain ethical approval (*Research Governance Framework for Health and Social Care*). The Economic and Social Science Research Council is funding a project to devise a *Framework for the Evaluation of Social Science Research Ethics* (www.york.ac.uk/res/ref). Part of the work of the European Union RESPECT Project is to provide guidelines for conducting ethical socio-economic research (see Dench et al., 2004). It is important, then, to recognize that all research that involves human subjects is increasingly subject to ethical scrutiny, and this includes research carried out by students – undergraduate as well as post-graduate. Many universities now require that all student research is subject to ethical approval as well as the research of staff, non-funded as well as funded.

Research ethics, however, need to be addressed throughout the whole life of a research project and not just at the outset. It is important that researchers stay alert to this. Making ethical decisions nearly always involves making judgements in the light of dilemmas. There are rarely right and wrong answers – rarely one straightforward answer, even. Ethical decisions have to be made by explicitly balancing basic ethical principles. The RESPECT guide lists 17 principles that the authors suggest are integral to ethical socio-economic research and that researchers should endeavour to meet (Dench et al., 2004).

1   The research aims of the study should benefit society and minimize social harm
2   Professional integrity should be balanced with respect for the law

3   In the commissioning and conduct of research there should be respect for and awareness of gender difference

4   In the commissioning and conduct of research there should be respect for all groups in society, regardless of race, ethnicity, religion or culture

5   In the commissioning and conduct of research there should be respect for underrepresented social groups and attempts made to avoid their further social exclusion

6   The concerns of stakeholder and user groups should be addressed

7   Appropriate research methods should be used, selected on the basis of informed professional expertise

8.   The research team should have the necessary professional expertise and support

9   The research process should not result in unwarranted material gain or loss for any participant

10   Findings should be reported accurately

11   Any potential disadvantage to participants should as far as possible be avoided

12   Reporting and dissemination of findings should be carried out in a responsible manner

13   Methodology and findings should be available for discussion and peer review

14   Debts to previous research should be fully acknowledged

15   Participation in research should be voluntary

16   Decisions to take part in research should be on the basis of informed consent

17   Data are treated with appropriate confidentiality and anonymity

Research participants are protected from undue intrusion, distress, physical discomfort, personal embarrassment or psychological or other harm. A first principle of research ethics – to be found in all the various codes of conduct imposed by professional and academic organizations – is that the subjects of the research should not be harmed by it. You might think this obvious, but some quite startling breaches of it have been committed in the course of research. In 1969, for example, a United States medical doctor called Godzeiher established a study to test the side-effects of birth control pills which involved a control group receiving only a placebo (a sugar pill) without their knowledge; seven unwanted pregnancies ensued. In the 1930s another US study sponsored by the US Public Health Service appears to have studied the course of syphilis by withholding treatment from 100 black sufferers, who were then examined and observed at intervals. These studies are discussed in Chapter 1 of Smith (1975). Among projects which involved closer and more personalized interaction with the 'subjects', we might cite Milgram's 1974 work on conformity to authority, which involved subjects being in the position of apparently administering near-lethal electric shocks to students in a learning task, and Zimbardo's 'simulated prison' experiment, where he divided up a group of students into 'prisoners' and 'guards' and set up a mock prison in a university basement (Haney et al., 1973). Milgram's experiment, as he reports himself, left students anxious and traumatized, and Zimbardo's had to be called off ahead of time because of the distress of some of the 'prisoners' and the behaviour of some of the 'guards'. Indeed, the American Psychological Association has banned replication of Milgram's experiments by its members.

The counter-argument which might be put forward (and was by Zimbardo in 1973) would be that the importance of the conclusions outweighed the pain caused by the research. Both Milgram and Zimbardo have justified their work by arguing that it was important to demonstrate in clear-cut and graphic terms the influence of situations on human behaviour. At a time when the atrocities of German and Japanese prison camps were being 'explained away' in terms of national character and the behaviour of some police and prison guards attributed to their character and/or rough working-class upbringing, Milgram and Zimbardo demonstrated, in their different ways, that ordinary, middle-class people will oppress inferiors, beat them up and even apply torture on the instruction of an authoritative other, or in response to their perception of the situation and its demands. Whether inflicting pain or distress is ever justified by the importance of a research topic is a question for each person to decide individually, but it is an *open* question. Even people vehemently opposed to murder might condone some particular act of assassination (for example, of Hitler), and there comes a point in many people's thinking where one strong principle has to give way to another aspect of the public good.

Whatever your stance on these extreme studies, you ought to note that precisely the same ethical problems are faced, though in less dramatic form, by all experiments and many other research studies. We would generally agree that in 'ordinary' research the subject/informant/respondent/participant should be protected from harm. It is for this reason, among others, that we generally promise informants confidentiality or anonymity in surveys or 'unstructured' interviewing projects; interviewing is intrusive, but having your personal details splashed in identifiable form across a research report is even more intrusive. (As we are using the term, *confidentiality* is a promise that you will not be identified or presented in identifiable form, while *anonymity* is a promise that even the researcher will not be able to tell which responses came from which respondent).

One ethical principle gaining increasing acceptance is that nothing should be done to the 'subjects' of research without their agreement, and that this agreement should be based on an adequate knowledge, supplied if necessary by the researcher, of what is implied by consenting. The concept of 'informed consent', however, is no easy answer to a set of moral dilemmas, because it is neither simple nor clear-cut itself. Very often, a researcher may be a practitioner within the area of social practice that is the target of the research and stands in a position of power or influence over the researched, or is identified with others who do so. The social worker, nurse, prison officer or teacher, researching his or her own clients, patients, prisoners or pupils, may have a direct power over the future of the people whom he or she wants as research informants. Even if not, there is an existing authority or dependency relationship such that the informants may feel bound to cooperate, however fairly the request is put. It is also not clear *whose* informed consent is required, in many cases. In research into the treatment or handling of elderly people, for example, do we need the consent of the elderly people themselves, or of their relatives, or of the district nurses and home helps who provide the immediate care, or of their general practitioners, or of the nursing and social service organizers, or of the management of the departments in which the practitioners work? All of these are 'interested parties' in the research, and many of them are or could be useful informants.

There is also the question of how far the consent can ever be 'informed'. To what extent, lacking the researcher's knowledge and background, can the other parties to the research ever understand fully what it is to which they are committing themselves and what use will be made of it? (We shall return to the problem of 'sharing knowledge' later in the chapter.) As researchers, we are trusted on the whole, by 'people out there', to behave honourably towards them, and they trust that the purpose of our research is important enough to justify the intrusion into their lives.

In some cases, the very process of giving information to researchers may itself cause people considerable distress and even long-term psychological problems. This may be the case, for example, if we want to research sensitive subjects. Examples of this type of research might include interviewing women who have been raped, women who have been beaten up by their partners, people who were sexually or physically abused as children or people suffering from life-threatening illness. Re-living distressing and painful experiences may be a very potent experience and could cause long-term psychological distress in some informants. There is also the issue of whether the gender of the interviewer is problematic. Should men, for example, undertake research that includes interviewing women about their experience of being sexually abused by their fathers? Should heterosexual people interview gay men and women about their sexuality?

A further problem concerns those in whose lives we do *not* intervene. In a well-known educational experiment (Rosenthal and Jacobson, 1968), the researchers picked children from a range of school classes at random and convinced the teachers that these had been identified as people likely to show a spurt of intellectual growth in the near future. Sure enough, some of these children did indeed do so, and the experiment is used as an example of the self-fulfilling prophecy in education. No one was directly harmed by the research; children were either advantaged or left alone. If you were one of the 'control' children, however, and you read about the experiment afterwards, might you not feel that you too could have shown a spurt if you had been picked for the experimental sample? The ethics of withholding a treatment which is expected to have a beneficial effect is a problem much discussed in practice research, in education and health care.

We should also note that, even in qualitative research such as participant observation, often considered ethically 'cleaner' because there is no direct manipulation or interrogation of 'subjects', ethical problems remain. The most difficult of these concern the relationships formed with participants and the use which is made of them. We tend to characterize participant observation and relatively unstructured interviewing as styles which give the participants a chance to express their own views and which treat them as people in their own right. In practice, however, the conduct even of ethnographic research can be quite Machiavellian. In Jack Douglas' book *Investigative Social Research* (1976) – which you will find refreshingly cynical or surprisingly realistic, depending on your expectations – the chapter on tactics of investigative research has as sub-headings 'Infiltrating the setting', 'Building friendly trust and opening them up', 'Setting them up' and 'Adversary discombobulating tactics'. In the first three of these, he points out how ethnographers and social anthropologists slip into the setting like spies, building relationships for the purpose of using them to extract information.

> the right use of friendly and trusting relations is not only a necessity of research, but also a powerful one ... the extensive cultivation of friendly and trusting relations with people in all kinds of settings has been vital ... In building affection and trust it does not matter whether the researcher is honest or merely doing presentational work ... But he must be convincing. (Douglas, 1976: 134–7)

Further ethical problems are raised by the extent to which a research project is rooted in the deception of those involved. It is clearly less reactive, for example, to measure people's lives in unobtrusive ways than to make them the subjects of a formal and public experiment; it may even be less harmful to them, to the extent that the knowledge of being watched or studied might cause distress or anxiety. However, another way of putting the term 'unobtrusive measures' is 'spying on people without their knowledge and consent'. Secrecy in research can be an issue in any style, but it is most evident and therefore most discussed in participant observation. Here the 'classic' project would be a covert one, with a researcher joining the social setting as a participant (or, indeed, already being there as one) or passing as a genuine participant, and conducting the research while trying to change the setting as little as possible – again, 'spying out the land' in a very real sense. The alternative is to do the research openly, declaring one's role as researcher, which is more reactive and therefore sometimes less effective, particularly when it is a disapproved behaviour, such as industrial corruption or racist discrimination, which is the topic of research. Nor is it clear that perfect openness occurs even in 'open' research. On the one hand, the researcher will not want to tell the actors how to behave or what to say in order to confirm the researcher's theories and, on the other, it is not clear that the aims of research can necessarily be explained to those who do not share the researcher's training and background (see the discussion of 'informed consent' above).

Less discussed are wider ethical problems to do with the selection of problems and of samples. By studying girls at school, do we disadvantage boys? By looking for ways to make community care more effective for those who are receiving it, might we be doing a disservice to relatives or professionals? Studying youth's behaviour in public, do we distract attention from their economic circumstances or the institutionalized behaviour of the police and the criminal justice system? People may be harmed if their interests are not reflected in research, perhaps sometimes as surely as if they were physically or psychologically damaged. It was argued at one time, for example, that the tendency for sociological research to concentrate on the behaviour and attitudes of working-class people was just one more facet of social control.

Another problem is the use to which our research findings are put – often completely unintended by the researchers themselves. Findings may be interpreted in ways that are much to the disadvantage of the researched. Some research on poverty, for example, intended by the researchers to demonstrate the hardships and difficulties of living on low incomes, has been interpreted by others as demonstrating that the problem is not insufficient income but the ways in which the income is spent. Can we absolve ourselves from blame by indicating that this is not what we intended our research to be used for? Are social scientists absolved from blame because the unintended use of their research does not have the fatal or harmful consequences of, say, the unintended misuse of chemical and physical research? In other words, if we say that our research should not harm anyone, we have to be very clear about what we mean by harm.

We have raised a number of questions in this section, and we shall raise more in the remainder of the chapter. We hope we have failed to answer most of them. This is because of the position we take on the nature of ethical dilemmas. We are inclined towards a *relativist* position: that there are a large number of ethical imperatives, sometimes in conflict with each other, and that knowing that there can be ethical arguments against a course of action does not absolve the individual from considering the consequences of taking or refraining from the action. Others, however, may take a more *absolutist* position: that some things are in themselves wrong and should never be done, whatever the consequences. We have also tried to indicate that even the basic concepts used when discussing ethics, such as 'harm' or 'consent', need themselves to be problematized: that what is meant by 'harm', for instance, can be a very narrow range of physical and/or mental outcomes, or a very broad range which includes remote social and political effects.

Politics and Research

Intelligence and the Politics of 'Race'

Intelligence tests are often portrayed as imperfect but *in principle* relatively neutral measures of an underlying quality inherent in people. However, the decision to measure a quality of people – expressing the concept that people differ in important ways with respect to that quality – is not a neutral act but one with political significance. Intelligence tests form a particularly obvious example of the political masquerading as the scientific, because their origins are blatantly political and embody the assumptions of particular periods of history. 'The interpretation of IQ data has always taken place, as it must, in a social and political context, and the validity of the data cannot be fully assessed without reference to that context. That is in general true of social science' (Kamin, 1977: 16).

The concept of 'intelligence' – general mental ability – and the desire to measure it, and classify the population with respect to it, predate the invention of the tests which are the means by which the measurement may be made. From the mid-nineteenth century there was growing neo-Darwinist concern about the deterioration of the 'national stock' – the notion that the physical and mental quality of the population was systematically declining. This was fuelled by military defeats abroad (for example, the defeat of Gordon at Khartoum), the poor physical condition of army recruits at the time of the Boer War, and the increasingly successful encroachment of Germany and the USA into areas of commerce and industry which had been seen as a British preserve.

'Deterioration' was seen as a multi-faceted condition of the disreputable poor: physical unfitness, 'mental inferiority', 'pauperism', prostitution, insanity, crime and delinquency were all seen as elements in a single 'weakening of the stock' with a common genetic origin. As the middle classes and the 'respectable' poor were beginning to limit family size, while the disreputable poor still bred without constraint, it was posited that bad hereditary traits were driving out good ones and the nation as a whole was declining in the same way that poorly bred cattle decline. A particular worry came to be people of low intelligence – 'feeble-minded' was the term used at the time – whose numbers became apparent with the introduction of universal schooling at the end of the nineteenth century.

The first IQ test, in 1905, was designed in France to pick out those children who were considered unteachable from those who were just badly taught, and it was a relatively pragmatic and untheorized object. It came into a social world which was very ready for it, however; a world in which the identification of 'defectives' and the monitoring and control of their rate of breeding was seen as of very great importance. The first promise of the test, to North American and British eyes, was that it at last provided a way of identifying 'borderline defectives', those with intelligence not much below the norm but who, in the eyes of eugenic scientists, were seen as fast and irresponsible breeders, likely to pollute and dilute the national stock, the gene pool.

> in the near future intelligence tests will bring tens of thousands of these high-grade defectives under the surveillance and protection of society. This will ultimately result in curtailing the reproducing of feeble-mindedness and in the elimination of an enormous amount of crime, pauperism and industrial inefficiency. (Terman, 1916: 16–17)

Thus the tests were welcomed as the first defence against what was seen as a very real 'threat from within'. Another group who welcomed them were those responsible for defence against the 'threat from outside' – the officials responsible for immigration control in the USA, where the problem of 'contamination of the national stock' was seen as even more severe than in the UK. *Within* the USA, eugenicists identified pockets of 'bad stock', where it was claimed that the inbreeding of 'degenerates' was spreading the disease of mental deficiency, pauperism, prostitution and crime. Immigration was the other problem, for it was firmly believed that 'races' differed in their innate ability. It was claimed that borderline mental deficiency

> is very common among Spanish-Indian and Mexican families of the Southwest and also among Negroes. Their dullness seems racial, or at least inherent in the family stocks from which they come ... The whole question of racial differences in mental traits will have to be taken up again ... The writer predicts that when this is done there will be discovered enormously significant racial differences which cannot be wiped out by any scheme of mental culture. (Terman, 1916: 91–2)

When the same methods of investigation were applied to the different kinds of European who were attempting to migrate to the USA, it turned out that white Northern Europeans of protestant stock stood at the peak of the intellectual pyramid, and other (e.g. Mediterranean) nationalities some way behind them. This gave a scientific method and a scientific justification for regulating immigration to preserve the quality of the population. Official control over immigration began with an Act of 1875 barring 'coolies, convicts and prostitutes', but 'lunatics' and 'idiots' were added to the list in 1882, 'epileptics' and 'insane persons' in 1903, 'imbeciles' and 'feeble-minded persons' in 1907, and 'persons of constitutional psychopathic inferiority' in 1917 – demonstrating, among other things, the changes that were occurring in psychological terminology.

There arose a public clamour for some form of 'quality control' over the inflow of immigrants. At first this took the form of a demand for a literacy test; but it could scarcely be doubted that the new science of mental testing, which proclaimed its ability to measure innate intelligence, would be called into the nation's service. The first volunteer was Henry Goddard, who, in 1912, was invited by the United States Public Health Service to administer the Binet test and supplementary performance tests to representatives of what he called 'the great mass of average immigrants'. The results were sure to produce grave concern in the minds of thoughtful citizens. The test results established that 83 per cent of the Jews, 80 per cent of the Hungarians, 79 per cent of the Italians and 87 per cent of the Russians were 'feeble-minded'. By 1917 Goddard was able to report:

that the number of aliens deported because of feeble-mindedness ... increased approximately 350 per cent in 1913 and 5670 per cent in 1914 ... This was due to the untiring efforts of the physicians who were inspired by the belief that mental tests could be used for the detection of feeble-minded aliens. (Kamin, 1977: 31)

The same tests, and others developed later, were very widely administered within the USA during and after the First World War, and it was their results that provided the first 'scientific evidence' for the alleged racial inferiority of Americans of African origin, something which was not of concern at the time but has since been elevated to a major scientific and political controversy. Carl Brigham, then an assistant professor at Princeton, developed a theory of races which paralleled and borrowed from what was being written in Germany at the time. He distinguished between people of 'Nordic', 'Alpine' and 'Mediterranean' origin, characterizing Nordics as rulers and aristocrats and Alpines as peasants and serfs. These ideas were widely taken up for a time, and they naturally allied themselves with the same sort of gratuitous anti-Semitism that characterized similar writing in Germany:

we have no separate intelligence distribution for Jews ... [but] our army sample of immigrants from Russia is at least one half Jewish ... Our figures ... tend to disprove the popular belief that the Jew is intelligent ... he has the head form, stature and colour of his Slavic neighbours. He is an Alpine Slav. (Brigham, 1923: 190)

The point we are making is not only that the tests were employed for political purposes, but also their use was scientifically illegitimate – a fact that was pointed out at the time but had little impact in the contemporary political climate. The employment of intelligence for this purpose was grounded in the discovery that certain populations tended on average to score less than 'native Americans' (by which term the proponents of the theory would have meant white settlers, not 'American Indians'); the differences were of the order of 10–15 score points, or one standard deviation. The plain fact is, however, that the tests of the time were not sufficiently precise for a difference of this order to be meaningfully attributed to genetic inferiority (and nor are current tests), for a number of reasons:

1 Although some attempt was made to overcome the problem, there can be no doubt that those for whom English was not a first language were at a disadvantage. Those who were functionally illiterate in American English will have included a disproportionate number of people from impoverished homes, including immigrants and citizens of African origin.
2 The items of which the tests were made up were selected as representing the familiar and common-sense world – but the familiar world of British and white North American people, not of Mexicans or Spaniards or Greeks.
3 The whole notion of test-taking, as we shall see below, is tied up with a certain approach to schooling. Those who came from other cultures may well not have learned this particular skill. (Few modern-day testers put the effects of practicing 'intelligence tests in general' at less than 10–15 score points.)
4 The best marks on tests go to those who are fundamentally motivated towards individual competition and keyed up to show themselves at their best (without being disruptively over-anxious). This state of mind, and the rules of the 'game' which demand it, are characteristic of people in advanced capitalist societies and much less characteristic of peasant ones.

5   Tests generally have a time limit within which the items have to be completed. This expresses and draws on a cultural norm of getting things done in a set time, which is much more common in advanced industrial societies, where time dominates the day's activities, than in non-industrial societies, where precise timing has less meaning.

In other words, the observed differences are as likely as not to be cultural, due to environment and upbringing rather than innate condition. Beyond this, the use of the tests for this purpose betrays the political stance of the scientists who advocated it, if only by their use or misuse of evidence. Sometimes the misuse is willful. Brigham, for example, somehow managed to cling on to a 'racial' theory of intelligence, even in the teeth of evidence that immigrants who had been in the USA for some time scored no worse than 'native' Americans. Sometimes the misuse is more subtle, but it still constitutes misuse. The tests of the 1930s showed a gender difference, for example. This was not hailed as a great discovery, but identified as a fault in the tests at a time when gender differences were not acceptable in this respect and eliminated by re-selection of items. When a 'racial' difference is found, however, it is hailed as a great discovery. Both reflect what was politically acceptable at the time.

Activity 12.1 (5 minutes)

Spend a few minutes thinking about what you have just read. Is the racism which has been displayed by intelligence testers – the tendency to cling to lines of argument even against evidence or valid criticism, and the use of tests to the deliberate disadvantage of people of certain ethnic origins – something which is avoidable, or is it inherent in the tests?
Make a note of your response before you continue.

It certainly still seems to be true that the concept of intelligence lends itself particularly well to the identification of supposed genetic differences between 'races' (itself a problematic and politicized concept here), and the faults of the tests are all too easily forgotten. (See Jensen, 1972, 1973, for an example of similar-sized differences in mean scores being interpreted as genetic inferiority.) In principle, however, a culture-fair test is possible (though it has yet to be shown how one can be constructed in practice), and certainly a culture-fair attitude within tests and among test-constructors is something which they themselves generally seek. A great deal of effort has been expended on trying to build tests which are not dependent on language or culturally common knowledge. Thus one might be inclined to argue that many of the problems arise from the misuse of tests by administrators and officials (though with the encouragement of scientists).

However, the point remains that the concept of intelligence emanates from a particular period of history in response to the perceived problems of that period. Historically its development has been much bound up with inequalities of race and class. Whether the concept would have been thought useful in a history where these particular inequalities were not crucial elements of social structure remains open to question. The need for the test, the concepts out of which it grew and the perceived social problems which these concepts addressed, grew up together to yield the tests and the concepts that we now employ. These concepts and this way of looking at people is now more or less taken for granted, part of the 'cultural stock of knowledge'. Whether present-day psychologists, who have grown up with quite different perceived problems, would have found a need for such tests and such concepts if they were not already a strong part of the discipline's 'knowledge', is not something we can readily determine.

Intelligence, Achievement and the Politics of Class

So far in this chapter we have looked at 'individualistic' ethics – the responsibility of the researcher for the 'subjects' of the research. We have examined the patent use of research concepts and their operationalized measures for political purposes. (It is the existence of the operationalized measure which makes the political action possible; if there were no tests of intelligence, groups could not be segregated or excluded on the basis of it.) Now we return to the measurement of intellectual potential and actual attainment, to look at a more subtle aspect of the way that research is grounded in politics.

We have seen that intelligence tests have been used for political purposes, though this use may perhaps not be inherent in their theory and construction. Achievement tests, by comparison, appear politically neutral; they simply test whether a form of teaching has 'taken' and a content been 'delivered'. There is a sense, however, in which both kinds of test play their part in the essentially political process, whereby a form of society reproduces itself. Both can be seen as elements in a discourse that is prevalent in our society – a discourse that defines people as necessarily having a place on a continuum of intelligence. Even if intelligence tests are not used, people are judged and classified on this criterion, and the attributed intelligence of a child is used to define the type of education to which he or she is exposed.

Intelligence testing grew up initially in reaction to fears about people seen as inherently 'feeble-minded', stoked by the introduction of mass schooling, which made it possible to count their numbers. Binet originally denied that the test he devised in 1905 was suitable for anything other than this specific purpose, but by 1908 it was being used to calibrate the development of 'normal' children, and the concept of the intelligence quotient as a measure standardized for chronological age was developed two years later. The measurement of intelligence as a routine way of identifying potentially able pupils took a little longer to become established, but eventually it became a standard feature of the schooling system.

Schools became an important part of the state/societal mechanism for maintaining order and discipline as the UK became increasingly an industrial society. Schooling which had previously been denied to working-class children began sometimes to be available, in one form or another, during the eighteenth century, but without any evidence of intent to gather up and socialize a whole social class; this was distinctively a nineteenth-century phenomenon. The factory system undermined the traditional family to some extent – the family of agriculture or cottage industry, with children socialized to production at home – and the traditional skills that might have been learned at home became increasingly inappropriate in an era of rapidly changing methods. Schools came to be seen as necessary, therefore, for the teaching of new skills, including basic literacy and numeracy. More important to those who were active in establishing schooling for working-class children, the school was a medium of socialization, including gender differentiation. It taught 'habits of industry' and accustomed male children to the discipline necessary for factory work, while giving female children the skills needed for domestic labour. It accustomed children to systematic, routine and often dull work and brought them to regard it as a normal part of life. It was also a chance to convey the moral precepts of the work ethic, directly through instruction or indirectly by example. In other words, it was a site of power in the sense in which Foucault (for example, 1982) often uses the term – a place where people can be moulded into understanding the world in the way in which the shaper wants them to understand it and behaving habitually in accordance with that view of the world. Schools may inculcate critical enquiry, but while doing so they also set the parameters of the society within which this enquiry is to take place.

This is not to suggest that schooling became some sort of monolithic repressive mechanism, aimed at the working class. Indeed, the same period was one of working-class struggle for education and access to schooling. Education was not just something imposed from above; its value was well realized by working-class people, and there was considerable individual and collective striving to make it more available to working-class children. Education became a major means of upward mobility for working-class children and made a wide range of occupations available to them which would previously have been beyond their reach. However, none of this changed the basic structure of the society. It changed the likelihood of particular people filling particular positions within it, and constructed thereby a fundamentally more open society, but the broad pattern of social structures and social relations remained unchanged.

Perhaps even more important, both for mobility and for the preservation of the social structure, education became a 'site of classification' – a mechanism whereby emerging adults could be assigned their place in the scheme of things. Testing is inseparable from our concept of schooling; one important function of schooling is the rank-ordering of children with regard to their abilities, by teachers' informal reports and by public examination. More insidiously, school plays a part in assigning some children to higher-grade occupations and others to lower ones by a process of self-shaping. Perceiving themselves as succeeding or failing in the tasks which schools set them and which are necessary for the successful completion of public examinations, children come to think of themselves as able or less able, suitable or not suitable for the higher reaches, as successes or failures. This process may occur even in schools which have a conscious rhetoric and policy of encouraging all children. Despite the efforts of teachers, some children succeed in the system and some fail in it; it is in the nature of the schooling system that children have to be located on a success/failure dimension. Because middle-class children have an advantage over working-class children in the 'schooling game' – they come into school 'knowing the rules', or at least some of them – the process of education is not a politically neutral one. Middle-class children are more familiar with the objects and procedures relevant to schooling – books, pencils, reading, counting, drawing, computers.

Middle-class parents tend to worry more (and to more effect) about how their children are labelled at school, to interact more with teachers to secure their children's advantage and to have the resources to supply additional schooling when the child appears 'not to be thriving' during the regular school day. They also tend to have more freedom to direct their children to schools according to their standing and more knowledge or access to knowledge on which such decisions can be based.

The development of intelligence testing in the first two decades of the twentieth century opened up the way to further stratification and the direction of children to types of school 'consonant with their needs and abilities' rather than just according to their parents' ability to pay. By about 1925 the division of schooling into 'academic' and 'vocational' was well advanced, and intelligence tests were well established as a way of determining which track should be followed. This process reached its most visible form in the tripartite system of grammar, technical and secondary modern schools which most Local Education Authorities established following the Education Act of 1944; here intelligence testing came into its own as a means of selecting the best children, irrespective of parents' ability to pay. There is research evidence that working-class children were still less likely to enter grammar schools than middle-class children of the same measured ability, but the tests acted in a more 'class-fair' manner than, for example, head teachers' recommendations. While we have retreated to some extent from this extreme separation over the past 30 years, vocational tracking still occurs in school practices (streaming and setting), in the nature of the curricula and in the nature of the examinations for which children 'of different abilities' are entered.

Achievement testing acts similarly to intelligence testing to differentiate, classify and assign pupils. The examination (and continuous assessment is included in this concept) provides documentation on the person and his or her abilities. The outcome of school practice – differential curricula, examining, profiling, testing – is therefore to produce a well-divided and ordered society. It does not necessarily preserve the status quo in the sense that only the children of advantaged parents finish up in advantaged positions (though there is a strong element of this), but it does tend to maintain the general shape and hierarchical nature of the society within which it is set. The existence of these divisions and the importance of correct allocation is the justification for a whole range of professional experts – teachers, lecturers, educational psychologists, sociologists of education. They in their turn have a stake in what these divisions shall be and some measure of power in determining what sort of people shall finish up in each of them.

School tests and examinations may be seen as arising out of, and at the same time reinforcing and reproducing, a particular discourse or way of viewing people and their social relations – one inherently typical of and adaptive for capitalist forms of social organization. Individuals are posited as truly individual rather than social, making their *own* decisions and 'naturally' in competition. They are seen as variously endowed, and it is this endowment which is seen as determining where they will finish up in the power hierarchy (but the fact that social background – class of origin – is part of this 'endowment' tends to be glossed over). The individual, in turn, is seen as being made up of – 'possessing' – qualities which are measurable and which enable us to compare one individual with another. During the period of industrialization a new 'knowledge-base' grew up around this increasingly dominant view of human nature, which eventually became the disciplines of 'individual' and 'social' psychology – terms developed to describe the human subject, and concepts developed in these terms which allowed the measurement of the subject's 'interior state'.

This leads us to the most important feature of the discourse: that it is aimed at the management of individuals. Mostly, it posits human beings as perfectible or change-able or curable by manipulation of their qualities or attributes. At the same time, it assigns them their place in society by reference to these qualities or attributes. Thus the activity of testing, however scientific its form, is far from neutral politically. It may form a ladder by which the few transcend their class position, but for the majority it reproduces the structure of society unchanged.

To say this is not necessarily to criticize it or denounce it as unjust, but to identify one of its functions, as an institution which permits upward mobility but tends on the whole to maintain the stability of the social system. The same point may be made about a much wider range of research areas – the criminal justice system, health, community care, income maintenance – all of which are grounded in existing social institutions which generate and are maintained by particular discourses, particular models of what people and the social order are like and what may be taken for granted about them.

Politics, Ideology and 'Research Style'

We have just looked at how theory, concepts and operationalized measures can embody ideologies or discourses, models of the world and of how questions about it are legitimately framed. Thus a line of research can be so imbued with a particular (unacknowledged) worldview that its conclusions must fall within that worldview and reinforce or validate it. In this section we shall look at the whole way in which research is conducted. It has been argued, as we shall see, that the 'stance' adopted in research itself expresses (and serves to validate) a particular model of how the social world is and should be.

It has been argued that to adopt one research style or 'stance' in preference to another is an implicitly political act, because research styles are not neutral or inter-changeable: they embody implicit models of what the social world is like or should be like and of what counts as knowledge and how to get it:

> Methods and methodology are not simply techniques and rationales for the conduct of research. Rather they must be understood in relation to specific historical, cultural, ideo-logical and other contexts ... when one ponders the questions – what methods will I use in my study? or, why was a certain method used for a given study? – these are not simply tech-nical issues ... (Reinharz, 1983:162–3)

In this section we shall explore a common criticism of 'conventional' research in the form in which it has been developed by feminist scholars and researchers. We should point out that the critique is by no means specific to feminism; elements of it have been expressed over the past 20 years by researchers in a number of quite disparate disciplines. (For a developed version emanating from humanistic psychology, for example, see Reason and Rowan, 1981.) Nor are we necessarily arguing that there is a distinctive 'feminist research methodology'. Feminist scholarship is one place, however, where issues of politics and power in research have been particularly sharply developed, and the discussion that follows owes a great deal to it. Two concepts of power are involved in our discussion of this scholarship: the direct power of the researcher over those researched, and the power of the researcher to 'set the agenda' of the research and declare and disseminate the results.

Activity 13.2 (5 minutes)

Think about the Reinharz quotation above and marshal your ideas about what form such an argument might take.

The arguments that feminists have put forward have tended to involve two separate (though related) issues. First, there is the criticism of quantitative research which conceives of itself as 'scientific', objective, value-free – the criticism of positivism. Feminists (and others) have argued that such research does not discover what the social world is like, but rather imposes its own conceptual schema on to the social world. A case in point would be social mobility research in the 1970s and 1980s, which *declared* women unimportant both for examining rates of social mobility over time and for theorizing about social mobility, rather than *discovering* that they were unimportant. (See Abbott and Sapsford (1987a) for a discussion of this.) Sociological theory defined women as dependent on male heads of households and therefore outside the concerns of class theory. Conversely, accepting that the social differences between men and women were natural (biological) and inevitable, sociology did not see sexual divisions as an area of sociological concern and defined the work that women did in the domestic sphere as of no sociological interest. When Ann Oakley wanted to start research on housework in the late 1960s, for example, she found it very difficult to find a supervisor and have the topic accepted, because housework was seen quite simply as something trivial, not something that constituted any sort of sociological problem. It was a very common experience of women sociology and psychology students in the 1960s and 1970s (and often still is today) to find a disjuncture between 'experience of the world … and the theoretical schemes available to think about it in' (Smith, 1974: 7); large areas of their lives and much of what really concerned them were declared non-existent, trivial, peripheral, not on the agenda for research or theory.

Feminists and others have argued that methods whose strength lies in the testing of theory are not suitable tools for research intended to develop new theory. Quantitative research is designed to obtain answers to researchers' questions; it does not yield an understanding of people's lives in depth nor, generally, leave space for them to indicate what they regard as the important questions. Quantitative methods typically isolate 'variables' for study, independent of the context in which they make sense and the sense which is made of them in that context: 'Concepts, environments, social interactions are all simplified by methods which lift them out of their context, stripping them of the very complexity that characterizes them in the real world' (Parlee,

1979: 131). Such criticism led to a call for relatively unstructured, qualitative methods which will 'take women's experience into account', explore the basis of women's everyday knowledge, let women 'speak for themselves' without the prejudgement and prestructuring of prior theory.

Positivistic science itself may reasonably be seen as expressing a discourse, a model of what truth is and how it is to be ascertained. The 'rules' of scientific discourse are that disputes are settled on the basis of evidence and logic – evidence in the form of careful, repeatable measurements whose relevance to the dispute can be readily justified, and logical argument from that evidence to a conclusion. These are the dominant 'rules of truth' in our current culture – the 'respectable' grounds on which arguments may be won. To say that something expresses a discourse is not to say that it is wrong; everything expresses some discourse, is framed according to some set of rules. The force of the scientific discourse, however, is to divert problematic issues from the arena of political debate – to 'depoliticize' them. 'Science' is not just a body of knowledge acquired for its own sake, but the basis of techniques which are used to solve problems. By accepting that certain kinds of issue are amenable to scientific solution – 'matters of fact' – we empower experts both to act on our behalf and ultimately to determine what our 'best interests' are. A part of the control, which this establishment of expertise exerts, is achieved

> by taking what is essentially a political problem, removing it from the realm of political discourse, and recasting it in the neutral language of science. Once this is accomplished the problems have become technical ones ... the language of reform is, from the outset, an essential component ... Where there [is] resistance or failure ... his [is] construed as further proof of the need to reinforce and extend the power of experts. (Foucault, 1982: 196)

The second criticism that feminists (and others) have raised is that much research is exploitative and oppressive – that it consists in a researcher with power controlling and manipulating 'subjects' for whom a better term might be 'objects'. Ann Oakley has raised as political/ethical the issue of the treatment of respondents in survey research, asking them identical questions in a set order and not being able to respond to issues they raise for fear of disturbing the standardized nature of the proceedings – in other words, treating human beings as like the objects of, e.g., research in physics or chemistry. This criticism is not confined to quantitative research, however; conventional participant observation research and 'unstructured' interview studies also come under fire. The process of research has been likened by some feminist scholars to the process of rape:

> the researchers take, hit, and run. They intrude into their subjects' privacy, disrupt their perceptions, utilize false pretences, manipulate the relationship, and give little or nothing in return. When the needs of the researchers are satisfied, they break off contact with the subject. (Reinharz, 1979: 95)

Thus research is criticized for the way it exercises power over its 'subjects'. A further criticism, however, might concern the power of the researcher to determine what is important in the situation, what needs researching, what the problem is. Here again the 'conventional' researcher has near-total autonomy and those who are researched may have little input (particularly in quantitative research).

These two criticisms have led some feminists and other researchers to call for fully collaborative research and the displacement of 'the researcher' from the control of the research process – or even, sometimes, for the abandonment of research in favour of participation in social action. As Maria Mies (1983) argues:

> The vertical relationship between researcher and 'research objects', the *view from above,* must be replaced by the *view from below* ...

> ... the hierarchical research situation as such defeats the very purpose of research: it creates an acute distrust in the 'research objects' ... It has been observed that the data thus gathered often reflect 'expected behaviour' rather than real behaviour ...

> [However,] Women, who are committed to the cause of women's liberation, cannot stop at this result. They cannot be satisfied with giving the social sciences better, more authentic and more relevant data. The ethical-political significance of the view from below cannot be separated from the scientific one ...

> The contemplative, uninvolved 'spectator knowledge' must be replaced by *active partici-pation in actions, movements and struggles* ... Research must become an integral part of such struggles. (Mies, 1983, in Hammersley, 1993: 68–9)

Activity 13.3 (5 minutes)

What problems do you see with the 'collaborative' approach to research? Spend a few minutes thinking about how it could be put into operation and what the implications would be for the researcher and the research.

Four problems occur to us:

1   We are inclined to think that adoption of a fully collaborative stance as an ethical imperative would abolish research into 'theory' and the use of research as an aid to scholarship and the development of ideas. If researchers are to avoid 'using' people for the researchers' purposes and confine their attention to helping to solve participants' problems, then all research becomes applied research. It is not clear, even, whether the researcher can initiate the research, or whether he or she has to wait to be 'commissioned'.

2   The adoption of a fully collaborative stance probably abolishes the role of researcher altogether. If the researcher is in no 'privileged' position – has no particular say in the planning of the research, no particular 'ownership' of the data, no special rights to use the material for publication – then it is difficult to see what he or she brings to the situation other than technical knowledge. Now, one may argue that researchers make their name and their living from studying the problems and miseries of others, and that the abolition of the role would be no bad thing, but one has to be clear that this *is* one possible consequence of this line of argument. We cannot take an authoritative position on this issue; as academics, we find it difficult to argue for the abolition of the academic role.

3   Most important of all, it is not clear that full power-sharing is possible, even in principle. In the extreme version of the collaborative stance, all participants are

to be equal, and the researcher's knowledge gives him or her no special position but has to be shared. 'Informed consent', in this position, involves the sharing of knowledge and experience so that all participants have the same power of understanding. Arguably, however, this would mean putting all participants through the same history of academic and research training and experience as the researcher has undergone, which is impractical and would not be desired by the participants. To the extent that it is not done, the power of knowledge necessarily remains with the researcher.

4   There is also the question of whom the researcher is collaborating with and who has given 'informed consent'. Research often involves several groups, where interests may not be the same; collaborating with one group may even reinforce power relationships, even if the research is intended to benefit all groups involved. For example, collaborative research with social workers into their practice still leaves the clients as research 'objects'.

We raise these objections not to decry the collaborative stance – we think that those who advocate it have alerted us to some very important ethical considerations, and that research should be strongly influenced by them – but to suggest that there are no easy answers to ethical and political dilemmas in research as in most walks of life.

Overview of Issues

We began this chapter with a discussion of research ethics, and this is where we have also finished up, but a lot of ground has been covered in between. We started with important questions of 'individualistic' ethics – for example, the design of research so that subjects/respondents/informants/participants are not harmed by it. We then went on, however, to look beneath the surface of the theories that are researched and the measures that are derived from them. It is easy to work as if qualities such as 'intelligence', 'achievement' or 'class' exist in some sense which is difficult to define but unproblematic, so that the problem is how to measure them. However, we looked at the background, history and usage of these variables to examine how the concepts have grown up, not as academic abstractions but ways of describing the social world for particular purposes. We discovered that social construction is an aspect of their 'existence': that they arise from certain theories or ideologies or discourses/world models and incorporate the assumptions implicit in their origins. The 'grand abstractions' of social science are not 'existent things', but ways of describing and abstracting from and characterizing the real 'existent things' – people and their social relations – and the notion that they might be constructed for a purpose, and deliberately or unwittingly incorporate theories about the social world, should come as no surprise. Going on to look at our own usual way of conceptualizing research as an activity, we found that even here there are taken-for-granted assumptions about the nature of the social world and the proper ('natural', 'inevitable') way that power and knowledge are distributed which are built into the way the enterprise is conducted and can shape its outcomes.

In other words, in looking at research papers or conducting your own research you need to be sensitive to the 'taken-for-granted'. Taken-for-granted ways of conceptualizing a problem area (or even taken-for-granted ways of conceptualizing aspects of social behaviour as 'belonging' to certain problem areas) shape how the problem is formulated, which restricts what can conceivably come out as results of any study undertaken. (Even more interesting, perhaps, is the way that disciplines and applied areas declare some questions to be 'real' problems and others as peripheral, trivial or 'not on the agenda'. Some selection *has* to be made – not everything can be researched – but the omissions sometimes add up to a systematic exclusion of some set of interests or points of view.) The question of the kinds of people who do and should appear in the sample again reflects a model of the social world with respect to the problem which has been formulated, as does the method of data collection adopted, the form of analysis chosen and even the form in which we choose to promulgate results and conclusions. In a sense, this is not a criticism, because it is a general statement about all conceivable research projects and all conceivable research reports. It is not possible to work in a vacuum; at the same time as some aspects of a situation are problematized, others must be taken for granted. However, an important aspect of the conduct of research, and an even more important aspect of reading research reports, is thinking about precisely *what* has been taken for granted and how it affects the conclusions.

The point has also been made that the use of existing and accepted methods of research, grounded in the 'knowledge base' of a discipline, may sometimes amount to taking sides in a potential dispute. We have used social class as an example of how gender issues may be prejudged, and intelligence and attainment as examples of implicit and (sometimes) unconscious prejudgement of issues related to 'race' and social class. It is inevitable that most research will proceed along established lines and within established paradigms – we cannot for ever question *everything* – and it is true that to use 'unconventional' methods and theoretical bases is equally to take sides. We need where possible, however, to identify what is being taken for granted in the methods we use and the disciplinary knowledge in which they are grounded.

Conclusion

This chapter has used the example of research into intelligence and achievement to make its points. The overall 'message', however, is that all research can be viewed from this kind of perspective and is open to this kind of critique. A major debate in research on the criminal justice system, for example, has been the ways in which social class is ignored or hidden or taken for granted in its analyses, while in sociology there have been significant criticisms of the ways in which social class has been both theorized and operationalized, resulting not just in the exclusion and marginalization of women but serving to justify (albeit unintentionally) a social structure in which women are subordinated to men. Research on families, health and community care is rightly, some would say, attacked for the way in which it tends to take for granted a particular set of relations between the genders and across the generations, thereby naturalizing women's work in the domestic sphere. Feminist research into the position

(Conclusion continued)

of women has been attacked for its tendency to ignore the important dimension of ethnic origins and for leaving in the shadows issues of masculinity. It is always a relevant form of critique to uncover the buried assumptions taken for granted by a piece of research, if only to show that they make no difference to the credibility of the conclusions. In other words, we need to be careful that something that is a *political* problem associated with the research is not turned into a *technical* problem, or indeed taken for granted as solved because of the research methods and design that are employed.

Further Reading

Smith, H.W. (1975) *Strategies of Social Research,* Ch. 1, Englewood Cliffs, NJ, Prentice-Hall.

Foucault, M. (1982) 'The subject and power', in H. Dreyfus and P. Rabinow (eds), *Michel Foucault: Beyond Structuralism and Hermeneutics,* Brighton, Harvester.

Reinharz, S. (1979) *On Becoming a Social Scientist,* San Francisco, Jossey Bass.

Dench, C., Iphofen, R. and Huws, U. (2004) *An EU Code of Ethics for Socio-Economic Research,* Brighton, Institute for Employment Studies, www.employment-studies. co.uk

Research Proposal Activity 13

This chapter has emphasized that ethics and politics are closely interconnected. It has also emphasized that both of them underlie all the decisions we make about research. Therefore, ethical and political issues need to be anticipated and addressed from the outset. By the time research has been carried out and a report published, it is too late to undo damage. In formulating a proposal for research, it is important to consider the questions given below. In doing so, it is useful to distinguish between 'micro' issues (for example, 'Are research procedures likely to harm particular individuals?') and 'macro' issues (for example, 'Does the research problem, as formulated, marginalize certain groups?'), and between the explicit (for example, 'What is the potential impact of data collection on the everyday lives of individuals?') and the implicit (for example, 'What are the taken-for-granted assumptions in the research problem as formulated?'). Key questions are as follows:

1   Are there ethical and/or political issues involved in the choice of research problem or the selection of particular samples to the exclusion of others (for example, in highlighting the interests of certain groups and ignoring those of other groups)?

2   Is the research sponsored, and are sponsors influencing the way in which the research problem is being defined, the way in which the research is designed, or the ways in which the data are likely to be interpreted and used. Should measures be taken to reduce the sponsors' influence? If so, what measures?

3 Is it anticipated that subjects of research will be harmed (for example, by research procedures such as withholding treatment from some subjects)? If so, does it matter that they are harmed? For example, is it believed that benefits derived from the research will outweigh potential harm to subjects? Is it considered that the research subjects do not deserve protection from investigative social research?

4 If it is felt that subjects should be protected, what precautions can be taken to reduce or prevent harm (for example, promises of confidentiality or anonymity)?

5 Should consent be obtained before research is carried out? If so, from whom should this consent be obtained (for example, from subjects themselves, or from gatekeepers to such subjects)?

References

Abbott, P.A. (ed.) (1988) *Material Deprivation and Health Status in the Plymouth Health Authority District,* Research report to the Plymouth Community Health Council.

Abbott, P.A. and Sapsford, R.J. (1987a) *Women and Social Class,* London, Tavistock.

Abbott, P.A. and Sapsford, R.J. (1987b) *Community Care for Mentally Handicapped Children: The Origins and Consequences of a Social Policy,* Milton Keynes, Open University Press.

Abbott, P.A. and Sapsford, R.J. (1994) 'Health and material deprivation in Plymouth: an interim replication', *Sociology of Health and Illness,* vol. 16, pp. 252–9.

Abbott, P.A. and Sapsford, R.J. (1998) *Research Methods for Nurses and the Caring Professions,* 2nd edn, Buckingham, Open University Press.

Abbott, P.A., Bernie, J., Payne, G. and Sapsford, R.J. (1992) 'Health and material deprivation in Plymouth', in P.A. Abbott and R.J. Sapsford (eds), *Research into Practice: A Reader for Nurses and the Caring Professions* 1st edn, Buckingham, Open University Press.

Allport, G.W. (1942) *The Use of Personal Documents in Psychological Science,* Social Science Research Council, Bulletin No. 49.

Althusser, L. (1971) 'Ideology and ideological state apparatuses', in L. Althusser (ed.), *Lenin and Philosophy and Other Essays*, London, New Left Books.

Bakhtin, M. (1986) *Speech Genres and Other Late Essays,* Austin, University of Texas Press.

Ball, S.J. (1981) *Beachside Comprehensive,* Cambridge, Cambridge University Press.

Ball, S.J. (1984) 'Beachside reconsidered: reflections on a methodological apprenticeship', in R.G. Burgess (ed.), *The Research Process in Educational Settings: Ten Case Studies,* Lewes, Falmer Press.

Bechtel, R.B. (1970) 'Human movement and architecture', in H.M. Proshansky, W.H. Ittelson and L.O. Rivlin (eds), *Environmental Psychology: Man and his Physical Setting,* New York, Holt, Rinehart and Winston.

Beck, A.T. (1967) *Depression: Causes and Treatment,* Philadelphia, University of Pennsylvania Press.

Becker, H.S. (1970) *Sociological Work,* London, Allen Lane.

Becker, H.S. (1974) 'Photography and sociology', *Studies in the Anthropology of Visual Communication,* vol. 5, pp. 3–26.

Becker, H.S. (ed.) (1981) *Exploring Society Photographically,* Chicago, Northwestern University Press.

Becker, H.S., Cleer, B., Hughes, B.C. and Strauss, A.L. (1961) *Boys in white: Student Culture in Medical School,* Chicago, IL, University of Chicago Press.

Bell, P.A. (1990) *Environmental Psychology,* 3rd edn, Fort Worth, TX, Holt, Rinehart and Winston.

Bennett, N. (1976) *Teaching Styles and Pupil Progress,* London, Open Books.

Berger, P. and Luckman, T. (1966) *The Social Construction of Reality,* Harmondsworth, Penguin.

Beynon, J. (1985) *Initial Encounters in the Secondary School,* Lewes, Falmer Press.

Billig, M. (1988) 'Historical and rhetorical aspects of attitudes: the case of the British monarchy' *Philosophical Psychology*, vol. 1, pp. 83–103.

Billig, M. (1991) *Ideology and Opinions: Studies in Rhetorical Psychology,* London, Sage.

Billig, M. (1997) 'Rhetorical and discursive analysis: how families talk about the royal family', in N. Hayes (ed.), *Doing Qualitative Analysis in Psychology*, Hove, Psychology Press.

Billig, M., Condor, S, Edwards, D., Gane, M., Middleton, D. and Radley, A. (eds) (1988) *Ideological Dilemmas: a social psychology of everyday thinking*, London, Sage.

Binet, A. and Simon, T. (1905) 'Methodes nouvelles pour le diagnostic du niveau intellectuel des abnormaux', *L'Année Psychologique,* vol. 11, pp. 191–244.

Binet, A. and Simon, T. (1908) 'Le developpement de l'intelligence chez les enfants', *L'Année Psychologique,* vol. 14, pp. 1–94.

Black, D. (1980) *The Manners and Customs of the Police*, New York, Academic Press.

Boelen, W.A.M. (1992) 'Street Corner Society: Cornerville revisited', *Journal of Contemporary Ethnography*, vol. 21, pp. 11–51.

Boelen, W.A.M. (1992) 'Street Corner Society: Cornerville revisited', *Journal of Contemporary Ethnography*, 21/1: 11–51.

Bogdan, R.C. and Taylor, S. (1975) *Introduction to Qualitative Research Methods*, New York, Wiley.

Bordia, P. (1996) 'Studying verbal interaction on the Internet: the case of rumour transmission research', *Behaviour Research Methods, Instruments and Computers*, vol. 28, no. 2, pp. 125–40.

Bottomore, T.B. and Rubel, M. (eds) (1963) *Karl Marx: Selected Writings in Sociology and Social Philosophy*, Harmondsworth, Penguin.

Boydell, D. and Jasman, A. (1983) *The Pupil and Teacher Record: A Manual for Observers*, Leicester, University of Leicester.

Boyle, J. (1984) *The Pain of Confinement*, London, Pan.

Brewer, J.D. (1991) *Inside the RUC: routine policing in a divided society*, Oxford, Clarendon Press.

Brigham, C.C. (1923) *A Study of American Intelligence*, Princeton, NJ, Princeton University Press.

British Sociological Association (1992) *Statement of Ethical Practice*, London, BSA.

Brophy, J.E. and Good, T.L. (1970) 'Teacher–child dyadic interactions: a new method of classroom observation', *Journal of School Psychology*, vol. 8, pp. 131–8.

Brophy, J.E. and Good, T.L. (1974) *Teacher–Student Relationships: Causes and Consequences*, New York, Holt, Rinehart and Winston.

Bryman, A. (1988) *Quality and Quantity in Social Research*, London, Allen and Unwin.

Bryman, A. and Cramer, D. (1990) *Quantitative Data for Social Sciences*, London, Routledge.

Buchanan, T. and Smith, J.L. (1999) 'Using the internet for psychological research: personality testing on the World Wide Web', *British Journal of Psychology* 90: 125–144.

Bulmer, M. (1980) 'Why don't sociologists make more use of official statistics?', *Sociology*, vol. 14, pp. 505–23.

Bulmer, M. (ed.) (1982) *Social Research Ethics: An Examination of the Merits of Covert Participant Observation*, London, Macmillan.

Burgess, R.G. (ed.) (1982) *Field Research: A Sourcebook and Field Manual*, London, Allen and Unwin.

Burgess, R.G. (1983) *Experiencing Comprehensive Education*, London, Methuen.

Burgess, R.G. (1984a) *In the Field: An Introduction to Field Research*, London, Unwin Hyman.

Burgess, R.G. (ed.) (1984b) *The Research Process in Educational Settings: Ten Case Studies*, Lewes, Falmer Press.

Burgess, R.G. (1987) 'Studying and restudying Bishop McGregor School', in Walford, G. (ed.), *Doing Sociology of Education*, Lewes, Falmer Press.

Campbell, D. (1969) 'Reforms as experiments', *American Psychologist*, vol. 24, pp. 409–24.

Campbell, D. and Ross, H.L. (1968) 'The Connecticut crackdown on speeding: time-series data in quasi-experimental analysis', *Law and Society Review*, vol. 3, pp. 33–53.

Capaldi, D. and Patterson, G.R. (1987) 'An approach to the problem of recruitment and retention rates for longitudinal research', *Behavioural Assessment*, vol. 9, pp. 169–77.

Chambliss, W. (1975) 'On the paucity of original research on organized crime', *American Sociologist*, vol. 10, pp. 36–9.

Cohen, G., Stanhope, N. and Conway, M. (1992a) 'How long does education last? Very long term retention of cognitive psychology', *The Psychologist*, vol. 5, pp. 57–60.

Cohen, G., Stanhope, N. and Conway, M. (1992b) 'Age differences in the retention of knowledge by young and elderly students', *British Journal of Developmental Psychology*, vol. 10, part 2, pp. 153–64.

Cohen, J. (1969) *Statistical Power Analysis in the Behavioral Sciences*, New York, Academic Press.

Cohen, S. (1972) *Folk Devils and Moral Panics*, London, Paladin.

Cohen, S. and Taylor, L. (1972) *Psychological Survival: The Experience of Long-term Imprisonment*, Harmondsworth, Penguin.

Connell, R. (1987) *Gender and Power*, Cambridge, Polity.

Conway, M., Cohen, G. and Stanhope, N. (1991) 'On the very long-term retention of knowledge acquired through formal education: twelve years of cognitive psychology', *Journal of Experimental Psychology*, vol. 120, pp. 395–409.

Coomber, R. (1997) 'Dangerous drug adulteration: an international survey of drug dealers using the Internet and World Wide Web', *International Journal of Drug Policy*, vol. 8, no. 2, pp. 71–81.

Corsaro, W.A. (1981) 'Entering the child's world: research strategies for field entry and data collection in a pre-school setting', in J.L. Green and C. Wallat (eds), *Ethnography and Language in Educational Settings,* Norwood, NJ, Ablex.

Couper, M., Blair, J. and Triplett, T. (1999) 'A comparison of mail and email for a survey of employees in US statistical agencies', *Journal of Official Statistics,* vol. 15, no. 1, pp. 390–456.

Cox, A., Rutter, M., Yule, B. and Quinton, D. (1977) 'Bias resulting from missing information', *British Journal of Preventative Social Medicine,* vol. 31, pp. 131–6.

Crawford, A., Jones, T., Woodhouse, T. and Young, J. (1990) *Second Islington Crime Survey,* Enfield, Middlesex Polytechnic.

Croll, P. (1980) 'Replicating the observational data', in M. Galton and B. Simon (eds), *Progress and Performance in the Primary Classroom,* London, Routledge and Kegan Paul.

Croll, P. (1986) *Systematic Classroom Observation,* Lewes, Falmer Press.

Croll, P. and Galton, M. (1986) 'A comment on "Questioning ORACLE" by John Scarth and Martyn Hammersley', *Educational Research,* vol. 28, pp. 185–9.

Crowle, A.J. (1976) 'The deceptive language of the laboratory', in R. Harré (ed.), *Life Sentences: Aspects of the Social Role of Language,* Chichester, Wiley.

Davies, B. and Harré, R. (1990) 'Positioning: the discursive production of selves', *Journal of the Theory of Social Behaviour,* vol. 20, pp. 43–65.

Davis, F. (1959) 'The cabdriver and his fare: facets of a fleeting relationship', *American Journal of Sociology,* vol. 65, pp. 158–65.

Day, C. (1981) *Classroom-based In-service Teacher Education: The Development and Evaluation of a Client-centred Model,* University of Sussex Education Area, Occasional Paper 9.

Delamont, S. (1984) 'The old girl network: reflections on the fieldwork at St Luke's', in R.G. Burgess (ed.), *The Research Process in Educational Settings: Ten Case Studies,* Lewes, Falmer Press.

Delamont, S. and Hamilton, D. (1984) 'Revisiting classroom research: a continuing cautionary tale', in S. Delamont (ed.), *Readings on Interaction in the Classroom,* London, Methuen.

Dench, C., Iphofen, R. and Huws, U. (2004) *An EU code of Ethics for Socio-Economic Research,* Brighton, Institute for Employment Studies, www.employment-studies.co.uk

Denzin, N. (1978) *The Research Act: A Theoretical Introduction to Sociological Methods,* 2nd edn, New York, McGraw-Hill.

Department of Employment (1990) 'Measures of unemployment: the claimant count and the Labour Force Survey', *Employment Gazette,* October, pp. 507–13.

Dey, I. (1992) *Qualitative Data Analysis,* London, Routledge.

van Dijk, J., Mayhew, P. and Killias, M. (1990) *Experiences of Crime across the World,* Deventer, Kluwer.

Donzelot, J. (1979) *The Policing of Families,* London, Hutchinson.

Douglas, J.D. (1976) *Investigative Social Research: Individual and Team Field Research,* Beverly Hills, CA, Sage.

Douglas, J.W.B. (1964) *The Home and the School,* London, MacGibbon and Kee.

Douglas, J.W.B. (1976) 'The uses and abuses of national cohorts', in M. Shipman (ed.), *The Limitations of Social Research,* London, Longman.

Eggleston, J., Galton, M. and Jones, M. (1975) *A Science Teaching Observation Schedule,* London, Macmillan.

Elliott, J. (1991) *Action Research for Educational Change,* Milton Keynes, Open University Press.

Ennis, P. (1967) *Criminal Victimization in the United States: A Report of a National Survey,* Washington, DC, President's Commission on Law Enforcement.

Erickson, B.H. and Nosanchuck, T.A. (1983) *Understanding Data,* Milton Keynes, Open University Press.

Eysenck, H.J. (1970) *Crime and Personality,* Harmondsworth, Penguin.

Fairclough, N. (1992) *Discourse and Social Change,* Cambridge, Polity.

Farrington, D.P. (1989) 'The origins of crime: the Cambridge Study of Delinquent Development', Home Office Research and Planning Unit, *Research Bulletin,* no. 27, pp. 29–33.

Fay, B. (1987) 'The elements of a critical social science', in M. Hammersley (ed.), *Social Research: Philosophy, Politics and Practice,* London, Sage, 1993.

Ferri, B. (2000) 'The hidden cost of difference: women with learning disabilities', *Learning Disabilities,* 10.

Festinger, L., Riecken, H. and Schachter, S. (1956) *When Prophecy Fails,* Minnesota, University of Minnesota Press.

Fielding, N.G. (1982) 'Observational research on the National Front', in M. Bulmer (ed.), *Social Research Ethics: An Examination of the Merits of Covert Participant Observation,* London, Macmillan.

Fielding, N.G. and Lee, R.M. (eds) (1991) *Using Computers in Qualitative Research,* London, Sage.

Finnegan, R. (1988) *Literacy and Orality: Studies in the Technology of Communication,* Oxford, Blackwell.

Finnegan, R. (1992) *Oral Traditions and the Verbal Arts: A Guide to Research Practices,* London, Routledge.

Fitzgerald, M. (1987) 'The telephone rings: Long-term imprisonment', in A. Bottoms and L. Light (eds), *Problems of Long-term Imprisonment,* Aldershot, Gower.

Flanders, N. (1970) *Analyzing Teaching Behavior,* Reading, MA, Addison-Wesley.

Foster, P. (1989) 'Policy and practice in multicultural and anti-racist education: A case study of a multi-ethnic comprehensive school', unpublished PhD thesis, Open University.

Foster, P. (1990) *Policy and Practice in Multicultural and Anti-racist Education: A Case Study of a Multi-ethnic Comprehensive School,* London, Routledge.

Foucault, M. (1970) *The Order of Things: an archaeology of the human sciences,* London, Tavistock.

Foucault, M. (1972) *The Archaeology of Knowledge,* London, Tavistock.

Foucault, M. (1973) *The Birth of the Clinic: an archaeology of medical perception,* New York, Pantheon.

Foucault, M. (1977) *Discipline and Punish: the birth of the prison,* London, Allen Lane.

Foucault, M. (1982) 'The subject and power', in H. Dreyfus and P. Rabinow (eds), *Michel Foucault: Beyond Structuralism and Hermeneutics,* Brighton, Harvester.

Foucault, M. (1990) *The History of Sexuality,* vol. 1, London, Penguin.

Frake, C.O. (1980) *Language and Cultural Description,* Stanford, CA, Stanford University Press.

Freeman, D. (1984) *Margaret Mead and Samoa: The Making and Unmaking of an Anthropological Myth,* Harmondsworth, Penguin.

French, J. and French, P. (1984) 'Gender imbalances in the primary classroom: an interactional account', *Educational Research,* vol. 26, pp. 127–36.

Gaiser, T. (1997) 'Conducting on-line focus groups', *Social Science Computer Review,* vol. 15, pp. 135–144.

Galton, M., Simon, B. and Croll, P. (1980) *Inside the Primary Classroom,* London, Routledge and Kegan Paul.

Garfinkel, H. (1967) *Studies in Ethnomethodology,* Englewood Cliffs, NJ, Prentice-Hall.

Garland, D. and Young, P. (eds) (1993) *The Power to Punish,* Aldershot, Gower.

Gergen, K. (2001) 'Self-narration in social life', in M. Wetherell et al. (eds) (2001a), *op. cit.*

Geuss, R. (1981) *The Idea of a Critical Theory: Habermas and the Frankfurt School,* Cambridge, Cambridge University Press.

Gibson, D.R., Drache, J.L., Young, M., Hudes, E.S. and Sorenson, J.L. (1999) 'Effectiveness of brief counseling in reducing HIV risk behaviour in infecting drug users: final results of randomized trials of counseling with and without HIV testing', *AIDS and Behaviour,* vol. 3, pp. 3–11.

Gillborn, D. (1990) *'Race', Ethnicity and Education,* London, Unwin Hyman.

Glaser, B. and Strauss, A. (1967) *The Discovery of Grounded Theory,* Chicago, IL, Aldine.

Glaser, B. and Strauss, A. (1968) *Time for Dying,* Chicago, IL, Aldine.

Glueck, S. and Glueck, E. (1950) *Unravelling Juvenile Delinquency,* London, Routledge and Kegan Paul.

Glueck, S. and Glueck, E. (1962) *Family Environment and Delinquency,* London, Routledge and Kegan Paul.

Goffman, E. (1959) *The Presentation of Self in Everyday Life,* New York, Doubleday.

Gold, R.L. (1958) 'Roles in sociological fieldwork', *Social Forces,* vol. 36, pp. 217–23.

Goodwin, C. (1981) *Conversational Organisation,* New York, Academic Press.

Goody, J. (1986) *The Logic of Writing and the Organization of Society,* Cambridge, Cambridge University Press.

Government Statisticians' Collective (1979) 'How official statistics are produced: views from the inside', in M. Hammersley (ed.), *Social Research: Philosophy, Politics and Practice,* London, Sage, 1993.

Green, P.A. (1983) 'Teachers' influence on the self-concept of pupils of different ethnic origins', unpublished PhD thesis, University of Durham.

Hakim, C. (1987) *Research Design: Strategies and Choices in the Design of Social Research,* London, Unwin Hyman.

Hall, S., Critcher, C., Jefferson, T., Clarke, J. and Roberts, B. (1978) *Policing the Crisis: Mugging, the State and Law and Order,* London, Macmillan.

Hammersley, M. (1979) Data collection in ethnographic research, in Block 4 of Open University course DE304, *Research Methods in Education and the Social Sciences,* Milton Keynes, The Open University.

Hammersley, M. (1980) 'A peculiar world? Teaching and learning in an inner city school', unpublished PhD thesis, University of Manchester.

Hammersley, M. (1990) *Reading Ethnographic Research: A Critical Guide,* London, Longman.

Hammersley, M. (1992) *What's Wrong with Ethnography?,* London, Routledge.

Hammersley, M. (ed.) (1993) *Social Research: Philosophy, Politics and Practice,* London, Sage.

Hammersley, M. and Atkinson, P. (1983) *Ethnography: Principles in Practice,* London, Tavistock.

Haney, C., Banks, C. and Zimbardo, P.G. (1973) 'Interpersonal dynamics in a simulated prison', *International Journal of Criminology and Penology,* vol. 1, pp. 69–97.

Hargreaves, A. (1981) 'Contrastive rhetoric and extremist talk: teachers, hegemony and the educationist context', in L. Barton and S. Walker (eds), *Schools, Teachers and Teaching,* Lewes, Falmer Press.

Harvey, L. (1990) *Critical Social Research,* London, Unwin Hyman.

Healy, J.F. (1990) *Statistics: A Tool for Social Research,* London, Chapman and Hall.

Hewson, C., Yule, P., Laurent, D. and Vogel, C. (2003) *Internet Research Methods: a practical guide for the social and behavioural sciences,* London, Sage.

Hindess, B. (1973) *The Use of Official Statistics in Sociology,* London, Macmillan.

Hobbs, D. (1988) *Doing the Business: Entrepreneurship, the Working Class, and Detectives in East London,* Oxford, Clarendon Press.

Hodkinson, P. (2000) 'The Goth Scene as Trans-Local Subculture', PhD thesis, University of Birmingham.

Holdaway, S. (1983) *Inside the British Police: A Force at Work,* Oxford, Basil Blackwell.

Holsti, O.R. (1969) *Content Analysis for the Social Sciences and Humanities,* Reading, MA, Addison-Wesley.

Homan, R. (1980) 'The ethics of covert methods', *British Journal of Sociology,* vol. 31, pp. 46–59.

Homan, R. and Bulmer, M. (1982) 'On the merits of covert methods: a dialogue', in M. Bulmer (ed.), *Social Research Ethics: An Examination of the Merits of Covert Participant Observation,* London, Macmillan.

Home Office (Annual) *Criminal Statistics: England and Wales,* London, HMSO.

Hopkins, D. (1985) *A Teacher's Guide to Classroom Research,* Milton Keynes, Open University Press.

Horn, S. (1998) *Clicks, Culture and the Creation of an Online Town,* New York, Warner Books.

Howells, D.C. (1985) *Fundamental Statistics for the Behavioural Sciences,* Boston, MA, PWS.

Huck, S.W. (1979) *Rival Hypotheses: Alternative Interpretations of Data-based Conclusions,* New York, Harper and Row.

Huff, D. (1981) *How to Lie with Statistics,* Harmondsworth, Penguin.

Humphreys, L. (1970) *Tearoom Trade,* Chicago, IL, Aldine.

Hunt, J. (1984) 'The development of rapport through the negotiation of gender in fieldwork amongst the police', *Human Organization,* vol. 43, pp. 283–96.

Hustler, D., Cassidy, T. and Cuff, I. (eds) (1986) *Action Research in Classrooms and Schools,* London, Allen and Unwin.

Irvine, J., Miles, I. and Evans, J. (1979) *Demystifying Social Statistics,* London, Pluto Press.

Jensen, A.R. (1972) *Genetics and Education,* New York, Harper and Row.

Jensen, A.R. (1973) *Education and Group Differences,* New York, Harper and Row.

Jones, T., Maclean, B. and Young, J. (1986) *The Islington Crime Survey. Crime, Victimisation and Policing in Inner-city London,* Aldershot, Gower.

Junker, B. (1960) *Field Work,* Chicago, IL, University of Chicago Press.

Jupp, V. (1989) *Methods of Criminological Research,* London, Allen and Unwin.

Jupp, V. and Norris, C. (1993) 'Traditions in documentary analysis', in M. Hammersley (ed.), *Social Research: Philosophy, Politics and Practice,* London, Sage.

Kamin, L. (1977) *The Science and Politics of IQ,* Harmondsworth, Penguin.

Kaplan, D. and Manners, R. (1972) *Culture Theory,* Englewood Cliffs, NJ, Prentice Hall.

Kendall, G. and Wickham, G. (1999) *Using Foucault's Methods,* London, Sage.

Kendall, L. (1999) 'Meaning and identity in "Cyberspace": the performance of gender, class and race online', *Symbolic Interaction,* vol. 21, pp. 129–153.

Kendall, M.G. (1952) *The Advanced Theory of Statistics,* London, Griffin.

King, R. (1978) *All Things Bright and Beautiful? A Sociological Study of Infant Classrooms,* Chichester, Wiley.

King, R. (1984) 'The man in the Wendy House: researching infants' schools', in R.G. Burgess (ed.), *The Research Process in Educational Settings: Ten Case Studies*, Lewes, Falmer Press.

Kinsey, R. (1986) 'Crime in the city', *Marxism Today*, May, pp. 6–11.

Kitson Clark, G. (1967) *The Critical Historian: Guide for Research Students Working on Historical Subjects*, New York, Garland.

Kitsuse, J. and Cicourel, A.V. (1963) 'A note on the use of official statistics', *Social Problems*, vol. 2, pp. 328–38.

Krantz, J., Ballard, J. and Scher, J. (1997) 'Comparing the results of laboratory and World Wide Web samples of the determinants of female attractiveness', *Behaviour Research Methods, Instruments and Computers*, vol. 29, pp. 246–9.

Krieger, S. (1979) 'Research and the construction of a text', in N.K. Denzin (ed.), *Studies in Symbolic Interaction*, vol. 2, Greenwich, CT, JM Press.

Kumar, K. (1984) 'Unemployment as a problem in the development of industrial societies: the English experience', *Sociological Review*, vol. 32, pp. 185–233.

Lacey, C. (1970) *Hightown Grammar: The School as a Social System*, Manchester, Manchester University Press.

Lacey, C. (1976) 'Problems of sociological fieldwork: a review of the methodology of "Hightown Grammar"', in M. Shipman (ed.), *The Organization and Impact of Social Research*, London, Routledge and Kegan Paul.

Lane, R.E. (1960) *Political Man*, New York, Free Press.

Lewis, O. (1959) *Five Families*, New York, Basic Books.

Lipsey, M.W. (1990) *Design Sensitivity*, Newbury Park, CA, Sage.

Lofland, L.H. (1973) *A World of Strangers: Order and Action in Urban Public Space*, New York, Basic Books.

Luria, A.R. (1972) *The Man with a Shattered World: The History of a Brain Wound*, New York, Basic Books.

McCracken, G. (1988) *The Long Interview*, Beverly Hills, Sage.

McIver, J., Carmines, E. and Zeller, R. (1980) 'Multiple indicators', in R. Zeller and E. Carmines (eds), *Measurement in the Social Sciences*, Cambridge, Cambridge University Press.

Mack, J. and Lansley, A. (1985) *Poor Britain*, Harmondsworth, Penguin.

Magnusson, D. and Bergman, L.R. (eds) (1990) *Data Quality in Longitudinal Research*, Cambridge, Cambridge University Press.

Malinowski, B. (1922) *Argonauts of the Western Pacific*, London, Routledge and Kegan Paul.

Malow, R.M., West, S.A., Corrigan, S.A., Pena, J.M. and Cunningham, S.C. (1994) 'Outcome of psychoeducation for HIV risk reduction', *AIDS Education and Prevention*, vol. 6, pp. 113–25.

Mann, C. and Stewart, F. (2000) *Internet Communication and Qualitative Research*, London, Sage.

Marsh, C. (1988) *Exploring Data: An Introduction to Data Analysis for Social Scientists*, Cambridge, Polity.

Marsh, P., Rosser, E. and Harré, R. (1978) *The Rules of Disorder*, London, Routledge and Kegan Paul.

Marwick, A. (1977) 'Introduction to history', in Open University course A101 *An Arts Foundation Course*, Milton Keynes, The Open University.

Mayhew, P. and Hough, M. (1982) 'The British Crime Survey', Home Office Research and Planning Unit, *Research Bulletin*, No. 14, pp. 207–24.

Mead, M. (1943) *Coming of Age in Samoa*, Harmondsworth, Penguin.

Middlemist, R.D., Knowles, E.S. and Matter, C.F. (1976) 'Personal space invasions in the lavatory: suggestive evidence for arousal', *Journal of Personality and Social Psychology*, vol. 33, pp. 541–6.

Mies, M. (1983) 'Towards a methodology for feminist research', in M. Hammersley (ed.), *Social Research: Philosophy, Politics and Practice*, London, Sage, 1993.

Milgram, S. (1974) *Obedience to Authority: An Experimental View*, London, Tavistock.

Mills, C.W. (1956) *The Power Elite*, New York, Oxford University Press.

Morris, L. (1994) *Dangerous Classes: the underclass and social citizenship*, London, Routledge

Mort, D. and Siddall, L. (1985) *Sources of Unofficial UK Statistics*, London, Gower.

Morton Williams, J. (1990) 'Response rates', Joint Centre for Survey Methods, SCPRILSE, *Newsletter*, vol. 10, no. 1.

Mowatt, C.L. (1971) *Great Britain since 1914*, London, Hodder and Stoughton.

Ochs, E. (1979) 'Transcription as theory', in E. Ochs (ed.), *Studies in Developing Pragmatics,* New York, Academic Press.

O'Connor, H. and Madge, C. (2000) *Cyber Parents and Cyber-Research: exploring the Internet as a medium for research,* University of Leicester, Centre for Labour Market Studies.

Ó Dochartaigh, N. (2002) *The Internet Research Handbook,* London, Sage.

Office of Population Censuses and Surveys (annual) *General Household Survey,* London, HMSO.

Office of Population Censuses and Surveys (1982) *Census 1981: Historical Tables 1861–1981,* London, HMSO.

Office of Population Censuses and Surveys (1984) *Census 1981: Household and Family Composition, England and Wales,* London, HMSO.

O'Neill, K., Baker, A., Cooke, M., Collics, E., Heather, N. and Wodak, A. (1996) 'Evaluation of a cognitive-behavioural intervention for pregnant injecting drug users at risk of HIV infection', *Addiction,* 91/8: 5.

Oppenheim, A.N. (1979) 'Methods and strategies of survey research', in Open University course DE304 *Research Methods in Education and the Social Sciences,* Milton Keynes, The Open University.

Oppenheim, A.N. (1992) *Questionnaire Design, Interviewing and Attitude Measurement,* London, Pinter.

Parker, H.J. (1974) *View from the Boys: A Sociology of Downtown Adolescents,* London, David and Charles.

Parker, I. (1992) *Discourse Dynamics: critical analysis for social and individual psychology,* London, Routledge.

Parlee, M. (1979) 'Psychology and women', *Signs,* vol. 5, pp. 123–33.

Patrick, J. (1973) *A Glasgow Gang Observed,* London, Eyre Methuen.

Pearson, K. and Lee, A. (1902) 'On the laws of inheritance in man. I: inheritance of physical characters', *Biometrika,* vol. 2, pp. 356–462.

Pellegrini, A.D. (1989) 'Elementary school children's rough and tumble play', *Early Childhood Research Quarterly,* vol. 4, pp. 245–60.

Pellegrini, A.D. (1991) *Applied Child Study: A Developmental Approach,* Hillsdale, NJ, Lawrence Erlbaum.

Platt, J. (1981) 'Evidence and proof in documentary research: 1, some specific problems of documentary research; 2, some shared problems of documentary research', *Sociological Review,* vol. 29, pp. 31–52, 53–66.

Plummer, K. (1983) *Documents of Life: An Introduction to the Problems and Literature of a Humanistic Method,* London, Allen and Unwin.

Potter, J. (1996) 'Attitudes, social representations and discursive psychology', in M. Wetherell (ed.), *op. cit.*

Potter, J. and Wetherell, M. (1987) *Discourse and Social Psychology,* London, Sage.

Potter, J. and Wetherell, M. (1995) 'Discourse analysis', in J.A. Smith et al. (eds), *op. cit.*

Pryke, K. (1979) *Endless Pressure,* Harmondsworth, Penguin.

Punch, M. (1979a) 'Observation and the police: the research experience', in M. Hammersley (ed.), *Social Research: Philosophy, Politics and Practice,* London, Sage, 1993.

Punch, M. (1979b) *Policing the Inner City: A Study of Amsterdam's Warmoesstraat,* London, Macmillan.

Punch, M. (1985) *Conduct Unbecoming,* London, Tavistock.

Rabinow, P. (ed.) (1984) *The Foucault Reader,* Harmondsworth, Penguin.

Reason, P. and Rowan, J. (1981) *Human Inquiry: A Sourcebook of New Paradigm Research,* Chichester, Wiley.

Reinharz, S. (1979) *On Becoming a Social Scientist,* San Francisco, Jossey Bass.

Reinharz, S. (1983) Experiential analysis. A contribution to feminist research, in G. Bowles and R.D. Klein (eds), *Theories of Women's Studies,* London, Routledge and Kegan Paul.

Reiss, A.J. (1971) *The Police and the Public,* New Haven, CT, Yale University Press.

Rex, J. and Tomlinson, S. (1979) *Colonial Immigrants in a British City,* London, Routledge and Kegan Paul.

Ropiequet, S. (ed.) (1987) *Optical Publishing,* vol. 2, Redmond, Microsoft Press/Penguin.

Rosenhan, D.L. (1982) 'On being sane in insane places', in M. Bulmer (ed.), *Social Research Ethics: An Examination of the Merits of Covert Participant Observation,* London, Macmillan.

Rosenthal, R. and Jacobson, L. (1968) *Pygmalion in the Classroom,* New York, Holt, Rinehart and Winston.

Rubinstein, J. (1973) *City Police,* New York, Ballantine.

Runkel, P.J. and McGrath, J.E. (1972) *Research on Human Behavior: A Systematic Guide to Method,* New York, Holt, Rinehart and Winston.

Rutter, M., Maughan, B., Morthnore, P. and Ouston, J. (1979) *Fifteen Thousand Hours: Secondary Schools and their Effects on Children,* London, Open Books.

Sapsford, R.J. (1983) *Life-sentence Prisoners: Reaction, Response and Change,* Milton Keynes, Open University Press.

Sapsford, R.J. (1993) 'Understanding people: the growth of an expertise', in J. Clarke (ed.), *A Crisis in Care: challenges to social work,* London, Sage.

Sapsford, R.J. (1999) *Survey Research,* London, Sage.

Sapsford, R.J., Stills, A., Miell, D., Stevens, R. and Wetherell, M. (eds) (1998) *Theory and Social Psychology,* London, Sage

Scarman, L.G. (1981) *The Brixton Disorders, April 10–12, 1981, Report of an Inquiry,* Cmnd 8427, London, HMSO.

Scarth, J. and Hammersley, M. (1986) 'Questioning ORACLE', *Educational Research,* vol. 28, no. 3, pp. 17–84.

Scarth, J. and Hammersley, M. (1987) 'More questioning of ORACLE', *Educational Research,* vol. 29, no. 1, pp. 37–46.

Schaerfer, D. and Dillman, D. (1998) 'Development of a standard email methodology: results of an experiment', *Public Opinion Quarterly,* vol. 62, pp. 378–397.

Schegloff, E.A. (1971) 'Notes on a conversational practice: formulating place', in D. Sudnow (ed.), *Studies in Social Interaction,* New York, Free Press.

Scherer, K.R. and Ekman, P. (eds) (1982) *Handbook of Methods in Nonverbal Behaviour Research,* Cambridge, Cambridge University Press.

Schnarch, D. (1997) 'Sex, intimacy and the Internet', *Journal of Sex Education and Therapy,* vol. 22, pp. 15–20.

Schofield, W.N., Heikens, G.T. and Irons, B. (1992) 'Methodological aspects of medical and nutritional studies in the community', *Journal of Tropical and Geographical Medicine.*

Scott, J. (1990) *A Matter of Record: Documentary Sources in Social Research,* Cambridge, Polity Press.

Simkin, C. (1992) *The Psychological Effect of Unemployment,* unpublished MSc dissertation, The Open University.

Slack, C. (1992) *Long-term Unemployment and Health Status,* unpublished MSc dissertation, The Open University.

Sissons, M. (1970) 'The psychology of social class', in Open University course D101 *Making Sense of Society,* Milton Keynes, The Open University.

Sissons, M. (1981) 'Race, sex and helping behaviour', *British Journal of Social Psychology,* vol. 20, pp. 285–92.

Smart, B. (1989) 'On discipline and social regulation: a review of Foucault's genealogical analysis', in G. Garland and P. Young (eds), *The Power to Punish,* London, Gower.

Smith, H.W. (1975) *Strategies of Social Research: The Methodological Imagination,* Englewood Cliffs, NJ, Prentice-Hall.

Smith, J.A., Harré, R. and Van Langenhove, L. (eds) (1995) *Rethinking Methods in Psychology,* London, Sage.

Smith, J.K. and Heshusius, L. (1986) 'Closing down the conversation: the end of the quantitative–qualitative debate among educational inquirers', *Educational Research,* vol. 15, pp. 4–12.

Smith, M.A. and Leigh, B. (1997) 'Virtual subjects: using the Internet as an alternative source of subjects and research environment', *Behaviour Research Methods, Instruments and Computers,* vol. 29, no. 4, pp. 496–505.

Sorenson, J.L., London, J., Heitzmann, C., Gibson, D.R., Morales, E.S., Dumontet, R. and Acree, M. (1994) 'Psychoeducational group approach: HIV risk reduction in drug users', *AIDS Education and Prevention,* vol. 6, pp. 95–112.

Sparks, R. (1992) 'The Prison Service as an organisation: 1979–91', in Open University course D803 *Doing Prison Research,* Milton Keynes, The Open University.

Sparks, R.F., Glenn, H.G. and Dodd, S.J. (1977) *Surveying Victims: A Study of the Measurement of Criminal Victimisation,* New York, Wiley.

Spencer, G. (1973) 'Methodological issues in the study of bureaucratic elites: a case study of West Point', *Social Problems,* vol. 21, pp. 90–103.

Sprent, P. (1988) *Understanding Data,* Harmondsworth, Penguin.

Stacey, M. (1960) *Tradition and Change: A Study of Banbury,* Oxford, Oxford University Press.

Stanton, J.M. (1998) 'An empirical assessment of data collection using the Internet', *Personnel Psychology,* vol. 51, no. 3, 709–725.

Steedman, C. (1982) *The Tidy House: Little Girls Writing,* London, Virago.

Stenhouse, L. (1984) 'Library access, library use and user education in academic sixth forms: an autobiographical account', in R.G. Burgess (ed.), *The Research Process in Educational Settings: Ten Case Studies,* Lewes, Falmer Press.

Stevens, R. (1995) 'A new vision of psychology: Developing our understanding of psychological understanding', *New Psychologist,* April.

Strauss, J. (1996) 'Early survey research on the Internet: review, illustration and evaluation', in E.A. Blair and W.A. Kamakura (eds), *Proceedings of the American Marketing Association Winter Educators' Conference,* Chicago, American Marketing Association.

Strauss, A. and Corbin, J. (1990) *Basics of Qualitative Research: Grounded Theory Procedures and Techniques,* Newbury Park, CA, Sage.

Stuart, I. and Ord, K.J. (1987) *Kendall's Advanced Theory of Statistics,* 5th edn, London, Arnold.

Swift, B. (1991a) *Teachers into Business and Industry: The Views of Users of the Pack,* Milton Keynes, The Open University, Institute of Educational Technology, Student Research Centre Report No. 56.

Swift, B. (1991b) *B886 MBA Dissertation: Student Perspectives,* Milton Keynes, The Open University, Institute of Educational Technology, Student Research Centre Report No. 46.

Swoboda, W., Muhlberger, N., Weitkunat, R. amd Schneeweib, S. (1997) 'Internet surveys by direct mailing', *Social Science Computer Review,* vol. 15, pp. 242–55.

Szabo, A. and Frenkl, M.D. (1996) 'Consideration of research on the Internet: guidelines and implications for human movement studies', *Clinical Kinesiology,* vol. 50, no. 3, pp. 58–65.

Taylor, L. (1984) *In the Underworld,* Oxford, Basil Blackwell.

Taylor, Lord Justice P. (1990) *The Hillsborough Stadium Disaster, 15 April 1989, Inquiry by the Rt Hon. Lord Justice Taylor, Final Report,* London, HMSO.

Terman, L.M. (1916) *The Measurement of Intelligence,* Boston, MA, Houghton Mifflin.

Tesch, R. (1990) *Qualitative Research: Analysis Types and Software Tools,* Lewes, Falmer Press.

Thomas, W.I. and Znaniecki, F. (1958) *The Polish Peasant in Europe and America,* New York, Dover Publications (first published 1918–20).

Tizard, B. and Hughes, M. (1984) *Young Children Learning: Talking and Thinking at Home and School,* London, Fontana.

Tizard, B. and Hughes, M. (1991) 'Reflections on young children learning', in G. Walford (ed.), *Doing Educational Research,* London, Routledge.

Tizard, J., Schofield, W.N. and Hewison, J. (1982) 'Collaboration between teachers and parents in assisting children's reading', *British Journal of Educational Psychology,* vol. 52, pp. 1–15.

de Vaus, D.A. (1991) *Surveys in Social Research,* 3rd edn, London, UCL Press.

Vietze, P.M., Abernathy, S.R., Ashe, M.L. and Faulstich, G. (1978) 'Contingency interactions between mothers and their developmentally delayed infants', in G.P. Sackett (ed.), *Observing Behaviour, 1: Theory and Applications in Mental Retardation,* Baltimore, MA, University Park Press.

Wadsworth, J. and Johnson, A.M. (1991) 'Measuring sexual behaviour', *Journal of the Royal Statistical Society, Series A,* vol. 154, pp. 367–70.

Walford, G. (1991) 'Researching the City Technology College, Kinghurst', in G. Walford (ed.), *Doing Educational Research,* London, Routledge.

Walford, G. and Miller, H. (1991) *City Technology College,* Milton Keynes, Open University Press.

Walker, A. (1991) 'The social construction of dependency in old age', in M. Loney, R. Bocock, J. Clarke, A. Cochrane, P. Graham and M. Wilson (eds), *The State Or The Market: Politics and Welfare in Contemporary Britain,* London, Sage.

Walker, J.C. and Evers, C.W. (1988) 'The epistemological unity of educational research', in J.P. Keeves (ed.), *Educational Research Methodology and Measurement: An International Handbook,* Oxford, Pergamon.

Walklate, S. (1989) *Victimology: The Victim and the Criminal Justice System,* London, Unwin Hyman.

Warren, C. (1988) *Gender Issues in Field Research,* Beverly Hills, CA, Sage.

Webb, E., Campbell, D.T., Schwartz, R.D. and Sechrest, L. (1966) *Unobtrusive Measures: Nonreactive Research in the Social Sciences,* Chicago, Rand McNally.

Weeks, M.F., Jones, B.L., Folsom Jr, R.E. and Benrud, C.H. (1984) 'Optimal times to contact sample households', *Public Opinion Quarterly,* vol. 48, pp. 101–14.

Weerasinghe, L. (1989) *Directory of Recorded Sound Resources in the United Kingdom,* London, British Library.

West, D.J. (1969) *Present Conduct and Future Delinquency,* London, Heinemann.

West, D.J. (1982) *Delinquency: Its Roots, Careers and Prospects,* London, Heinemann.

West, D.J. and Farrington, D.P. (1973) *Who Becomes Delinquent?*, London, Heinemann.

West, D.J. and Farrington, D.P. (1977) *The Delinquent Way of Life,* London, Heinemann.

Wetherell, M. (1996a) 'Group conflict and the social psychology of racism', in M. Wetherell (ed.), *op. cit* 1996b.

Wetherell, M. (ed.) (1996b) *Identities, Groups and Social Issues*, London, Sage.

Wetherell, M. (2001) 'Themes in discourse research: the case of Diana', in M. Wetherell et al. (eds) (2001a), *op. cit.*

Wetherell, M. and Stills, A. (1998) 'Realism and Relativism', in Sapsford et al. (eds), *op. cit.*

Wetherell, M., Taylor, S. and Yates, S.J. (2001a) *Discourse Theory and Practice*, London, Sage.

Wetherell, M., Taylor, S. and Yates, S.J. (2001b) *Discourse as Data*, London, Sage.

Whyte, W.F. (1981) *Street Corner Society: The Social Structure of an Italian Slum,* 3rd edn, Chicago, IL, University of Chicago Press.

Whyte, W.F. (1992) 'In defence of *Street Corner Society', Journal of Contemporary Ethnography,* vol. 21, pp. 52–68.

Willig, C. (2001) *Introducing Qualitative Research in Psychology: adventures in theory and method,* Buckingham, Open University Press.

Willis, P. (1977) *Learning to Labour: How Working Class Kids Get Working Class Jobs,* Aldershot, Gower.

Woods, P. (1979) *The Divided School,* London, Routledge and Kegan Paul.

Woolf, Lord Justice H.K. (1991) *Prison Disturbances April 1990, Report of an Inquiry by the Rt Hon Lord Justice Woolf (Parts 1 and 2) and His Honour Judge Stephen Tumim (Part 2),* Cmnd 1456, London, HMSO.

Worrall, A. (1990) *Offending Women,* London, Routledge.

Yates, F. (1935) 'Some examples of biased sampling', *Annals of Eugenics,* vol. 6, p. 202.

Zeller, R. and Carmines, E. (eds) (1980) *Measurement in the Social Sciences,* Cambridge, Cambridge University Press.

Zimbardo, P.G. (1973) 'On the ethics of intervention in human psychological research', *Cognition,* vol. 2, pp. 243–356.

Index